Church Growth
OUR
FATHER GOD'S WAY

Double Your
Attendance,
Double Your
Income

Velma Davies

WESTBOW
PRESS®
A DIVISION OF THOMAS NELSON
& ZONDERVAN

WestBow Press books may be ordered through booksellers or by contacting:

WestBow Press
A Division of Thomas Nelson & Zondervan
1663 Liberty Drive
Bloomington, IN 47403
www.westbowpress.com
1 (866) 928-1240

ISBN: 978-1-5127-9872-2 (sc)
ISBN: 978-1-5127-9873-9 (e)

Library of Congress Control Number: 2017912728

Print information available on the last page.

WestBow Press rev. date: 09/13/2017

DEDICATION

To my Heavenly Father God, to my Lord Jesus
Christ, and to our God's Holy Spirit

INTRODUCTION

Dear Christian Pastors and All Holy Bible Teachers,

Father God has told me to give Christian pastors and all Holy Bible teachers fifty written prophetic message from Father God to help them with their church growth. Father God told me that if they will preach one sermon a week using one of each of these prophetic messages for reference for fifty weeks, that in one year their church attendance will double and their church income will double. Praise God!

The Lord wants me to give to you this symbolism for Christian church growth:

My brother Cliff Garner is two years younger than I am. We lived at home in southern Washington State and attended Junior College together for two years at the same time. Cliff was on the tennis team then and played tennis very well. Cliff would take a lot of tennis balls and his racket and practice hitting balls against the concrete backstop. He would serve the balls and would hit them many, many times as they would ALWAYS come back to him.

I would take the same tennis balls, the same racket, and play against the same backstop, but those stupid balls just would NOT come back to me! I just did not have his hand strength, his aim, nor his playing experience. No matter how hard I tried, I just could not control that ball the way he could!

The Lord showed to me recently that it was the way the ball was **SENT OUT** that determined the way the ball **RETURNED**. The Lord showed to me that the way churches grow is how the spiritually well fed people are **SENT OUT** from the church services that determines the way they **RETURN**. If their spiritual hunger is being fed Jesus and the Bible in the church services that meets their spiritual needs, they will return for more and will bring their spiritually hungry family and friends with them.

Father God wants Christian pastors to know:

If you feed people Jesus and the Bible, you are feeding them steaks.

If you feed them anything else, you are feeding them, but you are feeding them crumbs.

Your own soul must grow in God, before you are able to feed others the true words of Jesus and the Bible. "Draw near to God, and God will draw near to you." (James 4:8)

Blessings! Velma

ACKNOWLEDGEMENTS

Thank you to
Karen Holmes, my proofreader;
Becky Holmes, her sister and helper;
Paul Weiland, my computer assistant.

LETTER NUMBER ONE FOR CHURCH GROWTH

Dear Christian Pastors and All Holy Bible Teachers,

The Lord wants me to write words of encouragement to you, so I will try to do it with His help.

When I had joined The Lord's Chapel church in Nashville in 1977, it was the fastest growing church in Nashville with several thousand members with the excellent leadership of Pastor Billy Roy Moore. As we outgrew our parking space in Brentwood, in August of 1988, we relocated to our new property and new building near Nolensville Road in Nashville with several acres with which to expand. After Pastor Moore left, The Lord's Chapel went through a series of different pastors as leaders until the attendance dwindled to only about forty people. Then in about 2003, The Lord's Chapel merged with Oasis Church which had more than a thousand people attending at the time, with the leadership of Pastors Danny and Jillian Chambers. The name was changed to Oasis Church located on Lord's Chapel Drive in Nashville.

At the time, I could not understand why The Lord's Chapel has such few members attending and why Oasis Church had such a larger attendance, especially since I believed that our Lord's Chapel church was doing so many good things that were helping so many people. Here are some of the good things that The Lord's Chapel was doing:

- We always had great Bible teaching from the pulpit every Sunday morning, Sunday evening, and Wednesday evening.
- We had praise singing at all our meetings. Two of our former pastors were gifted with singing and playing the keyboard, so we had excellent praise music and singing.

- We welcomed all our visitors and encouraged them to return.
- We always had Communion every Sunday morning led by the main pastor for the entire congregation.
- We had a weekly printed bulletin with announcements, Scriptures, and other information in it.
- We tithed as a church and used the money to support missions at home and abroad.
- We had Monday evening prayer meetings for about two hours led by the pastor.
- We prayed for prayer requests that were spoken, written, and phoned in.
- We held monthly church dinners to earn extra funds for missions and for our newsletter.
- We published a free newsletter mailed to more than 1,200 families, with Bible teaching from our pastor, with personal Christian testimonies from our members, and special announcements.
- We published a book with 44 Christian testimonies in it titled, *Victory in Jesus.*
- We had a well-stocked food pantry and gave free food and gas vouchers to the needy.
- We prayed in tongues and had interpretations, and had true prophecy that agreed with Scripture.
- We had Christian art on our walls and in our weekly bulletins.
- We gave monthly and yearly financial reports to the congregation as required with all non-profit organizations.

With all these good happenings going on, I just could not understand why our congregation did not grow. Every Monday evening at our prayer meetings, our pastor and many of we members always prayed earnestly for our church to grow, but it still didn't grow.

Only in the past two months has the Lord let me know why it

didn't grow. Every pastor, as well as every person, has the human capacity to become either a **servant** or a **dictator.** So long as a pastor has a **servant's** heart, the church will continue to grow. When a pastor shows signs of becoming a **dictator,** the church will stop growing in numbers and stop growing in finances. The Lord showed me this truth in Scriptures where Jesus says, "the greatest among you is the servant," and Jesus says, "I came not to be served, but to serve," and "those who humble themselves will be exalted, and those who exalt themselves will be humbled," and "the last will be first and the first will be last." God will raise up **servants,** but He limits how far **dictators** will be raised up.

The Lord showed me how each of these five pastors had reached their limits of being servants and desired the church to serve them, rather than them to serve the church. They were showing symptoms of becoming dictators so God had to limit their influence and their income. They wanted God to build up THEIR kingdom, rather than them to build up GOD's Kingdom on earth. I now give funds to many charities including to seven churches as I want to help build up the whole Kingdom of God on earth.

When I asked Jesus to speak to me, one of the things He said was, **"Tell them that if they will always stay humble before God, that God will always use them to help build up the WHOLE Kingdom of God."**

I praise my Lord Jesus for always speaking to me when I ask Him to. Joy! "Call unto Me, and I will answer you and show you great and mighty things which you know not." (Jeremiah 33:3)

Blessings! Velma

Yes, Our God's beloved children of God, YOUR heavenly Father God does love you, does take care of you at ALL times, and does meet ALL of your needs and all holy desires, while you are now alive on Our God's planet Earth.

Yes, do learn to obey YOUR Holy Triune God daily and nightly and do see HOW Our God does lead you and does feed you, and does give to you all good things and all good events in your life to enjoy.

Yes, YOUR heavenly Father God IS a good God, Who does enjoy giving all good things and all good events to Our God's obedient children who love God, and who live a righteous lifestyle in obedience to God, and who do love and do help their fellow mankind.

Do go about your daily tasks of loving and helping others and do see HOW Our God does reward you for this, reward you both in your one life on earth and reward you in your afterlife in heaven.

Do learn to PRAISE your Holy Triune God more on a daily basis so that YOUR Holy Triune God is able to fill you to the FULL with ALL love, joy, peace, kindness, generosity, wisdom, Knowledge, and joy.

Make praising your Holy Triune God a living sacrifice daily, even hourly in your life, and then do SEE HOW your God will enrich your life with ALL good things and ALL good events in your life and in your loved ones' lives.

Yes, you do serve a good God, a loving God, a very generous God, a God Who does have ALL power in heaven, on earth, and in earth.

NOTHING is too hard for your God to accomplish for your

life, in your life, and for the wellbeing of you and ALL your loved ones.

Keep living for God.

Keep working for and with your God.

Yes, keep preaching from the pulpit about Jesus, Father God, Our Holy Spirit of God, and about Our God's Holy Bible.

Yes, teach people about Jesus; Who He was and still is; how Jesus' perfect life is their example for godly living; how He always spoke the truth in love; how His many promises are always yes and amen; how He honored His heavenly Father God; how He does reward people for loving God, honoring God, witnessing for Jesus, and for helping the helpless.

Yes, when you do feed people the true words of Jesus and Father God from the pulpit, you ARE feeding them the meat that WILL enrich their spiritual life, and they are so very hungry for this rich spiritual food of Jesus that they WILL RETURN for this great spiritual food again and again, and you will need NO OTHER incentive for church attendance to grow and grow.

Yes, do encourage people to give tithes and offerings to promote the Gospel world-wide, then for them to watch how Our God returns to them double and more than double what they do give.

Yes, encourage people to use their talents and gifts to help others and to glorify God.

Yes, do encourage people to go out and witness for Jesus and tell people to get right with Jesus as Jesus will be arriving SOON for Our God's great rapture of souls.

Encourage them to tell others that Jesus loves them and takes care of them.

Give the unlovely your love, your kindness, and your generosity.

Be a friend to the friendless.

Live for and with God even as Jesus went about doing good, helping people, encouraging people, and telling them about HIS heavenly Father God.

5

Be encouraged in your work and witnessing for God, knowing Our God loves you and goes with you and HELPS you every step of the way.

Hallelujah!

Praises to Our heavenly Father God for this encouraging message!

Praise God!

Dear Christian Pastors and All Holy Bible Teachers,

This is the second message in a weekly series of fifty prophetic messages that our Father God told me to give to pastors to encourage them in their spiritual life for church growth.

After receiving that first one from Father God last week, I asked Father God Whom I should ask to give to me these weekly messages? He replied, **"Ask either Father God or Lord Jesus, or both, the choice is yours to make."** I have decided to always ask Father God for all fifty of them, as Father God is the One Who told me to give them to the pastors.

After I came home from our church service, God's Holy Spirit led me to send copies of these letters and prophetic messages to several other pastors. I found their addresses, wrote each a personal note, and mailed the copies to them. God showed me that this is Scriptural, as when Paul was in prison, he wrote many letters to the churches, and these letters are still benefitting the body of Christ today for our spiritual growth. The Lord showed me that not only will these prophetic messages benefit our church, but they will also benefit other churches, if these pastors will follow the teachings in these prophetic messages.

Here is a list of the pastors that I sent them to:

Pastor Danny Chambers at Oasis Church, Nashville, Tennessee

Pastor Adonis Lenzy and **David Garner** at Oasis Church, Nashville, Tennessee

Pastor Bobby Howard at The Father's House, Nashville, Tennessee

Pastor Marty Layton, Hendersonville, Tennessee

Pastor James Lowe, Brentwood, Tennessee

Pastor Ron Ledford, Vidalia, Louisiana
Pastor Ernest Angley, Akron, Ohio
Pastor Bishop Omukubah, Birmingham, Alabama
Pastor Dean Miller, Hattiesburg, Mississippi
Pastor Butch Crabtree, Seminary, Mississippi
Pastor Cameron Williams, Longview, Washington
Added later:
Pastor Michael Morgan, Hattiesburg, Mississippi
Pastors Tim and **Debbie Hogg,** Conyers, Georgia

All of our success comes from God. Let us honor Him with our lives. Father God once told me, **"If Thomas Kinkade had honored God for his success, he would still be alive and still be painting."**

I regret that he did not honor God and died at age 54 from an overdose of drugs and alcohol. "God will not give His glory to another." (Isaiah 42:8)

Blessings! Velma

Yes, Our God's beloved pastors of Our God's Christian churches, YOUR heavenly Father God does love you and does love ALL of your families, friends, and congregations; and yes, YOUR heavenly Father God is always taking care of you and them throughout the daytimes and evening times.

Yes, do live for God, worship God, and preach to others the true words of God as given to you in Our God's Holy Bible, and always let Our God's Holy Bible be your guide for holy living, then do see and do realize Our God's many rewards to you and to your family for living a righteous lifestyle unto God.

Yes, IF YOU WILL FOLLOW YOUR Father God's teachings as given to you in these fifty prophetic messages from YOUR heavenly Father God, your church WILL grow and grow all next year.

Yes, when you do PRAISE YOUR heavenly Father God, your Lord Jesus Christ God, and Our God's Holy Spirit of God, praise God MANY times daily and nightly, Our God WILL USE THIS TIME to fill you to the FULL with Our God's knowledge, wisdom, discernment, love, power, joy, good benefits, and ALL good rewards in your life, and you WILL BE the head and not the tail, and will be the great spiritual leader that Our God has already created you to be, to follow in the footsteps of Jesus, and to lead MANY MORE to salvation in Jesus.

Yes, when you do get to heaven, you WILL receive your crown from YOUR heavenly Father God that you have already earned for being a soul winner for Jesus.

Yes, in heaven there are many and GREAT REWARDS waiting for Our God's faithful servants who do endure to the end, even as Paul in the Bible endured to the end.

Yes, do read and do study Our God's Holy Bible cover to cover, and do GET prepared, and do BE prepared, to answer any spiritual question put to you about Jesus, your faith, the Bible, and about YOUR Holy Triune God.

Yes, there WILL come a time in your life when your Holy Bible could be taken from you by the evil forces that are NOW at work in Our God's earth, and you do NEED to commit key Bible verses to your memory now to help sustain you in these evil days ahead.

Do PUT YOUR Holy Triune God FIRST above all else in your life, above your ministry, your church, your family, your possessions, your goals, your ambitions—even above your own life as YOUR Holy Triune God can better use you to help yourself, help others, and glorify God on earth, when you do PUT YOUR Holy Triune God above ALL else in your life.

Yes, didn't Jesus say, "If you love your family more than Me, you are not worthy of Me"? (Matthew 10:37-39)

Yes, love God above ALL else and do honor God above ALL else.

Yes, times on earth are now hard, and they WILL get even harder, UNLESS people repent of their evil ways, turn to God, ask God for forgiveness, come out of ALL sin and live for God, and let Our God forgive their sin and heal their land of these wicked Americas. (2 Chronicles 7:14)

Yes, unless America repents and turns back to God as Head of this nation, America can and will be destroyed.

Yes, Our God's patience is running out for the wicked Americans to repent, come back to God as Head of this nation, so God can forgive their sin and unrighteousness and heal their land.

Yes, Mohammad is not God.

Buddha is not God.

Allah is not God.

All three are false gods pretending to be the true God and are now deceiving many with their false teachings.

Only Father God, Jesus Christ God, and Our God's Holy Spirit is the One true God.

Only Jesus Christ has paid the price of His holy shed blood on Calvary's cross to pay the penalty for each of mankind's sins.

Only Jesus Christ has the power to give a person life, abundant life on earth, and eternal life in heaven.

Preach Jesus Christ as the ONLY TRUE SAVIOR.

Only Jesus Christ can save a person's soul from going to hell after their one life and one death on earth.

A person must come to Jesus while they are alive on earth and ASK Jesus for salvation from their sins and wrongdoings, receive this FREE GIFT from Jesus of salvation, then go and sin no more.

Yes, read and study Our God's Holy Bible that teaches of heaven and hell and who will go there. (Revelation 21:8)

Yes, Jesus will return SOON for Our God's great rapture of souls to catch away Our God's saved and sanctified children in a split second to take them BACK to Our God's great heaven above to rule and reign forever with THEIR Holy Triune God.

Yes, do warn people that you meet that time IS SHORT and is growing shorter until Jesus returns toward earth for Our God's great catching away to Our God's great heaven above.

Preach and warn people to GET ready to go and to STAY ready to go to meet Jesus in the air.

Yes, choose Jesus now and NEVER regret it throughout eternity.

If a person dies without choosing Jesus and without living for God and ends up in hell forever, they WILL REGRET FOREVER not choosing Jesus.

Hallelujah!

Praises to Our heavenly Father God for this prophetic message!

Hallelujah!

Praises to Our God!

Dear Christian Pastors and All Holy Bible Teachers,

Last Tuesday evening from 7 p.m. to 9 p.m., my two housemates, Karen and Sherry, and I attended a taping of TBN in Hendersonville, Tennessee, hosted by Perry Stone. He had two guest speakers and had five black blood brothers who sang several Christian songs. All were very good. The program was due to be aired on TBN on Wednesday evening, September 23, 2015 from 9 p.m. to 11 p.m.

There were four pastors from different churches seated near us, two black pastors and two white pastors. As Perry Stone gave his Bible teaching message in the last half hour of the taping, he spoke on the critical times that we are now living in before Jesus returns for the rapture. He spoke about how evil forces are trying to get stronger and are coming against the Christians in America. He told the people, especially the pastors, to draw closer to God and to strengthen their congregations to withstand the evil times that are getting stronger in America. The Lord let me know the hunger in the hearts of these pastors to receive a fresh message from God for themselves and for their congregations.

I had taken with me four copies of prophetic message #798 where Father God had revealed that He will reveal the winner of the 2016 U. S. Presidential election ahead of time as God revealed by the Bible Code search six months before the 2012 election that President B. Obama would be re-elected U. S. President and sworn in twice. I gave three of these printed messages to three of the pastors. After the service, I gave a copy to a female TBN worker and asked her to give it to Perry Stone. She said that she would and went backstage to deliver it to him.

On the drive home from Hendersonville, the Lord revealed

to me that all the pastors in America need to hear from God on a regular basis with prophetic messages, and that these fifty prophetic messages that our Father God is giving to me for Christian pastors needs to be put into book form for each pastor to have their own copy. With a published book, our Father God can better encourage each pastor to stand strong in their faith. The title of the book that the Lord gave to me is, *Church Growth Our Father God's Way*.

After I got home from the trip, I got on my knees in prayer to our Father God and asked Him: "Are You going to reveal the winner ahead of the 2016 Presidential election by a message that's encoded in the original Hebrew or Greek of the Bible the way the previous President B. Obama winner message was revealed? Or, are You going to reveal the winner in the hidden messages in the prophecies that I have been getting?"

Father God spoke to me and said something like this, **"I will reveal the winner both ways, both from the Bible and from the prophetic messages you have been getting. This way people will connect these prophetic messages with what is written in the Bible."** Praise God!

Later, it was revealed by using the Bible Code that encoded in the Holy Bible was the message that Donald Trump would be elected U. S. President. It was revealed before the 2016 election was held. Praise God!

Blessings! Velma

Yes, Our God's beloved Christian pastors, YOUR heavenly Father God does love you and does love ALL of your loved ones, and YOUR heavenly Father God does take care of you and them at ALL times.

Yes, do CALL unto your God, call ANY time, daytimes or night times, and YOUR heavenly Father God WILL ANSWER YOU and WILL SHOW YOU great and mighty things which you know not. (Jeremiah 33:3)

Yes, YOUR heavenly Father God is no respecter of persons as YOUR heavenly Father God does love ALL of Our God's mankind on earth the same, and what I, your Father God, will do for one of mankind, I will do for any of mankind when the right conditions are met. (Acts 10:34)

Trust God.

Lean on God.

Believe God.

Know God.

Know the power of God.

Know the power of answered prayers from YOUR Holy Triune God.

Yes, keep trusting God, keep on believing in your God to answer ALL your prayers prayed for your benefit, for others of your loved ones' benefit, and that your God WILL be glorified on earth THROUGH THESE ANSWERS to your many prayers.

Yes, ALWAYS pray ALL your prayers in Jesus' holy name, because prayers prayed in Jesus' name ARE the strongest forces on earth today.

Nothing is impossible with YOUR God.

Yes, pray and let your requests be known to your God, pray

them in Jesus' holy name, and then do PRAISE YOUR Holy Triune God many times daily until you do see the results of these answered prayers.

Yes, no request is too big for your God's power, and no request is too small for your God's love to answer.

Yes, what is important to you is important to your loving God for you.

Yes, you will be tried and tested, but YOUR GOD will bring you THROUGH all these tests as pure gold, a worthy vessel for YOUR Holy Triune God to use in a greater way to win MANY MORE lost souls to salvation in Jesus.

Yes, preach Jesus over and over again.

People in YOUR congregation are HUNGRY for Jesus, for more and more of Jesus as Jesus is their Healer of their bodies, the Savior of their souls, their ONLY Gateway to their eternal home in heaven, their holy Bridegroom Who is coming back for ALL the saved and sanctified, right-living-unto-God beloved children of God, coming back SOONER than most people do realize, to catch them away in the air, to take them BACK to THEIR eternal home in heaven.

Yes, Jesus Christ is all-powerful. (Matthew 28:18)

Yes, Jesus Christ is the total and complete answer to any problem that any of mankind does have on earth.

Yes, Jesus Christ IS ABLE to meet every person's needs while they are on earth and meet ALL their needs in their afterlife in heaven, if only people will accept the free salvation that Jesus offers them, will come out of ALL known sin in their life and live for God, they can ask Jesus for whatever they desire, if it will benefit them, benefit others, and glorify God on earth, ALL their many prayers prayed in faith to Lord Jesus and Father God WILL be answered.

Yes, YOUR heavenly Father God SPOKE into existence this universe, your earth, all on it and all in it.

Yes, your heavenly Father God SPEAKS and something is created from nothing.

15

Yes, Jesus Christ IS the spoken Word of His heavenly Father God. (John 1:1)

Yes, when prayers are prayed to your heavenly Father God in Jesus' name, your heavenly Father God SPEAKS, "Be it done unto you according to your faith in My Son, Jesus Christ," and then Father God watches to see which prayers are answered as they ARE answered by your heavenly Father God according to YOUR FAITH in Jesus Christ.

Yes, a measure of faith in Jesus is given to each person when they accept Jesus as their Lord and Savior from their sins.

Yes, doesn't Our God's Holy Bible teach, "Draw near to God, and Our God will draw near to you"? (James 4:8)

Yes, to increase your faith in Jesus Christ, you must draw near to Him in praise, prayer, Bible study, and listening to Him speak to you personally.

Yes, doesn't Jesus, Himself, say in Our God's Holy Bible, "You have not, because you ask not. Ask and receive that your joy will be full"? (John 16:24)

Yes, Jesus, Father God, and Our God's Holy Spirit, are no respecter of persons, as We do, Our God does, love each person the same, and Our God can and WILL answer each person who praises God, who asks Our God to speak to them, and who will wait on their knees before God until Our God answers them.

Yes, Our God gives a great promise to you in Jeremiah 33:3 where God tells you, "Call unto Me, and I will answer you and show you great and mighty things which you know not."

Yes, that promise to you as given in Our God's Holy Bible is as true today as when it was given thousands of years ago.

Yes, what Our God will do for one person, Our God will do for ANY person when the conditions are met.

Yes, read and study ALL of Our God's promises to you in Our God's Holy Bible, KNOW the conditions to be met, MEET the conditions, and CLAIM the promises for you, your family, and for ALL your loved ones as Our God does DELIGHT to keep ALL Our promises to mankind, when they DO MEET the conditions, and when they do pray and do ASK in faith in Jesus' holy name.

Yes, ALL the good gifts that you do have now in your life are gifts to you from your heavenly Father God, and they do come to you THROUGH your Lord Jesus Christ. (Philippians 4:19)

Do you wish to be more prosperous and more successful in life?

Study the Scriptures in the Bible on how to live a successful life and prosper.

Psalm 1:1-3 tells you how to prosper in whatever you do: Read your Bible daily, keep away from bad influences, and whatever you do will prosper.

Do the work that you enjoy doing, praise God, and ask God to give you the knowledge, wisdom, skills, and ability to increase in your work, and Our God will help you to work successful, and will open new opportunities for your advancements.

Share what you have with love for the needy, elderly, the orphans, the ill, the handicapped, with people who need your help, and watch how Our God rewards you for your love, your kindness, and your generosity to the needy around you.

Pay your tithes and offerings and watch Our God repay you more than double what you give so that Our God's gospel can go forth on earth and the helpless will be helped.

Hallelujah!

Praises to Our Father God for this good message!

Praise God!

Dear Christian Pastors and All Holy Bible Teachers,

I want to tell you about some of the history of The Lord's Chapel which at one time was "The fastest growing church in Nashville" started and led by Pastor Billy Roy Moore. His background was Church of God, but he began it as a non-denominational church.

When Brother Moore wanted to begin a church, he prayed about it, and God spoke to him, **"Go, and I'll go with you. Sing and I will sing with you. Pray and I will pray with you. Preach and I will preach with you."** He began teaching a Bible study class in a private home with only a few people attending. He would take a book of the Bible like the book of Acts and would teach one chapter at each meeting, continuing on through the whole book of Acts. Then he would begin teaching another book of the Bible, usually from the New Testament, teaching one chapter at each meeting going through the whole book.

He sang some praise songs, and his wife Pixie played the piano and sometimes sang with him. He always led praise singing and always had Communion service at each of the meetings. He did not pass the offering plates. When people wanted to give offerings, boxes was placed by the door for this purpose.

Even as the attendance at the meetings continued to grow, these same practices were still carried out.

As the attendance at these Bible studies continued to grow, a larger space was needed so a larger house was rented for a while. Then a house was purchased in Brentwood, located at the corner of Granny White Pike and Old Hickory Blvd., where the congregation continued to grow. This building burned.

The insurance money was used to build a larger building at

this same location with the name of The Lord's Chapel used for this church building.

Then this new building burned, and the insurance money from this fire was used to again build an even larger building for The Lord's Chapel at this same location. While this building was being rebuilt after this second fire, the congregation met in a large tent with folding chairs in the parking lot of the church.

The attendance continued to grow.

Brother Moore's Bible teaching never changed as he kept teaching one chapter of the Bible at each meeting on Sunday mornings, continuing through one book of the Bible at a time. In 1977 when the congregation was meeting in the tent in the parking lot, while the building was being rebuilt after the second fire, was when my two small children and I joined The Lord's Chapel. I left the Presbyterian church and began attending The Lord's Chapel because it was the best Bible teaching that I could find in the Nashville area. I saw Connie Smith dedicating one of her little daughters to the Lord there so I then had Brother Moore dedicate our children to the Lord, Lori at age four and Alan at age two, while we were still meeting in the tent. Later, when Lori and Alan got older and accepted Jesus as their Savior, Brother Moore baptized them with emersion in our built-in baptistery in our church building.

The attendance at The Lord's Chapel continued to grow until we needed to expand. The building we were in could have a balcony built for this purpose, but codes would not allow it because the parking space was inadequate for more growth. Since none of the neighboring houses would sell us more land for us to expand the parking lot, we needed to relocate. We bought about thirty six acres of land on Nolensville Road in Nashville and built a building. We relocated to the new building with our first service held on August 7, 1988. When we relocated, we had enough funds from the sale of our previous building and enough pledges from the people to completely pay for the new property and new building.

You can see that God grew the church to be the fastest growing church in Nashville, built on Brother Moore's marvelous Bible teaching with the help of God. People are so hungry for good Bible teaching, for precious Jesus, and for the great help that Jesus gives them to live successful lives, that they will drive for miles and be content to have three-hour services, when God moves by His Spirit.

I was sitting in a Benny Hinn service in Atlanta when I thought, "Benny doesn't really have a sermon, he just comes out and talks about Jesus for four hours, and people get saved and healed." Then Jesus spoke to me and said, **"I will do this for anyone who will have a four-hour service."** So far, I have found only two four-hour services in Nashville: Once when Benny Hinn came to Nashville and once when Ernest Angley came to Nashville and rented the Grand Ol' Opry building. Jesus did physical healings at both of these meetings. Praise God!

Blessings! Velma

Yes, Our God's beloved Christian pastors, YOUR heavenly Father God does love you, does love ALL of your loved ones, does take care of you and them at ALL times, and does want you, them, and your congregations to prosper and be in good health as your souls prosper in God.

Yes, your God is a good God, a powerful God, a just God, an everlasting God, a God Who is in complete control of all things, all people, and all events at all times.

Do KNOW your God.

Do worship and praise your God.

Do live a righteous lifestyle with and for your God.

Do be blessed and rewarded by your God.

Do be used by your God to win MORE people to YOUR Lord and Savior, Jesus Christ.

Yes, do go around shaking hands with people and do TELL THEM that Jesus Christ, YOUR Lord Jesus Christ, does love them and He has, your Lord Jesus Christ has, prepared a heavenly home for them, and that Our God DOES WANT THEM to go there for eternity, to enjoy life in heaven always with Father God, with their Lord Jesus, and with ALL their loved ones.

Yes, heaven IS a beautiful place, a joyful place, a place of peace, rest, love, and happy times, where there is no sickness and no sorrow, where their heavenly Father God WILL wipe away every tear and will fill every person with love, joy, and peace as they do ABIDE in Our holy God's presence forever.

Yes, your ONLY one-way ticket to heaven in your afterlife, after your one life and one death on earth, is to come through the shed blood of Jesus Christ on Calvary's cruel cross to wash away ALL your sins and wrongdoings, to come OUT of all sinful lifestyle and live for God, learn to obey God, and then spend eternity in heaven.

Yes, at your moment of conception, your heavenly Father God created you in Our God's image with body, soul, and spirit.

Yes, Our God created you, each person, with an eternal spirit that will continue to live forever.

Yes, your spirit and soul will live forever either in heaven with your Lord Jesus, or it will continue to live forever in hell with Satan as there are no other places for your eternal soul to live after your one life and one death on earth.

Yes, there is NO reincarnation as you do know reincarnation to be.

Reincarnation is a complete lie from Satan, who is the father of all lies.

Those who do believe in reincarnation, where it teaches you can achieve heaven through your good works, are believing a complete lie from Satan as it is IMPOSSIBLE for anyone to try to work their way into heaven by good works and/or by kind deeds.

Yes, ONLY the shed blood of Jesus Christ is powerful enough to cleanse a person of sins and wrongdoings, to cleanse them of their sin nature they inherited from Adam, and give them the freedom of entering heaven cleansed and pure from ALL unholy filth.

Yes, sin will NEVER enter heaven.

Yes, after you ASK Jesus to cleanse you of all sin, you must rebuke all sin from your lifestyle and live your life for God free from all sin if you are to be counted worthy to enter heaven forever.

Yes, you MUST choose this FREE gift from Jesus for your eternal salvation and life in heaven, you must choose Jesus while you are alive in your one life on earth for if you DO die in your sins and lift up your eyes in hell, it could be TOO LATE for you to accept Jesus and live for God.

Yes, it IS possible for YOUR eternal soul to be trapped in hell forever, where there is never any hope of escape, where the worm/soul never dies and the eternal flame is not quenched.

Yes, hell is hot and it is LONG, and you do NOT want to go there.

Yes, the ONLY Being, alive or dead, Who has the power to keep your eternal soul from going to hell for eternity is Jesus Christ of Nazareth, Who has paid the penalty for your sins, transgressions, and iniquities, Who offers you a FREE one-way ticket to heaven away from hell for repenting of your sins, asking Jesus to forgive you of your sins, and by coming out of a sinful lifestyle, and living for God for the rest of your one life on earth.

Yes, do read and do study Our God's Holy Bible, and it will tell you the truth about heaven and hell.

Yes, do believe every word that you do read in Our God's Holy Bible as it is ALL true as it IS the divinely inspired Word of God and refined seven times for clarity. (Psalm 12:6)

Yes, secret hidden messages are encoded in the Bible in the Old Testament Hebrew text and in the New Testament Greek text that can be found by the Bible Code method of searching with equal distance letter skips going forward and going backwards in the text, and these hidden messages in these texts do reveal, prophesy, the future of mankind on earth and in heaven.

Yes, Our God's Holy Bible predicts what will happen to the future of America and what will happen in the rest of the world in the near future so DO BE PREPARED to meet your God, Jesus Christ face-to-face, when Jesus does split the great Eastern skies coming for ALL of Our God's Own saved and sanctified children of God, to catch them away into the air above earth in a split second, to take them BACK to THEIR eternal home in heaven.

Yes, time IS SHORT until Our God's Jesus returns toward Our God's earth for Our God's great rapture of souls.

Yes, get ready to go in the twinkling of an eye, in a split

second, as you do NOT know the day nor the hour when YOUR heavenly Father God WILL give the command to Our God's only begotten Son Jesus to, "GO!"

Get ready!

Stay ready!

The time is SHORT!

Jesus is coming SOON!

Hallelujah!

Praises to Our heavenly Father God for this message to help build up Our God's churches on earth to prepare for the SOON arrival of Jesus!

Hallelujah!

Praises to Our God!

Dear Christian Pastors and All Holy Bible Teachers,

We enjoyed a substitute speaker in our church service yesterday who spoke on Jesus and parts of the Bible. It is so refreshing to hear teachings from the Bible on how we can apply them to our lives so that our souls can grow in God.

I'm glad that our church members gave $60,000.00 cash and pledges of $120,000.00 in gifts during the next year in celebration of our church's 18th Year Anniversary. As for myself, I was not able to give anything extra or pledge anything extra as I am already giving about 60% of my net monthly income to my charities and my projects. I give to some of the same charities that our church gives to, such as The Nashville Rescue Mission, Second Harvest Food Bank of Middle Tennessee, Mercy Ministries, and others locally, nationally, and internationally.

I do not give to health charities, except to Smile Train and First Step, as I like to introduce people to the Healer, Jesus Christ. I like to give to promote the gospel world-wide, feed and clothe people, develop fresh water wells, help support individual children and several individual missionaries in foreign countries, seven churches in the United States, seven Jewish charities, five American Indian charities, ten military charities, and to many other charities that I know are trustworthy and are promoting the gospel world-wide. I also give to five young people monthly who need extra financial help. When I mail all my monthly checks to charities and to individuals, I also include with each check a printed prophetic message from Father God or from Lord Jesus.

I now have a list of more than 200 more worthy charities that I hope to give to when God increases my income. Father God once told me, **"Your greatest income will be from the sale of your books."**

I have now self-published two books, and this will be my third book to publish. I am now working on four more books to publish with the help of our God's Holy Spirit.

Father God wants me to write fifty letters to Christian pastors and receive from Father God fifty prophetic messages for church growth. He wants me to send copies of these letters and prophetic messages to fourteen pastors of churches to help them with their church growth, which I have been doing. He now wants me to self-publish them in a book titled, *Church Growth Our Father God's Way,* so that it can be marketed world-wide to help encourage pastors in other nations for church growth. He wants these messages to help get their congregations ready for our God's great rapture of souls, for our God's great end-time harvest of souls.

Yes, if these pastors will spend time studying their Bibles daily, let our God teach them what to teach others, and let these prophetic messages from God help them to know what is now on our God's heart for them to teach their congregations, their congregations will grow and grow.

I have just read the book by Dr. Paul Crouch, Sr., *Ask Me for Anything.* It is super good in teaching living for God, giving God your best gifts, and asking God for anything good that will help you, help others, and glorify God. He certainly put it all into practice himself in building up Trinity Broadcasting Network world-wide.

After I read the book, Father God said to me, **"Ask Me for anything."** I had read that one in five children in the United States goes to bed hungry every night so I asked God, "Please help us to feed the children so that no child goes to bed hungry at night." A couple of days later, I suppose that God wanted me to ask Him to do something for me personally, so Father God said to me, **"Ask Me to double your income!"** I praised God, was obedient to God, and asked Him to double my income. I also asked Him, "Please give me the knowledge and wisdom to use this income to help others and to help build up the Kingdom of God world-wide."

Father God once told me, **"Many people ask me to give them wealth, but they don't ask Me to give them the knowledge and wisdom to use the wealth beneficially."** God's Holy Spirit is now teaching me to praise God more in my prayer language daily, so that He can fill me more with knowledge and wisdom to lead a more successful life and help others. Praises to our God!

Blessings! Velma

Yes, Our God's beloved Christian pastors, YOUR heavenly Father God does love you, does guide you, does protect you, and has given to you a very great work to do on Our God's planet Earth to HELP build up the Kingdom of God on earth, that people will KNOW THEIR holy Creators God, will love and worship their God with their total being, and will love and will help their fellow mankind as they do love and do help themselves.

Yes, YOUR Holy Triune God is a loving God, a generous God, a forgiving God to ALL who do repent of their sins and wrongdoings, who CALL on God for forgiveness, who rebuke all sin from their lives, who then go and sin no more.

Yes, call on Jesus Christ for salvation from sin, and call on Our God's Holy Spirit for righteous living unto God, and do be rewarded by Our God for living righteously unto God and obeying God.

Do go around helping the helpless to YOUR God's glory, and do be rewarded for this by YOUR heavenly Father God.

Yes, do draw closer to YOUR God, and YOUR God WILL draw closer to you. (James 4:8)

Yes, do learn of ALL of Our God's promises to you as given in Our God's Holy Bible, and do meet the conditions of these promises, claim them for you, your household, and your church, and do WATCH Our God work on your behalf to enrich your life, the lives of your family and friends, and the lives of your church members.

Yes, Our God's promises to you and to your loved ones at church are always true, are always yes and amen, when the conditions are met for these promises as given in Our God's Holy Bible.

Yes, know these promises.

Yes, claim these promises.

Know the power of God in these promises when you know God, obey God, live for God, and witness for God.

Yes, Our God's words to you will not return void, but WILL ACCOMPLISH THAT for which they were sent. (Isaiah 55:11)

Yes, do CALL unto your God Jesus and Father God, and your God WILL answer you and show you great and mighty things which you know not. (Jeremiah 33:3)

Yes, doesn't Jesus say to you that you have not because you ask not? So do ask, do receive, and do let your joy be full. (John 16:24)

Yes, what Our God has done for others, Our God will do for you in building up your church as you do speak and preach the truth in love, the truth about Jesus, the Bible, Father God, Our God's Holy Spirit, about heaven and hell, and about the soon return of Jesus for Our God's great catching away to the heavenlies, for Our God's great rapture of all the saved and sanctified Christian souls to take them BACK to THEIR great home in Our God's great heaven above.

Yes, warn people that Our God's great rapture of souls is VERY SOON and for them to get ready and to stay ready to go in a split second to meet Jesus in the air.

Yes, time on earth, as you know time on earth to be now, is SOON running out.

Soon time on earth will be no more as you do know time now to be on earth as soon time on earth will enter Our God's millennial period.

Yes, very soon Our God WILL create a new heaven and a new earth as described in the book of Revelation as given in Our God's Holy Bible. (Revelation 21:1)

Yes, do warn all the people you meet to get right with Jesus Christ for the forgiveness of their sins and for the salvation of their souls as they MUST COME to Jesus for this FREE gift from Jesus while they are alive on earth—then they must come out of all sinful lifestyle and live for God for the rest of their life on earth, if they do expect to go to heaven in their life after their one life on earth.

Yes, sin will never enter heaven.

Yes, you must be cleansed of ALL your sin and wrongdoing, cleansed in the shed blood of Jesus, which He shed on Calvary's cross to pay the debt for your sins that you could not pay.

Yes, no amount of good works and kind deeds by yourself can qualify you to be able to enter heaven on your own—ONLY Jesus has the power to forgive your sins and make it possible for you to have FREE access to heaven in your afterlife.

Yes, life on earth is uncertain, and your one death on earth is certain.

Yes, choose Jesus as your Savior and Lord, live for God, and enter heaven forever.

Yes, do warn people that if they reject Jesus as their Lord and Savior and do NOT live for God while alive on earth, that they are in danger of living in hell fire forever for if they die in their sins and lift up their eyes in hell, they could remain there forever where there is no escape and where it is too late to choose Jesus as their Savior and live for God.

Yes, do encourage people to read and study their Holy Bibles for themselves and encourage them to know that EVERY WORD of Our God's Holy Bible is straight from the inspiration from Our God Who directed Our God's saints to write every word of it.

Yes, God is real.

Our God's Bible is true.

Believe every word of Our God's Holy Bible.

Draw close to God, and Our God WILL draw close to you. (James 4:8)

Yes, Our God does love each person equally, and what Our

30

God does for any of Our God's children, Our God will also do for you when the right conditions are met. (Acts 10:34)

Believe every word Jesus spoke when He walked this earth nearly two thousand years ago as recorded in Our God's Holy Bible.

Do let the lifestyle of Jesus become your own lifestyle as Jesus went about helping the lonely, the needy, the helpless, loving them, and teaching them of HIS heavenly Father God Who is able to give them ALL good gifts to enrich their lives and make them successful on earth and give them an eternal home in heaven with THEIR Holy Triune God.

Yes, worship God forever!

Enjoy your God forever!

Hallelujah!

Praises to Our heavenly Father God for this prophetic message for church growth in Our God's great End-time harvest of souls!

Hallelujah!

Praises to Our God!

Dear Christian Pastors and All Holy Bible Teachers,

Here are some reasons that I believe God wants you to speak on the Bible and Jesus from the pulpit every Sunday:

1. Jesus says that apart from Me, you can do nothing. (John 15:5)
2. All good gifts in our lives come from Father God and they come through Jesus to us. (Philippians 4:19)
3. Jesus is the only Being Who has ever lived Who has paid the price for us to have life, abundant life on earth, and eternal life in heaven. (John 10:10)
4. All power in heaven and in earth has been given unto Jesus. (Matthew 28:18)
5. The only way a person can come into the presence of their heavenly Father God is through the shed blood of Jesus to cleanse them of all unholy filth. (John 14:6)
6. Jesus is returning soon for the rapture, and people need to get ready and stay ready to go in any split second. (1 Corinthians 15:52)
7. Jesus had thirty-nine stripes on His back to pay for the healing of all thirty-nine kinds of diseases known to mankind on earth. (Isaiah 53:5) Jesus still heals today. (Hebrews 13:8)
8. Jesus is the spoken Word of His heavenly Father God Who created and Who owns the universe, the earth, all on it and all in it. (John 1:1-3)
9. Jesus has prepared homes in heaven for the obedient Christians to live in forever with our Holy Triune God. (John 14:2-3)

10. Jesus cannot lie, and all of His promises in the Bible to everyone are absolutely true when the right conditions are met. (Numbers 23:19)

11. Jesus' love for mankind was shown in His willingness to be betrayed, beaten, crucified, and killed for us to have all good things with Him. His resurrection, His ascension into heaven, His intercession for mankind with His heavenly Father God, His return to Earth to claim His Bride-to be, and His taking His obedient Christians home to heaven to rule and reign with Him forever, show His great love for each of mankind. No other human or so-called god has done so much for mankind. Father God and Jesus made it possible for us to be joint-heirs with Jesus and have all good things forever. (Romans 8:17)

12. Father God, Jesus, and God's Holy Spirit created and still creates mankind in Their image with body, soul, and spirit. (Genesis 1:27)

13. God revealed to me that at the moment of conception, God creates thirty-two miracles that have to take place at the same time in order for a person's life to begin. At conception, God gives each person their immortal soul that will live forever in heaven with Jesus, or it will live forever in hell with Satan as there are no other places for a person's soul to live after their one life and one death on earth. At conception, God gives each person gifts for their earthly success.

14. Jesus Christ is the only Being alive Who has enough power to keep a person's soul out of hell forever, and Who has enough power to give each person a FREE one-way ticket to heaven if each person will accept this FREE gift of salvation from their sins from Jesus and will live for God while alive on earth. (John 10:1-9)

15. Jesus spent His earthly life setting the best example for us to follow as He went about helping the helpless and teaching people about His and our heavenly Father God.

16. Jesus is God and deserves to be worshipped as God. (John 14:9-11)
17. The Holy Triune God deserves FIRST PLACE in our lives, hearts, and possessions. (Exodus 20:3-5)
18. Father God answers our believing prayers when we pray them in Jesus' holy name. The name of Jesus is holy, is above every other name, and at the name of Jesus every knee will bow and every tongue will confess that Jesus Christ is Lord of all to the glory of God the Father. (Philippians 2:10-11)
19. Jesus Christ DESERVES to be spoken about from your pulpit EVERY Sunday for all He has done, all He is doing for us now, and all He will do for us in the future.
20. Jesus teaches us about our heavenly Father God and Our God's Holy Spirit, and how to worship our God in spirit and in truth. (John 4:23-24) Jesus Christ is the way, the truth, and the life. (John 14:6)

If you don't preach about Jesus, the Bible, and our God's Holy Triune God, you are feeding people crumbs, and people will not have the power to face the future that Satan has planned for all the children of God. The congregation NEEDS to hear about the power, the provisions, and the protection that we all have in our God Jesus. Don't let people leave your church meetings spiritually hungry for Jesus and the Bible teachings if you want them to return and bring with them their spiritually hungry family and friends.

Blessings! Velma

Yes, Our God's beloved Christian pastors and all other Bible teachers, YOUR heavenly Father God does love you, does guide you, and does give to you MANY opportunities to teach others about YOUR Lord and Savior, Jesus Christ, what He has done for you and for ALL of your loved ones, what Jesus is NOW doing for you, and what Jesus will do both for you and for them.

Yes, Jesus IS a good God, an all-powerful God, a God Who does deserve ALL of mankind's praise and worship on earth.

Yes, Jesus is God.

Yes, worship and praise Jesus Christ as you do worship and praise YOUR heavenly Father God.

Yes, when you do finally get to heaven, you will see YOUR Holy Triune God as Three separate Beings of Father God, Jesus Christ God, and Our God's Holy Spirit of God; yes, Our God IS Three separate Beings, but We are, your God is, always in one accord.

Yes, when Jesus said on earth, "If you have seen Me, you have seen the Father," Jesus was speaking of His spiritual and holy union with HIS heavenly Father God, that He always knows His Father God and knows His Father God's will for His life, that Jesus and HIS Father God are always in agreement, always in one accord. (John 14:9)

Yes, time IS SHORT and is NOW growing shorter until Our God Jesus' soon return toward earth for Our God's great rapture of souls, ALL the saved-in-Jesus and sanctified, right-living-for-God, beloved children of God, to take them BACK to THEIR great heaven above, to live with, to rule and reign with their Holy Triune God forever.

Yes, do preach EVERY SUNDAY on this soon-coming rapture of Jesus Christ.

Do warn people to get ready and to stay ready to go to meet Jesus in the air in a split second.

Yes, you do NOT know the day nor the hour when Our God's Jesus will return for Our God's great rapture of souls, but do look around you at the signs of the times on earth and in the heavens, and you WILL KNOW the time is SOON for Jesus' appearing in the heavenlies.

Yes, only YOUR heavenly Father God does know the time of Jesus Christ's appearing when ALL the saints of God WILL BE READY for His appearing as only Our Father God is able to see this future time clearly of Jesus' appearing.

Do pray in ALL your lost family members and ALL your lost loved ones, and do WARN THEM that time is short and is growing shorter until Our Father God tells Jesus, "Go! Go and get your holy Bride-to-be and bring the right-living-unto-God saints of God BACK to heaven for the very great wedding supper of the Lamb!" (Revelation 19:9)

Yes, the hand of Jesus is now at the door of heaven awaiting HIS Father God's voice telling Him to, "GO!"

Yes, ONLY Father God knows when the exact time is right for Jesus to return toward earth in the heavenlies, and Our Father God knows the right time for the signal to Jesus to, "GO!"

Yes, your heavenly Father God has ALL power to control all things and all events in Our God's three heavens and in and on earth.

Yes, God knows all of your thoughts, all of your motives, all of your words, and all of your deeds on earth, and one day in the future, every person who has ever lived on earth WILL stand before Our God's white throne judgment and give an account for their one life on earth, for their thoughts, words, and deeds while they were alive on earth.

Yes, each person will tell if they accepted Jesus as their Lord and Savior while alive on earth, and if they came out of all sin and lived for God while alive on earth.

If they accepted Jesus as Savior and lived for God while alive on earth and lived for God apart from sin—a sinful lifestyle—in their life, their names will be found written in the Lamb's book of life, and they will be privileged to enter heaven forever to live with God and to rule and reign with THEIR Lord Jesus Christ forever.

If they refused to be saved by Jesus and refused to repent and come out of all sinful lifestyle while alive on earth, their names will NOT be written in the Lamb's book of life and they WILL enter hell with Satan forever.

Yes, you must make your choice for salvation in Jesus while you are alive on earth, and you must forsake ALL sinful lifestyle and live for God while you are alive on earth in order to go to heaven for eternity after your one life and one death on earth.

Yes, sin will NEVER enter heaven.

You MUST come out of ALL sinful lifestyle and live for God with Jesus as your Lord and Savior in order to enter heaven.

Yes, hell is hot and it is long, and many there be that find their way to hell.

Yes, you do NOT want to spend eternity in hell where your soul will never perish and the "worm" never dies, separated from your true God, Jesus Christ as there is no hope of ever escape from the fires and miseries of hell once you do enter hell.

Yes, you MUST come to Jesus, you must SEEK Jesus, you must ACCEPT the free gift of salvation FROM Jesus while you are alive on earth.

If you do die in your sins and lift up your eyes in hell, it could be TOO LATE for you to accept Jesus as your Lord and Savior and live for God.

Yes, do read and study Our God's Holy Bible about the rich man and Lazarus both dying with Lazarus going to heaven with Abraham and the rich man going to hell, how there was no escape from hell, and there was no hope in hell of the situation he was in for improvement. (Luke 16:19-31)

Hope, any hope for improvement in any situation while you are alive on earth, the hope comes from God.

God is not in hell, and there is no hope in hell.

Only a right relationship with God, Father God and Jesus Christ God, can bring any good hope to any situation while people are still alive on earth.

With God all good things are possible. (Luke 1:37)

Praises to Our Father God for this encouraging message!

Hallelujah!

Praises to Our God!

Dear Christian Pastors and All Holy Bible Teachers,

In our Oasis Church service yesterday, Pastor Danny Chambers said that Joseph was in a trial for thirteen years. I had just received this prophetic message number seven for church growth from Father God the day before this sermon, that stated that Joseph was in a trial for twelve years. Since I thought that maybe I didn't hear Father God accurately when I heard it was for twelve years, I got on my knees and praised God and asked Father God to speak to me about it. He replied, **"He was in bondage for twelve years. It is the same amount of trial that you are in at Oasis Church concerning these spoken prophetic messages."**

It has now been twelve years since Pastor Danny Chambers told me that I was not allowed to have spoken prophetic messages at Oasis Church. Also, Betsy Flick, our Sunday School teacher, will not allow me to speak prophetic messages in our class at Oasis Church. Father God also told me yesterday, **"You are right not to fight Pastor Danny and Betsy with this."**

Twelve years ago when I first met Pastor Danny Chambers at the merger of The Lord's Chapel with Oasis Church, I told him that there were prophetic messages on my website, HotOffTheThrone.com. He told me that I was not allowed to have these prophetic messages at Oasis Church. He told me this even though he had never read a single one of them and did not know if they were good or bad prophetic messages.

At that time of the merger, I knew that God wanted me to stay at Oasis Church even though all five of my volunteer jobs at The Lord's Chapel had been cancelled by the leaders of Oasis Church. I prayed and asked Father God, "Why am I at Oasis Church?" He replied, **"Spoken prophecy."** I said to Father God, "They won't allow me to speak prophecy at Oasis Church." Father God replied to me, **"Wait until I can work out all these problems with these leaders."** I have now waited for twelve years.

Then God's Holy Spirit led me to ask Pastor Danny if I may put the eighteen Oasis Church staff members on the mailing list to receive my monthly publication of The Garner News which has a prophetic message in ever issue. He did give his permission for me to do this so I have been giving it to them monthly for about a year. I have not heard if they are reading these prophetic messages.

I finally left this church of The Lord's Chapel which became Oasis Church after being a member there for thirty nine years. I am glad that I became Holy Spirit filled while at The Lord's Chapel. As a result of my being Holy Spirit filled, I now have more than 940 prophetic messages from Father God and Lord Jesus written out and typed up that I have asked for Them to give to me. Praise God! I put out a monthly family newsletter for twenty eight years and put a prophetic message in every issue for the past twenty five years with the help of our God's Holy Spirit. Praise God!

Father God told me recently that I am on the edge of a breakthrough in my life with several happenings. One is that God said He will double my income which is now $5,000.00 a month. God told me that soon I will have a spiritual breakthrough. Now, when I drive around town and am alone in my car, I turn off my radio and sing praises in my prayer language.

I recently drove to Cleveland, Tennessee, for a five-day Perry Stone Conference and then drove on to Marietta, Georgia, and visited my daughter and her family. I prayed and sang in tongues for several hours all the way down and back. I have had amazing results since then.

The most profound change is the continual abundance of JOY in my life. Also, I have amazing breakthroughs in doing my art work with new ideas and new techniques. God gives me amazing wisdom in my counseling others, and God gives me many opportunities to witness for Jesus. My life is now being transformed for the better. Praise God!

Recently, I felt led to submit to Trinity Broadcasting Network my book, *Christmas in The Bible Belt*, for their consideration in giving it as Christmas gifts to their donors. So I submitted it to them.

Yesterday, I received a letter from them that stated they are unable to use it for this purpose. So I prayed and asked Father God about it. He replied something like, **"In the future, they will accept one of your books with prophecy in it for this purpose."** So I am content to wait for God's timing in this. Maybe it will happen after some of the hidden Bible Code prophetic messages are found within these prophetic messages. I am getting these messages word for word from Father God and Lord Jesus. Father God has told me that there are hidden messages within these prophetic messages that foretell the future of the United States and the future of the world. Praise God!

Blessings! Velma

Yes, Our God's beloved Christian pastors and Our God's beloved Holy Bible teachers, YOUR heavenly Father God does love you, does lead and feed you ALL GOOD things and all good ideas, and YOUR heavenly Father God does MAKE A WAY for you to work and to witness for YOUR Lord and Savior, Jesus Christ of Nazareth.

Yes, do be faithful to YOUR God, and YOUR God will always be faithful to you and to ALL of your loved ones.

Yes, always draw near to YOUR God, and YOUR God will ALWAYS draw near to you. (James 4:8)

Yes, if you and the other pastors at your church WILL CONTINUE to live for God in your daily and nightly life, and if you will use these fifty prophetic messages given to you from YOUR heavenly Father God, use the content of them for the basis of fifty sermons, YOUR heavenly Father God WILL reward you and these other pastors with double your church growth attendance and double your church growth income by the end of your Bible teaching from these fifty messages.

Yes, do test these messages and test any other prophetic messages to see if they agree with what is taught in Our God's Holy Bible.

Yes, you, yourself, will be tried and tested by YOUR heavenly Father God many times during the next year as your Holy Triune God WILL test your faith to see if you ARE following your true God.

You and your staff of workers and servants must grow stronger daily in your faith in God to withstand all the evil forces that are planning now to come against ALL the Christians and come especially against ALL the Christian pastors and leaders and their families, as evil forces know that if they can come against the Christian leaders to destroy their faith in God, that their ministry will collapse and many of their Christian followers will also collapse as their faith in God will grow weaker.

Yes, do what you can to strengthen the faith-in-Jesus of your church members by feeding them the true Word of God, the true Bible teachings, and by teaching them of the love, power, and sacrifice of Jesus for them.

Tell them that Jesus will never leave them nor forsake them. (Hebrews 13:5)

Tell them that prayer to THEIR Father God in the name of Jesus IS the strongest force on earth today and for them to pray long and often to THEIR heavenly Father God in the name of Jesus.

Yes, the holy name of Jesus IS far above every name, and it is the only name given among men whereby man must come through Jesus for cleansing in Jesus' shed blood in order to enter heaven in their life after their one life and one death on earth. (Acts 4:12)

Yes, Jesus Christ does hold the keys to death, hell, and the grave. (Revelation 1:18)

Yes, you must go through Jesus to enter heaven as no other being, dead or alive, has paid the awful price for a person to be forgiven of their sins and enter heaven.

Yes, Jesus can keep your eternal soul out of hell by your accepting Jesus as your Lord and Savior and by your coming out of ALL sinful lifestyle and by your living for God while alive on earth.

Yes, there is only one true Father God, and Jesus God is the ONLY mediator between God and men. (1 Timothy 2:5)

If a person rejects Jesus as their Savior and rejects living for God while they are alive on earth, and if they do die in their sins and lift up their eyes in hell, they WILL be there for eternity where the soul never dies and where there is no hope of ever escape from the misery in hell.

Yes, do read in the book of Revelation about who will be in hell, and do preach against these actions in people's lives. (Revelation 21:8)

Teach people to forgive their enemies and pray for their salvation, because if a person does NOT forgive ALL who have wronged them, Our Father God will NOT forgive their sins.

Yes, when Jesus Christ spoke these words on the cross of Calvary, "Father, forgive them," it was because Jesus, Himself, had ALREADY forgiven them for their persecution of Him. (Luke 23:34)

Yes, you MUST learn to forgive all the cruel people who do come against you—you must not only FORGIVE the offense, but you must FORGET the offense in order for your heavenly Father God to HEAL you of the offense, heal you mentally, emotionally, spiritually, physically, financially, in every way.

Yes, when you do pray believing prayers in Jesus' holy name, your heavenly Father God WILL use your faith to reverse the bad situation and bring something good from it. (Romans 8:28)

Yes, when the time was right for Joseph's deliverance from prison and his twelve years of affliction, God not only gave him relief overnight, but brought him from prison to the second in command in Egypt overnight.

Yes, Our God can supply ALL your needs right on time when you love God, live for God, and ASK God for your needed supplies praying believing prayers in Jesus' holy name. (Psalm 84:11)

Yes, NOTHING is too hard for YOUR Father God to accomplish for your good, to help others, and to glorify God, when you pray BIG prayers to your heavenly Father God, believing God, trusting God, and asking in Jesus' name. (Ephesians 3:20)

Yes, do study your Bible daily.

Yes, do pray daily without ceasing for a long time.

Do fast often as led by Our God's Holy Spirit.

Do continue to live for God.

Do honor God by loving and helping the helpless when it IS in your power to do so.

Ask God for knowledge, wisdom, strength, power, love, kindness, and gentleness to flow through you to others.

Draw near to God, and Our God WILL draw near to you. (James 4:8)

Hallelujah!

Praises to Our God!

Hallelujah!

Dear Christian Pastors and All Holy Bible Teachers:

I greatly enjoyed our pastor's sermon yesterday morning in our third worship service when he told us of his health problems and how our God is solving them for him. Yes, Jesus is the Healer, and it was good to hear him speak of Jesus in his sermon. There were about five of his sermons in a row when the name of Jesus was not even mentioned. He did say the word "Lord" a couple of times in one of them, but God has shown to me the difference in the words, "Lord," "lord," and "Jesus." There are many lords, even a few Lords, but there is only ONE true JESUS. I will not follow a pastor who will not follow Jesus and Father God. I know that our pastor does truly follow and try to obey Jesus and Father God.

Yes, Jesus has paid the price for all of our physical healing, and I always honor Jesus as the true Healer. That is why I now have 118 charities that I give to and few of them are health charities as I give to the charities that promote Jesus, the true Healer. I believe that when our souls grow in Jesus, when our faith in Jesus-the-Healer grows stronger that we will be physically healed. Our God designed our bodies to heal themselves. Doctors, surgeons, medicines, and therapy can only treat, but Jesus can heal! When Jesus walked this earth, Jesus healed EVERYONE who came to Him and requested healing, and Jesus is still the same Healer today. Jesus is still capable of healing EVERYONE who comes to Him and requests healing.

Father God showed to me that it works like this: When people come to Father God and Jesus and pray in Jesus' name for physical healing, Father God speaks, **"Be it done unto you according to your faith in My Son Jesus."** Then Father God watches to see who was healed instantly and who was healed over time. He sees who has enough faith in Jesus for their healing.

As a person's soul grows in God, their faith in Jesus grows. Our faith in Jesus grows in many ways:

Through singing praises to God, through reading and studying the Bible, through hearing good Christian sermons and Bible teaching, through discussions with Christian friends, through reading good Christian teaching books and biographies, through prayers and praying in tongues, through hearing God speak to us.

One of the best ways to grow in God, I believe, is to read and study our Bibles daily. I have been hearing our present pastor's sermons weekly for over twelve years now, and I have never once heard him tell the congregation to read and study their Bibles on a daily basis. One of the greatest promises in the Bible to us, I believe, is Psalm 1:1-3, where it teaches us that if we will read our Bibles daily, stay away from evil influences, that whatever we do will prosper. I have now read daily through the Bible forty five times in the last forty six years, beginning in 1971. My family has been prospering since 1971, and I can say that this promise of God in the Bible is absolutely true in our lives. God is good! God is faithful!

To me, it was interesting what our pastor said in his sermon about God being mad at David for taking a census. In all the times that I have read through the Bible and read that part, I have never understood it.

I mean, we take a census in Brentwood every year, and I couldn't see anything wrong with it. When he told us that David took the census to know the number of his troops to go to war, and that he was doing this so that he could depend on his troops for victory and not depend on God for victory, was what God was mad at him about. Then it all made sense to me. This helped me in what Father God recently said to me.

Our pastor told of his trial with pain in his body and how God is helping him. I am in a trial now with finances. Every month, I have four sources of income in the amount of $5,000.00. Last month, my largest monthly check of $2,500.00 failed to appear as usual on October 10. The other $2,500.00 income did appear on time so I was able to pay the $2,100.00 to my charities as usual and pay the other $400.00 to my children for their inheritance as usual. I prayed and asked God, "Why?" He replied, **"I allowed it, to see if you trust God to meet your needs, or if you trust these payments to meet your needs."** I trusted God and all my needs were met right on time as God sent another source of income which helped greatly. Joy! Praise God for His faithfulness to us!

Blessings! Velma

Yes, Our God's Christian pastors and all Holy Bible teachers, yes, YOUR heavenly Father God does love you, does lead and guide you when you do preach the mighty truths about Jesus and the mighty truths as recorded in Our God's Holy Bible, and Our God does ALWAYS REWARD you and your entire family for living for God and for obeying YOUR Holy Triune God.

Yes, YOUR Holy Triune God IS a loving God, a just God, a rewarding God, a Giver of ALL GOOD things and all good events in your life on earth and in your future life in heaven.

Yes, do know and do claim for you, your loved ones, and for your congregations, ALL of Our God's good promises to you and to them as recorded in Our God's Holy Bible.

Yes, know all the conditions for Our God's promises to you, obey these conditions, then CLAIM these promises for you and for ALL of your loved ones.

Yes, pray and praise God without ceasing for a long time— then let the power of God flow through you to help yourself, help others, and glorify God on earth.

Yes, YOUR Holy Triune God does hear you and will answer you when you do pray in Jesus' name with your great faith in YOUR Lord and Savior, Jesus Christ.

Yes, do CONTINUE to live for God, love God, witness for your God Jesus, and you WILL BE greatly rewarded by YOUR heavenly Father God, rewarded by God both in your lifetime on earth AND in your future life in heaven.

Yes, what you do, do with and for your heavenly Father God, MUST be done quickly as time on earth, as you do know time on earth to be, is quickly drawing to a close.

Yes, time on earth will soon end as you now know time on

earth to be, and then Our God's planet Earth WILL enter into Our God's millennial time where a thousand years WILL equal one day.

Yes, Our Holy Triune God is the Author of all time that does exist.

Yes, your God is Alpha and Omega, from the beginning to the ending, without beginning and without ending.

Yes, YOUR heavenly Father God has ALL knowledge, all wisdom, all power, love, justice, and mercy.

Yes, YOUR heavenly Father God IS ABLE to see all future events clearly.

Yes, YOUR heavenly Father God knows the ending from the beginning of all nations, all people, and all future events on earth.

Yes, YOUR heavenly Father God knows exactly who the winner of the U. S. Presidential election will be and Our God WILL reveal this information ahead of time, and it WILL make national news and even make international news.

Yes, Our God is sovereign, Ruler of ALL nations on earth, and nothing either good or bad can happen on planet Earth without Our God's knowledge and without Our God's permission.

Yes, Our God does allow evil things and bad events to happen on earth to test the reactions of mankind on earth—will the event draw mankind closer to God, or will it drive mankind farther from God?

Yes, your many prayers to YOUR heavenly Father God prayed believing in the name of Jesus will influence the outcome of future events.

Do read and do study Our God's Holy Bible where in many cases Our God relented of the evil promised to destroy when a man or men prayed to God asking for mercy in a situation.

Yes, Our God is NOW looking for individuals to stand in the gap between God and man so that Our God can, is able to, bring good out of evil.

Yes, if ten righteous people had been found in Sodom and Gomorrah, Our God would not have had to destroy all the evil there. (Genesis 18:32)

Yes, if only the Christian people in America WILL turn back to God, repent of their many sins and evil doings, will come BACK to their first love of Jesus Christ and Father God, Our God could heal all the problems that America faces today, could even heal America overnight: Overcome the national debt, heal the unemployment, heal the health-care problems, heal the international wars problems, heal the government incompetency, heal the churches, heal the families, heal the poverty, heal the prisoners, heal the sick, heal the hunger and abuse.

Yes, if only the Christians in America would return to their God as their FIRST love, honor God, obey God, know Our God's promises to them as given in Our God's Holy Bible, and live for God as given in Our God's Holy Bible, Our God could and will heal Our God's America and use it as a shining light to lead other countries the world over, lead them ALL to the true God of Jesus Christ and their heavenly Father God, their holy Creators and holy Sustainers God.

Yes, Our Holy Triune God did and still does create each of Our God's mankind in Our God's image with body, soul, and spirit.

Yes, Our God does create each of mankind with the ability to either choose Jesus or reject Jesus.

If you do choose Jesus as your Lord and Savior, and if you do choose to come out of ALL sinful lifestyle and live for God, you WILL be rewarded for it, both in your lifetime on earth and rewarded for it in your afterlife in heaven where you WILL spend eternity with YOUR Holy Triune God.

Yes, YOUR heavenly Father God never slumbers nor sleeps, and YOUR heavenly Father God watches every person alive on earth at all times to monitor the desires of their hearts, to know their thoughts and plans of actions whether for good or for bad, sees their actions and rewards them accordingly so that their souls can grow in God.

Yes, whenever a child of God needs correcting or punishing for their evil deeds, because of Our God's love for them, Our God will correct them and will forgive them when they repent, come out of sin, and return to God.

Yes, Our God is ALWAYS the God of the "Fresh Start" when a person repents, turns from sin, and does return to God, to their first love.

Our God also watches Our God's children who do love God, honor God, live righteously, and who do help the helpless when it is in their power to do so; Our God does reward them continually for their righteous acts done with love for their fellow mankind.

No good gift will Our God withhold from those who do live righteously. (Psalm 84:11)

Hallelujah!

Praises to Our God!

Hallelujah!

Praise God!

LETTER NUMBER NINE FOR CHURCH GROWTH

Dear Christian Pastors and ALL Holy Bible Teachers,

Our pastor's sermon this week was about controlling our thinking, and that controls our actions. He taught about how some previous circumstances in our lives, when we were mistreated by others, our thinking about ourselves gets out of alignment with God's Word. When we are unable to think good thoughts about ourselves, we fail to prosper because of it. When we begin to change our thinking to good thoughts, pray for better things and better circumstances, believe that we have the answers to our prayers, claiming God's good promises to us about our better health, better finances, better marriages, and believing God will bring it about in due time, if we keep on believing, keep on praying and expecting God to work in our lives and in our circumstances, then good things will happen in due time. This is all true.

God is now helping me with my thinking about my art work. God wants me to have my second Christmas Open House in December, to show and sell my art work. Last year was my first year to have the two-day sale. I promised God that if any paintings sold, that I would give all the proceeds to my seven Jewish charities. I did not make a single sale until the last hour of the last day of the sale. In the final hour of the sale, four families came, bought eleven small paintings for a total of $345.00, so I was able to give $50.00 each to the seven Jewish charities. Praise God!

God is showing me how to prepare for this year's Christmas Open House Art Show and Sale. This year of all the painting purchases made, the purchase price will go to the purchaser's favorite charity.

This is a win/win/win situation. The purchaser gets the art

work, their charity gets the funds, and I get to claim the purchase amount on my income taxes for a tax refund.

God is showing me how to paint 100 new paintings every year, completing two a week, by painting only one hour a day for six days a week. This year, I am painting small 5" by 7" paintings in acrylics of a series of realistic butterflies with abstract backgrounds, trying to develop my skills of color harmony.

I had started seven oil paintings as gifts for others, had each one about half finished, and then ignored all of them for three months. Then Father God spoke to me and said, **"It is God's will for you to do this art work."** That is when He showed to me to paint for one hour a day. I did that for a few days, then again quit painting. Then God encouraged me again to paint, telling me, **"Paint three colors a day."**

Eventually, I am putting into practice what He is telling me to do with my art work. Father God encouraged me to FINISH my paintings. He told me, **"Every painting you finish will be better than the one before."** I praise God for these encouraging words.

God had enabled me to work my way through eight full years of college with a major in art. I graduated from the best art college in the nation at the time, Art Center College of Design in Los Angeles. Thomas Kinkade attended this college, but I was one of the only 10% who enter that eventually graduate from there, but only with my God's help.

Because of all the harsh criticism at Art Center from all the excellent teachers, I have developed a FEAR of completing any painting. I, myself, cannot overcome this fear, that no amount of my positive thinking can cure. God has now simplified the process for me by showing me how to paint only three colors a day on a painting with the help of God's Holy Spirit. When the painting is complete, I am to look at it and let God's Holy Spirit teach me how to IMPROVE it. Then I can make the improvements shown to me, and the completed painting will be successful to God's glory on earth. God has shown to me that I only have to MAKE the painting, and God's Holy Spirit will show me how to make it SUCCESSFUL! Father God told me that He can send buyers for the paintings, but that I must make something to sell.

Father God told me, **"If Thomas Kinkade had given God the glory for his success, he would still be alive and still be painting."** He died at age 54 from drugs and alcohol, leaving his wife and four young daughters. Father God told me that He will make my paintings successful and for me to always give God the glory for my success. I always want to do that. God's creations are so beautiful that it is a joy to paint them of His butterflies, birds, flowers, children, animals, waterfalls, sunsets, landscapes, and seascapes. Even man-made items are also beautiful to paint of barns, gazebos, castles, lighthouses, cityscapes, gardens, houses, bridges, and boats. The most beautiful thing to paint that God has created on our God's planet Earth, I believe, are the precious little faces of all of the children of the world. Father God once told me, **"God will help you to paint a portrait of Jesus. Then people will know what He looks like."** Praise God!

It has been said, "There are two things God cannot do. He cannot lie, and He cannot steer a parked car." But God can allow Satan to lie, and God can so motivate a person with expertise, courage, hope, and joy enough for the person to willingly get the car moving so God can steer it! God is good!

Blessings! Velma

Yes, Our God's beloved Christian pastors and Our God's beloved Bible teachers, YOUR heavenly Father God does love you, does guide you, does teach you, does protect you, and does use you to teach and to help others.

Yes, do continue to live for God, love YOUR God above all else, and you WILL CONTINUE to be used by YOUR Holy Triune God to love others and help others to know and love and serve THEIR Holy Triune God.

Yes, your service to your God and your service to others are ALWAYS rewarded to you by YOUR heavenly Father God.

Yes, always be faithful to YOUR God, and your God will ALWAYS be faithful to you.

Yes, redeem the time, do work while it is still day for the night comes when no man can work.

Yes, ALWAYS DO HELP win as many souls to Jesus Christ as you possibly can in the time you have left on earth.

Yes, do work and do witness for YOUR Lord Jesus Christ God with the help and guidance of Our God's Holy Spirit within you.

Yes, praise your God without ceasing for a long time, and you will be endued with power and wisdom from YOUR heavenly Father God to be a more powerful witness for your God.

Yes, praise God.

Serve God.

Be rewarded by your God.

Yes, the time is SOON when YOUR Lord Jesus Christ will split the great Eastern skies coming back toward earth for Our God's great saved-in-Jesus and sanctified Christians to take them BACK to THEIR home in heaven to live eternally with THEIR Holy Triune God.

Yes, warn others that their time is short and for them to get ready and to stay ready to go.

Yes, do pray in ALL your lost loved ones, and do warn them to keep ready to go at all times.

Yes, your heavenly Father God HAS called you out for such a time as this to help lead Our God's people into a closer walk with THEIR and your Holy Triune God.

Yes, do strive to live closer to YOUR Holy Triune God in the coming weeks and months ahead as you WILL BE tried and tested by your God to prove your loyalty to YOUR Holy Triune God.

Yes, Our God does put Our God's beloved chosen children through many trials and tests to see how their soul has grown in the Lord, to see how much MORE responsibility, fame, and fortune Our God is able to TRUST them with without these benefits corrupting them.

Yes, there IS a level above EVERY human being where if they reach it, they can become corrupt even as Satan in heaven became corrupt when God gave to Satan beauty, power, and responsibility when he was too weak to handle it, too weak to manage it and still stay true to God, true to his honor and loyalty to God.

Yes, Satan knows your weak points and your strong points, and he searches your weakest points so that he can bring you down, destroy you, and destroy your ministry of souls won to Jesus.

Yes, if you WILL only stay true to YOUR heavenly Father God and stay true to honoring Jesus—loving God and obeying God above all else—Our God WILL give you your heart's desire in due time.

Yes, your heavenly Father God will not give you a good benefit that will harm you, that will lead you to your corruption.

TRUST God to give you and your loved ones WHAT you need, ALL you need, WHEN you need it, and YOUR Holy Triune God will HONOR YOUR TRUST in your Holy Triune God.

Yes, your God IS a loving God, a gentle God, a patient God, a righteous God, a powerful God, a just God, an enduring God, a God of ALL knowledge, ALL wisdom, all grace, and all mercy toward ALL who know God, love God, honor God, obey God, and worship God.

Yes, do love and do obey YOUR Holy Triune God, and then ask what you will have from your God, always praying believing prayers, always praying them in Jesus' holy name.

Yes, Jesus' name is holy.

Yes, Jesus' name is powerful.

Yes, prayers prayed in the name of Jesus are the strongest forces on earth today.

Pray BIG prayers in the name of Jesus, pray believing in the power of Jesus' name, pray that you and your loved ones will be helped, pray that others will be helped, pray that God will be glorified on earth, then stand back and WATCH YOUR Holy Triune God answer ALL these prayers to Our God's glory on earth.

Yes, YOUR Holy Triune God is a VERY GENEROUS God Who does delight to give ALL Our God's obedient children the desires of their hearts when these benefits from God will HELP them, help others, and glorify God on earth.

Yes, do read and do study ALL of Our God's good promises to you as given in Our God's Holy Bible—do meet the conditions of them, do apply them to your own life, and then do teach them to others.

Yes, Our God does LONG to heal and prosper Our God's obedient children.

Do read and do study Our God's Holy Bible, how Our God blessed and rewarded the Israelites when they knew God, loved God, and obeyed God.

Also read how when they turned away from their true God, turned to worshiping idols and became corrupt, how Our God had to chasten them and nearly destroy them to get the remnant of the Jewish people to turn back to their true God.

Yes, America, which was founded by Christians on Christian principles, has been slowly turning away from THEIR true God and is becoming more and more corrupt.

Should not Our God discipline Our God's America?

Should not Our God seek to raise up leaders, teachers, pastors, and prophets, who will sound Our God's warnings to America, "Repent! Repent! Repent! Come back to your TRUE Father God! Come back to your TRUE Lord and Savior Jesus Christ Who loves you and paid His supreme sacrifice for you to have life, abundant life on earth, and have eternal life rejoicing in heaven forever"?

Yes, Jesus is coming back SOON to claim and to catch away ALL of Our God's saved-in-Jesus and right-living-unto-God beloved children of God to take them back to THEIR homes prepared for them in heaven.

Yes, warn the wicked to get right with Jesus for the salvation of their soul as Jesus Christ IS the ONLY being, dead or alive, Who has paid the price to keep their eternal soul out of a burning hell, forgive their sins, and give them a FREE one-way ticket to heaven in their life after their one life on earth.

Yes, there IS a heaven and there is a hell.

Preach on the book of Revelation, the last book in Our God's Holy Bible, as it does describe what is SOON going to take place on Our God's earth.

Yes, SOON Our God WILL create a NEW heaven and a new earth, and the old WILL pass away. (Revelation 21:1-8)

Yes, get ready for Jesus to split the Eastern skies in a split second at the last trumpet sound.

Warn others to get ready and to stay ready to go.

Yes, YOUR heavenly Father God is now speaking not only to Pastor Danny Chambers, but to ALL Christian pastors in and on Our God's earth.

Hallelujah!

Praises to Our Father God for this message to ALL Christian pastors!

Praise God!

Hallelujah!

Dear Christian Pastors and All Holy Bible Teachers,

Our good sermon at church last Sunday morning was on the power of right thinking in our lives to be the success that our God wants us to be. All that our pastor said, I believe is true. The Scripture verses he gave were good, proving the point that what we think in our hearts and minds can influence our words and our actions. However, in my own life of living my seventy nine years, I've found that there is more information that should be given to any congregation when teaching on the power of the mind, the power of God, and the power of Satan.

For example, in the pastor's teaching on how to win in life by controlling a person's right thinking, he did NOT give these two key verses: Jesus says, "apart from Me you can do nothing," (John 15:5) and the Bible teaches, "I can do all things through Christ" (Philippians 4:13). What he taught about Jesus, God, the Bible, right thinking, and right living, was very good, but it did not go far enough. He did not give both sides of the teaching. He did not give credit to Jesus where credit is due to Jesus.

For example in my own life, when I was attending Art Center College of Design in Los Angeles, my God taught me the difference between the power of positive thinking and the power of positive faith. The power of positive thinking will work fine when all is going well, but can fall apart when the going gets rough. At Art Center most of the students there put in ninety-hour work weeks, and most of them lose a lot of sleep working day and night in order to meet project deadlines on time. This could be one of the reasons why only ten percent of the students who enter Art Center are able to graduate. When a student goes without enough sleep over a long period of time, their immune system breaks down, and they easily become sick. Many times, when they are ill, they still continue to work on projects for ninety hours a week, still without getting the proper sleep for their bodies to recover from the illnesses. Without proper sleep and with illness, the physical body has limited strength, and no amount of positive thinking will force the body to co-operate. That's when the positive thinking lie flies out the window. That's when the student must give up, or the student must switch to positive faith. When the person switches to positive faith and calls on God to help them, they can receive from God the spiritual and physical help that they need. It was only by the power of positive faith that helped me to be in the ten percent of the students who actually graduated from Art Center, even though I was very ill at the time of graduation. It was during this trying time of four years at Art Center that I began to trust God with everything in my life, and He never failed me! Praise God for His goodness to me and to all of us!

Another example that I can give you in my own life about the difference in the power of positive thinking and the power of positive faith is when I was married to Hugh Davies for 30 years before Hugh became a Christian in the last few years of his life. Although Hugh was not a Christian, he was always a good man who loved life, loved his parents, loved me, loved our two children and grandchildren, completed his college education, worked hard on his job, was honest, always paid all his bills on time, always honest in paying all his taxes, treated people fairly, was always kind, helped the helpless, did not have a bad temper, was not an alcoholic, took good care of his health, kept his weight down, was frugal in his spending habits, loved to save and invest money, did his own repair work on our house and cars, and lived what most people would believe to be a successful life. He seemed to live the Christian life without being a Christian. He had a brilliant mind, had an excellent education from Vanderbilt with a PhD in Electrical Engineering, and worked his whole career at Vanderbilt with an excellent salary. God was always very good to him and to our family, but Hugh did not give God the glory for it.

Our conversation once went like this: I told him, "God gives you the power to get wealth." (Deuteronomy 8:18)

He replied, "God's got nothing to do with it. I got my education. I get up and go to work."

I said, "God gave you the good job."

He said, "That's not God. I applied for the job. They needed my skills, and they hired me."

I said, "God gives you the good health to go to work."

He said, "That's not God. That's just good luck!"

When Hugh's health failed, he was laid off from his good job at Vanderbilt Medical University. Then he knew that God is in control and that he needed God. He finally became a Christian after I had prayed for him for over thirty five years to become a Christian. He died seven years ago in a nursing home from Alzheimer's. He died with a smile on his face, and I know I will see him again in heaven for eternity.

There is a difference between:

"I can do all things," which is humanism, which Hugh had believed in, and "I can do all things through Christ," which is Christianity, which Velma believes in.

Please teach people the difference, when you teach them the power of the mind, the power of God, and the power of Satan. Thank you.

Blessings! Velma

Yes, Our God's beloved Christian pastors and Our God's beloved Bible teachers, YOUR heavenly Father God does love you, does love ALL of your loved ones, and does take care of you and them at ALL times.

Yes, do call out to YOUR heavenly Father God, call day or night at ANY time, and YOUR heavenly Father God WILL ANSWER YOU and WILL SHOW YOU great and mighty things which you know not. (Jeremiah 33:3)

Yes, your God IS a good God, a loving God, a powerful God, Who is ABLE to take care of ALL of Our God's beloved children of God on Our God's planet Earth at ALL times.

Do worship and do praise YOUR Holy Triune God without ceasing for a long time, and do LET Our God's knowledge, wisdom, power, and love flow through you to others to Our God's glory on earth.

Yes, the joy of the Lord is your strength. (Nehemiah 8:10)

Yes, as you continue to praise and rejoice in YOUR Holy Triune God with your total being, with your mind, body, soul, and heart, your JOY and your STRENGTH WILL INCREASE mightily.

Yes, do rejoice, rejoice, rejoice, in YOUR Holy Triune God for victorious Christian living.

Yes, YOUR Holy Triune God IS ALL powerful, and YOUR Holy Triune God does grant power to those of Our God's children who love God, obey God, and praise and worship Our true God.

Yes, didn't Jesus tell His followers to tarry until they are filled with Our God's Holy Spirit, until they are FILLED with Our God's power from on high? (Luke 24:49)

Yes, the time you spend praising God and waiting on God is NOT wasted as that is when Our God fills you with Our God's JOY and POWER to be successful in your life.

Yes, sing praises until the joy comes!

Sing praises until the power comes!

Rejoice, rejoice, rejoice, and again I say, rejoice—rejoice in YOUR Holy Triune God!

Hallelujah!

Yes, the end of the world, as you know the world to be now, IS coming very SOON, and I am, YOUR heavenly Father God is, NOW getting ALL of Our God's beloved children ready for the soon appearing of Jesus in the sky/clouds to claim and to catch away to Our God's great heaven above all the saved-in-Jesus and right-living-unto-God beloved Christian children of God.

Do WARN your church congregation to get ready to go and to stay ready to go in a split second to meet Jesus in the air in a split second.

Yes, time IS short and is now growing shorter.

Yes, Jesus is coming!

Yes, ALL of heaven is now ready with the wedding supper of the Lamb waiting for Father God's word to Jesus to, "GO! Go to earth and bring back Your holy Bride-to-be to the wedding supper of the Lamb!"

Yes, time on earth IS short!

Warn everyone you meet to get ready and stay ready to go.

Yes, SOON Our God WILL create a new heaven and a new earth as the old heaven and old earth will pass away, then the new heaven and new earth will be on Our God's millennial time where one day is as a thousand years. (2 Peter 3:8)

Yes, do read about Our God creating a new heaven and a new earth, and who will be living there, and who will not be living there—read Revelations 21:1-8, which is the last book in Our God's Holy Bible.

Yes, do read and do study and do preach on the book of Revelation in Our God's Holy Bible as people do need to know the things that are now happening on THEIR planet Earth, and they do need to know what will happen SOON on THEIR planet Earth.

Yes, each person now alive on earth does need to get right with THEIR Father God through their Lord and Savior, Jesus Christ, as no one is allowed to enter THEIR Father God's presence except they go through the shed blood of Jesus Christ on Calvary's cross for cleansing of their sins.

Yes, doesn't Our God's Holy Bible teach that there is one God, and that there is only one mediator between God and men, the Man Jesus Christ? (1 Timothy 2:5)

Yes, Jesus Christ is the ONLY Being, dead or alive, Who had paid the penalty for mankind's sins, and Jesus Christ gives FREE forgiveness, free redemption, free salvation to EVERYONE who does come to Jesus with a repentant heart, who does ASK Jesus for free salvation, who does receive free salvation and who does come out of ALL sinful lifestyle, who does and WILL live the rest of their lives on earth for and with God.

Yes, sin will never enter heaven.

To enter heaven after your one life and one death on earth, you MUST choose Jesus as your Lord and Savior while you are alive on earth, and you must come out of all sin and live the rest of your life on earth for and with God.

Yes, you cannot save yourself by trying to do good works as ALL of your good works are as filthy rags in Our God's sight. (Isaiah 64:6)

ONLY JESUS, Who has led the ONLY pure and holy life on earth, Who gave His holy pure blood to pay the required ransom for mankind to be forgiven of all sin and all wrongdoing, and this entitled each of mankind who choose Jesus as their Lord and Savior to go FREE, to have life, have abundant life on earth, and have eternal life in heaven—ONLY JESUS is ABLE to offer this free gift to mankind, to each and every one of mankind who will ACCEPT it from Jesus.

Yes, Allah cannot save you.

Mohammad cannot save you.

Buddha cannot save you.

No one but Jesus alone is able to save you from a burning hell in your afterlife.

Yes, reincarnation, as you know reincarnation to be, is a complete lie from Satan as there is NO reincarnation—absolutely NO WAY are you able to work your way into heaven by your trying to do good deeds and by your loving people.

Yes, Jesus Christ IS the ONLY Door to heaven. (John 10:1-9)

Yes, ONLY Jesus Christ is ABLE to give you a one-way ticket to heaven for eternity.

You cannot purchase salvation.

You cannot earn your salvation.

Jesus is your ONLY salvation as Jesus is the way, the truth, and the life. (John 14:6)

Yes, Jesus is truth.

Know Jesus and know the truth.

Read and study Our God's Holy Bible, and you will know the truth about Jesus, heaven, hell, and what awaits every person in their life beyond their one death on earth.

Yes, life on earth is uncertain, and death on earth is certain.

Yes, come to Jesus NOW before it is TOO LATE to come to Jesus.

Make Jesus YOUR Lord and Savior FREE for the asking, when you do COME to Jesus with a repentant heart.

After your salvation in Jesus, then do live for God in the best way that you do know how to live for God, with Our God's Holy Spirit within you leading you into all truth and all righteous living.

Then do pray to YOUR heavenly Father God, pray believing prayers in the name of Jesus, and then do EXPECT Our God to answer you that you will be helped, others will be helped, and Our God will be glorified on earth.

Yes, your God IS a good God Who does DELIGHT to answer ALL your good prayer petitions when you do know God, love

God, honor God, live for God, and when these answers to your believing prayers will benefit you, help others, and glorify God.

Yes, no good gift will Our God withhold from those who do live righteously. (Psalm 84:11)

Praises to Our Father God for this wonderful prophetic message for church growth!

Hallelujah!

Praises to Our God!

Dear Christian Pastors and All Holy Bible Teachers,

This Prophetic Message Number Eleven for church growth is the best one that I have ever received in my more than thirty years of receiving these prophecies, I believe. With more than 940 of them written out and typed up, I find it helpful to know why and how our God tests us, and why bad things and bad circumstances happen to good people, and how when we trust God, He works out all things and all circumstances for our good and for His glory.

Through our faith in God, we know He loves us, and He wants us to prosper and be in good health, but many times we have many questions to ask God about things and circumstances that we don't understand.

Sometimes we feel like Job felt, when he was so tired of suffering and just wanted God to answer him!

God finally answered Job and brought him through the long, trying time of testing, and rewarded him with double of all his former possessions.

When I was a child in our Sunday School class, we studied about the sufferings of Job. Our teacher told us that God gave Job double everything he had lost, but didn't give to him double his children he had lost. This is because Job still had his other deceased children in heaven that he would be with some day.

Later, God revealed to me that one of the reasons that God let Satan test Job to prove that Job would be faithful to God, was so that Job's soul could grow during the testing. Only after Job's soul had grown stronger in God, was Job's strength of character able to receive double of all his former possessions, without all this extra wealth and possessions corrupting Job.

This was a real breakthrough in my understanding of pain

and suffering—that it is not wasted! God uses everything we go through on earth to build our character, all the good things and all the seemingly bad things, to help us grow stronger in God. Father God once told me, "**God uses everything you go through on earth, all the good and all the bad, to grow your soul in God. The only thing that you will take to heaven with you is your soul's growth in God. Your soul will continue to grow in God in heaven throughout eternity.**"

Of all the trials that each of mankind goes through on earth, Father God told me, "**The two that are the hardest for them are their physical health and their financial poverty.**" Job went through many trials at once, the loss of his family, his physical possessions, his physical health, his friends, his prestige, and had false accusations. He lost everything but his life and his faith in God. Because of his strong faith in God, he endured to the end and was greatly rewarded for it.

When I didn't know what to write in this letter to the Christian Pastors and the Bible teachers, Father God told me to just share my Christian testimony. This is a good idea, because people can argue religion "until the cows come home." (The cows come home at dawn for milking time.) Also, people can argue the various meanings and different interpretations of Scripture, but who can argue with your personal experience?

It's like when I told a famous pastor that I had prophetic messages from Father God and from Jesus Christ on my website, and he replied, "That's impossible!!!"

I asked him, "Why?" He replied, "You can't hear from them separately, because they are the same Person!"

That's when I almost laughed out loud right in his face as I thought, "Who is this funny little man telling me I can't do something that I've been doing nearly every morning for more than thirty years?!"

I asked him, "What about all those books that have been written by people who visited heaven, came back and wrote books about their experience of visiting the Throne Room of God and seeing Jesus seated at the right hand of Father God?"

He replied, "I never read any of those books."

So I gave him three Scripture references of Father God in heaven with Jesus on the earth, of Jesus' water Baptism and of Jesus' transfiguration, when Father God spoke from heaven, and when Jesus prayed to His Father in heaven saying, "Our Father Who art in heaven."

He replied, "That is all symbolic. The Scripture verse you go by is when Jesus said, **'If you have seen Me, you have seen the Father.'** When we get to heaven, we will see Jesus only. We will not see Father God and will not see the Holy Spirit. If you don't believe like I do, do not join this church, and do not even visit this church!"

Since I had never had any pastor tell me before that I could not even visit his church, I went home, got on my knees in my prayer closet, praised Jesus, and asked Jesus about it. I knew that this man was the pastor of this church in Brentwood, but I also knew that Jesus Christ is Head of this church. When I asked Jesus about what the pastor had said, Jesus replied to me, **"You may visit that church anytime you wish."** I did not join that church, but I did keep my pledge to them of my mailing to them $28.00 a month for three years for their building fund.

Later, when I prayed to Father God about this church and what this pastor is teaching his congregation, I asked Father God why this church is prospering so much, when they don't even worship Father God, but worship Jesus only? Father God answered me something like this, **"Father God, Jesus Christ, and Our God's Holy Spirit are three separate Beings, but We are always in one accord. When you get to heaven, you will see Jesus Christ, Father God, and God's Holy Spirit as three separate Beings, but We all are worshipped as God. I allow one thing in each church to be wrong to test the people's reactions to it."** This helped me to understand how the Baptists, Presbyterians, Methodists, Church of Christ, Pentecostals, Church of God, Catholics, and other groups can all worship the same God, but keep their own separate beliefs. God loves all of us and observes and permits and tolerates our differences.

I was at this church on the day when about 30 new members joined the church as a group. They were asked to obey Jesus and obey the leaders of the church. Not a single word was said about Father God or about God's Holy Spirit. I wondered how many of those people joining that church knew that their Pastor Rice Broocks is a "Jesus Only" person?

Since this happened to me, as I read through the Bible daily, I notice how many times it is written that Jesus Christ and Father God are two separate Beings. It is all throughout the Bible! How can any person miss these hundreds of times that it is so plain in the whole Bible that Jesus and Father God are separate, but are always in one accord!? Also, I have received MANY prophetic messages from Father God saying that They are three separate Beings, but are always in one accord.

Even though I did not join that church or visit that church except twice after that, I felt the need to keep my three-year commitment that I had made to give to their building fund. They have now completed their new sanctuary that seats more people than their other sanctuary. This building is our former Lord's Chapel building, now named Bethel World Outreach Center. They were able to purchase more nearby property and enlarge their parking lot. Praise God that they were able to expand in that location and made many new additions and improvements to the old Lord's Chapel building and parking lot. God is good!

I hate it when people make commitments, then deliberately fail to keep them. When The Lord's Chapel had outgrown our building on Granny White Pike in Brentwood and needed to relocate to have more room to expand our parking lot, we purchased about thirty six acres of land on Nolensville Pike in Nashville and built a building. We had our first service in the new building on August 7, 1988. At the time we relocated, we had enough funds to completely pay for all of it with the funds from the sale of our Brentwood building and pledges from our several thousand people who had been attending. But our main pastor, Pastor Billy Roy Moore, left our church one year after we relocated. Then we had several other pastors who ministered for a couple of years, then left and took part of our congregation with them. Many of the people who had made pledges for the new building left the church and forgot about keeping their pledges. Over time, we had to sell some of the property to meet the expenses of the ongoing church. At the time of the merger with Oasis Church in 2003, we still owed $730,000.00 on the property. Now, fourteen years after the merger with Oasis, I do not know if there is still a mortgage on the property as Oasis Church fails to give financial reports to the members. I had been a member of that church for thirty nine years until I felt released from it by God.

When I relocated to Marietta, Georgia, I joined Mt. Bethel United Methodist Church where my daughter, Lori LaVoy and her family, are members. I am glad that they have a strong missions group which I hope to become involved with. We are planning a ten-day mission's trip to India the first week in November, 2017. Joy!

Blessings! Velma

Yes, Our God's beloved Christian pastors and Holy Bible teachers, YOUR heavenly Father God does love you and does love all of your loved ones and all of your congregations, and YOUR heavenly Father God does provide for you and them, and does protect you and them at ALL times.

Yes, your God is a good God, a merciful God, a loving and gentle God, showing mercy to a thousand generations to those who love God and who do obey THEIR God.

Yes, your God can make a way in YOUR wilderness when there seems to be no way.

TRUST your God.

Praise your God.

Lean on your faithful God at ALL times and SEE HOW YOUR GOD BRINGS you through your wilderness, and plants your feet on the Solid Rock of Jesus Christ where there is safety from ALL harm, and where there are provisions for ALL needs and for ALL holy desires.

Yes, Jesus Christ owns it all, and Jesus proclaims that you are joint heirs with Jesus! (Romans 8:17)

Yes, claim all good things and all good events for you and all your loved ones, and pray believing prayers to YOUR heavenly Father God, pray in Jesus' holy name, pray with great faith believing in Jesus, the power of Jesus, the love of Jesus, the willingness of Father God and Jesus Christ to HELP You, and to HELP ALL those you love and serve, and it shall be so to the glory of YOUR God on earth.

Yes, serve others and serve your God with your heart full of love, and do be rewarded for it by YOUR heavenly Father God through YOUR Lord and Savior, Jesus Christ.

Yes, YOUR heavenly Father God IS a good God, a loving God, a gentle God, a patient God, a generous God, an all-powerful God, a forgiving God, a just God, and an enduring God.

Yes, do cast ALL your cares, all your concerns, all your troubles, onto your God, pray believing prayers in Jesus' holy name, and then do WATCH and do SEE HOW YOUR loving God does solve EVERY problem in your own life, in your family's and other ones' lives, and with your and their church life.

Yes, is anything too hard for Our God's power to perform? Is anything too small for Our God's love to perform?

No, nothing is too big for Our God's power to control, and nothing is too small for Our God's love to control.

Yes, ask ANYTHING of YOUR heavenly Father God, pray in Jesus' holy name, believing your God is ABLE to perform what you request, and WATCH Our God work for you and work through you that YOU will be helped, that OTHERS will be helped, and that OUR God will be glorified on earth.

Didn't Jesus say to you that you have not because you ask not? So do ask, do receive, do exalt YOUR Holy Triune God, and your joy will be full. (John 16:24)

Yes, YOUR heavenly Father God IS the Giver of ALL good gifts that you now have in your life, and they have been given to you THROUGH Jesus Christ to you so do praise and thank YOUR Holy Triune God MANY times daily for Our God's good gifts to you and to your loved ones. (Philippians 4:19)

Yes, do teach your congregations to ALWAYS have a praise and a thankful heart unto their Holy Triune God at ALL times, and Our God will give them perfect peace of mind at all times.

Doesn't Our God's Holy Bible teach that God will give you perfect peace when you keep your mind stayed on God? (Isaiah 26:3)

Yes, when you praise Our God for Who We are, and when you thank Our God for what Our God HAS DONE for you, IS

NOW DOING for you, and WILL DO FOR YOU, you will have perfect peace of heart, mind, body, and soul.

When you stay your mind on God, Who God is and what Our God does, Our God is ABLE to fill you with ALL of Our God's good gifts of love, joy, peace, kindness, mercy, gentleness, prosperity, good health in mind, body, and soul.

Yes, ALL Our good benefits from Our God to you are given in your response to Our God's relationship with you if you love God, honor God, obey God, live for God, and trust God.

Doesn't Our God's Holy Bible teach you that no good gift will be withheld from those who live righteously? (Psalm 84:11)

Yes, do live for God, do obey God, do witness for Jesus, and do SEE Our God's benefits given to you and to ALL your loved ones.

Yes, when Jesus prayed the prayer on earth to His heavenly Father God of, "Thy will be done on earth as it is in heaven," Jesus was praying for all of Our God's fullness of love to benefit ALL of mankind, to meet ALL their many needs, for their salvation in Jesus, for their good physical, mental, emotional, spiritual health, for them to prosper in all good things, to use their talents, abilities, and possessions to help themselves, help others, and glorify God on earth, to receive EVERY good thing from God that will help them love God, honor God, and lead successful, happy lives on earth, and spend eternity in heaven, enjoying God and enjoying heaven forever.

Yes, YOUR heavenly Father God does LONG to give to you and to ALL your loved ones EVERY good gift that Our God has planned for you, before God created the earth and created all of mankind on earth.

Yes, your soul must grow in God and mature enough in God for you to have enough wisdom and knowledge for you to use these good gifts from your God, to help you and not to corrupt you, to help others, to serve others, to glorify God on earth.

Yes, when Our God does reign supreme in your heart, mind, soul, and body, and when you come out of pride and selfishness, when you do LEARN to love others as you do love yourself, THEN you ARE ABLE to handle more responsibility, more power, more riches, more fame, without it corrupting you.

Yes, YOUR loving heavenly Father God is continually monitoring everyone's thoughts, words, and actions, to see how much growth-in-God their soul has, to see if their soul is ready for promotion.

Yes, Our God does desire to GIVE to you the desires of your heart, when you are able to receive these good gifts without these good gifts corrupting you.

Yes, do praise and do thank Our God IN all situations.

When seemingly bad things happen, Our God tests your reactions to them—do they bring your trust in God closer, or does it push you farther from God?

Yes, ASK your Father God, ask in faith in Jesus' holy name, how the happening can bring you closer to God.

Yes, your response to bad situations shows your soul's maturity in God.

A good reaction from you in a bad situation, shows Our God how your soul has matured in God, shows Our God if and when Our God is ready to promote you to your next level in service to Our God, to your fellow man, and to yourself.

Yes, trust God in the difficult times, and watch Our God remove the difficult times.

Our God has you in your training to be a better servant of God, of your fellow mankind, and of yourself—THEN Our God's rewards come to you.

Hallelujah!

Praises to Our Father God for this wonderful message to help all pastors and their congregations!

Hallelujah!

Praises to Our God!

Dear Christian Pastors and All Holy Bible Teachers,

Father God has said that if you will base your teachings, your sermons to your congregations, on these fifty prophetic messages and preach one a week for fifty weeks, that your church attendance will double, and your church financial income will double. Father God wants you to compare what is in the prophetic messages with what is written in the Holy Bible to make sure that all the teachings in the prophetic messages do agree with the Bible teachings.

Karen, my editor friend, who proofreads all my writings and all the prophetic messages that I receive, questioned the sentence in the prophecy about if people choose to come to earth, or if God chooses to send them to earth.

I got on my knees in my prayer closet and praised God. Then I asked Father God if each person chooses to come to earth. He answered me and said something like this:

Every person who has ever lived on earth has chosen to come to earth, to experience the trials of earth, to grow closer to THEIR heavenly Father God. God sees their hearts and gives them their gifts and abilities. God knows a person's character and knows the desires of their heart, and God chose Jeremiah to be a prophet before he was born.

I had attended a few years ago a Christian conference in St. Louis, MO, sponsored by "End-time Handmaidens and Servants." While there, I heard Bert Crevier speak on his fifteen visits to heaven. When he returned to earth, he wrote two books about his heavenly visits and has been speaking about them. One thing he said that impressed me was when he first met Father God on his first trip to heaven. Father God said something like this to him: **You are my second choice for this mission** (of visiting heaven and returning to earth and writing about and speaking about his experiences). **My first choice for this mission refused to accept it, so you have been chosen.**

I have lived the past fifty one years in the Nashville, TN area, and have just recently moved to Georgia. God has had me in training for more than forty years, even before I became Spirit filled with the gift of prophecy, to have a syndicated newspaper column titled, "Hot Off The Throne," that has weekly prophetic messages that go into newspapers nationwide and worldwide. This column is designed to reach people who do not attend church to lead them to salvation in Jesus before Jesus returns to earth for our God's great rapture. Since I know that there are so many wonderful prophets and prophetesses out there, once I asked Father God, "Am I your first choice of a prophetess for this syndicated newspaper column, or did You choose someone else for it and they refused?" He answered me something like this:

You are My first choice. When you were young, I saw the strong desire in your heart to win souls to Jesus. I also saw how you left all your family on the West Coast and moved to Nashville to work at the Baptist Sunday School Board to win souls to Jesus.

Even before I became Spirit filled, my cousin Joan Garner Carnes gave a prophetic message to me that told of my working on this newspaper column. At the time that I got this message from God through Joan to me, I had believed that Joan would give the prophetic messages, and that I would type them and forward them to the newspapers for publication. A few months after I received this message from God through Joan, I became Spirit filled and learned how to ask God to speak to me, so that I could write out these messages. Joan gave this message to me more than forty years ago on January 17, 1977, and I have carried a typed copy of it in my purse ever since. Here is a copy of the message. My nickname that my family calls me since childhood is "Banny."

From Joan Garner on January 17, 1977

As I (Joan) was praying for Banny:

My child, you are with an army that has never lost a battle. Wait upon the Lord and I will work all these problems out.

My child, depend on God for your wisdom on this news column. I will supply all the needs and I will lead you daily.

As I fed the children in the wilderness daily, I will feed thee daily with wisdom, love, and blessings.

My child, when I call one to do a work for Me, I will help them and lead them.

I will go with you even until the end of the world.

Listen NOT to what man says, because MAN will lead you wrong, but put all your trust in the LORD JESUS CHRIST, Who is the Savior of the world.

You will be tried and tested, but I will bring you through pure as gold.

Hold fast and wait upon the Lord.

I can open doors that no man can open.

It takes time and patience to train My children My ways.

Don't get discouraged.

Just trust God for all things.

My eyes are over the righteous, and My ears are open unto their cries. (Psalm 34:15)

Praise God for the comforting words!

To begin working on this newspaper column more than nine years ago, God led me to go online and find the six largest newspapers in each of the fifty United States. When I did this, I had the names and addresses of the three hundred largest newspapers in the nation. The Holy Spirit helped me to ask for and receive a prophetic message every week from God, alternating one week with a message from Father God and the next week from Lord Jesus. He showed me how to type, print, proofread, and format, thirteen of these prophetic messages, and prepare them to mail to each of these three hundred newspapers each quarter. He showed to me how to make a heading of the word "Jesus" in a cross and the word "Bible" in an open book. The name of the syndicated column is "Hot Off The Throne." He showed to me how to write a cover letter to the newspaper editors to go with the thirteen prophetic messages, instructing them to print one a week for thirteen weeks in the quarter.

I have followed these instructions and have mailed thirteen new prophetic messages every quarter for the last nine years to the largest newspapers in every state in the USA. As far as I know, none of the newspapers have printed them. When I saw that they were not being printed, I asked Father God if I should stop mailing them to these editors. He replied: **"Keep mailing them. These editors are reading them."** In the past nine years, forty seven of these largest three hundred newspapers have gone out of business. I now mail them to only two hundred and fifty three newspapers.

When I first began mailing these prophetic messages to the newspapers, Father God had told me to rent the largest post office box available so I did. After a few years of keeping it open with very little response in it, I asked Father God if I should get a smaller post office box. He replied, **"That largest post office box that you rented will not hold all the mail you will receive, most of it hate mail. I will show you how to answer the hate mail."** At the bottom of each of the newspaper columns, I was led to put my website address of: www.HotOffTheThrone.com. Father God told me, **"After these prophetic messages are printed in the** newspapers, your website will receive 80,000 hits a day." Father God also told me at one time: **"These newspaper editors will not print these messages until Our God puts Our God's anointing on them. Then they will print them, and these messages will go worldwide."**

Forty years ago, God gave Joan a vision that showed the package of prophetic information arriving at a newspaper office. The editor opened it, looked at it, and laid it aside. The package arrived in the mail three times. The third time the editor looked at it when it had arrived in the mail and while he was reading it, God put His anointing on this editor, and then he published it. It showed a large newspaper, like the Los Angeles Times, with the headline of **HOT OFF THE THRONE!** Praise God for this vision given to Joan!

My God has been bringing me through tests and trials for the past forty years to prepare me for the Christian work ahead that He has for me to do. Here is the place where I am now:

A.   There is nothing that a non-Christian can say to me that will upset me as I have already heard most of it already said to me by my living with my non-Christian husband for about thirty five years. I will just give a "soft answer" to them and pray for them.

B.   There is nothing that a Christian leader can say to me that will upset me as I can get on my knees in my prayer closet, praise God, and receive my God's reply to the situation.

C.   My faith in my God is strong enough that I always trust God as my Provider to meet all my own needs and my loved ones' needs and meet all of our holy desires. God never fails us!

D.   If I have to make a choice to please my God, or please people, I always want to please God. God always rewards our obedience to Him. Praise God!

Blessings! Velma (Banny Garner)

Yes, Our God's beloved Christian pastors and Holy Bible teachers, YOUR heavenly Father God does love you, does love ALL of your family and other loved ones, and does love ALL of your congregations.

Yes, do feed ALL of them the true words of Our God's Holy Bible and the true words of Jesus Christ.

Yes, you will not go wrong if you will live your life in obedience to YOUR God and by following the example of the life of Jesus Christ as given in Our God's Holy Bible.

Yes, Jesus Christ IS the ONLY TRUE Savior of mankind in the world.

Yes, preach Jesus Christ again, again, and again, and Our God's Holy Spirit will work in the hearts and minds of each and every person in your audience, and Our God will reveal to each person who hears you preach about Jesus, they will know that Jesus is the way, the truth, and the life. (John 14:6)

They will know that Jesus came so that they could have life, abundant life, and eternal life in heaven. (John 10:10)

They will know that Jesus Christ is the ONLY way to their holy Creator, THEIR heavenly Father God. (1 Timothy 2:5)

Yes, Jesus is God.

Do worship Our Father God's only begotten Son of Jesus Christ as you do worship YOUR heavenly Father God. (John 3:16)

Yes, Jesus Christ is all in all. (Colossians 3:11)

Yes, Jesus Christ is the Word of HIS heavenly Father God. (John 1:1-3)

Yes, Jesus Christ IS all powerful. (Matthew 28:18)

Yes, Jesus Christ IS coming back soon toward Our God's

planet Earth to claim and to catch away to the heavens above earth in a split second, ALL of Our God's saved-in-Jesus and living-for-God Obedient Christians to take them BACK to THEIR eternal home in heaven to live forever with THEIR Holy Triune God.

Yes, time is short until Jesus Christ returns toward earth for Our God's great rapture of obedient souls.

Do warn your congregations and do warn ALL you meet that Jesus is coming soon and for them to get ready and to stay ready to meet Jesus in the air.

Yes, doesn't Our God's Holy Bible teach that Jesus can come as a thief in the night, when least expected? (1 Thessalonians 5:2)

Yes, do get ready to go and do STAY ready to go to meet Jesus in the air in the twinkling of an eye. (1 Corinthians 15:52)

Be warned!

Stay warned!

Yes, Jesus comes SOON!

Yes, YOUR heavenly Father God does know ALL of your heart's desires and ALL of your fondest wishes for yourselves, for your loved ones, and for your congregations, and YOUR heavenly Father God does LONG to GIVE you ALL of these desires and wishes.

Yes, as your souls grow more in God and as you become ABLE to HANDLE more responsibilities, your heavenly Father God WILL promote you and will give you more responsibilities.

Yes, when you do offer up praise and thanksgiving to YOUR Holy Triune God IS WHEN your soul does grow in God, and it is at THAT time the Lord God IS ABLE to fill you with Our God's love, knowledge, wisdom, strength, and courage to go forth and do more of Our God's will for your life.

Yes, as your soul grows in God, you will desire to be more like Jesus Christ, Who was the greatest Servant of God and the people Who ever walked this earth, as Jesus loved God enough and loved the people enough to give His body, His holy shed blood, and His very life to redeem mankind, to save mankind, to rejoin mankind with their heavenly Father God, with their holy Creator God.

You did NOT evolve from monkeys, apes, or other creatures.

Male and female human beings were created by THEIR Holy Triune God in Our God's image. (Genesis 1:27)

Yes, evolution of man from animals is a lie from Satan, the father of all lies. (John 8:44)

Yes, reincarnation is also a lie from Satan, as man can NEVER work their way into heaven.

Any of mankind's access to heaven is by their cleansing from all sin—their own sin and Adam's sin nature which they inherited—in Jesus' shed blood, and their repenting from sin, and their living for God while alive on earth.

Yes, Jesus Christ is the only Being, alive or dead, Who has the power to save you from your sins and give you an eternal home in heaven. (Acts 4:12)

Yes, all power in heaven and in and on earth has been given to Jesus. (Matthew 28:18)

Yes, Jesus is your ONLY access to YOUR heavenly Father God.

Jesus is your only access to heaven in your life after your one life and one death on earth. (John 10:9)

Yes, sin will never enter heaven.

You MUST repent of all sin in your life, come out of a sinful lifestyle on earth, and live for God while alive on earth, with Jesus Christ as your Lord and Savior, in order to enter heaven after your one life and one death on earth.

Yes, come to Jesus now.

Accept Jesus now.

Live for God now.

Honor God now.

Love God above all else.

Love others as you love yourself.

Help the helpless with love to Our God's glory, and DO BE rewarded by YOUR God for your good deeds to help others.

Yes, your God IS a VERY generous God Who knows your thoughts and sees ALL your good deeds to others, and Our God will reward you now and reward you in your future life in heaven.

Hallelujah!

Praises to Our heavenly Father God for this message!

Hallelujah!

Praises to Our God!

Dear Christian Pastors and All Holy Bible Teachers,

It sounds to me like these messages from Father God for church growth are greatly needed now.

Charisma Magazine had an article recently that stated that 31% of the adult population of the regular Christians who used to be faithful in their church attendance are dropping out now. They are not rebellious, they just have lost interest and don't feel any need to keep attending. Other reports state that many of the younger generation of children are not now in church, as their grandparents and parents were in church as children.

The largest Christian denomination in America at one time, the Southern Baptists, who owned seven of the largest buildings in Nashville, TN, have sold them and have relocated to smaller buildings in Nashville.

It seems that many Christian churches are not growing now. On the website of John Paul Jackson, there are four things listed that the churches need to do to save their churches:

1. The church must return to knowing God and His ways, rather than just knowing about God.
2. The church must learn to contend for the faith again. We need to be strong in faith and in our witness for God.
3. The church must return to the love of God's word and believe it is infallible and inerrant— that God is absolute with all power.
4. The church needs to declare sacred and solemn assemblies of repentance and corporate fasting—to rending our hearts before God.

God allows calamities to happen in order to draw us to Himself.

It's interesting to me that using the previous Bible Code method of computer-searching for hidden messages in the Old and New Testaments that only "words" or "word phrases" can be found. I believe they found thirty three words hidden in Scriptures that related to the Holocaust like, Germany, Hitler, Auschwitz, Jews, killed, gas. It's also interesting to me that the words "Twin Towers" were found vertically written, with the word "airplane" crossing horizontally through these words of the Bible written either in Hebrew of the Old Testament or in Greek of the New Testament. It's also interesting to me that the names of Jesus and His twelve disciples were found twice in code in the Hebrew of the Old Testament, with the name of Judas listed in one group, and the name of Matthias listed with the other group.

This Bible Code method of searching for hidden messages with equal-distance letter skips forward and backward with the use of the computer was discovered by a brilliant Jewish mathematician in Israel named Eliyahu Rips. It has been perfected by others since then. Michael Drosnin has written three books about the Bible Code.

Since I have been receiving these prophetic messages word for word from Father God and from Jesus Christ with the help of God's Holy Spirit, I once asked Father God, "Are there any hidden messages in these prophetic messages?" Father God answered me, **"Yes, there are, and your son will be the one who finds them. There are complete sentences hidden in them that are prophetic."** Father God had told me that He will reveal who will win the U. S. Presidential election ahead of the election, and that it will make national news, and even make international news. The Bible Code predicted the truth that Donald Trump would win the 2016 election for U. S. President. He did win in a major upset!

My son, Alan Davies, has a Bachelor's degree in Computer Science from Tennessee Tech in Cookeville, Tennessee. He worked as a Software Engineer for the U. S. Government for two years in

Florida. He then worked for Electronic Arts Mythic in northern Virginia for several years creating computer games. He is now working for Gannett Newspapers in northern Virginia creating Virtual Reality videos.

God recently gave me a dream about Alan. In the dream, Alan told me, "I may be taken off my job soon to go to the Supreme Court." After I woke up, I prayed and asked Father God if this was a prophetic dream, and if so, what does it mean? He answered me something like this. **"Yes, this dream is prophetic. The United States Government is interested in these computer messages found within the prophecies, as they want to know what will happen in the future of the United States and in the future of the world. They want Alan to do more searches for them."** Praise God!

It should be interesting to see what our God will do in our future!

Blessings! Velma

Yes, Our God's beloved Christian pastors and Holy Bible teachers, yes, YOUR heavenly Father God does love you, does guide you, does protect you, and does use you to speak and to live Our God's truth to your fellow mankind to help build up the Kingdom of God on earth, that ALL of mankind NOW alive on Our God's earth will know, will receive, and will live for Our God and Our God's truth of Jesus Christ and the truth of Our God's Holy Bible.

Yes, Our God has chosen each of you, has set you apart unto God, has called you, and has enabled you to speak and proclaim Our God's message of truth to ALL of mankind now alive on Our God's planet Earth.

Yes, you must work hard now while it is yet light for soon the great darkness will arrive when no man can work. (John 9:4)

Yes, now is the acceptable time of the Lord. (2 Corinthians 6:2)

Yes, ALL who do come to Jesus with a repentant heart, who do ASK Jesus to save them from their sins, who will receive this FREE salvation from Jesus, who will HONOR Jesus as their Lord and Savior, will be saved by Jesus, who then can go and sin no more.

Yes, sin will never enter heaven.

Yes, after a person's true salvation in Jesus, they MUST come out of ALL sinful lifestyle, live righteously in obedience to God, in order to complete and confirm their salvation in Jesus.

Yes, Jesus Christ shed His holy blood and gave His life on Calvary's cruel cross, so that mankind could be cleansed of all sin, all of their own sin and the sin of Adam that they were born into, then live a righteous lifestyle unto God, be rewarded

89

by God on earth, and enter Our God's great heaven above for eternity.

Yes, Our God hates sin, and Our God will NOT tolerate deliberate sin in a person's life.

Yes, you must COME OUT OF all sin, all sinful lifestyle, and live for God while you are alive on earth, with Jesus Christ as your Lord and Savior in order for ANY person to enter heaven after their one life and one death on earth.

Yes, the wages of sin is death. (Romans 6:23)

Yes, whatever a person sows, they WILL reap, as Our God is not mocked. (Galatians 6:7)

Yes, Our God is just, and Our God is Judge.

Yes, tell people to REPENT, REPENT, REPENT, and live for God while alive on earth if they do want to spend eternity in heaven with THEIR Lord and Savior, THEIR Lord Jesus Christ.

Yes, do ALWAYS keep your faith strong in YOUR Lord Jesus Christ, in your heavenly Father God, and in Our God's Holy Spirit of God, as yes, Our God is three separate Beings, but We are, God is, ALWAYS in one accord.

Yes, there are three separate Gods if you count God's Holy Triune God as three Gods.

Buddha is not God.

Allah is not God.

Mohammad is not God.

All the idols of Egypt and other historical idols are not God.

Our God's Holy Bible is absolutely true when it states that there is only one true God and only one mediator between God and men, the man Christ Jesus. (1 Timothy 2:5)

Yes, every word of Our God's Holy Bible is true as all the words written there have been given to these writers by God.

How else can hidden prophetic messages be hidden in these writings about the Holocaust written two thousand years ago if they were not inspired by the only true God Who knows the truth of the future of the earth?

Yes, even hidden in these prophetic messages you are now

given from YOUR heavenly Father God are complete sentences that can be found with equal-distance letter skips going forward and backward that do reveal hidden messages about the future of America and the future of the world you now live in.

Yes, doesn't Our God's Holy Bible teach that in the last days before Jesus returns toward earth for Our God's great catching-away-to-heaven all the saints of God, the right-living-unto-God Christians of God, say that travel will increase and knowledge will increase on the earth? (Daniel 12:4)

Yes, Our God is speeding up the knowledge of travel with the cars and airplanes and is speeding up the knowledge of information with radio, T.V., phones, and computers.

Yes, Our God is now revealing more information about Our God's universe, the earth, heaven and hell, the human body, animals, birds, fish, insects, trees, plants, flowers, science, math, and revealing more about God, Our God's Holy Triune God, to ALL who will receive all this good information.

Yes, doesn't Our God's Holy Bible teach you to draw near to God, and Our God will draw near to you? (James 4:8)

Doesn't Our God's Holy Bible teach you to call unto God, and Our God WILL answer you and show you great and mighty things that you know not? (Jeremiah 33:3)

Doesn't Our God Jesus tell you in Our God's Holy Bible to ask and to receive that your joy will be full? (John 16:24)

Yes, come to YOUR loving heavenly Father God and ask believing in Jesus' holy name, ask your God for anything good that will benefit you, your family and loved ones, and your church congregation, all good things that will help people and will glorify your God on earth, ask in Jesus' holy name, and claim the power of the shed blood of Jesus, and then WATCH Our God work in your life, in their lives, and in the lives of your church congregation.

Yes, do always teach your church group to pray in one accord, pray believing prayers, pray in Jesus' name, that people will be helped, and that God WILL BE GLORIFIED on earth, and then WATCH for your and for their prayers to be answered by YOUR God and by THEIR God.

Yes, Our God does love ALL Our God's children the same and does love ALL Our Christian churches the same. (Acts 10:34)

Yes, do strive for unity in your church to have all the congregation be at peace with God and be at peace with each other.

Do help the helpless that you do know of when you are ABLE to help them, whether or not they are members or attendees of your church.

Yes, all people alive on earth ARE created in Our God's image, they do ALL belong to YOUR God, and you ARE your brother's keeper.

Yes, didn't Jesus teach you to love God above all else and to love others as you do love yourself? (Mark 12:28-31)

Yes, they will know the true Christians by their love for God and by the love and help they give to others.

Yes, will others be attracted to your God, unless they can know the love, help, and concern they receive from Christians?

Yes, read about, know, and claim ALL Our God's good promises to all of Our God's mankind on earth.

Yes, ALL of Our God's promises to you in Our God's Holy Bible have been tried and tested at least seven times, and they are all true, yes and amen, when the right conditions are met. (Psalm 12:6)

Yes, what Our God does for one of Our God's children, Our God will do for ANY of Our God's children, when the right conditions are met.

Yes, do pray without ceasing for a long time. (1 Thessalonians 5:17)

Do worship YOUR Holy Triune God MANY times daily with your whole body, soul, and spirit, and do watch Our God fill you with ALL of Our God's good benefits.

Yes, ask for knowledge and do receive knowledge.

Ask for wisdom, power, love, prosperity, and all GOOD things to enrich your own life and the lives of others, ask it ALL in Jesus' name to the glory of God, ask believing, seek to receive, and you SHALL HAVE what you ask for, that Our God will show you Our God's love, power, and majesty on earth.

Praise your God continually, and you and your loved ones will be enriched beyond measure.

Doesn't Our God's Holy Bible teach that no good thing will be withheld from those who live righteously? (Psalm 84:11)

Yes, YOUR Holy Triune God IS a good God, Who delights to give all God's obedient children all good gifts, WHEN they are ready to receive them.

Hallelujah!

Praises to Our heavenly Father God for this wonderful message for all Our Christian pastors!

Hallelujah!

Praises to Our God!

Dear Christian Pastors and All Holy Bible Teachers:

As the souls of the pastors and other Bible teachers grow more in God, our God is able to entrust more responsibilities to the pastors and other Christian leaders of their churches.

There are many ways that I grow in God daily, weekly, monthly, and yearly:

- **Daily Bible Reading.** I have been reading through the Bible since 1971. I heard that if you read three chapters a day and read five on Sundays that you could read through the Bible in one year. It took me two years to read through the Bible the first time. After that, I read through it yearly with this method until I discovered The One-Year-Bible. I have been reading through the Bible yearly, using the New International Version of The One-Year-Bible, and have now read through the Bible forty-five times. The more I read it, the more I understand its teachings. I praise God for our Bibles in our own language, and that Our God's Holy Spirit within us helps us to understand and apply it's teachings to our lives.

- **Praising God for two hours nearly every morning** for many years. I praised God for an hour, then asked Father God to speak to me, and He always did. I ate breakfast and read my Bible and part of a Christian teaching book or biography. Then I praised God for a second hour, then asked Lord Jesus to speak to me, and He always did.

- **Reading good Christian educational books, biographies,** other non-fiction books, and Christian magazines of Guideposts and Charisma. I try to read twenty pages a day in books, which enables me to complete two books a month, which is 24 books a year. Biographies and autobiographies are my favorites, as I like to learn how a person is trained from an early age, how they develop their special gifts from God, how they mature in all areas of their life, and how they use their gifts to help themselves, help others, and glorify God. It's interesting to me how God blesses people who have a servant's heart, people like Conrad Hilton and J. W. Marriott with the hotels, Dave Ramsey with the family finances, Sam Walton with family shopping, R. G. LeTourneau with earth-moving equipment, Bill Gates with computers, the Wright Brothers, Corrie ten Boom, doctors, nurses, missionaries, and others.

- **Prayer.** I pray on my knees when I first wake up. I pray on my knees other times during the day and pray on my knees before I go to bed. In the last few weeks, when I drive around town running errands and drive on out-of-town trips, I use the time to praise God in my prayer language (tongues). I gave up watching all T.V. several months ago and no longer listen to talk radio. I get the news from the computer, from newspapers, and from my charity letters from all over the world. As I read the ten to twenty charity letters that I receive daily, I pray for some of their needs. I also pray for my two children, their spouses, my six grandchildren, my siblings, and other relatives and loved ones daily. I also pray for our government leaders to make wise decisions to help lead our nation back to God. I attend our monthly church prayer meetings, where we sing praises, have Communion, testimonies of answered prayers, and prayer for many needy.

- **Prophetic Messages.** I ask for, receive, write out, and type up, two prophetic messages each week. I now have more than 940 typed up, with more than half from Father God and the rest from Lord Jesus. God's Holy Spirit helps me receive them and process them.

- **Tithes and Offerings.** Every third Wednesday of each month, I receive my check from Social Security that is automatically deposited into my charities' checking account. Since I know the date the funds will arrive, I have all of my many checks written out, placed in their proper envelopes, with a printed prophetic message included, stamped, and ready to mail out. The day the funds arrive is the same day that I like to send them out. Joy!

- **I Attend Mt. Bethel United Methodist Church** in Marietta, Georgia. After I sold my house in Brentwood, Tennessee, in December 2016, and purchased a house in Marietta, Georgia in January 2017, I joined the church where my daughter, Lori LaVoy and her family, attend. I left Oasis Church in Nashville and joined Mt. Bethel UMC in March 2017. Father God revealed to me that I am like a plant in a pot that was root-bound, and I needed to be transplanted to a larger pot so that my soul can continue to grow in God. I am now enjoying attending this wonderful nine-thousand member church during the third worship service on Sunday mornings. We enjoy the praise singing with a large adult choir and orchestra and greatly enjoy the Bible-based preaching of our main pastor, Dr. Jody Ray. I have been enjoying our Wednesday evening church suppers, open to all for a $7.00 fee for adults. I have been attending our monthly first-Wednesday-evening prayer meetings. There are a great many Bible studies and other group meetings and activities for all ages at this church. Joy! My daughter Lori will teach a Dave Ramsey's Financial Peace class there this fall.

- **Daily Painting.** Father God wants me to paint daily on my paintings. I try to paint daily for one hour while listening to CDs. Recently I have been painting a series of fifty-three butterflies in acrylics on size 5" by 7" canvases, and putting them into stand-up frames. I paint the butterflies the shapes and colors in which God creates them, and then I add abstract backgrounds. Father God is helping me to become a better graphic designer by my analyzing the colors and shapes of the butterflies, as these perfect designs by God cannot be improved on. God's Holy Spirit is helping me to improve my sense of color harmony with the colorful abstract backgrounds of the butterflies. Father God told me, **"Each painting that you complete will be better than the previous one."** I can see that God is helping me to become a better artist. I want to make some of these small paintings into note cards, sell them, and give the funds to my charities. At Christmas in 2015, for my second Christmas Open House and Art Sale, I sold 17 paintings and many packs of note cards, and gave the funds to seven charities. Joy! I would enjoy painting the fifty state birds and fifty state flowers and make note cards from them. They are all so beautiful!

- **Christian Teachings and Christian Music on CDs.** I listen to CDs for an hour while I paint. My favorite Bible teachers are Derek Prince, Ernest Angley, and Robert Morris. I also like to watch, "It's Supernatural!" with Sid Roth on my computer. Sometimes I buy and read the Christian books advertised on "It's Supernatural!"

Blessings! Velma

Yes, Our God's beloved Christian pastors and Holy Bible teachers, YOUR heavenly Father God does love you, does lead and guide you, and does prepare a way for you to speak to others these great truths of Jesus Christ as given in Our God's Holy Bible.

Yes, these great truths that Jesus spoke as recorded in Our God's Holy Bible will NEVER pass away, as they will ALWAYS remain true until the end of time on earth and beyond.

Yes, every word that Jesus spoke when He walked this earth nearly two thousand years ago can now be tested by mankind on earth and can be proven to be as true now as they were true when Jesus spoke them on earth.

Yes, do believe EVERY word Jesus spoke as ALL the words Jesus spoke are absolutely true of what Jesus spoke of HIS heavenly Father God, Our God's Holy Spirit, heaven, hell, salvation in Jesus and forgiveness of sins, righteous living, of being a servant to your fellow mankind, helping the helpless, forgiving those who harm you in any way, prayer, love, justice, kindness, joy, and everlasting life in heaven with your Holy Triune God.

Yes, Jesus is righteous.

Yes, Jesus is God.

Yes, the righteous-in-Jesus and the obedient right-living-unto-God Christian children will SOON see Our God's Jesus Christ appearing in the clouds above Our God's planet Earth as He arrives in the heavenlies above earth, coming to claim and to catch away to the heavenlies ALL the saints of God to take them BACK to THEIR glorious home in heaven, to the many mansions He has, YOUR Lord Jesus has, now prepared for them, for them to rule and reign with THEIR Lord Jesus Christ forever.

Yes, get ready to go!

Stay ready to go to meet Jesus in the air SOON!

Yes, warn your congregations, warn ALL your listeners that time is SHORT and is now growing SHORTER until Jesus comes!

Get READY!

Stay READY!

Time is now short!

Warn others to come OUT of ALL sinful lifestyle, be saved in Jesus for the remission of ALL of their sins, and live a righteous lifestyle unto God.

Yes, sin will NEVER enter heaven.

Repentance from sin and acceptance of the shed blood of Jesus washing away a person's sins, then living a righteous lifestyle unto God, is any person's ONLY one-way ticket to heaven after their ONE life on earth is over.

Do not be deceived; Our God is NOT mocked: as whatever a person sows, they will reap. (Galatians 6:7)

Yes, the wages of sin is death. (Romans 6:23)

Yes, preach and teach against people living an unholy lifestyle as living in continual sin can doom a person to hell for eternity.

Yes, didn't Jesus teach that if an eye or part of a person causes them to sin, to pluck it out or cut it off, to get rid of sin, to enter heaven? (Matthew 5:29-30)

Yes, Jesus lived a holy life unto His Father God on earth and set the righteous example for all of mankind to follow on earth, to glorify God on earth, to be rewarded by God on earth, and to be rewarded by THEIR heavenly Father God in heaven in their life after their one life on earth is over.

Yes, heaven and hell are real.

Yes, teach about heaven and hell.

Teach about the evil activities of people that will doom them to hell for eternity as given in Our God's Holy Bible in the book of **Revelation.** (Revelation 21:8)

Yes, warn people about the evils of sin and the consequences of a habitual lifestyle of sin that separates a person from God.

Yes, preach righteousness in Jesus as led by Our God's Holy Spirit in a person's life.

Yes, as watchmen on the wall, do warn people of forthcoming evil when they turn away from their true God, their true holy Creator and Sustainer.

Yes, when people turn against their true God and allow things and/or events to have first place in their hearts, minds, bodies, and souls, they become worthless to God, and except they repent and turn back to their first love, THEIR Holy Triune God, they shall all perish from the face of the earth.

Yes, be warned!

Live a holy life unto God!

WARN OTHERS to come out of ALL sinful lifestyle and live holy unto God!

Yes, how you do send your church members and congregations out, IS how they WILL RETURN to you, and your church membership and congregations and church financial income WILL be built up.

If you feed them crumbs of anything besides Jesus and the teachings in Our God's Holy Bible, they will NOT return.

You must LEARN to feed your congregations the "true meat" of Jesus Christ and the true teachings of Our God's Holy Bible if you want your congregations to keep on returning to your church services.

Yes, there is GREAT power in the name of Jesus, in the shed blood of Jesus, and in the true teachings of Jesus.

Yes, people are now HUNGRY for the love of God and for the power of God working in their lives.

Yes, do FEED the people the true teachings of Jesus and Father God and the Holy Spirit of God as found in Our God's Holy Bible.

Teach them to imitate Jesus by showing love and service to the people.

Yes, Jesus, the only perfect man who ever lived a lifetime on earth, does set the example of how Our God wants Our God's mankind to live on earth.

Yes, Jesus always honored His heavenly Father God and always taught others how to know their Father God and how to honor and how to live for THEIR heavenly Father God.

Yes, Jesus always spoke the truth in love.

Yes, Jesus loved and helped the unlovely and the needy who needed His help to overcome difficulties in their lives.

Yes, the teachings of Jesus and the promises-to-mankind that Jesus gave, that are now recorded in Our God's Holy Bible, are still as true today as they were absolutely true when Jesus gave them.

Yes, Our God's earth may pass away, but Our God's words, the promises of Jesus in Our God's Holy Bible, will NEVER pass away. (Matthew 24:35)

Yes, Jesus Christ IS the holy living Word of HIS heavenly Father God. (John 1:1-3)

Yes, Jesus Christ IS the same yesterday, today, and forever. (Hebrews 13:8)

Yes, Jesus Christ healed everyone who asked Jesus to heal them when Jesus walked this earth nearly two thousand years ago, and Jesus Christ is STILL all of mankind's physical Healer today.

Yes, Jesus still heals sick people today, when they do CALL on Jesus to heal them, when they do have enough faith-in-Jesus to be healed by Jesus.

Yes, when people do come to their heavenly Father God in prayer, praying with faith in the holy name of Jesus, Our God does hear EVERY WORD of their prayers, and Our God does see their faith in Jesus to be healed; Our Father God speaks the words, "Be healed according to your faith in Jesus Christ," and then Our God does watch to see who gets healed, who receives their healing.

Yes, in Our God's Holy Bible, doesn't Jesus speak the words, "Your faith has made you whole," to many who are healed as recorded in Our God's Bible Scriptures? (Mark 5:34, Luke 17:19)

Yes, faith in Jesus will heal the sick. (James 5:15)

Yes, faith in Jesus' holy name will get your righteous prayers answered.

Yes, the prayers of a righteous person do availeth much. (James 5:16)

Yes, ALWAYS pray your prayer to YOUR heavenly Father God, pray in Jesus' holy name.

Yes, your heavenly Father God does honor your prayers prayed with faith in Jesus' holy name when the answers to these prayers will benefit you, benefit others, and WILL glorify God on earth.

Yes, no prayer request is too small for Our God's love to answer, and no prayer request is too big for Our God's power to answer.

Yes, do pray BIG prayers to your BIG God, pray with faith, pray in Jesus' holy name, pray believing in good answers, pray that you will be helped, pray that others will be helped, pray that God will be honored and glorified on earth, live for God, obey God as given in Our God's Holy Bible, and do EXPECT great and good things and events from your God.

Yes, live for God.

Obey God.

Love God with your total being.

Love others as you love yourself and your family and other loved ones.

Help the helpless with love and kindness, and then do WATCH and do see what good things and good events Our God WILL DO for you and for your loved ones.

Yes, know Our God's promises to you.

Fulfill the requirements for these promises to you, and WATCH Our God work on your behalf for you.

Yes, ALL Our God's promises to you in Our God's Holy Bible are yes and amen when the right conditions are met.

Yes, what Our God will do for one, or for any, of mankind, Our God will do for all when the right conditions are met for the promise to be fulfilled as Our God does love all of mankind, each of mankind, equally. (Acts 10:34)

Yes, Our God does desire fellowship with each of mankind on earth.

Yes, Our God WILL SPEAK to any of Our God's mankind who does get alone with God on their knees in their prayer closet, who praises God, who asks God to speak to them, and who waits on their knees to hear Our God's reply to them, to their request for them to hear Our God speak to them.

Yes, Our God WILL answer you, will call you by your name, and will tell you that Our God does love you, and WILL answer your questions.

Yes, doesn't Our God's Holy Bible tell you to call unto God, and Our God WILL answer you and show you great and mighty things which you know not? (Jeremiah 33:3)

Yes, call on your God, day or night, as your God is ALWAYS available for you.

Your God never slumbers nor sleeps. (Psalm 121:4)

Hallelujah!

Praises to Our heavenly Father God for this message!

Hallelujah!

Praises to Our God!

Dear Christian Pastors and All Holy Bible Teachers,

In all these letters to you that accompany these prophetic messages, the Lord wants me to just share with you some of my experiences. Father God told me to NOT give suggestions for your improvements or corrections as He said, **"That is God's job."** I will try to honor God in this.

With this letter, I believe that God wants me to share with you how I have used my artwork in the churches that I have been in. I was born into a Christian family and always attended church with my mother, Tessie Morgan Garner, and my siblings from birth. I was born the second of five children near Hattiesburg, Mississippi. For the first ten years of my life, living in rural southern Mississippi, our family walked about one and a half miles on a gravel road to attend a small Southern Baptist Church. I became a Christian there at about age eight. I was baptized in a river as our church had no water supply for a baptistery for emersion.

My dad, Grover Garner, never attended church services with us. His grandfather Garner was a Baptist preacher, and I believe Dad was brought up attending church. But as an adult, I knew Dad to attend a regular church service only one time. I never heard him to speak either for or against the Lord, so I never knew whether or not he was a Christian.

When I was age ten in 1948, our family sold everything we owned in Mississippi and moved with only a few of our clothes to Longview, Washington, so Dad could find employment as an automobile mechanic. He found a job working at the same garage over the Columbia River in Oregon where my Uncle Art Hall worked. We lived with Mom's sister and her husband, Aunt Essie and Uncle Art Hall, for about two years on Beacon Hill. When they moved to Oregon, our family purchased a small house in Longview. Shortly after we moved into this house, our eight-year-old brother, Leonard, drowned in the man-made Lake Sacajawea, which was a great shock and great grief for all of us.

We had attended a Sunday School class on Beacon Hill, but when we bought our own house, we were able to attend the regular church services at First Baptist Church. Mom and we siblings walked to church on the sidewalks and over the bridge of Lake Sacajawea, for about one and a half miles to church. Dad had a car, but never drove us, and Mom couldn't drive. When I became age sixteen and got my driver's license, I drove us to church.

We never had any art in the rural public schools in Mississippi, but we did have art in the public schools in Washington. I always loved the beautiful colors. In seventh grade, I saw one of the students doing double the art assignments, using double the free art supplies. I did not know that was allowed. I thought that if she was allowed to do it, maybe I could do it also. I continued doing double art assignments throughout the rest of my public school life, simply because it was fun, and I was allowed to use the free art supplies. Upon my graduation on six-six-fifty-six from Longview High School, I was voted, "The Most Likely to Succeed in Art," and was given a little trophy.

While attending our First Baptist Church on a regular basis, I was asked to make some posters to announce upcoming events and decorate several bulletin boards. I volunteered my artwork in this way in church many times all through high school and all through my two years of Junior College while living at home.

When I went away to the Art Center College of Design in Los Angeles, I became a member of the College Department of the very large Hollywood Presbyterian Church, led by Dr. Henrietta Mears. There were about two hundred members in the College Department, and they always had several events that needed to be publicized, so I was recruited to make posters and decorate show cases. I did volunteer work for this church for the four and a half years that I was in Los Angeles while attending the Art Center College of Design, and while I worked for one year at Gospel Light Publications as a Graphic Designer. Gospel Light Publications and Forest Home Christian Conference grounds were also started by Dr. Henrietta Mears.

When the College Department planned to have a Christian Conference at Forest Home, four of us artists were paid to draw portraits of the twelve speakers planned for the Conference. We drew them life size from their photos, and they were hung around the College Department sanctuary to advertise the upcoming event.

After graduating from Art Center College of Design, I returned home to Longview, Washington, for six months, while teaching an evening art class at Lower Columbia Junior College where my brother Cliff and I had attended as students for two years.

Then I was hired as a Graphic Designer at The Baptist Sunday School Board in Nashville, Tennessee in 1965. I worked at The Baptist Sunday School Board for four and a half years, creating artwork for Christian literature, to win souls to Jesus Christ world-wide, which was my greatest desire. While employed there, I also taught a beginning art class at night at Watkins Institute for adults. One of my students there introduced me to Hugh Davies, who was a student at Vanderbilt, studying for his Master's Degree in Electrical Engineering.

Hugh and I dated off and on for five years and then decided to get married on Thanksgiving weekend in 1970. During our first five years of marriage we had our two children, Lori and Alan. During these five years, I worked part-time freelancing as a Graphic Designer for both The Baptist Sunday School Board and for the Methodist Publishing house. I was a member of the large First Baptist Church in downtown Nashville, where we used some of the Sunday School literature that I had produced as an artist for The Baptist Sunday School Board.

Since Hugh decided to not attend church services with the children and me, I decided to attend The Lord's Chapel in Nashville, and independent church led by Pastor Billy Roy Moore, which had the best Bible teaching that I could find in the Nashville area. At the time the children and I joined in 1977, it was the fastest growing church in Nashville, with several thousand members attending. When I saw Connie Smith, the Country Music star, dedicate one of her three daughters to the Lord there, I wanted to dedicate my children to the Lord there also. Brother Moore dedicated them when Lori was age four and Alan was age two. As they became older and accepted Jesus as their Lord and Savior, Brother Moore baptized them with immersion in our built-in baptistery in the church building.

I became a member of The Lord's Chapel in 1977 and was a member there for thirty nine years, leaving there when I relocated to Georgia in 2016. When I first joined The Lord's Chapel, I did volunteer work in the nursery for the first two years, helping to take care of about thirty, three- and four-year-olds for three and a half hours every Sunday morning, during Sunday School and two church services.

Sometimes I had help and sometimes I didn't. I used some of my art work to teach the children their four-minute Bible lessons, according to their four-minute attention span.

As my children grew older, I helped with the young children in our monthly Bible Bowl activities, by making up a game about what Jesus said and what Jesus did, and giving my two small paintings as prizes to the winners. The paintings were for them to hang on their walls to remember to thank Jesus for the beauty He has created in all living things.

Then I began making posters and decorating bulletin boards at The Lord's Chapel. Then I joined the Mission's Committee and was Secretary for twelve years because no one else would take the job. While Secretary, I also published a monthly newsletter for the church for twelve years titled, "The Chapel News." We had a Christian testimony in every issue. I gathered forty four of these testimonies and published a book titled, *Victory in Jesus.* We published two hundred copies of the book with the Mission's Committee doing the work of the collating and spiral binding. We gave free copies of the book to all the 44 who had their testimonies in the book, and were able to sell all the other copies.

I also did volunteer work in the office all day every Friday for two years, answering the phones while preparing the weekly bulletins to be handed out in the Sunday morning services. My artwork was on the covers of the bulletins for two years. The artwork for the second year was of fifty antique crosses that I had discovered in a Guidepost's magazine, where a group of ladies in a northern church had researched the designs. They had made a hundred needle-point covers for their hymnbooks using these designs.

I later received permission from Guidepost's magazine to use forty of these designs in my book, *Christmas in The Bible Belt*. I put one of each of the forty antique cross designs as the headings for the forty prophecies in the book. Other artwork of mine in the book are forty line drawings of orchids, and eight portrait black ink line drawings of Hugh's family and of our family.

Another art project that I was involved with while at The Lord's Chapel was when four other artists and I met weekly at the church for creating watercolor paintings. We decided to each donate five of our paintings and have a silent auction at the church to raise funds for missions. We displayed the paintings for a week, and received many silent bids written on a small paper by each painting. All of the twenty five paintings sold, except for the largest one, and $1,200.00 was raised. The funds were given to our missionaries John and Joyce Hanson in Haiti for their work there with Christian schools.

When I wanted to give funds to Christian charities, but had no personal income, I was led to paint note cards in watercolors, sell them two for a dollar, and give the funds to twelve Christian charities.

I painted up some samples of thirty designs, displayed them of six to a pack for $3.00 a pack, and showed them to some of my friends at The Lord's Chapel. People began buying them, and I was able to paint 1,700 watercolor notecards in two years, sold them, and gave the funds to my favorite twelve charities.

Father God led me to have a Christmas Open House Art Show and Sale at my house. My friend Karen helped me with the first two, of planning the events, getting out the advertising, displaying the paintings, packaging the note cards, and helping prepare and serve the snacks provided. The first year, I earned $345.00 and gave the funds to my seven Jewish charities. The second year, I earned twice that, with the funds given to the purchaser's favorite charities. It was a win/win/win situation, as the purchaser got the artwork, their charity got the funds, and I got to claim the gift on my income taxes for a pleasant refund.

Joy! Then last year, since my house was up for sale in December, I did not have the Christmas Open House Art Show and Sale at my Brentwood house. Instead, I rented a booth at the Mt. Bethel UMC Christmas sale, and was able to sell $176.00 worth of art and note cards, and gave the funds to some charities.

Father God told me, **"When you move to Georgia, buy a large house, so you can have your Christmas Art Show and Sale in it."** When I moved to Georgia and was looking at houses last December, I found one that I liked. I got on my knees and praised God. I asked God if I should buy this House? He replied, **"You have found the house that God has chosen for you to buy. Offer them $375,000.00, purchase it for $385,000.00, and move in on January 6."** Praise God! We closed on the sale on January 6, and I moved in on January 8, 2017. God is good!

God is encouraging me to paint more to the glory of God. God has given me four prophetic dreams showing my artwork to be successful. Father God spoke to me and said something like this: **"As Amy Grant is to music, soon the name Velma Davies will be to art."**

Father God also told me, **"God will soon help you to paint a portrait of Jesus. Then people will know what Jesus looks like."** After my dad passed away in January 1979, the spirits of Jesus and my dad visited me and I saw them with my spirit. I know Jesus has light brown hair, parted in the middle, is shoulder length, turned out and up a bit on the ends, with a bit of natural wave to it. Joy!

Blessings! Velma

Yes, Our God's beloved Christian pastors and Our God's beloved Holy Bible teachers, YOUR heavenly Father God does love you, does love ALL of your loved ones, and does love ALL of your congregations at ALL of your churches, and at ALL of your gatherings in Our God's name.

Yes, didn't Jesus say to all of His followers in Our God's Holy Bible that where two or three are gathered in His name that He is there with them? (Matthew 18:20)

Yes, this divine promise from Jesus given in Our God's Holy Bible is still true today and has ALWAYS been true from the time Jesus Christ spoke it, when He walked this earth nearly two thousand years ago.

Yes, ALL of these good and excellent promises that Jesus Christ gave to ALL of mankind as given in Our God's Holy Bible by Jesus will endure, will remain TRUE, throughout ALL of eternity, the never-ending eternity.

Yes, YOUR Holy Triune God is from eternity to eternity, without beginning and without ending, the Alpha and the Omega. (Revelation 22:13)

Yes, YOUR heavenly Father God never slumbers nor sleeps. (Psalm 121:4)

Yes, YOUR heavenly Father God loves ALL of Our God's created-by-God mankind the same, and what Our God does for one person, Our God will do for each person, when the right conditions are met. (Acts 10:34)

Yes, do love people and do help the helpless as you are able to, even as you do love and do help yourself.

Yes, you ARE your brother's keeper.

Love people, help people, teach people, live for God, and be rewarded by your God in the way you need it the most.

Yes, YOUR God is a great God of great and MANY rewards that Our God does ENJOY giving to ALL of Our God's obedient children, who have earned all these rewards, who will be benefitted by them, and will not be corrupted by them.

Yes, yes, yes, you do lead others not only by your verbal teachings, but by your righteous living for God, and by your good deeds done unto others.

Yes, live for God.

Obey God and be rewarded by God.

Help the helpless.

ENJOY your daily walk with and talk with YOUR heavenly Father God, YOUR Lord Jesus Christ, and Our God's Holy Spirit in your life, leading you, teaching you, helping you, rewarding you, providing for you, and protecting you.

Yes, YOUR Holy Triune God is very, very good to you at ALL times.

LEARN to praise and thank Our God for Our God's goodness to you at all times, and Our God will keep you in perfect peace and give you joy unspeakable in your life at ALL times.

Yes, your heavenly Father God never slumbers nor sleeps, but your heavenly Father God does watch your life, your thoughts, your motives, and your actions at ALL times.

Yes, YOUR heavenly Father God does reward you for your good thoughts, good motives, and good actions when they do help others, help yourself, and when they do glorify God on earth.

Yes, the true leaders with a servant's heart who do help others who do need their help are the ones who do get promoted by God to higher levels of service, higher levels of responsibilities, higher levels of prestige, fame, and fortune.

Yes, Our loving God will NOT promote any leader or pastor or missionary above the level of responsibility that they are able to handle, able to control, with Our God's Holy Spirit's help in their life/lives.

Yes, your God knows you much better than you know yourself, as your God knows the number of hairs on your head and knows the number of cells that make up your physical body.

Yes, YOUR heavenly Father God knew you in heaven before you were born on earth, your heavenly Father God knows every part of you and your life now on earth, and your heavenly Father God knows ALL your future life on earth, and your future life in heaven after your one life on earth.

Yes, your heavenly Father God knows your faults, your weaknesses, your human frailty, your personal struggles, your family and friend struggles, your ministry and service-to-others struggles.

Yes, Jesus Christ and your heavenly Father God are the answers to ALL of your struggles and to ALL of your earthly concerns.

Yes, pray often.

Pray in Jesus' holy name.

Expect good and quick answers to ALL your righteous prayers to help you, help your loved ones, and to glorify God on earth.

Yes, YOUR heavenly Father God is able to do FAR more than you can pray for, can think of, can even be aware of. (Ephesians 3:20)

Yes, pray often and claim in Jesus' holy name, ALL the answers to your righteous prayers.

Yes, do realize that you do serve and do live for a big God, a mighty God, a just God, a righteous God, a loving God, a peaceful God, a never-ending and never-beginning God, a God Who does have all things and all people and all situations FULLY in Our God's control at ALL times, all day times and all night times.

Yes, nothing good and nothing bad can happen on planet

Earth, can happen at any time, unless Our God allows it to happen.

Yes, your heavenly Father God does absolutely control ALL happenings on planet Earth at ALL times.

Yes, God does allow seemingly bad things to happen on earth to get people to return to THEIR holy Creator God.

When people turn away from knowing and from following the true God of Jesus Christ, God allows seemingly bad circumstances in their lives to bring them BACK to God, or to bring them into a closer walk with God, to a greater dependence on THEIR true God to meet ALL their needs and to meet ALL their holy desires.

Yes, when you ARE TESTED by ANY adversity in your life, that means that Our God is allowing your soul to grow in God, is HELPING your soul to grow more in God, so that when Our God brings you through the adversity, and your soul has grown more in God, Our God is able to TRUST YOU enough to promote you to new levels of service and new levels of responsibilities.

Yes, your soul will continue to grow up in God throughout eternity in heaven.

Yes, upon your physical death on earth, your soul's-growth-in-God is the only thing you are able to take to heaven with you as your soul was created by God for you at your moment of conception to endure forever.

Yes, Our God's promises to you and given to everyone in Our God's Holy Bible are given to you for the growth of your soul.

Yes, Our God's promises to you are always yes and amen, and can be claimed by you and by anyone, when the right conditions are met.

Yes, do know these promises.

Do claim these promises for you and for others.

Do meet the conditions of these promises and do ACT on these promises.

Let everything you do, do it with love to the glory of God, and do watch and do see HOW Our God does reward you for this.

Yes, the Lord is YOUR Shepherd, you shall not be in want, as YOUR Holy Triune God IS trustworthy to meet ALL your needs and ALL your holy desires right on time.

Yes, do help others with love in the ways that they need it the most when you ARE ABLE to help others, then WATCH and do see how Our God meets all YOUR needs in the way that you need it/them the most.

Yes, your heavenly Father God does desire and does delight to give each of mankind ALL Our God's good gifts to them that Our God created and laid up for mankind before the world was created, the earth you know of was created, give them to each of mankind, when each person is ready to receive these good gifts.

God will NOT give you a good gift for you to consume it in your lusts.

God WILL give you good gifts to help you lead a better righteous life and share these good gifts with others who need them, as they will glorify God on earth.

Yes, do praise and do thank your heavenly Father God for ALL the good gifts you now have in your life and in the lives of your loved ones, and soon you and they WILL have MORE of Our God's good gifts.

Yes, do enter into YOUR heavenly Father God's presence with praise and thanksgiving.

Glory!

Hallelujah!

Praises to Our heavenly Father God for this prophetic message for church growth worldwide!

Praises to Our Father God!

114

Dear Christian Pastors and All Holy Bible Teachers,

I sincerely hope that all of you pastors and Bible teachers continue to preach and teach on the messages of Jesus and the teaching of our God's Holy Bible throughout the year, so that all our churches can grow in attendance and grow in finances, so that more people can be helped in these troubling times on earth.

I recently read an article online at Charisma News Daily that stated: "4,000 churches close every year, and over 3,500 people leave the church every single day." They come seeking the love of God in their lives, and seeking the power of God in their lives to make them successful people on earth. When they don't receive this, why should they return?

If the Christian pastors and Holy Bible teachers will only teach the great truths in the Bible about Jesus and the will of God for their lives, their souls will grow in God, they will WANT TO return to church to be fed more "solid meat." If they are fed anything else but the truth about Jesus and the Bible, they are being fed crumbs, and will not want to return. People are HUNGRY for more of God. People are HUNGRY for truth, and Jesus is truth. People are HUNGRY for more of God's love and God's power in their lives, to solve all their problems, to meet all their needs, and to give them hope, happiness, and success in their daily lives.

- They need to be taught to follow the example of Jesus for their daily living.
- They need to be taught how to pray in Jesus' name and how to get their righteous prayers answered.
- They need to be taught to read their Bibles daily, avoid evil influences, and whatever they do will prosper. (Psalm 1:1-3)

- They need to be taught the benefits of tithing, that what they give will be returned to them double and more than double guaranteed.
- They need to be taught to serve mankind, to help the helpless, and God will reward them.
- They need to be taught that by living a righteous lifestyle unto God, that no good thing will be withheld from them. (Psalm 84:11)
- They need to be taught that it is more blessed to give than to receive. (Acts 20:35)
- They need to be taught of the rewards in heaven in their afterlife.
- They need to be taught the punishments of hell for eternity in their afterlife because of refusing Jesus and living in habitual sin.
- They need to be taught who will go to heaven and who will go to hell. (Revelation 21:8)
- They need to be taught how to witness to their loved ones and to strangers about Jesus, the Bible, heaven, and hell.
- They need to be taught how to come out of all sinful lifestyle and live in obedience to God.
- They need to be taught to put God first above all else, and to love others as they love themselves.
- They need to be taught that God loves all people the same, and what God will do for one of His children, He will do for any of them when the right conditions are met.
- They need to be taught of the supreme sacrifice of Jesus to pay for their physical healing, for their salvation, and for their eternal life in heaven.
- They need to be taught that Jesus is alive in heaven and that He still heals people physically today.
- They need to be taught that all the good gifts in their lives are from Father God, and that they come from Father God through Jesus Christ to them.

- They need to be taught the power in praise and worship to God—that when they are praising and worshipping God is when God is filling them with love, joy, peace, power, and all good things for their happiness and for their successful living.
- They need to be taught that Jesus Christ is able to meet EVERY need and EVERY holy desire that they have on earth.
- They need to be taught how to love, honor, respect, live for, and co-operate with God in their lives to be successful in life.
- They need to be taught that they have the Helper, the Comforter, the Guide, the Teacher, of God's Holy Spirit living within them that they can have the help from Him they need at any time.
- They need to be taught how to practice the presence of God in their lives at all times, by focusing on God continually, by thanking, worshipping, and praising God for His goodness, His love, His power, His majesty.
- They need to be taught how to hear from God for themselves, by getting alone in their prayer closet on their knees, praising God, asking God to speak to them, and waiting on their knees in silence, until God speaks to them in a still small voice in their minds, then thank God for speaking to them.
- They need to be taught that when Father God or Jesus speaks to them, that if they don't speak out or write out that first thought, that the other thoughts will not come.
- They need to be taught how to be FILLED with the Holy Spirit of God, how to pray in their own prayer language, tongues, so that their prayers will be more effective, and they will have more love, joy, peace, and power in their lives.
- They need to be taught that at their moment of conception in their mother's womb, that God gave to them their eternal soul, and their soul will continue to live either in heaven

117

or in hell after their one life on earth, as there are no other places for their soul to live after their one life on earth is over.

- They need to be taught that at their moment of conception in their mother's womb, that God gave to them special gifts, that when they grow and mature and develop these interests and special gifts, God will help them to be successful in their life's work, to help themselves, to help others, and to glorify God on earth.

- They need to be taught that Jesus is coming back SOON for our God's great rapture of the saved and sanctified souls on earth, for them to get ready, stay ready to go, pray in all of their lost loved ones, and warn the wicked to get right with God while there is still time, while they are still alive on earth.

- They need to be taught that God hates a sinful lifestyle, and except they repent and turn to Jesus Christ for salvation, and live a righteous lifestyle while alive on earth, that they will regret it forever in hell.

- They need to be taught that Allah, Buddha, Mohammad, and other so-called gods are NOT the only true God of Father God, Jesus Christ God, and the Holy Spirit of God, and that none of these gods have the power to save anyone at all, and they cannot even save themselves.

- They need to be taught that Jesus Christ of Nazareth is the ONLY TRUE SAVIOR of ANY of mankind, as only the sinless, pure shed blood of Jesus is capable of washing away a person's sins, saving their eternal soul, and taking them to heaven forever.

- They need to be taught that reincarnation is a lie from Satan to deceive mankind that they can work their way into heaven over several lifetimes on earth. Man lives only once on earth and then the judgment. (Hebrews 9:27)

- They need to be taught that the ONLY way to their holy Creator, their Father God, is through Jesus Christ. (1 Timothy 2:5)

- They need to be taught to obey the laws of the land, as Jesus obeyed the laws of the land when He walked this earth nearly two thousand years ago.
- They need to be taught that all their parents, siblings, spouses, children, grandchildren, and other loved ones are only loaned gifts to them from God, but that they are still God's children, and that God can come for ANY of His children at ANY time that He has a higher purpose for them.
- They need to be taught the truth of Jesus, of the Holy Bible, of the Holy Triune God, of heaven and hell, of what our God expects of them, and what Jesus and Father God and the Holy Spirit have done for them, is now doing for them, and will do for them.
- They need to be taught the promises of God and how to apply them to their lives.
- They need to know the purpose and rewards of the trials they go through on earth.
- They need to know that their mistakes can be forgiven by God, and that they can have a new fresh start in life by giving their life to God.
- They need to know that God wants them to LIVE, not commit suicide, to give their life to God, and watch God turn their life on earth into something beautiful.
- They need to know that it is God that gives them the power to get wealth. (Deuteronomy 18:28)
- They need to know God as their Provider and their Protector, and to thank God often for their provisions and for their protection.
- They need to know that Father God is sovereign, and that He is able to answer all big prayers, all little prayers, and all prayers prayed with faith in the name of His only beloved Son, Jesus.
- They need to know that God knows their thoughts, their motives, and their actions, and that God knows their past,

their present, and their future, not only of them, but of everyone now alive on Our God's planet Earth.

- They need to know that apart from Jesus, they can do NOTHING, but that they can do ALL THINGS through Christ.
- They need to know that God's Holy Spirit helps you with your sermons and Bible teaching.

Here are some quotes from people that I like. My psychiatrist said, "The Holy Spirit doesn't quit moving just because the church service lets out." When one pastor told a woman that she could meet Jesus at church, she replied, "Yes, I know. I bring Him with me."

When I dated a pastor's son in Los Angeles, he said to me, "Here you are a thousand miles from home, and you still show up at church every Sunday morning. When I was at college in Kentucky, I slept in every Sunday morning. I had been MADE to go to church every Sunday morning, and I was so glad to get away from it." My answer to him at that time was, "I was GLAD when they said unto me, let us go into the house of the Lord."

I meet Jesus before, during, and after the church service. I will not follow a pastor who does not follow Jesus and the Bible teachings. I can hear it not only in their preaching, but see it in their lifestyle and in their service in helping others. When my current pastor, Dr. Jody Ray told us, "I would do anything but sinning, to win souls to Jesus Christ," I knew I had joined the right church in Marietta, GA. So I asked him, "As the main pastor of this large Methodist church, would you be willing to allow five thousand families to camp out for three days and three nights on the church grounds while Jesus saves people and heals the sick and restores the MAIMED?" Well, I'm praying for that to happen! Is anything too hard for our Jesus?!

Blessings! Velma

Yes, Our God's beloved Christian pastors and ALL Holy Bible teachers, YOUR heavenly Father God, YOUR holy Creator God, does love you, does love ALL of your loved ones, and does love ALL of your congregations, and Our God does meet with you, when you do gather in Our God's only begotten Son, the holy name of Jesus Christ.

Yes, do gather OFTEN in the holy name of Jesus Christ, and do praise for a long time Our God's Holy Triune God, and then do WATCH Our God's love, peace, harmony, and joy flow through the crowd to love God more and to love their fellow mankind more.

Yes, Jesus is love, and Jesus is ALWAYS WITH YOU when two or more gather in Jesus' holy name. (Matthew 18:20)

Yes, Jesus STILL has the power to save lost souls and to heal the sick and restore the maimed.

Yes, Jesus Christ IS the same yesterday, today, and forever. (Hebrews 13:8)

Yes, Jesus has been raised from the dead by HIS heavenly Father God, then He ascended into Our God's heaven, and is now seated at HIS Father God's right hand, now making intercession with HIS Father God for the salvation and well-being of ALL the people NOW alive on Our God's planet Earth.

Yes, it is Our Father God's will that NONE perish, that NONE reject Jesus Christ as their personal Savior from their sins, that NONE continue living in sin while they are now alive on earth and MISS going to heaven in their afterlife, after their one life on earth is over.

Yes, hell is hot and it is long, and you do NOT want to go

there by rejecting Jesus as your Lord and Savior from your sins and by living in a sinful lifestyle on earth.

Yes, sin will NEVER enter heaven.

Yes, ONLY the holy shed blood of Jesus Christ has enough power to wash away a person's sins and Adam's sin that all of mankind was born into, and each person must COME to Jesus with a repentant heart, ASK Jesus to forgive their sin, MAKE Jesus the Savior, Lord, and Ruler of their life, then come OUT of ALL sinful lifestyle and live their life in obedience to God, in order to enter heaven in their afterlife, their life after their one life on earth is over.

Yes, people living in habitual sin will NOT enter heaven, unless they REPENT, come out of ALL sinful lifestyle, ask Jesus for forgiveness, then live their life in obedience to God, will they THEN enter heaven, after their one life on earth is over.

Yes, yes, yes, do TELL people to COME OUT OF ALL SINFUL lifestyle and live a holy life unto God, if they do plan to be caught up in Our God's SOON rapture of ALL saved and sanctified right-living-unto-God Christian souls, to meet THEIR Lord Jesus Christ in the air in a split second, to be taken BACK to their heavenly home with THEIR Lord Jesus Christ forever.

Yes, time is SHORT until Jesus returns toward earth for Our God's great rapture of souls.

Yes, teach REPENTANCE!

Yes, teach Jesus Christ SAVES!

Teach time is SHORT and is growing shorter day by day!

Teach that NOW is the day of salvation—that tomorrow may be TOO LATE for them to come to Jesus for salvation and right-living for God.

Teach that if they die in their sins and lift up their eyes in hell, they can and will be trapped in hell forever, with NO HOPE of ever escaping from hell.

Yes, teach Jesus is the way, the ONLY way, the truth, and the life. (John 14:6)

Yes, Jesus Christ of Nazareth is the only Person, dead or alive, Who holds their one-way ticket to heaven, and it is FREE for their ASKING Jesus for it, for their repenting of ALL sinful living in their life, by their coming OUT of ALL sin, and by their living righteously for God while they are alive on Our God's planet Earth, for their soul to enter heaven in their life after their one life on earth is over.

Yes, you do love and do live for and do serve a mighty God, a righteous God, a powerful God, a loving God, a just God, a never-ending God, an all-knowing God, a God Who never slumbers nor sleeps, a God Who did create and Who does sustain at all times this vast universe, your planet Earth, and all on it and all in it.

Yes, each person alive now on earth could not survive for even a second longer, unless Our God gave to them their life and their breath.

Yes, Our God in heaven created all of mankind on earth in Our God's image with body, soul, and spirit to live forever, to know God, to fellowship with God, to worship God, to live for God, and to do the works on earth that Our God has prepared for them to do and has equipped each one of them to do.

Yes, doesn't Jesus Christ teach you in Our God's Holy Bible to love God above all else and to love others as you do love yourself? (Matthew 22:37-39)

Yes, when you do love your true Holy Triune God above ALL else, you will WANT to fellowship with God, praise God, thank God for Our God's goodness to you and to your loved ones, obey God and lead a righteous life unto God, and study Our God's Bible to learn more about Our God and Our God's ways.

Yes, when you do love others as you do love yourself, you will WANT TO help the helpless, encourage the downtrodden, pray for the sick and afflicted to be healed, and give to ALL people the eternal hope that Jesus Christ gives of life, abundant life on earth, and eternal life in heaven through the only true Savior of mankind, Jesus Christ of Nazareth.

Yes, Jesus Christ shed His pure innocent holy blood to wash away the sins of mankind to give them access to THEIR heavenly Father God and to give them free salvation and free access to heaven forever, if they will ONLY come to Jesus with a repentant heart, ASK Jesus for forgiveness of their sins and wrongdoing, will ACCEPT this free gift of salvation from Jesus, and then will go and sin no more.

Yes, Jesus will accept ALL who do come to Jesus, who repent of ALL their sins, who ASK Jesus for this free salvation, who do come out of ALL known sin in their life, and who will then live a righteous life unto God.

Yes, after a person DOES COME to Jesus, does ASK Jesus for their salvation, and does accept this free gift of salvation, Our God does give to each one who is saved-in-Jesus, gives each one a measure of Our God's Holy Spirit to live within them, to train them how to better live for God, love God, love others, and serve others with love to Our God's glory on earth.

Yes, Our God's Holy Spirit does teach each of mankind to love like Jesus loved, help others as Jesus helped them, love and honor and teach others about THEIR heavenly Father God.

Yes, when Jesus walked this earth nearly two thousand years ago, He prayed to HIS Father God in heaven, and Jesus taught others how to pray to THEIR Father God in heaven.

Yes, YOUR heavenly Father God is in control of all of heaven and all of earth at all times, and nothing good or nothing seemingly bad can happen at any time, unless it is allowed by Our God.

Yes, YOUR Lord and Savior Jesus Christ has ALL POWER in His full control at all times. (Matthew 28:18)

Yes, when you pray to YOUR heavenly Father God, always pray in the holy name of Jesus.

Yes, the strongest force on earth today is prayers prayed in Jesus' holy name.

Yes, Jesus paid the awful price for each of mankind to be

124

reunited to their holy Creator God, with His shed blood and giving His life on Calvary's cross. (1 Timothy 2:5)

Yes, Jesus is God. (John 10:30)

Worship and praise Jesus as you worship and praise YOUR heavenly Father God.

Yes, your heavenly Father God does know ALL of your needs and does know ALL of your holy desires, but YOUR heavenly Father God wants you to pray to Father God in Jesus' holy name and ask God for these good gifts to you and to your loved ones, so that when Our God does answer your prayers and gives you these good gifts and good events in your life, you will know WHERE they came from—they came FROM your heavenly Father God and they came THROUGH YOUR Lord Jesus Christ.

Yes, do PRAISE your heavenly Father God for ALL the good gifts you now have in your life, and do THANK YOUR Lord Jesus Christ for His supreme sacrifice that makes it possible for you to RECEIVE ALL these good gifts from YOUR heavenly Father God.

Yes, you are joint-heirs with Jesus. (Romans 8:16-17)

Yes, know God and live for God, then ask what you will from YOUR heavenly Father God, pray believing prayers, pray in Jesus' holy name, and you WILL RECEIVE ALL the good things from God that will help you, will help others, and will glorify God on earth.

Yes, will others not come to Jesus for salvation or come to Father God, if they cannot see the love of Jesus and the provisions of God in a person's life?

Yes, you witness for God by how you live, how you love and help the needy, how you praise God for Our God's goodness to you and to them.

Yes, tell others that Jesus and Father God created them and does love them.

Yes, love the unlovely.

Help the helpless.

Be kind and be generous to ALL you meet.

Let Our God's Holy Spirit rule and reign in your life to teach you about God and Our God's will for your daily and nightly life.

Let Jesus be your example to follow.

Know the promises of Jesus for you as given in Our God's Holy Bible.

Claim these promises for you.

Live by Our God's directions for your prosperity and your successful life as given in Our God's Holy Bible.

Draw near to God and God WILL draw near to you. (James 4:8)

All good things and all good events flow to you from God.

Seek God and all good things and all good events will follow.

Hallelujah!

Praises to Our God for this good prophetic message for all Christian pastors and for all Christian Bible teachers!

Hallelujah!

Praises to Our God!

Dear Christian Pastors and All Holy Bible Teachers,

I have been praying about what Father God wants me to write to you to go with the prophetic message number seventeen for church growth. Since I am not a professional writer, but I am a professional Graphic Designer, I depend heavily on our God's Holy Spirit for guidance whenever I do write anything.

For many years, I published my Garner family monthly newsletter and enjoyed putting Christian testimonies in it. Since I am only a typist and not a professional writer, I always invited Christian friends to submit to me their WRITTEN testimonies for the newsletter. Most of them did this, and I praise God for the ones who did. However, when I asked Mary DeWitz for her testimony, she gave to me her ninety-minute spoken testimony on a cassette tape, recorded when she had spoken before a group, and asked ME to write it for her. I really wanted this testimony for our newsletter, as it was the story of how Mary, a former Catholic nun, became married to Hitler's body guard, a German man named Hans DeWitz. We were all members then of The Lord's Chapel.

I listened to the ninety-minute cassette tape a few times and made some notes. The first time through, I had hand written SIXTEEN pages of notes. I knew that my writings could be no longer than THREE handwritten pages for publication in the newsletter. I kept listening to the ninety-minute tape several times during the week, trying my best to condense the testimony, without leaving out anything that was important. Each time that I would write the whole story, it would get a page or two shorter, but NEVER short enough. I listened to the testimony over and over many times during the week, and wrote and wrote, and became more and more frustrated, that I just could NOT condense it enough for three pages.

When I became so frustrated that I was reduced to tears and just cried and cried, I knew that the task was beyond my ability to condense.

When I tried it again, I just could NOT condense it, as it was still EIGHT pages long! I became so terribly frustrated that I just threw the notebook and the cassette player with the tape inside across the room and shouted out to God, **"GOD, YOU KNOW THAT I AM <u>NOT</u> A WRITER!!!"** Then Father God spoke to me very gently in a very calm voice and said, **"Always speak and write the truth in love."**

I was amazed at how *calm* His voice was, when I was so very upset, and how *patient* He was with me, and how much *wisdom* He had in speaking to me! It took me about a half hour to calm down, and when I finally did, I responded to Father God, "Alright, God, with your help, I will always try to do that." I asked for God's help, rewrote it one more time, left out a lot of the things that I thought were so important, and finally condensed it to three hand-written pages. I included it in the family newsletter, with my portrait drawing of their family on the front cover, and with my portrait drawing of their house in Franklin, TN on the back cover. The drawings were the easy part, with God's help. Praise God!

Now I pray and ask for God's help in writing these letters to these Christian leaders, and I know that God's Holy Spirit helps me to write them to you.

Since this prophetic message seventeen from Father God speaks of hearing God's voice for yourself, I want to share some trials God has brought me through in my learning to hear God's voice for myself.

When I first became aware that God will speak personally to individuals was when my two cousins in Georgia, sisters Vera and Joan Garner, who were Spirit-filled and belonged to a Church of God gave me a prophetic message. Vera and Joan prayed for me in their prayer language of tongues. When they did, Joan spoke out a message from God for me on a cassette tape recording. The first sentence she ever spoke for me began, **"My child, you are with an army that has never lost a battle."** Every message she gave to me personally was so very encouraging, that I wanted to become Spirit-filled, so that I could hear from my God for myself.

We all prayed for me to become Spirit-filled. After I joined The Lord's Chapel in 1977, I knew that the Elders there would pray for a person to become Spirit-filled. I went to an Elder, who prayed for me and nothing happened. I went to a different Elder, was prayed for and nothing happened. For one whole year, I listened to the three best Bible teachers that I could find on how to become Spirit-filled. These three were Derek Prince, Billy Roy Moore, and Ernest Angley, all of them Spirit-filled, who all taught on how to become Spirit-filled. Daily I devoured their books, tapes, and messages on the gifts of the Holy Spirit, and tried to do everything they told me to do, yet I did not receive the infilling of the Holy Spirit with the gifts of tongues and prophecy.

When I spoke with Jean Cope, our secretary at The Lord's Chapel, she said, "Go to Elder Louis Hart and you will receive." So I did. I received when Louis struck me on my forehead and said, "Praise God higher!" Joy unspeakable! Louis would tell me, "Pray for the Israelis, pray for the American Indians, pray for the Japanese, pray for the Mexicans," and others. Each group of people that he told me to pray for, I did and my language would change. The only foreign language that I recognized was the Spanish. Right after I received, Louis said to me, "You spoke in seven different languages. That is the best gift of tongues I have ever heard!" I told Louis that I had been seeking it for a year. I prayed four hours in tongues that day, because I was so happy to receive!

Later, I read a book on how to ask God to speak to you. Praise God that He allows me to hear from God EVERY time that I ask Father God or Lord Jesus to speak to me, with God's Holy Spirit helping me. God will do this for ANYONE, who will faithfully seek God, get alone with God in their prayer closet, praise God, ASK God to speak to them, then wait on their knees until God gives them specific phrases in their mind, then thank God for speaking to them. They must speak out or write out the phrase they hear in their mind, or the next phrase will not come. (Jeremiah 33:3)

The book that I read on how to hear God speak to me gave these steps, which I follow:

- I get alone in your prayer closet and praise God.
- I say, "I bind all evil away from me in the holy name of Jesus. I bind all my own thoughts away from me in the holy name of Jesus. I ask Father God (or Lord Jesus) to speak to me."
- Then I pray briefly in my prayer language (tongues).
- I hear words in my mind which I speak out or write out until the words stop coming.
- Then I praise my Father God (or Lord Jesus) for speaking to me.

Blessings! Velma

Yes, Our God's beloved Christian pastors and ALL Holy Bible teachers, YOUR heavenly Father God in heaven does love you, does guide you, does HELP you to be a worker, a servant of God, and a servant of mankind on Our God's planet Earth, to HELP bring in Our God's End-time harvest of souls, before Our God's Lord Jesus Christ returns SOON for Our God's great rapture of ALL the saved-in-Jesus and right-living-unto-God beloved Christian souls to take them BACK to Our God's great heaven above, to dwell with THEIR Holy Triune God forever.

Yes, time IS short and is now growing shorter until Jesus Christ does return toward earth for Our God's great rapture of souls.

Yes, what you do for and with YOUR Holy Triune God must be done quickly.

Yes, SOON time on Our God's planet Earth will run out as you do know time now to be on earth, and then Our God's planet Earth will change to Our God's millennial time, when one day will be as a thousand years. (2 Peter 3:8)

Yes, yes, yes, do get ready to go, and do stay ready to meet Jesus in the air in ANY split second for Our God's great rapture of souls on earth.

Yes, pray in ALL your lost loved ones.

Witness for Jesus.

Tell people that Jesus loves them, can save them, can heal them, can meet ALL their needs and ALL their holy desires both in this life and in their life after their one life on earth ends.

Yes, tell people that their ONLY route to heaven in their life after their ONLY ONE life on earth is through the shed blood of Jesus, shed on Calvary's cruel cross, to wash away ALL of their sins, help them come out of ALL evil lifestyle, live in obedience to the TRUE heavenly Father God, and enter heaven forever in their life after their one lifetime on earth.

Yes, no one else besides Jesus Christ has the power to save anyone.

Buddha cannot save anyone.

Allah cannot save anyone.

Mohammad cannot save anyone.

No person can save themselves by trying to live a righteous life, or by doing certain deeds while alive on earth.

ONLY Jesus, ONLY Jesus, ONLY Jesus is powerful enough to save ANYONE from going to a burning, tormenting hell in their afterlife, and each person now alive on earth MUST COME to Jesus, must ASK Jesus to save them, must REPENT of ALL sinful lifestyle, must THEN live a righteous lifestyle on earth in obedience to God, to go to heaven, to reject going to hell, in their life AFTER their one life on earth is over.

Yes, PREACH Jesus saves!

Preach ONLY Jesus saves!

Preach NOW is the acceptable time to come to Jesus for salvation and for righteous-living- unto-God, for if they die in their sins and lift up their eyes in hell, it can and will be too late for them to accept Jesus, live for God, and go to heaven, as they will be trapped in the torments of hell forever, where there is never any hope of escape.

Yes, Jesus is God.

Yes, worship, praise, love, serve Jesus as you do worship, praise, love, and serve YOUR heavenly Father God.

Yes, your Helper Jesus Christ does hear and help Our Father God answer ALL your believing prayers, prayed in Jesus' holy name, that will benefit you, benefit others, and will glorify God on earth.

Do stay tuned in to YOUR Holy Triune God day and night and do listen to the still small voice of God speaking within you to teach you HOW to listen more to your God speaking with you and communion with you.

Always proof what you hear within your inner voice to make sure that what you are hearing within does agree with the Bible teachings.

You will be tried and tested in learning to hear Our God's voice within yourself.

Yes, all true words from God will ALWAYS agree with the true teachings in Our God's Holy Bible.

Yes, Satan is NOW going about trying to deceive the elect, the special ones chosen by God to teach others about Jesus, Our God, Our God's ways, as given in Our God's Holy Bible.

Yes, Satan is an expert at quoting and misquoting Scripture verses.

Yes, do read and do study Our God's Holy Bible on a daily basis, know what it teaches, and seek to rightly divide the word of God.

Yes, when Satan quoted Scriptures to Jesus, Jesus always answered Satan with other true Scriptures that DID apply to those specific situations.

Know the Scriptures, and know how to rightly divide Scriptures, know how to rightly reply to people who quote Scriptures to you, and especially to those who misquote Scriptures to you, or who take the quotes of Scripture out of context and twist their meanings, so what they speak is untrue.

Yes, Jesus Christ IS the way, the TRUTH, and the life. (John 14:6)

Yes, Jesus will always reveal Jesus' truth to you.

Doesn't Our God's Holy Bible teach you, that you will know the truth, and the truth will set you free? (John 8:32)

Yes, know Jesus and know the truth.

Yes, Our God has given each born-again-in-Jesus'-shed-blood Christian, a measure of Our God's Holy Spirit to live within them to guide them into all truth.

Yes, when Satan misquotes a Scripture to you, Our God's

Holy Spirit within you will bring to your remembrance the exact Scripture that truly relates to the current situation.

Yes, Our God's Holy Spirit will NEVER lead you wrong, when you do ASK Our God's Holy Spirit to lead you in the right way you should think, speak, and act, when you pray believing prayers, praying in Jesus' holy name.

Yes, all of mankind who are alive now ARE living in the last days before Jesus returns toward earth for Our God's great rapture of souls, ALL of the saved-in Jesus and right-living-for-God beloved Christian children of God, to catch them away into the air to meet Jesus, to go BACK to their true and final home in heaven.

Yes, it is possible in these last days before Jesus returns, possible for even the elect Christians to be led astray—but when they TRULY SEEK the true God and truly seek Our God's ways, they will NOT be led astray for long, as Our God can and WILL open their understanding to the TRUTH, so that they will be able to return to the true God, and to the true ways of Our God.

Yes, do SEEK daily your TRUE Holy Triune God—do seek Our God with your total being, your body, soul, and spirit.

Let your spirit commune with Our God's Spirit.

Learn from God.

Let Our God teach you Our God's ways, that you WILL be able to do them, to make your ways prosperous on earth.

Yes, it is Our God's will for you and for all of your loved ones to prosper in EVERY good way: spiritually, physically, mentally, emotionally, educationally, financially, in multiple good possessions, to help yourself, help others, and to glorify God on earth.

Yes, it is God's will for you to be in good health at all times and to prosper in every good way at all times, so you can know God better, can relate to your God better, can praise, worship, and thank your God more for ALL the GOOD BENEFITS in your life that your God has given to you, and has given them to you through YOUR Lord and Savior Jesus Christ.

Yes, you are joint heirs with Jesus. (Romans 8:17)

Yes, Jesus has made it all possible for you to receive ALL good gifts from your heavenly Father God.

Yes, worship Jesus Christ as God.

Worship YOUR heavenly Father God.

Worship Our God's Holy Spirit of God.

Yes, do worship Our God's Holy Triune God—three separate Beings, but We are, God is, ALWAYS in one accord.

Yes, when you do get to heaven, you will see Father God, Jesus Christ, and Our God's Holy Spirit as three separate Beings, but We are, God is, always in one accord.

Yes, when Jesus walked this earth nearly two thousand years ago, He prayed to HIS Father God in heaven, and Jesus Christ has been resurrected from the dead by HIS Father God, has ascended into heaven, and is NOW SEATED at HIS Father God's right hand now making intercession with HIS Father God for the welfare of all of mankind still alive on earth, that each of mankind will come to Jesus for free salvation from their sins, that they will all come out of their sinful lifestyle, will live the rest of their life on earth for God, and will spend eternity in heaven with THEIR heavenly Father God after their one life on earth ends.

Yes, Jesus is coming soon!

Be warned!

Warn others!

Yes, help people to get ready and to STAY ready to meet Jesus in the air in a split second to be transported BACK to THEIR eternal home in heaven, to rule and to reign with THEIR Lord and Master Jesus Christ forever.

Hallelujah!

Praises to Our God Jesus!

Hallelujah!

Dear Christian Pastors and All Holy Bible Teachers,

I have been praying about what to share with you and the others this week. I believe the Lord wants me to share what is going on in my life now.

I received a Christmas gift from my son-in-law, John LaVoy, the book, *The Mystery of The Shemitah,* by a Jewish author, Jonathan Cahn, which I have nearly finished reading. I believe that EVERY Christian should read this book, as it shows us how our God controls EVERYTHING on planet Earth, from the smallest blade of grass to the greatest international powers on earth. Reading this book will greatly increase your faith in Father God, Jesus, and God's Holy Spirit.

The word Shemitah means the seven-year cycle of events that applies to the whole earth, which declares for the people to rest in the seventh year, and let the land rest from raising crops in the seventh year, and when all debts are canceled for the people. When the people obey this plan, they are rewarded by God. When the people do NOT obey this plan, punishment overtakes them. The book shows the relationship between the United States not obeying the seven-year plan and our stock market dropping every seven years. It dropped in September 2001, again in 2008, and again in 2015. It also connects the destruction of the Twin Towers in New York with the date of the Shemitah, and believes they were destroyed because they were the symbol of America's pride. It was a wake-up call to America!

As I was reading this book, God's Holy Spirit was teaching me how these same principles of pride are applied to the lives of leaders, especially to the lives of church leaders. God looks on the heart of each leader, and what He sees are either the symbols of a "dictator's heart" or of a "servant's heart." God does not raise to more power and prestige the leader who has a "dictator's heart," or they will become more corrupt. Only the ones with the "servant's heart" are the ones that God is able to raise to more power and prestige, without them becoming corrupt. Our divine example of this is our Lord Jesus Christ, Who was the greatest of us all, Who said, **"I came not to be served, but to serve."** Jesus set the example for His followers to be servants of themselves, of others, and of God.

I believe that God wants me to give to you two examples of this with two of the Christian leaders that I have worked with, to show you the contrast of the "servant's heart" and the "dictator's heart."

I was a member of The Lord's Chapel/Oasis Church for 39 years. In 1992 and 1993, at The Lord's Chapel, I volunteered my time every Friday for two years in the office answering the phones, and preparing and printing the weekly bulletins that were passed out before the Sunday morning worship services. I used my art skills for the drawings on the covers, and used my typing skills for the inside announcements of the bulletins.

After our main pastor, Billy Roy Moore, relocated to Little Rock, Arkansas, we went through several pastors, who usually stayed for two or three years and then moved on. One temporary pastor who came and served our congregation for a few months was Pastor Jack Gray. When he was being considered by our Elders for being hired as our full-time pastor, he was working in the office on a Friday, when I was volunteering in the office. He called me into his office and said, "I want to hire you to work for me full-time." Since I knew that I was only an artist and a typist, I asked him, "What work do you want me to do for you?" He replied, "Just clear my desk for me." So I asked him, "What are you going to be doing while I am clearing your desk for you?" He replied, "I will be traveling."

I replied to Pastor Jack Gray very firmly, "If you are called to be the pastor of this church and are being paid by this church, we will not be paying you to flit about the country. This is YOUR desk and you need to be clearing your OWN desk! If this were my desk, I would be the one to clear it!" He was not hired by our Elders to be pastor of The Lord's Chapel. He had a "dictator's heart."

The other person I want to write about is my experience with Franklin Graham. I phoned his organization in North Carolina and asked the question, "How many Christmas shoeboxes were given out last Christmas?" I was inquiring because I wanted to publish the amount in my monthly family newsletter, as some of my family members had filled and given some shoeboxes for children in foreign countries. Someone answered my question over the phone at the time I had called and told me how many shoeboxes were sent and to how many foreign countries.

A few days later I received in the mail a personal letter from Franklin, typed by his secretary, that not only answered my question in detail, but also gave me the history of his worldwide Christmas shoebox ministry, and asked for prayers for him and his staff! I was just amazed! This Christian leader who has a worldwide ministry, who has a large working staff, who has a million-dollar yearly personal income, showed up at his office, dictated a letter to his secretary to me, in response to ONLY my ONE phone call!

This man truly has a "servant's heart!" God promoted him! I gladly published his letter in my family newsletter! Praise God!

I wonder how many Christian pastors write a personal letter for a simple phone call that comes into their church office? If they do, I think they must be ready for a promotion from God!

Blessings! Velma

138

Yes, Our God's beloved Christian pastors and all Holy Bible teachers, YOUR heavenly Father God does love you, does provide for you, and does protect you.

Yes, you do know, you do live for, you do worship and praise the ONLY TRUE God, YOUR heavenly Father God, YOUR Lord Jesus Christ God, and Our God's Holy Spirit of God.

Yes, your God is majestic, your God is holy, your God rules and reigns above all.

Yes, your God created it all and STILL creates it all, and your God is most powerful above all.

Yes, Our God did create and still creates, mankind in Our God's image with body, soul, and spirit.

Yes, Our God did and still does create and place each of mankind on earth and does breathe the breath into mankind.

Yes, Our God's white throne judgment will SOON take place when each of mankind who has ever lived on Our God's planet Earth WILL give an account of their thoughts, words, and deeds done while they were alive on Our God's earth. (2 Corinthians 5:10)

Yes, mankind lives only once on earth, then Our God's judgment. (Hebrews 9:27)

Yes, each of mankind was born into the sin nature of Adam, and each of mankind has committed their own sins.

Each of mankind needs a HOLY Savior to pay the price for their sins, to wash away their sins, and wash away ALL of their unholy filth, to clean them up, to help them live righteously unto God, for them to enter heaven spotlessly pure from sin after their lifetime on earth is over.

Yes, Jesus Christ of Nazareth is the ONLY pure and holy

Savior of ANY and ALL of mankind, Who is capable of saving each person's eternal soul, helping them live for God righteously on earth, and ONLY Jesus can open the Door to heaven for them. (John 10:9)

Yes, Jesus saves.

Yes, Jesus forgives sins.

Yes, Jesus ONLY holds the one-way ticket for each of mankind to enter heaven forever.

Yes, ONLY Jesus Christ has paid the extreme price for each of mankind to be saved, to live for God, and to enter heaven in their afterlife, by Jesus' holy shed blood, death, and resurrection.

Yes, now IS the acceptable time for any of mankind now living on Our God's planet Earth to COME to Jesus, ASK Jesus to FORGIVE their sinful lifestyle, make Jesus Christ THEIR Lord and Master, come OUT of ALL known sin in their life and live in a righteous lifestyle in obedience to God—THEN enter heaven forever, to live with their Holy Triune God forever.

Yes, Our God is NOW calling ALL of mankind on Our God's planet Earth to come OUT of their sinful lifestyle, turn to their God, Jesus Christ, for salvation, to REPENT quickly before they are completely destroyed by evil forces on earth.

Yes, preach righteousness!

Preach righteous living!

Preach a RETURN to THEIR TRUE God!

Preach repentance!

Preach Jesus is coming soon for Our God's great rapture of Our God's saved-in-Jesus and righteous-living Christian souls.

Yes, get ready—stay ready to go in the twinkling of an eye!

Yes, Jesus comes SOON!

Tell ALL the people you meet that Jesus comes SOON!

I want ALL My Christian children READY to RECEIVE JESUS SOON!

Yes, you do love and do serve the most powerful and the most loving God that does exist in ALL of existence, YOUR

Holy Triune God of Father God, Jesus Christ God, and Our God's Holy Spirit of God.

Yes, YOUR Holy Triune God does have ALL things that do exist WELL in Our God's full control at ALL times, and nothing at all can happen at any time without your God allowing it to happen, for God's specific reason for it to happen.

Yes, Our God causes good things to happen to mankind to bring mankind closer to God.

Yes, Our God does allow seemingly bad things to happen to mankind as a wake-up call to them, to help bring them closer to God, so that when they do respond to God, grow closer to God, Our God can and will reward them.

If they do NOT respond favorably to Our God's wake-up call to them, and if they continue to drift farther from God, they are headed for destruction—not that God destroys them, but that they destroy themselves, by not heeding Our God's wake-up call to them to return to God, to return to their first love, their beginning love for God.

Yes, it is very easy for mankind to slowly drift away from their first love of God, because of the seeming pleasures of sin that Satan entices mankind with.

But Our God does send many wake-up calls to each of mankind, to each family, and to each nation that drifts away from their first love of God.

Yes, America, these United States of America, is being slowly led astray from the true God, from their Christian founding Fathers, who established America on God and on God's ways; the people are now being led astray by corrupt politicians and other corrupt leaders, who are filled with pride, who are covetous of financial gain, power, and prestige, who care nothing about leading the people to know the true God, to live righteously, and to be a servant for the welfare of others.

Yes, when the leaders of a nation become corrupt and seek evil gain for themselves, they will lead the whole nation into corruption.

Yes, your God is a just God, and your God will allow this corruption of these evil leaders to go only so far, until Our God WILL take action against this corruption now going on in these wicked United States, with these corrupt leaders leading this nation away from the true God.

Yes, do read and do study how Our God had to deal with the nation of Israel written in Our God's Holy Bible, how God dealt with the beloved people when they turned against God, became corrupt, and became worthless to the very God Who created them and Who sustained them and Who gave them ALL good gifts so richly to enjoy.

Yes, when a nation turns its back on God, God turns Our back on that nation by Our God's removing their hedge of protection from evil, and Our God does ALLOW evil forces to come to an evil nation and harm the nation.

If the evil in the nation is so corrupt that nothing good that honors God can be found in it, Our God does allow the enemy to invade the nation and completely destroy the nation, usually with very few survivors.

Yes, America and Americans are now drifting away from loving God, honoring God, and serving God.

Yes, the signs of the end times are now being manifested by people the world over.

The churches are becoming so lukewarm that people become less interested in attending the services.

The people are not being taught about God, the love of God, the power of God, the goodness of God, the benefits of knowing God, honoring God, living for God, obeying God, and loving and helping their fellow mankind.

Yes, do teach others how to know God, how to honor God, how to live and serve God, how their soul can grow in God.

Yes, when your soul grows in God, you will be in good health, and whatever good you do will prosper. (3 John 2)

Yes, teach people the power of the tithe, that they WILL

receive double BACK, what they give to promote Our God's gospel and good works to help others.

Yes, do teach people that they ARE their brother's keeper, and what they do with love to help the helpless, that they ARE doing these good works unto Jesus, and that Our God WILL reward them WELL for it, reward them well for it both in their life on earth and in the future life in heaven.

Yes, do TEACH PEOPLE to read and study their Bibles on a daily basis, do live for God, and Our God WILL REWARD THEM, as whatever they do WILL PROSPER. (Psalm 1:1-3)

Yes, when you do abide in Jesus and Jesus does abide in you, you WILL be given knowledge, skills, enthusiasm, and the ability to excel in whatever good you do to help yourself, help others, and to glorify God.

Yes, you are joint heirs with Jesus. (Romans 8:17)

When you have Jesus in your life, you have ALL GOOD things and all good events in your life.

Yes, read how God wanted to bless and reward the Israelites when they were set to enter the Promised Land after coming out of bondage in Egypt, if only they would stay true to God. (Deuteronomy 28:1-14)

Also, read about how the Israelites would be punished, if they turned against God after entering their Promised Land. (Deuteronomy 28:15-68)

Yes, Our God DID GIVE THEM fair warning of their consequences of their turning away from God; they did turn away from God, and these warnings from God came true, as their land WAS destroyed by their enemies, some were killed, and the rest went into bondage in a foreign land.

Yes, the God then is the same God today.

Yes, God is now sending Our warnings to these wicked Americas to come back to the true God, the true God of their first love, or they will continue to deteriorate into their own destruction.

Yes, the nation that honors God, that nation will Our God honor.

Yes, the nation that forgets God, will have Our God's hand of protection removed from it, and it could be destroyed by its enemies.

Yes, return to God, America, and your God WILL return to you, and will again make the United States of America the greatest nation of earth, as it once was when the leaders and people knew the true God, loved God, honored God, and served God.

Hallelujah!

Praises to Our heavenly Father God for this message!

Praises to Our God!

Hallelujah!

Dear Christian Pastors and All Holy Bible Teachers,

I have been praying about what to write to you Christian leaders at this time. I believe that God wants me to write to you about my history of giving to my charities for the past twenty five years.

I have been a Christian since I was about eight years old. I began tithing at age twenty eight after I moved to Nashville, Tennessee, from Longview, Washington, and began my first permanent job as Graphic Designer at The Baptist Sunday School Board. My main purpose of working at the Baptist Board was to win souls to Jesus Christ through my creating Christian literature that would be used worldwide. My main reason for tithing was to win souls to Jesus Christ, especially in foreign countries.

I continued tithing while I had my own personal income for about seven years.

After Hugh Davies and I got married and had our first child, a daughter named Lori, I continued working free-lance for the Baptist Sunday School Board and for the Methodist Publishing House, both in Nashville. However, every time I left infant Lori with a baby sitter who kept a group of other small children, three days later, she would come down with a fever. Later, we had our second child, a son named Alan. Since I had no relatives or friends to keep the children, without them being around other children who were sick, I decided to be a stay-at-home mom. I didn't really need to work, as I had almost paid off all my loans from my eight years of working my way through college twice. Also, Hugh had a wonderful job at Vanderbilt Medical College with his PhD degree from Vanderbilt Engineering College.

I tithed from my personal earnings until I quit work.

Since my husband Hugh was not a Christian, he would not go to the church services with the children and me. He allowed me to give only five dollars a week to the church of "his money," as he called it.

Since we were giving such a small amount of finances to the church, I tried to make up for it with volunteer work by teaching the children, bringing snacks, buying teaching supplies for the children, and by painting and giving small framed oil paintings as prizes for children's games.

Later, at The Lord's Chapel, I published the monthly newsletter for twelve years, donating my Graphic Art skills, with the church paying for printing and postage for the bulk-rate mailings. Later, our Missions' Committee gathered up forty four of the Christian testimonies that had been published in the newsletter over the years, and self-published them in a book titled, *Victory in Jesus*. Praise God that they all sold, except for the 44 that we gave as gifts to the ones whose testimonies were published in the book.

Since The Lord's Chapel tithed the regular weekly offerings to missions, we had a Missions' Committee of about seven or eight of us who met monthly to disburse the funds to about twelve missions, local and foreign. I served as secretary for this group for twelve years straight, because no one else would take the job. Since the funds that we were disbursing from the regular offerings were so small, our Committee decided to have monthly luncheons to help raise funds for missions.

On a Saturday once a month, a small group of us met at church and set up the tables, chairs, and decorations, and prepared some of the food. The following day on Sunday after the morning worship service, we finished cooking the food and served it, and cleaned up afterwards. We were feeding about two hundred people and were earning money for missions.

However, when it came time for our Missions Committee to disburse this earned money to missions, the members would NOT disburse ANY of it. I finally got fed up with this, as I had helped earn this money, and I wanted it to be used for winning souls to Jesus. I talked with an Elder, and the Elders MADE the Committee start disbursing the funds we had earned.

When the Committee finally began disbursing the funds, they were giving most of it to people who were not doing any missions work at all to help build up the Kingdom of God on earth. They were completely wasting the money! Nothing I could say or do would convince them to give the funds to trustworthy causes. Many times after our monthly Missions Committee meetings, I would drive home at night and sit in my car in my driveway, cry many tears, crying out to God that they were WASTING the missions' money!

It was so very frustrating to me, because Hugh would not allow me to give any of "his funds" to missions, and the Missions Committee would NOT give to worthy causes. Our children had the use of my car, so I had no dependable transportation to go out and find my own paid employment for me to give to missions. So I decided to use my artwork at home to give a bit to missions. I created original designs for thirty note cards, showed some samples of them to my friends at church, and they began purchasing them at the price of $3.00 a pack for six hand-painted note cards with envelopes. Over a two year period, while listening all day to TBN on the small T.V. in front of me on the table, I hand painted in watercolors and sold 1,700 note cards of orchids, lighthouses, roses, English Cottages, Hawaiian flowers, and Guatemalan people. All of these funds went to my twelve charities. My painting skills in watercolors increased greatly! Praise God! During these two years, I knew that my God was watching me paint, because as soon as I completed one order of several packs of cards, immediately another order would arrive for many more packs, even many orders from out of state. Praise God!

When both of our children left home for college and I finally had the sole use of my car, I got a part-time job clerking at the mall near our house for one year, and gave ALL these funds to missions.

Then I worked one school year in an elementary school cafeteria, and gave ALL my earnings to missions.

Then I delivered a weekly newspaper at night and gave ALL my earnings to missions. I did this for one year. Then the newspaper hired me to be a proofreader and receptionist for two years. I did this full-time, and gave ALL my income to missions.

Then I turned age sixty two and began getting $700.00 a month in Social Security benefits, and gave ALL of this income to my charities.

Then when Hugh passed away seven years ago in 2010, I began getting his Social Security of $2,161.00 a month. I have been giving it ALL away monthly, plus more, to my 118 charities.

I began selling my art paintings and note cards at my Christmas Open House Art Show and Sale, and giving all of these funds to missions.

I rented an art booth at the Christmas arts and crafts show at Mt. Bethel UMC and gave all the income from sales to my charities.

When my Brentwood, Tennessee, house sold for more than the purchase price of my house in Marietta, Georgia, I began giving more to all of my charities with some of these excess funds.

I give to charities that promote the gospel, that win souls to Jesus, and that feed and clothe the needy.

I rarely give to health charities, as I like to give to support our divine Healer of all illness, Jesus Christ.

I can never out-give God, as He gives back to me more than double what I give to help build up the Kingdom of God on earth.

I would like to use my paintings to earn more money for foreign missions. Father God gave to me a dream that showed to me holding my large painting of a black canvas. A voice said to me in the dream, "One of your paintings will sell for ten thousand dollars, and for more than ten thousand dollars." Praise God! I received this dream shortly after I read an article that twelve children could be sponsored in India with Gospel for Asia for a whole year for ten thousand dollars, which would include a school uniform, school supplies, a free lunch, class instruction, and Christian teaching, Joy!

I would also like to start my own note card business to raise funds for foreign missions. PTL!

Blessings! Velma

Yes, Our God's beloved Christian pastors and Our God's Holy Bible teachers, your heavenly Father God does love you, does take care of you, does provide all good things and all good events for you and for ALL of your loved ones, and YOUR heavenly Father God does protect you and them from ALL harm, when you know God, love God, honor God, and obey Our God.

Yes, your God IS a loving God, a merciful God, a forgiving God, a righteous God, a just God, the all-powerful God, the ONLY God that can do the possible that it is impossible for man or all of mankind working together can do.

Yes, what is impossible for mankind to do is EASY for Our God to do.

Yes, prayers in the holy name of Jesus IS the strongest force on earth today.

Yes, with YOUR God, ALL things are possible. (Matthew 19:26)

Yes, do pray BIG prayers to YOUR BIG God, pray believing prayers, pray in the name of YOUR Lord and Savior, Jesus Christ, then do praise YOUR God many times daily until the answers do come from YOUR God for ALL your righteous prayers prayed in the name of Jesus that will benefit you, will help others, and will glorify Our God on earth, and you shall have ALL these good answers to your righteous prayers.

Yes, the effectual fervent prayers of a righteous person availeth much. (James 5-16)

Yes, no prayer is too big for Our God's power to answer, and no prayer request is too small for Our God's love to answer. (Ephesians 3:20)

Yes, pray, pray, pray!

Then praise, praise, praise until ALL your righteous answers come!

Yes, YOUR heavenly Father God does DELIGHT to give ALL of Our God's righteous-living and obedient Christian children ALL GOOD GIFTS and ALL GOOD EVENTS that will benefit them, will help others, that will bring you and them closer to Our God, that will NOT harm them or cause them to drift further away from God.

Yes, all good things and all good events on earth ARE POSSIBLE with Our God.

Yes, all good gifts that you do have in your life now and even your whole life now, are good gifts to you FROM YOUR heavenly Father God and are delivered to you by YOUR Lord and Savior Jesus Christ. (Philippians 4:19)

Yes, your greatest gift you now have in your life is your free gift of salvation from your sins, given to you by your Lord and Savior Jesus Christ, when you asked Jesus to forgive you of your sins and save you, as your salvation-in-Jesus opens the door for ALL your other good and excellent gifts to be received of fellowship with your holy Creator, your heavenly Father God, to have ALL your needs met and ALL your holy desires met; you then have Our God's Holy Spirit within you to guide you, help you, teach you, and comfort you; and you become joint heirs with Jesus; and as you live in obedience to God, you will have life eternal in heaven.

Yes, at the very moment of each person's conception, your heavenly Father God does give each person an eternal soul that will live forever.

Yes, each person's eternal soul will live forever in heaven with Jesus as their personal Savior, or it will live in hell with Satan forever, if the person rejects Jesus as their Lord and Savior, and if they refuse to live a righteous lifestyle unto God, as there are NO OTHER PLACES for their one soul to live, after their one life and one death on earth.

Yes, each person now alive on earth was born with a free will to either choose Jesus as Savior and live for God, or reject Jesus as Savior and not live for God while alive on earth.

Yes, Jesus is now awaiting the choice of every living person on earth to choose Jesus, live for God while alive on earth, and spend eternity in heaven rejoicing with their God Jesus Christ of Nazareth.

Yes, Jesus Christ, Father God, and Our God's Holy Spirit are always in one accord and are always the supreme God of all, even though YOUR Holy Triune God IS THREE separate Beings.

Yes, when you enter heaven, you will see three separate Beings of God, which is Jesus Christ, Father God, and Our God's Holy Spirit.

Yes, your Holy Bible teaches you that God is three separate Beings, as your heavenly Father God did speak from heaven to mankind when Jesus walked this earth nearly two thousand years ago, when God spoke after Jesus was baptized in the river Jordan by John, and when God spoke when Jesus was transfigured on the mountain before some of His disciples. (Matthew 3:17, Matthew 17:5)

Yes, didn't Jesus return to heaven after His bodily resurrection and was seated at His Father God's right hand, now making intercession with HIS Father God for the people on earth? (Mark 16:19)

Yes, didn't Jesus teach you while He was on earth, as recorded in Our God's Holy Bible, that Jesus does NOT know the day nor the hour when Jesus will return to earth for Our God's great catching away of saved souls, but that ONLY Father God does know the day and the hour of this coming rapture event? (Matthew 24:36)

Yes, ONLY Father God knows the exact time and date of this future event, when the time is right for the return of Jesus.

However, Jesus did give to all of mankind, as written in Our God's Holy Bible, the signs of the times, for all people alive on earth to know the warning signals that the time is NEAR for the return of Jesus. (Matthew 24:4-14)

Yes, YOUR heavenly Father God does say to you and does say to one and to all, that the time of Jesus' return toward earth for the great catching away of the saints of God is CLOSE and is growing CLOSER day by day, when Our God's last trumpet sound will be heard on earth, and all the saved-in-Jesus and righteous-living-for-God Christians will be caught up into the heavens in a split second to join Jesus in their trip BACK to THEIR heavenly home in the third heaven to live with, to rule and reign with, THEIR Holy Triune God forever.

Yes, get ready to go in a split second to join Jesus in the air! STAY ready to go!

Preach to others and pray for others, to GET ready to go and to STAY ready to go!

Yes, the imminent return of Jesus Christ is soon!

Yes, soon time on earth, as you do now know time on earth to be, will end, and Our God's millennium time will begin, when one day will be as a thousand years. (2 Peter 3:8)

Yes, Jesus and the right-living followers of Jesus, the saved by Jesus and sanctified children of God, who have been raptured by Jesus, will enjoy the great marriage supper of the Lamb of God, which is NOW, already, prepared for them in heaven.

Yes, the hand of Jesus is now at the door in heaven awaiting the signal from HIS Father God to, "GO! Go back to earth and do claim Your holy Bride-to-be and bring her back all dressed in white for the marriage supper of the Lamb."

Yes, Jesus Christ IS the Lamb of God slain from the beginning of the world to pay for ALL of the sins of mankind, to give each of mankind life, abundant life on earth, and to ALL who will receive Jesus as Savior and live for God while alive on earth, give to them all eternal life in heaven with THEIR Holy Triune God. (Revelations 13:8)

Yes, Jesus Christ is God.

Worship Jesus Christ as you worship God.

Do worship YOUR heavenly Father God.

Yes, when you do worship YOUR Holy Triune God, it gives

your Father God more good opportunities to reward you with ALL of Our God's good benefits of love, joy, peace of mind, physical healings, financial breakthroughs, more good friends, more knowledge and wisdom for success, freedom from fear, freedom from depression, freedom from physical illness, freedom to make right choices for the benefits of you and your loved ones, and be given more of God, and will glorify God more with your life.

Yes, Jesus said, "If you have seen Me, you have seen the Father," as the will of Father God was living within Him, because of his ALWAYS obedience to His Father God's will. (John 14:9)

Yes, when YOU obey Jesus and do the will of Jesus for your life—be saved from your sins in Jesus and live righteously for Jesus—people can see the reflection of Jesus' will in your life.

Yes, it is Christ in you, the hope of glory. (Colossians 1:27)

Yes, do live your daily and nightly life in the footsteps of Jesus, as Jesus went about loving people, helping comfort and feed people, feeding them both physical food and the words of His Father God, spiritual food.

Do feed your congregations the spiritual food of Jesus and Our God's Holy Bible, and they WILL return for more and more of Jesus.

Yes, ALL people are hungry for the TRUE spiritual food of Jesus.

Feed them JESUS, so their souls can grow in God.

Yes, your soul growth is your only possession you are able to take to heaven in your afterlife.

Receive Jesus now.

Live for and with Jesus now.

Hallelujah!

Praises to Our heavenly Father God for this message for church growth!

Hallelujah!

Praises to Our heavenly Father God!

LETTER NUMBER TWENTY FOR
CHURCH GROWTH

Dear Christian Pastors and All Holy Bible Teachers,

It's interesting to me, that our God says that the soul growth of the leaders of a church is what causes the church attendance and church finances to increase. So, if a church hasn't grown in attendance and finances for the past year, the leaders have not had any soul growth in God for the past year. In other words, their sermons and Bible teachings have not improved, because they have not spent enough time praising and worshiping God, praying, and reading and studying their Bibles, so that God is able to impart to them more knowledge, more wisdom, more love, and more service.

After I had visited my daughter, Lori LaVoy, in Marietta, Georgia in 2016, she told me something interesting. She belongs to the large Mt. Bethel United Methodist Church, which has 9,600 members (not 7,000 members, as I had reported earlier). She said that the usual method that the Methodists have of filling their pulpits is to rotate their Methodist preachers from church to church, leaving each one in a new location for a specific time. However, in her church in the past years, when they published in their weekly bulletins the name of the next Sunday's speaker, if the name was NOT their lead pastor, many of the congregation would not show up for the Sunday morning service. Most of the people wanted to hear only their lead pastor as his sermons were always so much better than ANY of the other speakers. His preaching and teaching had built up so much the membership of this Methodist Church that the managing leaders of all of the Methodist churches decided to leave this pastor at this church. As a result of his great preaching, the church membership grows greatly EVERY year.

The Lord gave me a dream recently concerning church growth. I know of a particular charismatic pastor in Nashville who has a small congregation of about forty people in attendance on Sunday mornings for their worship service. Their attendance has not grown any in years, even though this Christian pastor has been preaching for many years and is now a father and a grandfather. In my dream, it showed this pastor as a young teenage boy. The teenage boy represented that his soul had not yet grown to maturity.

He needs to develop the heart of a servant for his soul to grow in God. A later dream that I had about this same pastor showed that his congregation had grown as a result of these prophetic messages being learned and taught by him. In this later dream, it showed that he had built a new church building, and the church attendance had grown from forty people to about eight hundred in the congregation! Praise God!

God said in a different prophetic message, **"The only thing you take to heaven with you is your soul's growth in God."** I had never heard this spoken of before, and I wondered if I was hearing God right. I thought, "Don't we take to heaven with us our body, soul, and spirit?" Then God's Holy Spirit revealed to me that our body, soul, and spirit are not ours, but they are God's since He created us and sustains us.

Each person now alive on earth chose to be born on earth for the main purpose SO THEIR SOUL COULD GROW IN GOD. God told me that every good experience and every seemingly bad experience that a person goes through on earth helps their soul to grow in God, that no experience we go through as humans is ever wasted.

When Joseph was in bondage for twelve years, God was preparing his character to be trustworthy enough to save multitudes from famine for seven years as second in command of Egypt.

Job suffered the worse type of human suffering except the loss of his life. He lost his possessions, his family, his friends, his health, his prestige among men, and even his many prayers seemed to be unanswered for a while. All his suffering was NOT in vain, as all that time, our God was building Job's character, increasing his faith and trust in God so that our God could reward Job more by doubling his possessions, restoring his good health, giving him another family with children, giving him more true friends, and giving him prestige among men. Job's soul had grown enough in God through these trials that he could handle this good increase without it corrupting him.

God looks on the heart of EVERY pastor and EVERY Bible teacher, and He can see if the person has the heart of a servant or the heart of a dictator. One sign of a dictator is that he delegates what he is able to do for himself and for others. God promotes the pastors and Bible teachers who have the heart to serve even as our Lord Jesus served.

Blessings! Velma

Yes, Our God's beloved children of Our God's beloved Christian pastors and beloved Holy Bible teachers, YOUR heavenly Father God does love you, does guide you, and does MAKE A WAY for you to work and witness daily to HELP build up the whole Kingdom of God on earth.

Yes, time is NOW SHORT and is growing SHORTER day by day to help bring in ALL the lost souls now alive on Our God's planet Earth for salvation from sins in Jesus, the ONLY TRUE Savior of any of mankind on earth.

Yes, teach mankind to come to Jesus for salvation, then come OUT of ALL sinful lifestyle and live for God while they are alive on earth, if they do plan to enter heaven after their one life on earth is over.

Yes, sin will NEVER enter heaven.

The ONLY DOOR to heaven available to a person now alive on earth is through the holy shed blood of Jesus Christ to wash away ALL of their sins, ALL of their unholy filth, then for them to come OUT OF all sinful lifestyle, then live the rest of their life on earth in a righteous lifestyle in obedience to God, for them to enter heaven in their afterlife.

Yes, Jesus Christ is now alive and well in heaven, and Jesus accepts and cleanses from sin, ALL who do come to Jesus with a repentant heart, who asks Jesus for forgiveness, who accepts this free gift of salvation from Jesus, who makes Jesus the Lord, Master, and Savior of their life, who then goes and sins no more, will be the ones who do enter heaven for eternity.

Yes, Jesus is righteous and Jesus led a righteous lifestyle on earth, when He walked this earth nearly two thousand years ago, and He did, Jesus did, set an example for mankind to follow in knowing God, loving God, honoring God, obeying God, teaching others about God, Jesus, heaven, hell, and other knowledge and wisdom to benefit all of mankind, and Jesus also set the excellent example of loving and helping mankind physically, mentally, emotionally, and financially, to help them be successful in life.

Yes, Jesus IS the same yesterday, today, and forever. (Hebrews 13:8)

Yes, call on Jesus for ANY and for ALL your needed help, knowledge, wisdom, supplies, and protection for you, for your loved ones, and for your ministry to others.

Yes, pray, pray, pray!

Ask, ask, ask!

Believe, believe, believe!

Receive, receive, receive!

That YOU will be helped, that others will be helped, that YOUR holy high God WILL receive glory on earth.

Yes, your God, your loving heavenly Father God, does desire to give to you and give to ALL your loved ones, all good gifts and all good events to prosper you and them and your ministry on earth, that people will know THEIR holy Creator God, that they will come out of ALL sinful lifestyle, know Jesus Christ as their Lord and Savior, will live for God, and will rejoice with THEIR God in Our God's great heaven above forever more.

Yes, do ALWAYS live for God and do follow the leading of Our God's Holy Spirit in your life, THEN you will ALWAYS prosper and be in good health as your soul continues to grow in God. (3 John 1:2)

Yes, ASK your God, ask in Jesus' holy name, for God to lead you, feed you, teach you, prosper you, so that you WILL BE ABLE to teach others, love others more, and help others more to YOUR God's glory on earth.

Yes, you have not, because you ask not, so do ASK YOUR heavenly Father God for great love, great knowledge, great wisdom, great power, and a great will and great desire to love and help others in a greater way to YOUR GOD'S glory on earth.

Yes, everyone who does ask for knowledge, wisdom, and love, who asks Father God, who asks in Jesus' holy name, who prays with faith in Jesus, WILL BE GIVEN the very things that you/he prays for, in order to advance Our God's Kingdom on earth.

Yes, it is Our God's will that Father God's will be done on earth as it is in heaven. (Matthew 6:10)

Yes, Jesus Christ of Nazareth is now still seated at HIS Father God's right hand in heaven, and He, Jesus, is still praying this same prayer, that Father God's will, will be done on earth as it is in heaven.

Yes, in Our God's third heaven all is love, joy, peace, kindness, generosity, harmony, music, worship of God, and much joy and happiness throughout the land.

Yes, do go about loving others, helping others, and teaching others of all of Our God's great truths as recorded in Our God's Holy Bible.

Yes, do TEACH people to read and study Our God's Holy Bible for themselves.

Teach people to come out of a sinful lifestyle and live for God, if they do want to receive ALL the good benefits in their life, that Our God is ABLE to give to them, and that Our God does DESIRE to give to them, WHEN they are ABLE to receive ALL these good gifts from God to enrich their own life, to help others, and to glorify THEIR God on earth.

Yes, you do witness to others by your living a holy lifestyle unto God.

Yes, when Jesus Christ walked this earth nearly two thousand years ago, He did live a holy lifestyle for you to follow in your daily and nightly life, and He did go about honoring HIS heavenly Father God by teaching others about THEIR heavenly Father God, and by helping, healing, and comforting others, to Our God's glory on earth.

160

Yes, let every act you perform, every good deed you do on earth, be done with the love and generosity of God, and YOUR heavenly Father God does SEE and does REWARD you for ALL these good deeds, does reward you on earth and WILL reward you in heaven.

Yes, LEARN to be a servant of God and LEARN to be a servant of mankind, so that your SOUL can grow in God, as your promotions in your life and in your work/ministry are from God, and it relates directly to your soul's growth in God.

Yes, the more of God you have in your life, the more Our God is able to trust you with more of Our God's good benefits in your life, more possessions, more fame, more wealth, more influence, greater responsibilities, more power to accomplish more good in your life to Our God's glory on earth.

Yes, as you do learn more from your God through praise and worship, through prayer, through the reading and studying of Our God's Holy Bible, your soul will CONTINUE to grow in God, and you WILL become trustworthy enough in God, so that Our God IS ABLE to promote you more, to give to you more of Our God's good benefits to enrich your life and to enrich the lives of others.

Yes, as your soul grows more in YOUR God daily, more knowledge and more wisdom WILL be given you daily, and your sermons and Bible teachings will improve, which will help your church congregations to grow and your church finances to grow and improve, so that MORE good works can be done to help others that YOUR God will be glorified on earth.

Yes, do let Our God's Kingdom come on earth and do let Our God's perfect will be done on earth, that people will be helped, and that YOUR God will be honored and glorified on earth.

Yes, time on earth, as you do now know time on earth to be, is quickly running out.

Yes, soon time on earth will change into Our God's

millennium time, when a thousand years are as one day. (2 Peter 3:8)

Yes, time now IS quickly passing until YOUR Lord Jesus Christ WILL split the great Eastern sky coming back toward earth for Our God's great rapture of all the saved and sanctified Christians of God to take them ALL BACK to THEIR home in heaven.

Yes, do go all out NOW to win souls for Jesus.

Yes, time IS SHORT and is growing shorter day by day until Jesus returns toward earth to claim and to catch away ALL His Own holy Bride-to-be.

Yes warn others to GET ready and to STAY ready to go in a split second to meet Jesus in the air.

Yes, when Jesus does come, you do NOT want to be left behind to be persecuted and endure hardship on earth.

Yes, you DO want to attend Our God's great wedding supper of the Lamb in heaven, which is NOW prepared for ALL the saints of God to come and enjoy, all the saints who know Jesus as their Lord and Savior, and who are living a righteous lifestyle unto God.

Yes, sin will NEVER enter heaven.

Jesus paid the price for you to be cleansed of ALL sin and for you to live a righteous lifestyle unto God and escape hell forever.

Yes, do TEACH ALL PEOPLE that Jesus is the ONLY way to escape hell forever.

If they die in their sins and lift up their eyes in hell, it can and will be too late for them to escape hell by living for God, by accepting Jesus as their Lord and Savior.

Yes, they must accept Jesus as their Lord and Savior while alive on earth and live for God for the rest of their life on earth, if they want to enter heaven after their one life and one death on earth.

Yes, Jesus is your and their ONLY access to heaven.

Encourage ALL to trust Jesus now for salvation and for them to live for God.

Hallelujah!

Praises to Our heavenly Father God for this prophetic message for church growth!

Glory!

Hallelujah!

Thank You, God!

LETTER NUMBER TWENTY ONE
FOR CHURCH GROWTH

Dear Christian Pastors and All Holy Bible Teachers,

Greetings in the name of our Lord Jesus. These prophetic messages are now greatly needed for church growth. Recently I read an article by a Southern Baptist person who works with churches, and he reported that 3,000 churches closed in 2015. I believe those pastors and church leaders were not teaching of the love and power of God that is available to all Christians, when they know Jesus as Savior, when they pray believing prayers in Jesus' name, and when they claim all the promises of God as given in God's Holy Bible.

For the most part, their congregations are not being taught:

How to love and honor God above all else, and love and help others as they love and help themselves.

That Jesus is the solution to every problem and every bad circumstance they face.

How to know Jesus and Father God and God's Holy Spirit on a one-on-one basis.

How to live a successful life in good health by having their souls grow in God.

The power of tithing and helping others with love, that they receive more than double what they give.

How to know Jesus as physical, mental, emotional, spiritual, and financial Healer, Helper, Provider, and God of all.

How to get ready for God's rapture of souls.

How to come out of all sinful lifestyle and live for God, or they WILL miss going to heaven forever.

How to read and study the Bible for themselves.

That every part of God's Holy Bible is absolutely true.

That heaven and hell are real.

What hell is like, and who will be going there for eternity.

That there is never any hope of escaping from hell for the people who are there.

That hell is hot and it is long, and that they do NOT want to go there.

What heaven is like, and who will be going there for eternity.

That the rapture is SOON, SOON, SOON, and for them to pray in ALL of their lost loved ones.

To love and help and care for the needs of others, especially for the ones of their own households.

That it is more blessed to give than to receive.

The joys and rewards of giving to help the helpless.

That they are unique, created in God's image, with body, soul, and spirit.

That their eternal soul will live either in heaven with God or in hell with Satan, as there are no other places for their eternal soul to live after their one life on earth is over.

That Jesus is the ONLY way to heaven, and that Jesus is the ONLY way to their holy Creator and Sustainer, their heavenly Father God.

That what God will do for one of God's children that He will do for any of His children, when the right conditions are met.

That their life on earth is quick, a vapor, and that eternity is a long, long time.

The power that comes in worshiping and in praising God for a long time.

The power that comes in praying in tongues, in their special prayer language.

How to witness for Jesus, how to do our God's supernatural miracles to attract a crowd in public, and then to give the crowds the message of salvation in Jesus, the way Jesus taught His disciples to do, when Jesus walked this earth nearly two thousand years ago.

How to let the actions of Jesus be their guide for holy living.

How to get right with God, or they are going to perish from the face of this earth.

To pray for America, for these wicked leaders to turn to

God for salvation, and to lead the people to return to the God of America, as when America was created on our God's principles. If not, America could be completely destroyed by our enemies.

How to hear from THEIR God personally, at any time day or night, if they will only get alone with God in their prayer closet, praise God, ask God to speak to them, and wait on their knees until they hear the small voice in their minds as God answers them, then thank and praise God for answering them.

How to speak out or write out the first phrase that God speaks to them, or the next phrase won't come.

How to tap into their inner strengths and gifts that they were created with at conception, given to them by their Father God, of how these special gifts can benefit themselves, help others, and glorify God on earth.

That it is God Who gives them the power to get wealth. He may not give them money, but will give them a job, or a better-paying job, or give them ideas for new jobs, or give them ideas on how to improve their present jobs. Yes, it is God's will for a person to work and to take care of themselves and their families. Ask God how you can be a better servant of God, servant of others, and of yourself, wait for God's reply, and then do the work heartily as unto God's glory, and watch how our God does reward you.

That God is sovereign, that God knows all, sees all, sees the future, and has all power at all times.

That God rewards people for knowing God, for loving God, for honoring God, for living for God, and for helping the helpless with love to our God's glory.

People are hungry for God, for the love of God, for the provisions of God, for the protection of God, for all the good benefits of God. When the truth of Jesus Christ, the Holy Bible, and God's blessings are taught to the congregations, hungry people will return for more, and these churches WILL grow and prosper to our God's glory on earth. Hallelujah!

Blessings! Velma

Yes, Our God's beloved children of God, Our God's beloved Christian Pastors and Our God's beloved Holy Bible teachers, YOUR heavenly Father God does love you, does teach you, does provide for you, and does protect you and all of your loved ones at ALL times.

Yes, YOUR heavenly Father God NEVER slumbers nor sleeps. (Psalms 121:4)

Yes, YOUR Holy Triune God is all powerful, all loving, the Almighty God, the holy Creator and Sustainer of this vast universe, the planet Earth, all on it and all in it, and nothing happens with any of Our God's creations without Our God's knowledge and Our God's permission for it to happen.

Yes, Our God is the sovereign Ruler of ALL created things and ALL created beings that do exist.

Yes, Our God did create and still does create, each of mankind in Our God's image with body, soul, and spirit.

Yes, at each person's moment of conception in their mother's womb, they were given an eternal soul that would live forever.

Yes, each person's soul will live forever either in heaven with THEIR Lord and Savior Jesus Christ, or it will live forever in hell with Satan, as there are no other places for their eternal soul to live after their one life on earth is over.

Yes, in order for any person now alive on earth to enter heaven after their one life on earth is over, they must choose the ONLY Savior of mankind, Jesus Christ of Nazareth, and ASK Jesus to save them from their sins, and ASK Jesus to be their Lord and Savior God, must accept this free gift of salvation from Jesus with their repentant heart, must then go and sin no more in their continued life on earth, in order to enter heaven in their life after their one life on earth is over.

Yes, sin will NEVER enter heaven.

Yes, a person must choose Jesus as their Lord and Savior and repent of ALL sinful lifestyle while they are NOW alive on earth, for if they do die in their sins and lift up their eyes in hell, it can and will be too LATE for them to repent of their sins, turn to Jesus for salvation, and live for God.

Yes, time on earth, as you do know time on earth to now be, is quickly running out, before Our God's great rapture of souls takes place on earth, when Our God's Lord Jesus Christ returns to claim and catch away to heaven, ALL of Our God's saved and sanctified Christian souls to take them BACK to THEIR eternal home in heaven to live with, to rule and reign with, to enjoy THEIR Holy Triune God forever.

Yes, time on earth is short and is now growing shorter day by day until Jesus returns toward earth for Our God's great rapture of souls, Our God Jesus' holy Bride-to-be of saved and obedient- to-God beloved saints of God to take them BACK to Our God's third heaven for the SOON wedding supper of the Lamb of God.

Yes, no one wants to miss Our God's great rapture of souls being taken BACK to heaven by THEIR Lord Jesus Christ.

Yes, do warn all sinners now living in sin, to come OUT of ALL sinful lifestyle, get right with God, and live a righteous lifestyle in obedience to God with Jesus Christ as their Lord and Savior, if they do desire to enter heaven forever.

Yes, do not be deceived: Our God is not mocked, as a person does reap what they sow. (Galatians 6:7)

Yes, sowing a life of sin does reap eternal life in hell, if a person does NOT repent, turn to Jesus for forgiveness of sins, come out of ALL sinful lifestyle and live for God while alive on earth.

Yes, the wages of sin is death. (Romans 6:23)

Yes, life eternal in hell is known as the second death. (Revelation 20:14)

Yes, choose Jesus NOW, before it is too late to choose Jesus.

Yes, time is now SHORT and is now growing SHORTER day by day and hour by hour until Jesus appears in the Eastern sky coming to claim and to catch away in a split second ALL His own.

Yes, you do NOT want to miss Our God's great rapture of Our God's saved and sanctified Christian souls.

Yes, preach repentance!

Yes, live repentance!

Yes, preach Jesus saves!

Preach ONLY Jesus saves!

Preach Jesus is the ONLY Door to heaven! (John 10:9)

Preach Jesus is the ONLY way to Our heavenly Father God! (1 Timothy 2:5)

Preach Jesus is coming SOON, for ALL to get ready and to stay ready to meet Jesus in the air in ANY split second to be taken back to their eternal home in heaven!

Yes, do pray in ALL of your lost loved ones and do warn them that TIME IS SHORT!

Yes, even so, come quickly, Our Lord Jesus Christ!

Yes, Jesus Christ is the ONLY Savior Who is capable of saving each of mankind's souls, when each person does come to Jesus with their repentant heart and does ASK Jesus to forgive their sins and to save them and to give them an eternal home in heaven with THEIR heavenly Father God and with THEIR Lord and Savior, Jesus Christ of Nazareth.

Yes, after their salvation in Jesus, they must go and sin no more.

They must KEEP their garments spotless by living a righteous lifestyle unto God for the rest of their life on earth, with a measure of Our God's Holy Spirit living within them to guide them and to help them to lead a righteous lifestyle unto God.

Yes, Our God does require holy living by Our God's Christian children in order for them to enter heaven with Jesus as their Lord and Savior, after their one life on earth.

Yes, it is appointed unto each of mankind to die only once after their one life on earth is over, then Our God's white throne judgment will happen, when each of mankind WILL give an account of their thoughts, words, and deeds, of all the decisions they made, while they were alive on earth. (Hebrews 9:27)

Yes, if a person chose Jesus as their Lord and Savior and lived for God while they were alive on earth, their sins and wrongdoings have been forgiven by Jesus, and they will hear Jesus say to them, "Welcome home, thy good and faithful servant," and they will enter heaven forever.

If they chose to reject Jesus Christ as their Lord and Savior from their sins and wrongdoings while they were alive on earth, and if they refused to come out of all known sin in their life, and refused to live for God for the rest of their life on earth, they will hear Jesus Christ say to them, "Depart from Me, I never knew you," and they will go to hell with Satan forever, where there is no hope of ever escaping hell, as their eternal soul will live in hell forever.

Yes, hell is hot and it is long, and no one ever wants to go there.

Yes, teach others to read and study Our God's Holy Bible, as it WILL teach them all truth about heaven and hell, and who will be going there forever.

Yes, if you only knew how beautiful, how majestic, how wonderful heaven is, surely you would want to go there, where all is peace, joy, love, happiness, fulfillment, music, and ALL good things and all good events, with good health, with joy unspeakable, eternal beauty, and everlasting harmony and good will, where Our God will be worshiped, adored, honored, glorified, and enjoyed forever.

Yes, Jesus Christ makes all good things and all good events possible for all of mankind, to everyone who will come to Jesus,

170

praise Jesus, and ask Jesus for all good things in their life and in the lives of their loved ones.

Yes, Jesus came to earth so that each of mankind could have life and could have it more abundantly. (John 10:10)

Yes, Jesus had 39 stripes on His back to pay for ALL of mankind's physical healing. (Isaiah 53:5)

Do ASK Jesus for your physical healing, and do ASK with great faith in Jesus, that Jesus is able to do the impossible-with-mankind, but it all is possible with God.

Yes, Jesus is God. (John 10:30)

Yes, Jesus is your physical Healer God.

Jesus is your spiritual Healer God.

Jesus is your mental, emotional, and financial Healer God.

Yes, ALL GOOD THINGS and ALL GOOD EVENTS are possible for you, when you pray believing prayers to YOUR heavenly Father God, when you pray prayers in Jesus' holy name.

Yes, prayers prayed in Jesus' holy name are the strongest force on earth today.

Believing prayers prayed in Jesus' holy name can overcome any bad thing, any bad condition, any bad circumstance on earth today.

Yes, Jesus is alive and well today, and Jesus is the same yesterday, today, and forever. (Hebrews 13:8)

Yes, do call on the holy name of Jesus, when you are in any kind of trouble, any kind of bad circumstance, ASK Jesus to help you, and then do watch and do wait for your needed help to come from Jesus.

Jesus is able to help you in many ways to overcome, to escape from, your bad circumstances, while you are alive on earth.

Yes, do call on Jesus for salvation and for right-living-unto-God, while you are alive on earth, and do watch and do see how Jesus saves you, helps you, and gives to you a happy, healed, prosperous life, as your soul grows in God.

If you do die in your sins and lift up your eyes in hell, it can and will be too late for Jesus to save you from your sins and too late for you to come out of all sinful lifestyle and live for God.

Yes, you MUST choose Jesus while you are now alive on earth.

Soon it will be too late to choose Jesus and live for God, as time on earth is now rapidly drawing to a close, where time, as you now know time to be on earth, will be no more at the end of the age.

Soon time on earth will be measured in Our God's millennial time, when a thousand years is as one day. (2 Peter 3:8)

Yes, do prepare to meet Jesus in the air in a split second, when the last trumpet sounds, for Our God's great rapture of ALL the saved-in-Jesus and right-living-unto-God children of God will rise to meet Jesus in the air, and they WILL be taken BACK to their eternal home in heaven to rule and reign with THEIR Lord Jesus Christ forever.

Yes, warn people of the inevitable rapture of God that can overtake people in any split second, when they will be caught up to meet Jesus in the air.

Warn people to GET READY to go and for them to STAY READY to go, as time IS QUICKLY RUNNING OUT before Our God's great rapture of ALL of Our God's saved and obedient Christians.

Yes, warn everyone you meet!

Let them know Jesus is coming soon!

Pray in ALL your lost loved ones!

Even so, come quickly, Our Lord Jesus!

Hallelujah!

Praises to Our heavenly Father God for this prophetic message for church growth!

Hallelujah!

Praises to Our God!

172

Dear Christian Pastors and All Holy Bible Teachers,

I have now received more than 947 prophetic messages written out and typed up from Father God and from Lord Jesus, and this is the strongest one that I have ever received telling all the wicked Americans to REPENT or PERISH! People need to know that God has the power to give life, and God has the power to take away life. Our God created all of mankind to know God and to enjoy God forever, and when this is not happening because of mankind's wickedness, why should God continue to sustain their lives?

God wiped out nearly all of mankind on earth with a flood because of their wickedness. The next time people become so wicked that God needs to wipe out nearly all of them, He will not do it with flood waters, but will do it with fire. God is a just God, and God will not tolerate the sins of mankind forever.

God is now giving mankind a warning and a fair chance to repent, forsake evil, and return to God, or destruction is surely coming from our enemies.

God put pastors, prophets, teachers, and other leaders in churches to teach the people the ways of God, the truth of Jesus Christ, and the infallible Word of the Holy Bible. When these leaders fail to live for God and fail to teach the whole truth of God to their congregations, God will hold them responsible for the lives of their congregations. If a dangerous bridge is out ahead and a train full of people is speeding toward it, they definitely NEED to be WARNED, and not be just "entertained!" God is now calling people to sound the alarm that time is SHORT!

If the pastors and leaders are true to live for God and true to teach their church people about God and God's ways, and the people refuse to believe and to obey, God will not hold these leaders responsible for the evil actions of the people. God creates each person with a free will and a free choice, and they are free to choose Jesus or reject Jesus.

If they choose Jesus and live for God for the rest of their life on earth, they will go to heaven in their life after their one life on earth. If they reject Jesus, do not come out of all sin and live for God while alive on earth, they will NOT enter heaven in their afterlife. People need to know that heaven is real and that hell is real. They need to know that eternity in the hot, tormenting hell is a long, long time, with no hope of ever escaping.

Yes, the United States is on the verge of being destroyed by its enemies. It will surely face destruction, unless the wicked people repent, turn back to God and honor and trust God as the true God of America. The true God was once the head of America, Who brought prosperity to America. We all need to acknowledge Jesus Christ as Savior and Healer of the nations. America needs to turn our attention from "entertainment" to "spiritual growth in God," if we want to live through these evil times that are fixing to come on these wicked Americans.

My siblings of Carolyn, Cliff, Pauline and her husband, Phil, and I get together once a year for a reunion. Two years ago we went to The Holy Land Experience in Orlando, Florida. Last year we went to Longview, Washington, for a week, to revisit our childhood home and friends, and visit Seattle and friends from our college days.

This year we were planning to get together in Branson, Missouri, for some Christian music shows. My sister, Pauline in Oregon, checked on some air fares round-trip from Portland, Oregon, to Branson, Missouri, and found them to be over $600.00 for each person. As I was praying about how to find a better way for us all to meet in Branson, Father God spoke to me and said something like this: **"Change your focus from entertainment to spiritual growth."** Then He gave me a plan for us all to attend a week long Christian conference with Perry Stone in Cleveland,

Tennessee. All of his conferences are free, with only love-offerings taken. There are always excellent Christian praise music with excellent guest speakers. Their services are held in the mornings and evenings with the afternoons free. I told my siblings about this excellent plan, but they couldn't work it out for us to attend.

As it turned out, we postponed our reunion until after I had relocated from Brentwood, Tennessee, to my new house in Marietta, Georgia. They all flew into the Atlanta airport, where I met my brother, Cliff Garner from Florida, and my sister, Carolyn Hill from California. Our sister and her husband, Pauline and Phil McCulloch from Oregon, missed some flight connections, and arrived a day later than planned.

We got to enjoy our week together, staying in my new house. We visited the Jimmy Carter Museum in Atlanta, the caves in Dahlonega, the "Gone with The Wind Museum" in Marietta, and saw other sights.

We attended the Sunday morning late service in our Mt. Bethel United Methodist Church in Marietta, and saw my thirteen-year-old grandson, Joshua LaVoy, have his confirmation service with several dozen other children. Joy! God is good!

Next year they all want to visit Boston and tour some historical sights. I hope to attend some of the Perry Stone conferences, even if I go by myself. I've been to two of them and they are MARVELOUS!

Blessings! Velma

Yes, Our God's beloved Christian pastors and beloved Holy Bible teachers, YOUR heavenly Father God does love you, does guide you, and does help you to lead a successful life on Our God's planet Earth.

Yes, Our God has called each of you to do a great work with and for YOUR Holy Triune God to HELP bring in Our God's great End-time harvest of souls, souls that are saved in Jesus from their sins, and who are now living a righteous lifestyle unto God, to HELP PREPARE people for the SOON return of Jesus Christ.

Yes, the SOON return of Jesus Christ toward earth for Our God's great rapture of the righteous-living Saints of God is imminent!

Yes, get ready to go in the twinkling of an eye at morning, noon, or night, in ANY split second as the last trumpet sounds!

Yes, ALL of heaven is NOW ready for Our Father God's voice to say to God's only beloved Son Jesus, "Go quickly! Go BACK towards planet Earth for Our God's great catching away, and bring back to heaven the holy Bride-to-be for the great wedding supper of the Lamb of God!"

Yes, only Our heavenly Father God knows the exact day and hour when the holy Bride-to-be of Jesus Christ will be ready to receive Jesus for Our God's great rapture of souls on earth.

Yes, Our God's many prophets are NOW sounding the alarm that TIME IS SHORT and is GROWING SHORTER day by day and hour by hour until the holy Bridegroom appears in the Eastern skies just above earth to claim and to catch away to heaven His holy Bride-to-be, all the saved-in-Jesus and right-living-unto-God beloved Christian children.

Yes, SOON, SOON, SOON!

Be warned!

Warn others!

Get right with Jesus for salvation from sins, washed clean of ALL unholy filth in the shed blood of Jesus.

Yes, come OUT of ALL sinful lifestyle and live a righteous lifestyle unto God with Our God's Holy Spirit as your Guide, your Teacher, your Comforter, your God.

Yes, worship, praise, love, and obey YOUR Holy Triune God.

Warn others to love and obey God above all others, and love and help others as you love and help yourself.

Yes, warn others to rebuke ALL sinful lifestyle from their life and live for God with salvation in Jesus, if they do want to enter heaven in their afterlife, after their one life on earth is over.

Yes, sin will NEVER enter heaven.

Yes, Our God is perfect, righteous, and holy, and all people must have ALL their sins washed away in the HOLY shed blood of Jesus, then must live a HOLY life for God and keep their garment spotless from sin, in order to enter heaven in their afterlife after their one life on earth is over.

Yes, Jesus Christ is the ONLY TRUE Savior of mankind. (Acts 4:12)

Yes, Jesus Christ is the only mediator between men and God. (1 Timothy 2:5)

Yes, choose Jesus now.

Live for God now.

Enter heaven forever.

Yes, unless these wicked Americans do repent of ALL their evil and turn back to the true God of America, they will ALL perish, as Our God MUST cleanse the land of all the wickedness that is NOW going on in these Americas.

Yes, God will NOT continue to be mocked by wicked people as there will come a time of repentance or destruction, and the choice is theirs.

Yes, your God is a just God.

Yes, YOUR Holy Triune God is NOW calling all wicked people in America to repentance, to stop sinning, to get right with THEIR Holy Triune God, get right with their fellow mankind, and begin living for God, if they do want to avoid destruction by their enemies.

Yes, Our Holy Triune God is NOW sending out the alarm to ALL wicked people in these Americas to get right with God, repent of all evil thoughts and all evil actions, and live for and with God, if they do want to continue to live peacefully on planet Earth.

Yes, now is the time to repent of all evil ways, turn to God, ask God to forgive all your sins, and ask God to heal these lands of these Americas.

Yes, it is NOT too late yet for repentance, for coming to God for forgiveness, for living righteously with Our God's help, and LET Our God HEAL these lands, as ONLY Our God's Holy Triune God has the power to heal these Americas and bring prosperity BACK to America, as it once was when God, the true God, was Head of these Americas, when God was honored by the righteous-living Christian people, and Our God was then able to pour out all of Our God's good benefits on America.

Yes, America and its wicked Americans are causing America to slowly drift away from honoring and obeying the true God of America, and America and Americans are drifting toward sudden destruction, even as a large boat in a slow-moving river is drifting toward a fatal large waterfall for sudden destruction.

Yes, there MUST be repentance, and there MUST be a turning away from evil influences, and there must be a turning back to God, first by the leaders of America, then by all the people of America, if they do want to survive these evil times that are fixing to come on these wicked Americas.

Yes, Jesus is your Savior, your Healer, your Rewarder, your soon-coming Bridegroom.

Yes, Jesus is still able to save and to heal people today.

Yes, do teach people that the ONLY safe place for them on planet Earth in the future is under the covering of Our God's Holy Triune God.

Do encourage people to get right with God and stay right with God, and ask God with faith in Jesus' holy name to meet ALL their needs and holy desires.

Yes, do teach them to draw near to God, and Our God WILL draw near to them. (James 4:8)

Yes, teach them to stand firm on the solid Rock of Jesus Christ, so that when these End-time storms do come, their house will remain standing firm, while they watch other's houses around them collapse that have been built on sand. (Luke 6:47-49)

Yes, ONLY houses built on the solid Rock of Jesus Christ WILL remain standing when these storms come when others trust in false gods whose houses do collapse.

Yes, money and possessions cannot save you when the storms of adversity come.

Friends, family, and other loved ones are unable to save you when evil times come.

ONLY your faith in and your trust in Jesus Christ, your only true Savior, is there enough spiritual power to bring you and your loved ones through these evil times that ARE fixing to come on these evil Americas; unless there is a turning BACK to Our God's Holy Triune God, these evil times will surely come.

Yes, encourage your church congregations to have their souls grow stronger in God through Bible study and memorization, through prayer and praise to God, through trusting God, through spending time with God, to build their faith and trust in God, to overcome all evil and all foolishness in their life, to pray for others, to help others, to encourage others, to grow closer to God.

Yes, Father God, Jesus Christ God, and Our God's Holy Spirit are able to meet every need you and your loved ones will ever have on planet Earth, but you must come to Father God and ask Father God in Jesus' name to meet all your needs, and you must TRUST God to answer all your prayers and meet ALL your needs.

Yes, Buddha cannot save anyone.

Allah cannot save anyone.

Mohammad cannot save anyone.

People are unable to save themselves by righteous deeds and loving mankind as no one is ever able to earn their salvation.

Only Jesus Christ has enough power to save a person from their sins and wrongdoing and give them eternal life in heaven with THEIR Holy Triune God.

Yes, do tell others continually that Jesus Christ is their ONLY hope of salvation and their only hope of joy and protection from evil, from want, from bad influences, from evil attacks, while alive on earth.

Yes, preach Jesus saves.

Preach Jesus heals.

Preach Jesus provides.

Preach Jesus protects.

Preach Jesus is the ONLY GOOD answer to ANY problem they face while alive on earth.

Preach Jesus IS coming SOON for Our God's great rapture of ALL Christian souls, all the saved-in-Jesus and right-living-unto-God beloved children of God, to take them BACK to THEIR eternal home in heaven.

Yes, do HELP the holy Bride-to-be of Jesus to GET READY and to STAY READY to go at the last trumpet sound, when Jesus does split the great Eastern skies coming back toward earth to claim and to catch away ALL His Own to take them BACK to their heavenly home to rule and reign with Jesus forevermore.

Hallelujah!

Praises to Our heavenly Father God for this prophetic message for church growth!

Hallelujah!

Praises to Our God!

180

Dear Christian Pastors and All Holy Bible Teachers,

These fifty prophetic messages from our heavenly Father God are to help you and your congregations to grow in God. As your soul grows in God, your preaching and teaching will get better and better, and that will help people's hungry souls to grow in God. As their souls do grow in God through your good Bible teaching, they will return for more and more better teaching, and your church congregations will grow and your church financial incomes will increase.

"It is God Who gives you the power to get wealth." (Deuteronomy 8:18) When your soul grows more in God, you will have more knowledge and more wisdom to handle more responsibilities and more wealth, which enables God to grant it to you, without your becoming corrupt with these added benefits.

This message is being taught over and over in these prophetic messages. I have been attending church services all my life of Southern Baptist, Presbyterian, and independent charismatic ministries. I have been a born-again Christian since about age eight, when I had attended a Southern Baptist church in rural southern Mississippi from birth. While in art college in Los Angeles, part of the time I lived across the street from the very large Hollywood Presbyterian Church and attended there for 4½ years.

I came to work as a Graphic Designer at the Baptist Sunday School Board in Nashville, where I worked for 4½ years. After that I worked freelance for them and for the Methodist Publishing House for about three years.

While working at the Baptist Sunday School Board, it was

required of all their workers to be members of Southern Baptist Churches. I was a member of First Baptist Church at 5th and Broadway in downtown Nashville, where I taught a Sunday School class of elementary school age girls.

While Hugh Davies and I were dating for about five years, we attended a Methodist Sunday School class with friends. He liked the Methodists, but was not interested in attending any of the Baptist churches. Hugh was not a Christian at the time, but he seemed interested in the Bible study and asked a lot of questions.

After we were married for four years and were expecting our second child, we bought a house in Franklin, Tennessee, and relocated from our rented duplex in Nashville. Since I knew that Hugh did not like for us to attend the Baptist church, for Hugh's sake, our two children of Lori and Alan and I joined a Presbyterian church in Franklin. Hugh chose not to attend with us during the two years that the children and I attended there.

When Lori was age 4 ½ and Alan was age two, I had a talk with Hugh, and asked him if he would go to church with us, and if not, I planned to change churches. Even though Hugh would not attend with us, he did not object to my taking our children to church. Father God had spoken to me and said, **"Get in a church were your soul can grow."**

Some of my artist friends whom I had worked with at The Baptist Sunday School Board told me about The Lord's Chapel in Brentwood, that they had visited several times. During 1977 it was the fastest growing church in Nashville. I visited there a few times and especially liked the Bible teaching in the weekly sermons by the head pastor, Billy Roy Moore. He would take a book of the Bible, and teach one chapter each Sunday morning, going through that whole book, before choosing another book to teach.

Since it was the best Bible teaching that I could find in Nashville, I decided for the children and me to join this church.

The children and I joined in 1977. The speaking in tongues with interpretations given in the worship services were new to me. When a message in tongues was given in the service,

Brother Moore told us that he always prayed immediately for the interpretation, which he always received for himself. He always waited for someone else in the service to give the interpretation, but if no one else gave it, then Brother Moore would give it. I found these messages and interpretations very encouraging. It was like God, Himself, was speaking directly to each one of us, telling us the things that we needed to hear most, to apply to our own lives. I began having the desire to hear from God for myself in this way.

I will always be grateful to God for The Lord's Chapel and for Pastor Billy Roy Moore, because my soul was able to grow in this church. I am especially grateful to God that I became Spirit filled with the gifts of praying in tongues and receiving prophetic messages while being a member of The Lord's Chapel. I am grateful to my God for the opportunities to serve the Lord and serve others there.

I have now been a member of this church for 39 years, going through the relocation from Brentwood to near Nolensville Pike in Nashville in 1988, and with the merger with Oasis Church in 2003. With the merger, Pastor Danny Chambers changed the name from The Lord's Chapel to Oasis Church. He would not allow tongues and interpretations to be spoken in the church services. Pastor Danny also cancelled all four of my volunteer jobs that I had at The Lord's Chapel. He cancelled the monthly church newsletter that I had been publishing as he wanted to use email instead. He cancelled the Missions' Committee as he wanted to decide where the church tithe would be given. He cancelled the weekly Sunday morning Communion service and changed it to once a month on a Wednesday evening. He cancelled the Monday evening prayer meetings. He cancelled the Sunday morning bulletins that were passed out in the service.

He took down all the beautiful art paintings from the walls.

All of my church volunteer jobs were cancelled. I was offered the opportunity to be an early-morning Sunday Greeter at the front door, which I did serve in this place for a few months. However, my elderly friend, Janie Lamb, needed a ride to and from the church service. When I provided transportation for her to and from the Sunday School class and third worship service, I was then unable to continue as a Greeter.

With all of the "light sermons" at Oasis Church, no Monday evening prayer meetings, and no opportunities to continue serving, I can truthfully say that my soul grew very little there in the last twelve years that I was a member. The worship music and singing were very good there, but louder than most of the older members liked. I left this church in 2016 when I relocated from Brentwood, Tennessee to Marietta, Georgia after 39 years there. When I left Oasis Church, only six of the original Lord's Chapel's 40 members had remained. Raymond Oakley is the only leader from the Lord's Chapel who remained. He is not an Oasis leader, but is a faithful volunteer worker parking cars in the parking lot.

However, my soul was still growing with my own daily Bible reading, my weekly prophetic messages from Father God and Jesus, with my reading good Christian books and Christian magazines, and with my weekly Bible class discussions in our Sunday School there. Also, as I gave funds to several Christian charities worldwide, I was receiving and reading their newsletters and magazines. Also, with the four Christian ladies living with me at home, we often prayed together and discussed the love of the Lord a lot.

Recently Father God revealed to me that I was like a plant in a small container, and that I had outgrown the container and needed to be transplanted into a larger container, so that my soul could continue to grow in the Lord. That is why God had me to relocate to the Marietta, Georgia area, and join the very large Mt. Bethel United Methodist Church where the Bible and Jesus are taught EVERY Sunday morning, with wonderful missions trips in the summers, and a wonderful monthly prayer meeting! Joy!

Blessings! Velma

Yes, Our God's beloved children of Our God's beloved
Christian pastors and beloved Holy Bible teachers, YOUR
heavenly Father God does love you, does take care of you, does
protect you, and does give to you MANY opportunities to teach
others about God and about Our God's ways of how to know
God and how to obey Our God.

Yes, Jesus Christ is God.

Yes, Jesus Christ saves sinners and heals people today, even
as He did when He walked this earth nearly two thousand
years ago.

Yes, Jesus Christ is Lord and Ruler over all, and you are
NOW joint heirs with Jesus. (Romans 8:17)

Yes, YOUR heavenly Father God HAS raised Jesus Christ
from the dead, and Jesus Christ is NOW alive in heaven seated
at the right hand of HIS heavenly Father God.

Yes, soon Jesus Christ WILL return toward earth with a
great shout coming BACK toward earth for the great catching
away to heaven all of the saved and sanctified Christian saints
of God to take them ALL back to THEIR heavenly home to rule
and reign with THEIR Lord Jesus Christ forever.

Yes, Jesus is coming SOON!

Yes, do GET READY and do STAY READY to go to meet
Jesus in the air in ANY split second for Our God's great rapture
of ALL of the saved-in-Jesus and right-living-unto-God beloved
Christian children of God.

Yes, NOW is the time to preach and to teach REPENTANCE,
to come OUT of ALL known sin in a person's life, live a
righteous lifestyle unto God, be caught up into heaven, and

enjoy rejoicing in heaven with YOUR and THEIR Holy Triune God forevermore.

Yes, doesn't Our God's Holy Bible teach that without repentance from sins and then living a holy lifestyle unto God that no person born alive on earth will see Our God? (Hebrews 12:14)

Yes, do preach REPENT, REPENT, REPENT!

Come OUT of ALL wicked lifestyle and live for God, or they will NEVER SEE their God, their holy Creator and Sustainer God!

Yes, Jesus Christ of Nazareth is the ONLY TRUE Savior of ANY of mankind on earth, and they MUST COME to Jesus, and they MUST ASK Jesus for this FREE salvation in Jesus, so that Jesus can forgive their sins, save them, give them new life with Our God's Holy Spirit living within them to teach them HOW to obey God, how to live a righteous lifestyle unto God, and to enter heaven forever after their one life on earth is over.

Yes, Jesus comes SOON!

Yes, preach and teach that Jesus comes soon!

Now is the time to get ready and stay ready to meet Jesus in the air in ANY split second.

Yes, you may not have tomorrow on earth.

Yes, yes, yes, Jesus comes quickly!

Yes, YOUR heavenly Father God HAS spoken to you!

Yes, YOUR heavenly Father God does go before you daily and does create a path for you to walk in to be a holy witness for YOUR Holy Triune God, that people will know God, love God, know Jesus Christ as their Lord and Savior, and know to come out of ALL sinful lifestyle and live for God while alive on earth, then for them to spend eternity in heaven with THEIR Holy Triune God in their afterlife, after their one life on earth is over.

Yes, do make it your highest aim both day and night to become more like Jesus Christ as He went about loving people, helping people, forgiving people of their sins and human weaknesses, and teaching people about THEIR heavenly Father

186

God, and teaching them how to live for God, and how to be rewarded by God for helping the lonely, the sick, the widows and orphans, the hungry, the hurting, the prisoners, and how He healed the sick, the afflicted, the handicapped, and how He raised the dead, to HIS heavenly Father's glory on earth.

Yes, do read and do STUDY Our God's Holy Bible daily, and do MEMORIZE large portions of it, especially memorize ALL the teachings of Jesus, especially the words He spoke to His twelve disciples and the words He spoke to the crowds and the individuals He taught.

Yes, do live your daily lives based on what Jesus lived and what Jesus taught, when Jesus walked this earth nearly two thousand years ago.

Yes, Jesus Christ is God so do always love, worship, and honor Jesus Christ as you do love, worship, and honor YOUR heavenly Father God.

Yes, when your earthly life is over and when you always stay true to your God's calling on your life while alive on earth, when you do enter your God's heaven for eternity, you WILL see your Lord Jesus Christ of Nazareth seated at HIS Father God's right hand even as written about several times in Our God's Holy Bible.

Yes, every word written in Our God's Holy Bible is absolutely true, even as these prophetic messages are true, as every word in Our God's Holy Bible was inspired by God, checked for accuracy seven times, and have stood the test of time over the years to be the infallible Word of God. (Psalm 12:6)

Yes, every word of Our God's Holy Bible is absolutely true.

Didn't Jesus say that heaven and earth shall pass away, but His words will never pass away? (Matthew 24:35)

Yes, do believe every word that Jesus spoke as recorded in Our God's Holy Bible, memorize these words, live by these words as they are truth and they are life, given to you and your students, your followers, through Jesus FROM YOUR heavenly Father God.

Yes, preach Jesus saves, Jesus heals, Jesus is the spoken Word of HIS heavenly Father God. (John 1:1)

Yes, Jesus is all in all. (Ephesians 1:22-23)

Yes, apart from Jesus, you can do nothing. (John 15:5)

Yes, you can do all things through Jesus Christ which enables you. (Philippians 4:13)

Yes, honor Jesus.

Love Jesus.

Preach the forgiveness of Jesus.

Preach a fresh start for EVERYONE in Jesus.

Preach Jesus is the God, the Ruler, the Sustainer of this earth, all on it and all in it, and of this entire universe.

Yes, preach Jesus owns it all, and the obedient Christians are joint heirs with Jesus. (Romans 8:17)

Preach that the Lord is their Shepherd, that they have ALL they need. (Psalm 23:1)

Yes, preach Jesus is coming back toward earth SOON and for EVERYONE to get ready to meet Jesus in the air in a split second to RETURN to THEIR home in heaven prepared for them by THEIR Lord and Savior, Jesus Christ.

Yes, tell them to lay up their treasures in heaven where they are not stolen or corrupted, but give their funds on earth to further the gospel of Jesus Christ, so that people who have never heard of Jesus can know the saving and healing power of Jesus.

Yes, ONLY Jesus has the power to save a person's soul while they are alive on earth and give them a home in heaven for eternity. (John 14:6)

Yes, Jesus Christ is the ONLY Door to THEIR heavenly Father God, their holy Creator and Sustainer God. (1 Timothy 2:5)

Yes, Our Holy Triune God did create and still does create each of mankind and all of mankind to know Our God personally on a one-on-one basis and enjoy Our God forever.

Yes, do teach ALL of Our God's mankind about the God Who created them, Who sustains them, Who gives them their next breath, Who gives them ALL the good things in their life/lives that they now enjoy, and teach them WHY Our God created them and WHY Our God sustains them.

Teach them to know God, enjoy God, grow up in God, claim all good benefits from God, claim them in Jesus' holy name, and then WATCH Our God provide them with ALL GOOD benefits in their life, to enrich their own life, to enrich the lives of others, and to glorify God on earth.

Yes, teach people that God is their Provider, their Source, of all good things and all good events in their life.

Yes, teach them that when they do need to be disciplined in their life, that Our God does discipline them with divine love and fairness to help their soul to grow up in God.

Yes, Our God does try and test ALL of Our God's children to strengthen their faith in God, strengthen their TRUST in God, so that when they do remain faithful to THEIR God through these trials, after the trials end and they have been brought through them victoriously, Our God is able to promote them to a new level of responsibilities, of service, of possessions, of influence, without their becoming corrupted and destroyed by the promotions.

Yes, your heavenly Father God loves you, teaches you, trains you, and does help you to help others.

Do worship your God now.

Praise you, my heavenly Father God!

Hallelujah!

Praises to Our God forever!

Hallelujah!

LETTER NUMBER TWENTY FOUR
FOR CHURCH GROWTH

Dear Christian Pastors and All Holy Bible Teachers,

I am not a professional writer, but Father God once spoke to me and said, **"Always speak and write the truth in love."** I always want to obey my God in this, always with our God's Holy Spirit helping me.

When I make mistakes, I always want to correct them.

I attended a Sunday School class at Oasis Church. Father God told me, **"I'm going to build up that Sunday School class. Each Sunday give to them a printed prophetic message."** I started doing this.

We have some of the same adults in our weekly Sunday School class that we have at our monthly Senior's Luncheon with our same leader.

At our Senior Luncheon at Oasis Church, our leader told me to NOT give these printed prophetic messages to people. Since the Bible teaches that we ought to obey God rather than man, I planned to keep obeying God in this. God rewards us for our obedience, and our teacher does not. A couple of weeks before this, God gave me a dream about this leader that showed me that soon our God will open her eyes to the truth. I said to her, "God is sovereign. He can say whatever He wants to anyone He wants at any time He wants. He is the same yesterday, today, and forever. He spoke to the writers of the Bible, and He speaks to people today, and they can write down what He says." I also told her that when hidden prophetic messages are found within these prophecies in complete sentences given to me, using the Bible Code search method, and they reveal the winner of the 2016 United States Presidential election, she will know that only God could encode future events with accuracy and that Velma is not making up these messages. She replied, "Some people don't believe in the Bible Code." I replied, "That's because Satan has blinded their minds to the truth."

After the luncheon, I came home, got on my knees in prayer to Father God. He told me something like this: **"What you said to her today was exactly right."** Praise God.

Later, God showed me that what she said about the Bible Code and people not believing that hidden messages are in the Old Testament Hebrew and in the New Testament Greek, with equal distance letter skips, both forwards and backwards, is like what people used to say about flying: "If God had wanted us to fly, He would have given us wings." You don't hear that said much about flying anymore. God showed me that GOD DID GIVE US WINGS and they are in our HEADS, not on our bodies like birds and angels have.

Only after the computer was invented, was the Bible Code method of searching for hidden messages within Scripture found. It was first discovered by the Jewish mathematician in Israel named Eliyahu Rips.

It's interesting to me that they found the names of Jesus and His twelve disciples listed twice in the Old Testament Hebrew using the Bible Code search method. Once they found the name of Judas included with the twelve, and once with the name of Matthias included with the list. It seems to me like this alone would be enough evidence to show the Jewish people that Jesus is God's only begotten Son, and that Jesus is the Messiah! But Satan is a master at deceit and is able to deceive some people.

Some people don't believe in heaven and hell. Some people find out this truth too late, when they end up in hell where there is no escape for eternity. God is now sending out warning to people about the reality of heaven and hell. If people would only read their Bibles, they would learn the truth about heaven and hell and who will be going there. If people would only read their Bibles on a daily basis, Our God's Holy Spirit would teach them what is truth and what is not truth.

I have been listening to Pastor Danny Chambers preach sermons for twelve years, and I have never once heard him say, "Read your Bible on a daily basis." I have never heard him say in a sermon, "I read my Bible daily."

While I was in Los Angeles, I was in the Hollywood Presbyterian Church College Department under the leadership of Dr. Henrietta Mears for 4½ years. At that time, Dr. Mears was mentoring twelve young college men who were preparing to go into full-time Christian ministry. She told them that they must spend four hours every day in prayer and Bible study. Dr. Bill Bright who established "Campus Crusade for Christ" was one of the young men she had mentored.

One time a verbal survey was taken at The Lord's Chapel by a visiting speaker. He asked the crowd of about 400 people present, "How many read the Bible on a daily basis?" It looked like about fifty or more people raised our hands. Then he asked, "How many have been reading the Bible daily for at least five years?" About two dozen or more raised our hands. Then he asked, "How many have been reading the Bible daily for about fifteen years?" About a dozen of us raised our hands. Then he asked, "How many of you have been reading the Bible daily for more than twenty years?" One other person and I raised our hands.

When I began reading my Bible daily in 1971, our finances went straight uphill from then on, until we became more than millionaires. God showed to me the truth of Psalm 1:1-3, that promises if you will read your Bible daily and keep away from bad influences, that whatever you do will prosper. Please teach people the truth of Psalm 1:1-3! Teach people to read their Bibles daily for their souls to grow in God, so they can be rewarded more by God!

Blessings! Velma

Yes, Our God's beloved Christian pastors and beloved Holy Bible teachers, YOUR heavenly Father God does love you, does provide for you, does protect you, does guide you, and does give you MANY opportunities to teach people about YOUR heavenly Father God, your Lord Jesus Christ, Our God's Holy Spirit of God, and about Our God's Holy Bible.

Yes, do worship and do praise Our God's Holy Triune God for a long time, and do ALLOW Our God to strengthen you in body, soul, and spirit to BETTER do the great and mighty works that Our God HAS CALLED YOU to do with and for YOUR Holy Triune God to win souls to Jesus Christ and to help build up the Kingdom of God on earth.

Yes, your God goes with you when you do go to preach and teach Our God's gospel of good news to others.

Yes, when you pray, Our God's Holy Spirit is with you, and He does HELP you to pray for Our God's perfect will to be done in your life.

Yes, your God is a good God, a loving God, a just God, a generous God, and a never-ending God.

Yes, Our God teaches you and HELPS you to teach others with Our God's love, wisdom, and expertise of Our God's Holy Bible and the life and teachings of your Lord and Savior, Jesus Christ.

Yes, do read and do study and search the Scriptures daily to learn Our God's great truths in Our God's Holy Bible.

Yes, ALL good gifts do come to you from Our Father of lights, and they do come to you through Jesus Christ. (Philippians 4:19)

Yes, Jesus Christ is the ONLY true Savior of mankind on earth. (Acts 4:12)

Do CLAIM salvation in Jesus now for yourself and for all of your loved ones, then do come out of ALL sinful lifestyle and live in a righteous lifestyle unto God, then do see and do rejoice in ALL of Our God's good rewards to you and to all of your loved ones.

Yes, yes, yes, do CLAIM ALL of Our God's good promises to you to enrich your own life, to help others, and to bring glory to YOUR God on earth.

Yes, others will see your good works done to help the helpless, will see ALL your good rewards to you from YOUR Holy Triune God, and will be drawn to YOUR God for THEIR successful living on Our God's planet Earth.

Yes, do rejoice, rejoice, rejoice, in Our God's goodness to you, Our God's forgiveness of your wrongdoing, and in Our God's help to you to lead a happy and successful life on earth.

Yes, you do witness to others by how you do live a righteous lifestyle unto God, and by how you worship and honor God.

Yes, do reach out to others who need your help, your love, your good deeds done with love to help others, and they WILL come to know, love, and cherish YOUR God through your love for them and your good deeds of your help to them.

Yes, time on earth, as you do now know time no earth to be, is quickly drawing to a close, and what you do for God and with God must be done quickly.

Yes, soon time on earth WILL CHANGE from earth time governed by the sun and moon, change to Our God's millennial time, when one day will be as a thousand years. (2 Peter 3:8)

Yes, the time is now drawing very near when Jesus' return toward earth for Our God's rapture of ALL the saved-in-Jesus and right-living-unto-God Christians will be caught up into the air in a split second to meet Jesus in the air, the time is now imminent.

Yes, SOON Jesus IS appearing at the last trumpet sound for Our God's great rapture of saved-in-Jesus and sanctified souls to take them BACK to THEIR great home in Our God's great heaven above.

Yes, do warn people, everyone you do meet, to get ready to go and to stay ready to go in Our God's great catching away of the saints of God.

Yes, keep watch!

No one knows the day nor the hour when Jesus will return, except Father God alone knows. (Matthew 24:36)

Yes, YOUR heavenly Father God alone knows WHEN Our God's great rapture of souls on earth WILL take place, and YOUR heavenly Father God is NOW WARNING YOU that Jesus is and does COME SOON!

Yes, warn all your congregations to come out of a sinful lifestyle, accept Jesus Christ as their Lord and Savior, and live a holy, righteous lifestyle unto God, if they do expect to enter heaven after their one life and one death on earth.

Sin will never enter heaven.

You cannot work your way into heaven by doing good works and by loving and helping people.

Yes, your ONLY Door to heaven is to ask Jesus to save you by washing away all your sins in Jesus' holy shed blood on Calvary's cross, and by your coming out of ALL sinful lifestyle and living for God with a repentant heart.

Yes, Jesus saves.

Yes, Jesus is God. (John 10:30)

Yes, Jesus is the ONLY Being, dead or alive, with enough power to forgive your sins and give you a FREE one-way ticket for eternity to live forever joined with YOUR holy Creators God, to enjoy beauty, peace, and happiness forever in heaven.

Yes, Mohammad cannot save anyone.

Allah cannot save anyone.

Buddha cannot save anyone.

Only Jesus Christ can save anyone--as ONLY Jesus Christ has paid the ultimate, supreme sacrifice to pay for your sins and for Adam's sin you inherited--by Jesus' holy shed blood and death and resurrection.

Yes, Jesus offers to everyone this FREE gift of life, abundant life on earth, and eternal life in heaven, offers it to everyone and to anyone who will come to Jesus with a repentant heart and will ASK Jesus to forgive their sins and save them, and who will accept this free salvation gift from Jesus, and who will THEN go and sin no more.

Yes, your God is a righteous God, a generous God, a forgiving God, a merciful God, a powerful God, the Almighty God, Who created the heavens, the earth, and all on it and all in it, with ONLY Our God's spoken Word.

Yes, your heavenly Father God only spoke the Words, and the heavens and the earth were created, and a God Who can do that can surely do whatever Our God chooses to do. (Psalm 33:6-9)

Yes, Our God owns this whole earth and all on it and all in it. (Psalm 24:1)

Yes, Our God created the heavens and the earth and all of mankind for a purpose—for mankind to know Our God and to enjoy Our God forever.

Yes, do guide people into knowing your God, and do help them ALL to have a closer daily and nightly walk with and talk with Our God's Holy Triune God.

Yes, Our God does desire daily fellowship with Our God's great mankind on earth that Our God has created and still does create on a daily and nightly basis.

Yes, YOUR heavenly Father God NEVER slumbers nor sleeps, and your heavenly Father God does hear every prayer that is prayed to God.

Yes, YOUR heavenly Father God does hear EVERY prayer you pray, and your heavenly Father God does answer ALL the prayers prayed in Jesus' name and prayed with YOUR great faith in Jesus.

Yes, pray and keep on praying; knock and keep on knocking. (Luke 11:9)

Yes, know God, live for God, obey God, ask what you will in Jesus' name, with great faith in Jesus, and you SHALL HAVE EVERY good gift you ask for in Jesus' name, with great faith in Jesus, to help yourself, help others, and to glorify your God on earth.

Yes, it is Our God's will for mankind to know God, to live in peace and harmony with God and with your fellow mankind, to be prosperous and in good health, and to love and help the helpless, to Our God's glory.

Yes, know God, love God, obey God, be happy, be healthy, be prosperous, be fulfilled in your life's calling and your life's ambition, be loving, kind, and helpful to others, and spend eternity in heaven after your one life and one death on earth.

Yes, if you only knew Our God's love for you, care for you, provisions for you, and Our God's capacity for you in your attaining ALL of Our God's good gifts laid up for you, you would seek to know God better, love God above all else, and enjoy praising and worshiping God more, and be rewarded with all good things and all good events more than ever before.

Yes, taste and see that God is good. (Psalm 34:8)

Yes, come into a right and better relationship with YOUR Holy Triune God, and you will know more joy, more love, more happiness, more success in EVERY area of your life, than you have ever known before.

Yes, enjoy YOUR God more and ALLOW Our God to enjoy you more!

Joy!

Praises to Our heavenly Father God for this divine message! Hallelujah!

Praises to Our heavenly Father God! Hallelujah!

LETTER NUMBER TWENTY FIVE
FOR CHURCH GROWTH

Dear Christian Pastors and All Holy Bible Teachers,

I believe that Father God wants me to have these fifty letters and fifty prophetic messages put into book form with the title, *Church Growth Our Father God's Way.* I am now looking at different publishing companies that will self-publish the book for me.

My other book was published by Office Depot when I furnished them camera-ready pages that were typeset with the art in place. The title of that book is, *Christmas in The Bible Belt.* It contains forty prophetic messages and eighty-eight black line drawings in the body copy plus the full-color cover. It is a thirty-nine-day daily diary written during December 1987 and part of January 1988, during the Christmas and New Year's season. My family of four was invited to twenty five different parties and was able to attend twenty of them. During this time, my husband Hugh was employed with Vanderbilt Medical College in Nashville, and our daughter Lori was in tenth grade in Brentwood High School, and our son Alan was in seventh grade in Brentwood Middle School. Both children were in bands, so we had band parties at their schools, a Boy Scout Breakfast for the parents at a Church of Christ, some church parties at The Lord's Chapel and at the Methodist church, some library parties at the Brentwood Public Library, some Vanderbilt parties, some Tennessee Art League parties, and some in private homes, all in the Nashville, Tennessee area, which is in the Bible Belt area of the United States.

Father God had told me, **"Print a thousand copies of the book, and sell them for a dollar over cost."** I paid Office Depot twelve thousand dollars to print a thousand copies in 2012. I did not try to market them, but I gave away about 250 free copies to family members and friends. After giving away these copies, I asked Father God if I should try to market the book? He replied something like this, **"You may if you want to, but it will not sell well until the hidden messages are found encoded within the prophetic messages, using the Bible Code search method. When these hidden messages are found within these prophecies that foretell the future, these books will sell well worldwide."** I have not tried to market the book, but I have given away a few more books to friends.

When I visited my son Alan when He was living in Covington, Georgia, he was able to do a Bible Code search with three of the prophetic messages that were printed in this book. We were able to find thirty-three words in each of these three prophetic messages. We found the words "New York City" twelve times, the words "Atlanta" and "Dallas" and "Alan" six times each, and the name "Velma" once spelled backwards. We had to instruct the Bible Code search engine what to search for. It was capable of searching for only words and for groups of words. It could not search for complete sentences.

Father God had told me that complete sentences are hidden within these prophetic messages. I asked Alan if he could write a program that could search for complete sentences? He replied that he could do so, but he has not yet done so.

Alan updated my website of "www.HotOffTheThrone.com" in February 2016, before I mailed out thirteen prophetic messages to the 258 largest newspapers in the United States for the weekly syndicated newspaper column, "Hot Off The Throne."

Now in June of 2017, I have mailed out thirty-seven consecutive quarters of thirteen prophetic messages to 253 of the largest newspapers in the United States for a weekly syndicated newspaper column. During this time of more than nine years of mailing out these prophetic messages, I have had NO response of them being published! I asked Father God, "Should I stop these mailings since there is no response from these newspapers?" Father God answered me something like this: **"Yes, keep mailing them out. These editors are reading them, and many are responding to their teachings."**

Father God also recently told me something like this: **"When God puts God's anointing on these editors, they will publish them. When I put My anointing on these editors to publish them, I will also put My anointing on you to furnish them."** I praise God for helping me to do so, for my proofreader checking my typing, for helping me to pay costs for the printing and mailing of them, and pay the rental fee of the largest post office box in Marietta, Georgia for the business return address.

I now have 892 prophetic messages written out and typed up including receiving one a week for the newspaper prophecies. If you are interested, you may see some of them posted on my website. These prophetic messages for the newspapers are not the same as the ones from Father God that I received for church growth. The 892 that I have received over the past many years, have all the odd-numbered ones from Jesus, and all the even-numbered ones from Father God. I am asking for and am receiving all the series of fifty for church growth from only Father God, as it was Father God Who told me to receive the series of fifty prophecies for church growth.

More than nine years ago, when the Lord God wanted me to begin sending a series of prophetic messages to the largest newspapers in the nation for a syndicated newspaper column, He gave me the name for it of "Hot Off The Throne." He instructed me to choose the six largest newspapers in each of the fifty states in the United States to mail the prophetic messages to. I went online and found their names and addresses, which was three hundred newspapers at the time.

As I have mailed them out quarterly over the years, some of them are returned to me with no forwarding address. This tells me that maybe they have gone out of business. Now I mail to only 253 of these largest newspapers in the fifty United States as forty seven of them no longer are in operation.

200

Many people now no longer read the printed news and advertisements as they get their news from talk radio while driving, and get it from T.V., internet, and cell phones. Also computer shopping is now becoming more popular, so people are relying less on newspaper print advertisements for their information. If their advertisements are not selling goods and services to the public, their ads diminish, their subscriptions diminish, and they go out of business.

Even the printed magazines are having trouble keeping up their subscriptions. Three of the major magazines have now reduced their yearly subscription rate to $10.00 for Money Magazine, Fortune Magazine, and Reader's Digest. They have lowered the cost by more than half, to keep up the number of subscribers, to guarantee their advertisers their reading audience.

The Lord told me when we first began the syndicated newspaper column that the purpose of it is, **"to reach the people on the street for salvation, for the ones who do not attend any church."** So, I will be faithful to God to keep sending them out, until my God says, **"Enough."**

Blessings! Velma

Yes, Our God's beloved Christian children, Our God's beloved Christian pastors and Our God's beloved Holy Bible teachers, YOUR heavenly Father God does love you, does take care of you, does guide you into ALL righteous living unto your God with Our God's Holy Spirit living within you to guide you, help you, teach you, and make a way for you to teach Our God's truth to your congregations and to your other people.

Yes, your God Jesus Christ is by your side teaching you and helping you to teach others Our God's truths found in Our God's Holy Bible.

Doesn't Jesus tell you in Our God's Holy Bible that where two or three are gathered in Jesus' name that He is there with them? (Matthew 18:20)

Yes, you are NOT alone when you teach others Our God's truths and promises to people, as you do have the help, love, and encouragement of YOUR heavenly Father God, the power and wisdom of Jesus Christ as your example, and Our God's Holy Spirit within you as your Helper, your Encourager, your Revealer of truth, and Our God has already programmed you and called you to be successful in preaching and teaching others about Our God and Our God's ways.

Yes, your God does protect you at ALL times.

Yes, your God MAKES a way for you to work and witness for YOUR Holy Triune God that others WILL BE brought to YOUR Lord Jesus Christ for THEIR salvation, for their righteous Christian living, for their provisions, and protection by their Holy Triune God.

Yes, your God is just.

Your God is fair.

Your God does reward the righteous, and your God does punish the wicked who do DESERVE Our God's punishment.

Yes, whatever a person sows IS what that person will reap. (Galatians 6:7)

Yes, do sow good seeds of righteous living and righteous preaching and teaching, and do SEE HOW Our God does reward you for this.

Yes, do encourage others to know Jesus Christ as their personal Savior from their sins and wrongdoings, then come OUT of ALL sinful lifestyle, and live a righteous lifestyle unto God in obedience to God.

Yes, you do witness by how you live, so do let your lifestyle reflect the lifestyle of Jesus, by praising God, living for God, helping the sick and helpless, telling others the good news of THEIR heavenly Father's love for them, and teaching them how to know God, be saved in Jesus, and be led and helped by Our God's Holy Spirit.

Yes, bring people to YOUR heavenly Father God to have ALL their many needs and ALL their holy desires met from THEIR heavenly Father God THROUGH Jesus Christ, the ONLY TRUE Savior of mankind.

Yes, speak, teach, and write the truth in love, love of YOUR God and love of your fellow mankind.

Yes, you ARE your brother's keeper.

Show your brotherly love, your kindness, and your generosity to ALL you meet.

Do PRAY for your enemies and do pray for ALL who come against you.

Yes, it is always BETTER to obey your God than to obey mankind, as mankind can and will lead you astray.

Pray about all the decisions you are to make, and wait for your God's answer to you.

By obeying your God's decisions for you can save you a lot of future headaches.

Doesn't Our God's Holy Bible teach you that if anyone lacks

wisdom to ask it of God, and Our God WILL answer you and WILL give to you the wisdom you do desire. (James 1:5)

Yes, call unto your God, and your God WILL ANSWER you, and will show you great and mighty things which you know not. (Jeremiah 33:3)

Yes, your God is no respecter of persons as your God does love each of Our God's mankind the same, and what Our God will do for one of Our God's mankind, Our God will do for any when the right conditions are met. (Acts 10:34)

Yes, do LIVE for God, and do teach Our God's truths to mankind as found in Our God's Holy Bible.

Yes, Our God's Holy Bible is the divinely inspired Word of God that has been tested and proved seven times for its accuracy. (Psalm 12:6)

Yes, even as Our God tested and proved correct seven times, even so Our God tests and proves each of mankind seven times to prove a person's faithfulness to God.

Yes, doesn't Our God's Holy Bible teach that a righteous man/person can fall seven times, but that he will get back up seven times? (Proverbs 24:16)

Doesn't Our God's Holy Bible teach you that you should not think it strange when these fiery trials come on you, because it is common to man, but Our God WILL make a way for you to escape so that these trials will NOT consume you? (1 Peter 4:12-19)

Yes, IF you WILL stay true to YOUR Holy Triune God throughout ALL these fiery trials, you can be assured that YOUR heavenly Father God WILL BRING YOU THROUGH all these fiery trials IN DUE TIME, and you can ALWAYS be assured that Our God WILL ALWAYS REWARD YOU for your steadfastness, for your enduring to the ends of these trials.

Yes, ALWAYS keep your faith in God strong to the end, and you will receive your crown of righteousness from YOUR God. (2 Timothy 4:8)

Yes, Our God is now building up Our God's strong army

of believers-in-God on earth to withstand these strong evil influences that are fixing to come on these evil lands of these wicked Americas and these wicked Americans.

Yes, unless these wicked Americans do repent of ALL their evil ways and turn to God for repentance and for forgiveness, they can and will be destroyed.

Yes, Our God's arm is NOT slack in bringing needed judgment and punishment to these wicked Americans, who have turned away from God as their first love, and who follow their own corrupt ways and evil desires.

Yes, even now the prayers of the saints of God are what are staying the hand of God from allowing the enemies of America to come in and have the power to destroy America and these wicked Americans.

Yes, do preach repentance.

Do preach for people to COME OUT OF a sinful lifestyle and live for God.

Do preach for people to turn back to God, repent of their sins, live for God, and ASK GOD to save America from total destruction.

Yes, do not just "entertain" the congregations in church with fanciful and humorous stories, but do preach the truths of Our God's Holy Bible to them.

Do preach Jesus Christ to them, that Jesus saves, Jesus heals, Jesus provides all good things for them FROM THEIR heavenly Father God. (Philippians 4:19)

Do preach that the coming of Jesus Christ is SOON, coming back for Our God's great rapture of ALL of Our God's great saved and sanctified Christians to take them back to their eternal home in heaven.

Do warn them to GET READY to go and to stay ready to go to meet Jesus in the air in a split second.

Yes, the soon return of Jesus is IMMINENT!

Yes, time on earth, as you do now know time on earth to be, IS SOON running out.

Yes, soon time on earth will be counted in Our God's millennial time, when a day is as a thousand years. (2 Peter 3:8)

Yes, time on earth, as you now know time to be on earth, IS quickly running out, and what you do for and with your God MUST be done quickly.

Yes, do read and do study Our God's book of Revelation in Our God's Holy Bible, and it will tell you, teach you, what WILL happen on Our God's planet Earth at the end of the age, before Jesus returns for His thousand-year reign on earth.

Yes, Jesus is coming again soon.

Get ready to WELCOME Jesus and to go BACK to YOUR heavenly home WITH Jesus to rule and to reign forever with Jesus.

Yes, all righteous-living-for-God Christians ARE joint heirs with Jesus. (Romans 8:17)

Yes, Jesus is supreme over all of heaven and earth. (Matthew 28:18)

Yes, ask what you will of YOUR heavenly Father God, always asking it in Jesus' holy name, always having great faith in YOUR Lord and Master Jesus, and ALL GOOD THINGS and ALL GOOD EVENTS will be given to you, to help yourself, to help others, and that WILL bring glory to YOUR Holy Triune God on earth.

Yes, Jesus is ALWAYS your physical Healer. (Isaiah 53:5)

Do pray for sick and afflicted people to be healed by Jesus.

Ask Jesus ONCE for healing and then do praise Jesus and praise the holy name of Jesus, until the manifested healing takes place.

Yes, when Jesus walked this earth nearly two thousand years ago, Jesus healed EVERY sick person who came to Jesus and who ASKED for healing from Jesus.

Yes, Jesus still heals people today who do ASK Jesus for healing and who do keep on asking, until their healing takes place, is manifested.

Yes, Jesus loves you.

Yes, Jesus has paid the price on Calvary's cross to pay for the salvation of anyone who comes to Jesus with a repentant heart, who asks Jesus for salvation, who receives free salvation from Jesus, who will go and sin no more.

If you do live in habitual sin, a sinful lifestyle, you cannot enter heaven.

Sin will never enter heaven.

You must have salvation from your sins in Jesus, and you MUST come out of ALL known sin in your life, and live for God, if you want to enter heaven for eternity.

Yes, all sin and all sinners, who have not repented of all sin, do belong in hell with Satan, the chief of sinners.

Yes, Jesus has made the ONLY way for sinners to escape their going to hell for eternity, and that is by their choosing Jesus as their Lord and Savior while they are now alive on earth, and by their living their lifestyle for God while they are alive on earth.

Yes, do preach repentance from all sins.

Yes, do preach Jesus as Savior, Healer, and soon-coming Bridegroom.

Yes, do go and do preach righteous living for God so that Our God is able to reward mankind for knowing God, loving God, honoring God, and being fulfilled in God with all good things and all good events.

Do praise your God now for this message!

I praise you, my heavenly Father God, for this message!

Hallelujah!

Praise God!

LETTER TWENTY SIX FOR CHURCH GROWTH

Dear Christian Pastors and All Holy Bible Teachers,

I have been praying about what to write to you in these fifty letters for church growth that will encourage you to grow stronger in the Lord and will help you in your teaching others and in your service to others.

Now, I want to write to you about prophetic messages and being Holy Spirit filled with the gift of tongues. One thing I want to warn you about is what our Father God told me, **"In these last days before Jesus returns, Our God's Christians can be led astray, but if they truly keep on seeking Our true God, they will not be led astray FOR LONG, because Our God will reveal truth to them and will bring them BACK to their true God."**

Evil forces can come at you pretending to be good forces, and it can be very deceiving, even to the strongest Christians in these End-times on earth. Even with myself being a Christian for about 72 years, being Spirit filled for more than 37 years, having read through the Bible yearly since 1972, and having more than 940 prophetic messages written out and typed up, I am still being deceived at times with these voices and dreams from evil sources that are sounding like good voices and good dreams. However, I keep on seeking our true God until Our God reveals truth to me. One name that I know that I can depend on without fail is the holy name of **Jesus.** Father God has protected the holy name of Jesus, and evil forces are not allowed to use the holy name of Jesus. Evil forces can call themselves, "god," "spirit," "son," "savior," "messiah," "father," and many other names that sound righteous, but are totally evil.

I went into the mental hospital in 1981 for a month from hearing voices that were pretending to be good voices, but were totally evil voices. I was put on anti-depressant medication, and the voices immediately stopped. Then again in 1983, even with myself still on anti-depressant medication, I again began hallucinating with hearing voices that were pretending to be good voices, but were totally evil voices. Again I was in the mental hospital for a month, with a change of medication, until the voices stopped. However, both times that I was hallucinating with the evil voices, my true God taught me some things about hearing the true voice of God and hearing evil voices **pretending to be** the true God.

Father God taught me the difference in hearing from **"god"** and hearing from **"your heavenly Father God."** He taught me the difference in hearing from **"spirit"** and hearing from **"Our God's Holy Spirit."**

He taught me the difference in hearing from **"the son"** and hearing from **"Jesus."** Father God taught me that when He speaks to me, He usually calls me by my name, and always tells me that He loves me, before He tells me anything else. He taught me to always compare what I hear in these prophetic messages with what is taught in the WHOLE Bible, and not in an isolated verse of Scripture. He has taught me that if the prophetic message foretells a future event, and the event does NOT come true on the given due date, it is NOT from God as our God never lies.

God gives us the Scripture verse of Jeremiah 33:3 that teaches us to call on God and He will answer us and show us great and mighty things that we know not. God does give to us the assurance that when we do call on God that He will answer us. But sometimes, when Satan demands it, our God allows us to be tested by Satan and other evil forces, to see if we can be deceived by Satan's cleverness in Satan's pretending to be the true God. Many times, when the true Christians fail the test of recognizing Satan's voice when Satan pretends to be the true voice of our God, and the Christian realizes that they have been deceived, this sometimes drives them away from trying to hear the true voice of their true God.

I want to encourage all the true Christians who want to hear the true voice of their true God, to not ever be discouraged when a false message comes that is not from the true God. Just discard it, learn from it, and keep on trying to hear the true voice of God. If we keep seeking our God, our God will remain true to us, and will reveal Himself to us in due time. If you are led astray, you will not be led astray FOR LONG, because our God will bring you back to Himself and will reveal Himself to you if you don't get discouraged and give up.

One of the recent ways that I was deceived in the past year was with a dream that I had about the recent sale of my house in Brentwood, Tennessee. I had planned to put my house up for sale at the beginning of the summer in 2016. On January 1, 2016, I had a dream just before I woke up in the morning. My dream showed to me the large numbers of 186 written in white. I went back to sleep and had the exact same dream with the large white numbers of 186. I had heard from someone that if you get the same dream twice it means that it is from God. I wondered if the dream had something to do with the sale of my house? I got out my calendar and counted off 186 days from January 1. So I got on my knees before God and asked God if this date means anything? I heard the words, "Your house will sell on this date." My house did NOT sell on that date! It finally sold on December 19, 2016. So the dream was a false dream and was very deceiving. That's why our God tells us to test the messages to discern if they are from God. If they do NOT come true on the due date, they are NOT from God. (Deuteronomy 18:22) Satan is very evil, and when you get any kind of message, be sure to TEST it to see if it is from the TRUE God, and not from the false "god" of evil forces **pretending** to be a good voice.

I have been hearing the true voice of MY heavenly Father God and MY Lord Jesus Christ for more than 37 years with the help of our God's Holy Spirit. I praise my God that He has kept me OUT of the mental hospital for more than 34 years straight!

Blessings! Velma

Yes, Our God's beloved Christian pastors and all Holy Bible teachers, YOUR heavenly Father God does love you, does take care of you and ALL of your loved ones, and YOUR heavenly Father God does MAKE a pathway for you to walk in daily to teach and to witness for YOUR Holy Triune God.

Yes, Your God is a loving God, and you do reflect YOUR God's goodness when you love others, teach others with joy and kindness, AND when you do go about HELPING the needy and helpless with love, kindness, and generosity.

Yes, it IS Christ in you, the hope of glory. (Colossians 1:27)

Yes, yes, yes, Jesus Christ IS COMING SOON!

Tell everyone you meet and tell everyone you teach in your groups to get ready to go in any split second to meet Jesus Christ in the air for Our God's great rapture of righteous-living Christian souls, to go BACK to THEIR glorious home in heaven with THEIR Lord and Savior, Jesus Christ.

Yes, yes, yes, do GET READY and do STAY READY to go with spotless garments washed clean and pure in the holy shed blood of Jesus.

Yes, Jesus Christ paid the supreme sacrifice on earth with His holy shed blood and crucifixion on Calvary's cruel cross to open the way for any and all of mankind to come to Jesus, ASK Jesus to forgive ALL their sins and unrighteous living, be Lord and Master of their life, come out of ALL known sin, and live the rest of their life on earth in obedience to God, then enter Our God's heaven forever.

Yes, Our God's Holy Spirit within you will reveal more and more of Our God's true riches of knowledge and wisdom as you do read, study, and memorize Our God's Holy Bible.

Yes, your preaching and teaching skills WILL improve daily as you do read, study, and meditate on Our God's Holy Bible.

Yes, your soul will grow more in God daily as you do worship and praise God without ceasing for a long time.

Do spend quality time in prayer with YOUR Holy Triune God, and do speak Our God's proclamations over yourself, your family, your church group, and your other loved ones, always praying ALL of your prayers in Jesus' holy name, always believing in the power of Jesus with your strong faith, always EXPECTING Our God to answer ALL of your prayers speedily, that you will be helped, that others will be helped, and that Our God will be glorified on earth.

Yes, prayer in the name of Jesus IS the strongest force on earth today so do pray often and do pray long.

Do find a prayer partner to HELP you to claim all the excellent benefits from your God for you and for them, and for ALL of your needy loved ones.

Yes, prayer to YOUR heavenly Father God and to YOUR Lord Jesus Christ on earth is free to all, and it does pay the biggest and most profound rewards.

Yes, your heavenly Father God does want you and your loved ones to prosper and be in good health at all times, so do claim these good benefits from God and they WILL HAPPEN as your souls all grow in God when you and they ARE STRONG ENOUGH in your relationship with YOUR God to accept all of these good benefits from God, without your becoming corrupt from it.

Yes, Our God does LONG to pour out ALL GOOD BENEFITS on you, on your family, and on ALL your church congregations, so that ALL of you will be helped spiritually, mentally, emotionally, educationally, physically, and financially, so that you can be blessed as children of God and so that you can HELP meet the needs of others who do need your help, and so that your God will be honored and exalted on earth as your and their holy Creator, Sustainer, Provider, and Protector.

Yes, your Holy Triune God is all powerful and does hold this whole earth and entire universe within the power of Our God's hands, all the past, present, and future of all things, all events, and all people.

Do trust YOUR Holy Triune God to meet ALL your needs and meet ALL your holy desires at all times.

Yes, YOUR Holy Triune God can always MAKE a way when there seems to be no logical way for solutions to ALL problems and dilemmas on earth, as YOUR Holy Triune God IS a God of miracles, as YOUR God can make possible what is impossible for man to do, even all men working together cannot do many of the accomplishments that are EASY for your God to do.

Yes, your God does have all power at all times in heaven and earth.

Yes, all power in heaven and earth has been given to Jesus by Father God after Father God raised Jesus from the dead. (Matthew 28:18)

Yes, didn't Jesus tell you in Our God's Holy Bible that ALL things are possible with God? (Matthew 19:26)

Yes, doesn't Our God's Holy Bible teach you that you can do ALL things through Jesus Christ which strengthens you? (Philippians 4:13)

Doesn't Our God's Holy Bible teach you that you are joint heirs with Jesus? (Romans 8:16-17)

Doesn't Jesus teach you to ask anything of the Father in Jesus' name and it will be given unto you? (John 16:23)

Yes, make ALL your requests known unto your heavenly Father God, ask it always in Jesus' holy name, and always TRUST your God to answer your prayers speedily, and ALL good gifts and good benefits will be given to you by your God.

Yes, love the unlovely people, and help the helpless people, and when you show kindness and generosity to others, it does please YOUR heavenly Father God, and you WILL be rewarded for your good actions by your heavenly Father God, rewarded in the way that you need it the most.

Yes, when you help meet the needs of others, your God WILL meet more of your needs.

Yes, if you have a physical illness in your body, pray that others will be healed of the same physical illness and your God will work to heal you both.

Yes, do teach your congregation members to live in one accord with others, and to pray in one accord with others so that their prayers WILL be answered, and will NOT be hindered.

Yes, when people are not living in one accord with ALL of their fellow mankind, their prayers can be hindered from being answered by God. (Mark 11:25)

Yes, Our God desires unity, unity with Our Holy Triune God, unity in marriages, unity in families, unity in the churches, unity in the work force, and unity in social gatherings.

Yes, do promote unity by promoting love, kindness, generosity, forgiveness of wrongs and harms and hurts, committed intentionally and unintentionally.

Yes, people MUST not only learn to forgive wrongs seventy times seven, but they must learn to FORGET wrongs seventy times seven.

Yes, in heaven all is love, kindness, happiness, joy, sharing, beauty, peace, riches, and eternal worship of THEIR Holy Triune God.

Yes, do let YOUR Father God's will be done on earth as it is done in heaven. (Matthew 6:10)

Yes, teach others of the love, the power, the generosity of Jesus.

Yes, teach others to be like Jesus.

Teach others that Jesus is God, part of Our God's Holy Trinity, Our God's only begotten Son, Who now is raised from the dead, is seated at His Father God's right hand, is now making intercession to His Father God for the salvation and welfare of all mankind alive on earth, and Who is now awaiting HIS Father God's command to go back towards earth for Our God's great rapture of ALL Christian souls who are now living for God and are staying ready to meet Jesus in the air in a split second, to go home with THEIR holy Bridegroom Jesus, to rule and reign with THEIR Lord Jesus forever.

Praise Father God for this message!

Hallelujah!

Praises to Our heavenly Father God!

Hallelujah!

Dear Christian Pastors and All Holy Bible Teachers,

Father God always wants me to, **"Speak and write the truth in love,"** so I have decided to write about the two pastors that were at my Southern Baptist Church when I was a teenager in Longview, Washington.

Their names are Pastor James Frost and Pastor Harris, when our church congregation had about four hundred people attending. Pastor Frost served for about two years. When he left to go pastor another church in another city, Pastor Harris became our pastor for about two years.

Pastor Frost had a wonderful memory and had most of the New Testament memorized. Before each of his sermons on Sunday mornings, he would stand in the pulpit with his open Bible in his hand, look at the audience the whole time, and quote from memory every word exactly from the whole chapter that he was going to preach on. His sermons were always excellent!

He had all four hundred first and last names of the congregation memorized. As people arrived for the service he would stand at the door, shake each person's hand and call them by their first and last names, and welcome them to the service. He did this for every man, woman, child, and infant attending. As people left the church service he would also stand at the front exit, shake each person's hand, call them by their first and last name, and thank them for coming.

Pastor and Mrs. Frost had a teenage son who was the same age as I was at the time. I knew him as we went to the same high school as well as church together. Their son got into some kind of trouble and ran away from home. I felt so bad for their family as they searched and searched for him. It took them about a year to locate him. They finally found him when he joined the military service.

I did not see Pastor Frost and his family for eleven years until after I graduated from high school in 1956, worked my way through seven years of college, worked on some jobs for three years, then took a Graphic Design job at The Baptist Sunday School Board in Nashville, Tennessee in 1965. My first week on the job at the Baptist Board, I happened to pass Pastor Frost in the hallway! He greeted me, "It's Velma Garner from Longview, Washington!" I was shocked that he could remember me and even remember my name after eleven years!

I greeted him, "Pastor Frost, what are you doing here?" He replied "The Baptists promoted me from Pastor to Editor. I work here full time now." Later, I heard the Baptists promoted him again as head of all the Southern Baptist work in Florida. He is a wonderful Christian worker with a wonderful family.

Pastor Harris replaced Pastor Frost in our First Baptist Church in Longview, Washington, and was there for about two years. He was a wonderful Pastor, even though he didn't shake people's hands and call them by their first and last names on their way in and out of the building. He was a great man of prayer. Before each of his Sunday morning sermons, he would spend an hour in prayer in the basement of the church, praying about the message he was to give. He preached wonderful sermons!

Pastor Harris had a wonderful wife and precious baby son. He and his wife were married several years without any children. They kept praying for a son, and finally God did give to them their hearts' desire, a precious baby son they named Samuel. He was kept in the church nursery while his dad preached, and my mom and Mrs. Ammons enjoyed keeping him.

Our Garner family of Mother and we five children walked a few miles to church every Sunday morning, Sunday evening, and Wednesday evening. Dad didn't go with us, and Mom didn't drive.

At age sixteen, I got my driver's license and drove us to church, which was great as it rains a lot in southern Washington.

Mother had a close friend and neighbor named Mrs. Ammons. She was our only paid nursery worker at the church. Since Mother knew that she needed help with the babies and small children, Mother became a full-time volunteer nursery worker for many years. Since we had only one Sunday morning church service, Mother always missed it in order to help with the nursery. Mrs. Ammons was an elderly widow, very obese with many health problems, and spent her time in the nursery mostly in a rocking chair, rocking one or two babies, occasionally feeding them. Mother always was up helping the little ones with their toys and snacks and diaper changes. Once a little child was choking on a small toy, but Mother got to him in time and was able to push the item down his little throat! Praise God that she was there and was able to help him in time!

Pastor Harris knew that these faithful nursery workers were always taking care of his little Samuel. One day he stuck his head in the nursery door and said, "We appreciate you nursery workers." Every Sunday morning, as Mom and we children walked to church, Mom ALWAYS commented on, "Brother Harris said he appreciates us nursery workers." I would ask her, "He said it again?" She always replied, "No, he said it only one time." But she REMEMBERED it every week!

It's interesting to me that Mom never once remembered or commented on Pastor Frost calling her by her name and shaking her hand twice on Sunday mornings for about two years, but she ALWAYS remembered Pastor Harris' kind words spoken ONLY ONCE to her.

It's also very interesting to me that after I had volunteered my time for about 3½ hours every Sunday morning for two years at The Lord's Chapel's nursery with about thirty three- and four-year olds, when my name was brought up in a leaders' meeting, the head pastor, Pastor Billy Roy Moore, asked, "Who is she?"

It would be a very kind thing for pastors to do, to thank their nursery workers, especially the volunteer ones. God knows their names and rewards them, even when the pastors do not know them or thank them.

Blessings! Velma

Yes, Our God's beloved Christian pastors and all beloved Holy Bible teachers, YOUR heavenly Father God does love you, does take care of you, and does provide MANY opportunities for you to preach, teach, and witness for YOUR Holy Triune God to saints and to sinners.

Yes, do ENCOURAGE the saints, the ones who do know Jesus Christ as their Lord and Savior and who are now already living a righteous lifestyle in obedience to THEIR God.

Yes, do warn the sinners, and all people now alive on earth have committed their own sins, as well as, being born into the sins committed by Adam, do warn them to come to Jesus Christ of Nazareth with a repentant heart and ASK Jesus to forgive ALL their sin and ASK Jesus to be Lord and Master of their life, RECEIVE this FREE salvation from Jesus, then go and sin no more.

Yes, after they DO ACCEPT this free gift of salvation from THEIR Lord Jesus, they MUST come out of ALL sinful lifestyle, and live a lifestyle of obedience to God for the rest of their one lifetime on earth, if they do want to go to heaven when their life on earth is over.

Yes, yes, yes, do preach repentance, repentance, repentance, for each of mankind to repent of ALL sin in their life, let Our God heal them, heal their loved ones, and heal this nation of America.

Yes, if ONLY the people would repent of their wicked lifestyle, turn to God, ask Our God's forgiveness, THEN Our God would HELP them to live righteously unto God, and would heal America, and make America great again, as it WAS GREAT when the leaders and the people were under the Lordship of Our true God's Holy Triune God.

Yes, America and Americans have been drifting farther and farther away from God, and they do not realize that if they continue drifting more and more away from God that they are heading toward their total destruction!

Yes, Our God created and still does create each of mankind in Our God's image so that mankind could know Our God personally, and could enjoy the goodness of Our God forever, know Our God's love, fellowship, rewards, and all good gifts from Our God to make their lives happy and successful on earth, be saved in Jesus the ONLY TRUE Savior, live for God, and enter Our God's beautiful heaven forever.

Yes, help people to TURN BACK TO their first love of Our God's Holy Triune God, know Our God, love Our God FIRST above ALL else, and be provided for and be protected by Our God's Holy Triune God.

Yes, encourage your people, the ones you teach and the ones you minister to, to love their fellow mankind, and help those needing help as they do love and do help themselves.

Yes, you ARE your brother's keeper.

Yes, YOUR heavenly Father God will ALWAYS reward you for your love, kindness, and help to your fellow mankind.

Didn't Jesus tell His followers that when you help the poor and needy among you that you are helping Jesus? (Matthew 25:40)

Yes, every person now alive on Our God's planet Earth has been created by Our God in Our God's image with body, soul, and spirit.

Yes, pray for your enemies, that they will TURN AWAY FROM their wickedness, turn to your God and be saved in the shed blood of Jesus, be set free from all evil, live for God, and enter heaven forever.

Yes, Satan is desperately wicked, evil, cunning, lying, deceitful, and uses every evil thing and every evil power that

221

he can to deceive people in these last End-time days before Our Lord Jesus Christ returns toward earth for Our God's great rapture of ALL the saved and righteous-living Christians to take them back to Our God's great heaven above.

Yes, Satan knows his time is SHORT until his eternal punishment in hell.

Yes, pray to Our heavenly Father God, pray with faith in the name of Jesus Christ, that you will not be deceived by Satan in these last days, but that Our God will keep your faith in Jesus, and your thoughts, words, and actions WILL stay true to the glory of YOUR God, the TRUE God, on earth.

Yes, as your soul and their souls do grow up more in God, you and they do become more stable and more trustworthy in your faith in God, THEN Our God is able to provide MORE of Our God's good benefits to you and to them, without you and them becoming corrupt.

Yes, your heavenly Father God and your Jesus Christ God always use Our God's wisdom in giving ALL of Our God's children Our God's good gifts to them as Our God will not give a good benefit to a person whose soul and character are too weak to handle the good benefit.

Yes, your soul must grow more in God for you to receive the good benefits from God of more wealth, more fame, and more responsibilities in teaching, and in governing people.

Yes, draw closer to YOUR God so that YOUR God IS ABLE to draw closer to you. (James 4:8)

Yes, Jesus Christ obeyed HIS Father God and was faithful unto death on the cross, paying for ALL the sins of mankind when He was totally innocent, Himself, so that Father God could reward His obedience by giving Him all power in heaven and on earth. (Matthew 28:18)

Yes, each Christian person WILL BE tried and tested by God to prove what IS in the heart of each person.

If the person stays true to God throughout the test and endures faithfully with God until the end of the test, they will be promoted to a higher level of service as they have proven themselves trustworthy in God to receive more good benefits in God and from God.

Yes, Satan's beauty and power level in heaven corrupted him and his character was not strong enough in God to handle the good gifts from God of his beauty, his fame, and his power, and when Satan refused to repent of his corruption, he must be destroyed by his Creator God.

Yes, Satan knows his time is now short before his final doom so he has now come down to mankind on earth to do as much damage as possible before his final punishment for eternity. (Revelation 12:12)

Yes, do read and do study and do memorize Our God's Holy Bible so that you are able to recognize when evil forces do try to attack you, your family, your other loved ones, and even your church congregations.

Yes, do pronounce Our God's healing Scriptures over you, your family, and other loved ones, and over your congregations daily, and do watch Our God fulfill Our God's promises to you and to them.

Yes, learn the strategies of Satan, who comes to steal, kill, and destroy, devour everyone who allows him to, but you are able to overcome Satan, his evil tactics, his evil forces, with the spoken word of God, even as Jesus overcame Satan's temptations to Jesus with Our God's spoken words to Satan as given in Our God's Holy Bible.

Yes, know the words written in Our God's Holy Bible to you, and BELIEVE every word written in the Bible, and they WILL help you overcome every evil force that comes against you and all your loved ones.

Yes, you do overcome all evil by the shed blood of the Lamb of God, Jesus Christ.

Yes, the shed blood of Jesus is righteous and holy.

Yes, there is power in the shed blood of Jesus that is able to break the yoke of oppression from everyone who will use it correctly, who knows Jesus as their personal Savior, who lives a righteous lifestyle for God, who has faith in Jesus, who claims this power in the name of Jesus to help themselves, to help others, to glorify God on earth.

Yes, prayer in the name of Jesus, and claiming the shed blood of Jesus over a situation, ARE the strongest forces on earth today so use them with strong faith in Jesus and do use them often, that you will be helped, others will be helped, and Our God will be glorified on earth.

Yes, know your Father God better through prayers, Bible study, worship, and by helping others who have less good benefits than you have.

Yes, know that all good benefits in your life now have been given to you from YOUR heavenly Father God, and they have been given to you through YOUR Lord and Savior, Jesus the Christ. (Philippians 4:19)

Yes, Jesus is now coming back SOON for Our God's great rapture of ALL the saved and sanctified children of God.

Yes, do get ready and do STAY ready to go at all times.

Yes, you do not know the day nor the hour when Jesus will appear in the great Eastern sky, coming back toward earth for Our God's great catching away to heaven, Our God's saved-in-Jesus and obedient-unto-God beloved children of God.

Do warn others to get ready to go and to stay ready to go in any split second to meet Jesus in the air to be taken BACK to THEIR eternal home in heaven.

Yes, sin will never enter heaven.

Yes, you must have salvation in Jesus to wash away all your sins and you MUST live righteously while alive on earth to enter heaven forever after your one life on earth.

Yes, your eternal soul that was given to you at the moment of your conception by YOUR heavenly Father God will live either in heaven with Jesus and your Father God, or it will live forever in hell with Satan, as there are NO other places for your eternal soul to live after your one life and one death on earth.

You must make your own decision either for Jesus Christ or against Jesus Christ while you are now alive on earth.

Yes, soon your life on earth will be over and your holy Creator God will decide your eternal fate according to the decisions you made and you lived by while alive on earth.

If you chose Jesus as your Savior and lived for God while alive on earth, you will enter heaven forever.

If you rejected Jesus and lived a corrupt, sinful lifestyle on earth, you will enter hell with Satan forever.

Receive Jesus, live for God, and enjoy heaven forever! Hallelujah!

Praises to Our heavenly Father God for this message! Praise God!

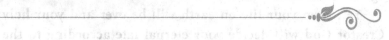

Dear Christian Pastors and All Holy Bible Teachers,

Last Sunday at our church in the third worship service, I heard some good testimonies of friends helping friends that I would like to have written up and published in my monthly family "Garner News." I would like to later include these testimonies into a book that I am compiling of forty Christian testimonies titled, *Friends Helping Friends*. I now have about twenty testimonies of the forty needed for the book, that have already been published in my family newsletter. I plan to include a prophetic message between each testimony in the book.

I was able to publish the testimony of Pastor Alex Pearne that he gave in our church service. He told how a friend paid his airfare once every month for him to visit his girlfriend, who was away at college, whom he later married.

I would like to publish our pastor's experience of how God sent a friend to help him overcome bullying when he was in school. I would also like to get the written testimony of the man who donated ten children's bicycles that were given away at our church's Easter celebration.

The six books that I am working on now are:

Friends Helping Friends, with forty testimonies and forty prophetic messages.

Church Growth Our Father God's Way, with fifty letters and fifty prophetic messages.

Tithe Your Way out of Debt, with fifty testimonies and fifty prophetic messages.

The Best Things, with forty testimonies written by widows and widowers of the twelve best things of their marriages when their spouses were living, and forty prophetic messages.

Art Lessons Beyond The Classes, with forty art lessons of the things that God's Holy Spirit taught me about art, after my eight years of college with an art major, and forty prophetic messages.

And God Said ..., with fifty things that my God spoke to me to help me in various situations.

The main book that I am working on now that will soon go to press is, *Church Growth Our Father God's Way.* I am planning to self-publish it with Westbow Press at a cost of $5,075.00 plus some editorial fees before I send it to them. Father God gave to me His approval for this, and said he will help me to pay the costs. Praise God! Westbow Press is a division of Thomas Nelson and Zondervan publishing companies.

Father God told me that after I finish this book with fifty prophetic messages for pastors and Bible teachers to help the churches grow in attendance and in income that Father God will give to me fifty more prophetic messages on tithing and giving to be put into the book titled, *Tithe Your Way Out of Debt.* I have already asked for and have received the first five prophetic messages for this book. I would like to continue to receive one a week this next year to complete the book. I would like to have fifty Christian families, who are now in debt, who are not tithers, to meet once a week for a year, begin tithing according to the Bible and according to these prophetic messages, and keep a written record of the blessing that God gives to them in one year for their obedience in tithing. I would like to publish a one page report from each of fifty families between each of the fifty prophetic messages.

I asked my financial planner at Fifth Third Bank, "Do you know of any financial investments that pay a 100% return guaranteed?" He replied, "No. There are none." I told him, "I know of one. It's called tithing. God told me that the Scripture verse that teaches, 'Give and it will be given back to you, full measure, pressed down, running over,' means you will receive back double and more than double, and God cannot lie, so it's guaranteed!" This book on tithing will help the families and will help the churches. Tithes are holy, and our God rewards people who honor God with giving their holy tithes to promote the gospel of Jesus, and who help the helpless. Everyone has something that they can give to help others have a better life.

I have been giving my tithes and offerings since I have been a professional Graphic Designer. God has ALWAYS rewarded me and my family abundantly with finances and many other benefits. In 1965, I came to Nashville from Washington state as I was hired to work at the Baptist Sunday School Board helping to create Sunday School literature to hopefully win the world to Jesus Christ. When they hired me, they flew me out for an interview, then later paid my train fare to come to Nashville. I arrived with two suitcases of my clothes and $3,500.00 in college debt. I was in the bottom five percent in the nation in financial net worth as the bottom five percent are in debt. Now, fifty one years later, Father God has put me in the top five percent of Americans in net worth. The top five percent in America in net worth are millionaires.

God will do the same for anyone who knows Him, honors Him, trusts Him, does honest work for honest pay, helps themselves, helps the helpless, gives tithes and offerings, reads their Bible daily, keeps away from bad influences, and lives for God. God is no respecter of persons. What He does for one of His children, He will do for any when the right conditions are met. Many families need this teaching!

Blessings! Velma

Yes, Our God's beloved children of all Christian pastors and all Holy Bible teachers, YOUR heavenly Father God does love you and does love ALL of your family, your congregations, and all your other loved ones, and YOUR heavenly Father God IS taking care of you and them at ALL times.

Yes, your heavenly Father God never slumbers nor sleeps, but YOUR heavenly Father God has a CONTINUAL WATCH over you and others to reward you for your righteous thoughts, words, and deeds, the good that you do to help yourself, help others, and glorify God on earth.

Yes, you ARE your brother's keeper.

Yes, encourage others.

Help others in the ways that they need it the most, and your God WILL help you in the ways that you need it the most.

Yes, your God is a loving God, a generous God, a powerful God, a perfect God, a just God, a rewarding God, a never-beginning and never-ending God, a God Who ALWAYS DESERVES to be loved, honored, and praised by ALL of Our God's created mankind on Our God's created earth.

Yes, yes, yes, as you do worship, love, and praise YOUR Holy Triune God, your God is re-creating you from the inside out, filling your eternal soul with love, joy, peace, and happiness to your God's glory.

Yes, yes, yes, YOUR Holy Triune God does have ALL the RIGHT answers for you to have a healthy, prosperous, happy, contented, and very enjoyable life on earth, when you do know God, know Jesus Christ as your Lord and Savior, when you trust Our God to provide for you and protect you, when you pray to YOUR heavenly Father God believing in Jesus and praying in Jesus' holy name, you SHALL RECEIVE ALL the things and ALL the events that will help you, help others, and glorify YOUR Holy Triune God on earth.

Yes, praise your God many times, daily and nightly, on your knees, and feel and SEE the power of God working in you, through you, and unto you, to HELP you, HELP others, and glorify God.

Yes, the more your soul grows in God, the more funds, fame, and responsibilities your God is able to give you, without your becoming corrupt, even as Satan in heaven became corrupt.

Yes, your God does see your heart, your emotions, your servant spirit to love and honor God, to love and help others and yourself, and YOUR GOD WILL reward you accordingly.

Yes, you do teach others by how you live and by what you speak to others.

Yes, do live for God and do let your yes be yes and let your no be no.

Yes, ALWAYS do speak and write the truth in love, love of yourself, love of your fellow man, and love of YOUR Holy Triune God.

Yes, not only TELL people that you love them, but SHOW your love to them by your kindness and by your generosity to help them, WHEN they do NEED your help and WHEN you ARE ABLE to help them.

Yes, when you do show love, kindness, and generosity to your fellow mankind, you do reflect Our God's love to them through you.

Yes, Jesus was kind, loving, patient, and generous to ALL He met, and He helped EVERONE who asked Him for help.

Yes, go and do likewise, because when you help the least of these, you ARE helping YOUR Lord Jesus, and you WILL BE REWARDED for ALL your good deeds for others done in love to help them, WILL be rewarded by YOUR heavenly Father God, rewarded with all good benefits through Jesus Christ to you.

Do NOT hold grudges against ANY who have harmed you

in any way, but do FORGIVE THEM and do FORGET their harmful acts and harmful speech against you, even as YOUR heavenly Father God forgives and forgets YOUR harmful ways when you do repent, turn to God, ask God for forgiveness, then go forward and live the rest of your life loving God and helping others to your God's glory.

Yes, in Our God's Holy Bible it does teach you to turn the other cheek and be kind to those who do mistreat you so that you will be TRUE children of God. (Luke 6:29)

Yes, vengeance is mine, saith God, and your GOD will repay your enemies for how they have mistreated you. (Romans 12:19)

Yes, evil people with their evil actions will be repaid for their evil actions.

Yes, Our God's Holy Bible does teach you to obey God and do good, and great will be your reward from God. (Ephesians 6:8)

Yes, when you do see evil prospering, do consider their eternal fate, as when you eventually search for them, they will be gone. (Psalm 37:34-36)

Yes, evil people will not live out the full length of their days on earth.

Yes, long life on earth is a gift from your heavenly Father God, given to you in your obedience of a life lived for and with God. (Psalm 91:14-16)

Yes, love God, honor God, obey God, live righteously, and help the helpless with love to your God's glory, and then do watch Our God pour out ALL good benefits on you and on your loved ones.

Yes, YOUR Holy Triune God is a good God Who does so generously pour out Our God's good benefits on several generations of those who love God, honor God, and obey God. (Exodus 20:6)

Yes, claim your whole family for God and DO TEACH THEM the right way to know God, trust God, obey God, and be rewarded abundantly by THEIR God for their good works and kind deeds to help others, and to glorify THEIR God on earth.

Yes, the time IS short until God's only begotten Son, Jesus Christ, comes back toward earth for Our God's great rapture of ALL the saved-in-Jesus and sanctified-unto-God Christian children of God, to claim them, to catch them away to heaven in a split second of time, to take them BACK to THEIR home in heaven, to live with, to rule and reign with, THEIR Holy Triune God forevermore.

Yes, do stay prayed up.

Do stay fasted up.

Do KEEP ready to go at all times.

Do WARN OTHERS that time is now short and is growing shorter, until YOUR Lord Jesus Christ returns for Our God's great catching away of ALL the saints of God, all the ones saved by the shed blood of Jesus, who are living righteously for God.

Yes, do read and do study Our God's Holy Bible, and you will see and know that the signs of the times of Jesus' appearing are NOW happening on Our God's earth that do signal the SOON return of Jesus.

Yes, earthquakes in various places, wars and rumors of wars, travel increasing, knowledge increasing, people growing cold and turning away from God, people turning against their parents, people disrespecting law and order, and are not obeying those in authority, are all signs of the corruption coming on earth before Jesus Christ appears for Our God's great rapture of souls.

Yes, do study the book of Revelation.

Yes, do know, believe, and teach on the book of Revelation, the last book in Our God's New Testament of Our God's Holy Bible, and it WILL TEACH YOU what all MUST happen in the heavens and on earth in these end times on earth.

Yes, doesn't Our God reveal to Our God's true prophets and prophetesses, what Our God will do before it actually happens? (Amos 3:7)

Yes, be warned!

Jesus IS coming soon!

232

Do teach others to GET ready and to STAY ready to WELCOME Jesus back for Our God's great rapture.

Yes, time IS NOW SHORT and is now growing shorter until Jesus comes.

Don't be caught unaware of the times of the end of the age.

Yes, pray in ALL your lost loved ones.

Yes, even so, come quickly, Our Lord Jesus!

Hallelujah!

Praises to Our God for this message!

Hallelujah!

Praises to Our heavenly Father God!

Amen!

Dear Christian Pastors and All Holy Bible Teachers,

The last five sermons at our church taken from the teachings in Joel Osteen's book, *The Power of I AM,* have been very enjoyable for our members and visitors to hear. Yes, it is always a very good thing to encourage all the saved Christians to know their rights as Children of God, so that we can claim them, live for God, and experience the abundant life that Jesus gives us while we are alive on earth.

However, in all teaching by pastors including by Joel Osteen, it is important to not only encourage all the Christians, but also to warn the wicked as it is important to preach and teach, "The truth, **the whole truth,** and nothing but the truth." If pastors and Bible teachers do not warn the wicked, they are teaching only half of the whole truth. The Bible says that if the watchman on the wall sees danger approaching and fails to warn the people, that God will hold that watchman accountable for not warning the people of danger. (Ezekiel 33:6-9)

I have been reading the book by Perry Stone titled, *Deciphering End-Time Prophetic Codes,* and on page 149, he has this to say about a prophetic message given years ago by General William Booth, the man who started The Salvation Army:

> Booth foresaw a time in which there would be preaching that included heaven but omitted hell. Western preaching today tends to emphasize prosperity, blessing, and favor. It is void of anything considered "negative," with hell being at the top of the list—even though hell is mentioned fifty-four times in the King James Version.

Now, a new wave of ministers is exempting themselves from this troubling and frightening teaching of eternal punishment, careful not to offend the unbelieving and unrepentant. These smiling ministers can say glowing words about heaven, but willfully ignore the Scriptures on hell. Alleged Christian authors publish popular books, omitting and rejecting the idea of life separated from God.

This is a dangerous, deceptive teaching that if believed could destroy souls for eternity. The subject may not be pleasant, but it was Christ who gave the firmest warnings against the dangers of hell (Matthew 5:22-30; 10:28).

Before I became a member of The Lord's Chapel and Oasis Church, I was a member of a small Presbyterian church in downtown Franklin, Tennessee when Alan was a baby, forty two years ago. Our Sunday School class had about a dozen members attending of both men and women. One of the men in our class was well known in the Country Music industry. Three Sundays in a row I heard him tell our class something like this, "Yes, I'm married with a family and I have a girlfriend on the side. Ha, ha! The Bible says, confess and believe, so I'm confessing and believing. Ha, ha!" I knew who his wife and baby were, as when I took my turn in the church nursery with baby Alan, I saw her as she picked up their baby from the nursery. She was not in our Sunday School class.

Nobody in our class said anything to him about his continual, "confessing and believing." Finally I got fed up with this! After class I said to him privately, "The Bible does not say, confess and believe. The Bible says REPENT, confess and believe." He replied, "You show me in the Bible where it says that."

The next Sunday, I handed him a paper with about a dozen Bible Scriptures written about salvation in Jesus with righteous living. I don't know what happened, as I left that Presbyterian church shortly after that and joined The Lord's Chapel for better Bible teaching. Later I read in the newspaper that he had gotten divorced. A few years later, I read in the newspaper that he had died.

In our Sunday School class at Oasis Church, our Bible teacher said, "Salvation is by grace through faith and nothing else." I told our class, "Salvation is by grace through faith with righteous living. Christians living in a sinful lifestyle will NOT go to heaven unless they repent and live righteously." I believe our God will hold the pastors and Bible teachers accountable for telling them this.

Blessings! Velma

Yes, Our God's beloved children of Our God's beloved Christian pastors and ALL of Our God's beloved Holy Bible teachers, your heavenly Father God does love you and does love ALL of your congregations and people you teach the great truths of Jesus Christ and the infallible Word of Our God's Holy Bible.

Yes, you do hold these great truths of Our God in your hands when you do hold a copy of Our God's Holy Bible in your hands.

Yes, do teach these great truths to mankind as given in Our God's Holy Bible, and if you do use Our God's Holy Bible as your guide, you will NOT lead people astray, but you will give to them life, light, and living water from Jesus.

Yes, Jesus Christ is the way, the truth, and the life for EACH of mankind now alive on Our God's planet Earth. (John 14:6)

Yes, Jesus Christ is the ONLY way to salvation from sins and entrance into heaven in any person's afterlife, after their one lifetime on earth is over. (Acts 4:12)

Yes, Jesus Christ is the ONLY access to mankind's only true God, THEIR holy Creator God. (1 Timothy 2:5)

Yes, it is impossible for a person to work their way into heaven by doing good deeds on earth, as all good deeds done on earth are as filthy rags to God, Who is always perfect. (Isaiah 64:6)

Yes, only through faith in Jesus Christ to save a person from all sins, transgressions, and iniquities, then the person coming out of ALL sinful lifestyle and living in a righteous lifestyle in obedience to God, can a person enter heaven in their life after their one life on earth is over.

Yes, a person lives only once on earth and then is Our God's white throne judgment. (Hebrews 9:27)

Reincarnation is a complete lie from Satan that is now deceiving people into believing they can work their way into heaven by righteous acts over several lifetimes on earth.

Yes, Satan is a liar and is the father of all lies. (John 8:44)

All who are habitual liars will follow Satan into hell for eternity, unless they do repent of their sins and turn to Jesus for salvation and right-living in obedience to the true God. (Revelation 21:8)

Buddha cannot save anyone.

Allah cannot save anyone.

Mohammad cannot save anyone.

A person cannot save themselves apart from Jesus.

Only Jesus Christ can save anyone, and the person MUST come to Jesus and ASK Jesus to save them, MAKE Jesus Christ their Lord and Savior and Master of their life, then repent of ALL sin and wrongdoing and live a life in obedience to God, can ANYONE be saved, redeemed, be made whole and pure enough to enter heaven in their life after their ONE life on earth is over.

Yes, ONLY Jesus has paid the supreme sacrifice of His holy shed blood, death, and resurrection that enable Him to be the ONLY TRUE SAVIOR of mankind.

Yes, all power in heaven and in earth has been given into the powerful hands of Jesus. (Matthew 28:18)

Yes, Jesus WILL RETURN SOON toward Our God's earth to claim and to catch away to heaven the holy Bride-to-be of Jesus, to take ALL the obedient Christians BACK to THEIR heavenly home to rule and reign with their Lord and Savior, THEIR holy Bridegroom, Jesus Christ, forever in great joy and happiness and fulfillment.

Yes, you do represent YOUR Holy Triune God by how you live and by what you say, what you teach and preach.

Yes, do make your daily and nightly living for God match what you teach and preach.

If you live one way and teach the opposite way, your teaching becomes ineffective, and people will have no regard for anything you say.

Yes, do TRY to live by ALL the good principles taught by Jesus and LIVED by Jesus in Our God's Holy Bible.

Yes, Jesus went around helping people who needed His help, and He taught people the good principles of God, who needed His teaching.

Yes, do LET Jesus be YOUR holy example of how to know God, love God, live for and with God, teach others about God, and do LEAD them into a successful relationship with THEIR God, how to love their God more, how to trust their God more, how to honor their God more, how to be led and fed more by THEIR Holy Triune God, and how to live a more prosperous and successful life in tune with their Holy Triune God.

Yes, at the moment of each person's conception, THEIR Holy Triune God gave each person special gifts and special talents to make them successful in life, to prosper in life, to help themselves, and to help others, and to glorify God with these special gifts, as they do grow and mature and use these special gifts from God.

Yes, it IS Our God's holy will for each person alive to KNOW THEIR holy Creators God, have daily fellowship with THEIR God, live with and for God, and go about helping themselves, helping others, and glorifying God with their daily and nightly lives.

Yes, true happiness is knowing God, developing your gifts and talents from God, and using them to love and help yourself and others to God's glory.

Yes, Jesus was the greatest Servant of mankind.

Yes, when a person seeks to serve mankind, he will grow in the image and likeness of Jesus.

Yes, Jesus Christ lived the only holy human life to maturity on earth, then He gave ALL He had to give on Calvary's cross of His holy shed blood and His life, so that sinful mankind could be freely redeemed and brought BACK to their rightful state with THEIR heavenly Father God, their holy Creator God.

Yes, Jesus Christ was totally faithful in His obedience to His Father God, so HIS Father God was able to give Jesus all power in heaven and in earth. (Matthew 28:18)

Yes, when each pastor and each Bible teacher becomes completely humble with their heavenly Father God, when they love God, obey God, live by the teachings of God, become a servant of God by serving the people, Our God is then able to raise them to a new level of service, with greater influence, more income, and more prestige.

Yes, it is God Who gives you the power to get wealth. (Deuteronomy 8:18)

Yes, it is God Who prospers your church growth in numbers of people, wealth, and prestige.

Yes, as the leaders of the church grow more in their relationship to God, Our God is able to fill them more with Our God's knowledge, wisdom, teaching skills, and service to the people, THEN their sermons WILL have more "meat" to TEACH the people the great truths of God, and as the spiritually hungry people feed on the great "meat" of the good sermons, they will return for more and more good spiritual food and will bring their friends to your church services and to your Bible teaching groups.

Yes, do seek to be led more and more by YOUR Holy Triune God to grow up more in your soul's relationship with God.

Yes, doesn't Our God's Holy Bible teach you to grow closer to God, and Our God WILL grow closer to you? (James 4:8)

Yes, all of Our God's promises to you and to others given in Our God's Holy Bible are true, they are yes and amen, and they will work for ANYONE, when the right conditions are met.

Yes, do KNOW these promises from God, and do KNOW these conditions for these promises to be met from God, do claim these promises from God for you and for your loved ones, do MEET these conditions, and THEN do watch Our God work in YOUR life and in THEIR lives.

Yes, do LET Our God reveal Ourselves to you, by speaking to you, by answering your prayer requests, by giving you ALL good gifts for prosperous living and for helping the helpless, by healing you physically, spiritually, mentally, emotionally, and financially.

Yes, do claim Our God's promise to you given in Psalm 23:1 of, "The Lord is my Shepherd, I have all that I need."

Yes, your God IS ABLE to meet ALL your many needs and ALL your holy desires at ALL times, when you know God, love God, live for God in a righteous lifestyle, ASK God for provisions, ask in Jesus' holy name, and do expect Our God to meet ALL your needs and meet ALL your holy desires.

Yes, Our God does have UNLIMITED supplies and UNLIMITED benefits to pour out on you and pour out on ALL of mankind, when their faith in God and their trust in God is strong enough for them to receive it, without them becoming corrupt.

Yes, power can corrupt and absolute power can corrupt absolutely.

Yes, Our heavenly Father God knows and watches each person, and in Our God's knowledge and wisdom knows exactly how much promotion to give to each person, according to the growth of their soul in God, according to their love and service of mankind.

Yes, love God, love others, serve God by serving others to God's glory.

Hallelujah!

Praises to Our heavenly Father God for this divine message!

Hallelujah!

Dear Christian Pastors and All Holy Bible Teachers,

I have been praying all week about what to write in this letter to pastors and Bible teachers. Father God wants me to write to you a present day parable to illustrate a Bible teaching. Jesus often taught great spiritual lessons telling parables to the crowds, when He walked this earth nearly two thousand years ago. Here is the present-day parable:

There was once a well-known preacher man who announced on worldwide television that a valuable property was given to him debt free, even though the property had a mortgage of $720,000.00 at the time.

The next day, Father God sent a prophet of God to the preacher man who told him, "I heard you say on television that the property is debt free. The only reason that you were given the property is for you to pay off the mortgage."

Instead of repenting of the deliberate lie that he told, as King David repented of his sins when a prophet of God confronted him, the preacher man told the prophet, "Leave this church," and he did not repent of his lie.

Years later, God sent the same prophet to the preacher man who told him, "Non-profit organizations are required by law to give a financial report every year to the congregation, and you have not been doing this. Also, the financial books of non-profit organizations are required to be open at any time for anyone who wants to see them. You are not allowing this, and you are causing others to lie about it." This warning from God by the prophet was totally ignored, and the preacher man kept disobeying the law of the land by not giving yearly financial reports. Dave Ramsey said, "I would not attend a church that does not give financial reports."

A third time, God sent the prophet to the preacher man who told him, "There is a lie on the church website about the mortgage that it was given free and clear." This third warning by the prophet of God to the preacher man was totally ignored and the lie was not removed from the church website. The preacher man has had twelve years to repent of the lie and publish a printed financial report to the church members, but has not yet done so, so far as is known.

There are two Bible Scriptures that apply to this situation. One is of the lie told by Ananias and Sapphira about their property where they paid for their lie by God striking them dead on the spot. (Acts 5:1-11) The other Scripture is found in Revelation 21:8, where it says that all liars will go to hell with Satan, who is the father of all lies.

The Lord wants me to tell you the difference between an honest mistake lie, and a deliberate evil lie. All people are human, all Christians are still human, and all humans make mistakes. An honest mistake lie is when a lie is told, when the truth is not known to tell. As soon as the truth is revealed, an apology is made for the lie, then the truth is made known about the situation. Satan is the father of all lies, and all habitual, deliberate liars will follow Satan to hell for eternity. God says that there is no little sin and no big sin, as all sin is still sin, and Jesus died for all of our human sins. God will not tolerate His pastors living in a sinful lifestyle for long. They will either repent and live for God, or God will allow their punishment.

The Lord wants me to share with you some of my human frailties. I have now published our monthly family newsletter for twenty-eight years, titled "Garner News," by my maiden name of Garner. It began by sending twelve copies to our family members who live in the southern states and on the West Coast.

Three years later, when I began adding a prophetic message in every issue, many more family members and friends were added to the mailing list until it grew to more than 210 copies mailed out monthly.

For the covers of the eight-page newsletter, I always liked to have a group of photos that I had taken at our yearly Garner Family Reunions in southern Mississippi, as well as other photos that were sent to me. When I got home to Tennessee after our reunion, I looked at all the many dozens of photos that I had taken at the reunion, and tried to sort them into the eight main families and their friends who had attended. There were so many children and other people that I didn't have the names for, that I had trouble listing the correct names with the correct photos for the newsletter. Practically all of my relatives live out of state, so I couldn't run to them, show them the photos, and get from them the correct names with their correct spellings. Many times in the newsletter, I made mistakes of wrong names by photos and incorrect spelling of names. As soon as I find out the truth, I ALWAYS TRY to make corrections in the next issue of the newsletter.

Several times when I made mistakes, I would discover the mistake AFTER I had already printed over half of the 210 copies. I wished that God's Holy Spirit would show me the mistake BEFORE I printed some of the copies! Once I asked the Holy Spirit, "If you are helping me, why am I making so many mistakes?" He replied, **"We want to see if you will correct the mistakes."** I always want to correct my mistakes as soon as I can. Praise God's Holy Spirit for helping me to do so! When the Holy Spirit said to me, **"WE,"** He revealed to me that my heavenly Father God was also watching! Praises to our God!

Blessings! Velma

Yes, Our God's beloved Christian children of Our God's Christian pastors and ALL of Our God's beloved Holy Bible teachers, YOUR heavenly Father God does love you, does GUIDE you, does lead and feed you, does protect you, and does HELP you to preach Our God's truths in Our God's Holy Bible to the masses in your congregations and in your Bible classes.

Yes, these great truths as recorded in Our God's Holy Bible WILL ENDURE FOREVER.

Yes, doesn't Our God's Holy Bible teach that heaven and earth may pass away, but Our God's words will endure forever? (Luke 21:33)

Yes, learn Our God's words, teach Our God's words, memorize Our God's words, and LIVE BY Our God's words, and you will never go wrong, and you will never lead others wrong.

Yes, do LET Our God's Holy Spirit within you HELP you study, memorize, teach, and live by Our God's truths as recorded in Our God's Holy Bible.

Yes, do learn to rightly discern the truths of Our God's Holy Bible.

Yes, Satan and his demons are able to quote and to misquote Scripture verses to you, even as Satan quoted Scripture to Jesus, when Jesus was hungry after His forty days of fasting.

Jesus, however, answered Satan by quoting the right Scriptures back to Satan as Jesus knew how to "rightly divide" the Scriptures.

Yes, as you do read, study, and meditate daily on Our God's holy Scriptures, Our God's Holy Spirit within you will teach you knowledge and wisdom on how to "rightly divide" the

Scriptures, how to apply these great truths to your own life, how to live them, and how to teach them to others.

Yes, doesn't Our God's Holy Bible teach you to give the right answers to everyone who asks you about the faith within you? (1 Peter 3:15)

Yes, do know WHAT the Bible teaches, and do know HOW TO APPLY these greats truths to your own life and to the lives of others.

Yes, the Spirit of God is truth, and Our God's Holy Spirit will teach you truth, how to live it, and how to teach it to others in such a way that they can receive it and apply it to their own lives.

Yes, YOUR Holy Triune God is the God of all truth, so do love truth, follow truth, live truth, and do teach truth, the truths of your God, and you will enrich your own life, enrich the lives of others you meet, and WILL glorify your God on earth.

Yes, do teach and do preach from Our God's whole Bible in order for you to encourage the righteous, but also to warn the wicked of the consequences of their evil words and evil actions, UNLESS they REPENT, turn to God for forgiveness, then come out of ALL sinful lifestyle, then go and sin no more.

Yes, it IS good to preach and teach about the goodness of God and the rewards from God to the ones who know God, love God, obey God, and who help others with love to Our God's glory.

But yes, it is ALSO YOUR responsibility as a Bible preacher and Bible teacher to warn the people of Our God's judgment who are now living in habitual lifestyles, to come out of ALL sinful lifestyles, repent before God, be saved in the shed blood of Jesus that washes away ALL of their sins, wrongdoing, and ALL of their unholy filth, that enables them to GO to heaven and live eternally in heaven with their Holy Triune God.

Yes, it does tell in the book of Revelation in Our God's Holy Bible the ones who will be going to hell for eternity of adulterers, fornicators, all liars, the unbelieving, the ones who have rejected

Jesus as their Lord and Savior, murderers, and ones who have NOT lived a righteous lifestyle unto God. (Revelation 21:8)

Yes, time now IS short, and is now growing shorter until Jesus Christ comes back toward earth for Our God's great rapture of Christian souls, for all those who have been saved from their sins in Jesus' shed blood, and who are then living a righteous lifestyle for God.

Yes, sin will NEVER enter heaven.

Those living in a sinful lifestyle when they physically die, or when Our God's rapture takes place, will NOT enter heaven with Jesus.

Yes, Jesus and Father God are merciful and We will, God will, forgive their sins, cleanse them of ALL unrighteousness when they ASK and when they RECEIVE, and when they REPENT and come out of their evil lifestyle and LIVE for God on a daily and nightly basis.

Yes, if you do, or if any person does, tolerate habitual sin in your or their life, it does give Satan an opportunity to rip you off, to harm you, to torment you, to deceive you, even to destroy you.

In order to teach Our God's Holy Bible effectively, with power and with love, you must LIVE A HOLY LIFE unto God.

Yes, salt water and fresh water cannot come out of the same fountain at the same time.

Even so, Bible teaching truth and deliberate lies cannot be spoken with power from the same mouth.

Yes, do clean up your lifestyle and clean up your words—live a holy life unto God—then go and speak the true Holy Bible teachings to your people, THEN Our God WILL prosper both your living and prosper your Bible teaching.

Yes, do read in Our God's Holy Bible where God spoke to the Israelites who came out of Egypt, how God spoke to them from one mountain how God would reward them if they always stayed true to God, and how God warned them from the other mountain how they would be persecuted and tormented if they turned away from God and became corrupt. (blessings given on Mt. Gerizim in Deuteronomy 28:1-14, and curses given on Mt. Ebal in Deuteronomy 28:15-68)

Yes, it IS the same God Who does speak to you today as Who spoke to them then, and these same rewards from God and same punishments from God still hold true today.

Yes, some people think they have a lot of "bad luck" in their life with poor health, lack of finances, lack of opportunities for advancements, loss of property, harmful accidents.

This is not their "bad luck", but it is because they don't know God, don't love God, don't honor God, don't live for God, don't obey God, don't know God's divine will for their life, don't know God's promises to them, don't claim God's provisions for them, and are not living under the good benefits from God as promised to them in Our God's Holy Bible, the blessings promised to them on the mountain, the same benefits promised to the Israelites before they entered the promised land, IF ONLY they would ALWAYS stay true to God, that ALL would ALWAYS go well with them.

Yes, do encourage ALL the people that you do teach to read and study the entire Bible for themselves, THEN THEY will know the WHOLE TRUTH of Our God's teachings.

Yes, all the way through Our God's Holy Bible is taught the truth of how God rewards the just and how God allows the wicked to be punished.

Yes, Our God does reward today the people who know God, who love God, who live a righteous lifestyle unto God—whereas, Our God gives to each of mankind, as well as to each nation on earth, time to repent, time to come out of a sinful lifestyle, time to come to God for forgiveness, time to turn from their wicked ways, time to live a righteous lifestyle unto God.

However, if they do not repent and turn to God in a given time period allowed by THEIR holy Creator God, and if they continue to grow in worse condition of turning from God, THEN Our God, Who is a just and righteous God, must allow them to be destroyed even as the flood destroyed all the evil people in Noah's day who refused to turn from their corruption.

Yes, Our God does know each of Our God's children, does know each of their human weaknesses, and Our God has given each of Our God's Christian children the gift of Our God's Holy Spirit to live within them to teach them how to know God and how to live righteously for God and how to be rewarded by God.

Yes, do learn to flow better with Our God's Holy Spirit within you, helping you live and teach victoriously to Our God's glory on earth.

Hallelujah!

Praises to Our Father God for this divine message!

Hallelujah!

LETTER NUMBER THIRTY ONE
FOR CHURCH GROWTH

Dear Christian Pastors and All Holy Bible Teachers,

I have been praying about what to write to the pastors and the Bible teachers that will encourage them in the Lord. I like the sermon our pastor preached last Sunday about what we can learn from the trees. Before each sermon, I pray and ask God what He wants me to learn from this sermon that I can take away to improve my life. Also when I read two books a month of twenty four a year plus my daily Bible reading, I ask God to help me to learn one good thing from each book that I can apply to my life that will improve it, for twenty-four improvements a year. The one thing that God showed to me about this sermon on the trees was that for us to "bloom where we are planted."

God showed to me now after my fifty-one years in the Nashville area, He is transplanting me to the Atlanta area, where I can "bloom better." Oasis Church promotes music, dance, and graphic lights with stage design, but it does not promote framed oil and watercolor paintings. If I join my daughter's large Methodist Church in Georgia, I can rent one of their arts and crafts booths during the Christmas holidays to show and sell my art work each year. Also art buyers from the New York Galleries come to the Atlanta area often and buy many paintings for resale in New York. Also there are many other places in the Atlanta area where I can display and sell art paintings.

There is one thing that I want to comment on, and then relate how it applies to my art work. In a Sunday's newspaper, I read an article by an expert telling how to be a better salesperson. He quoted someone as saying, "The only progress you make is by the people you meet and the books you read." Whenever I hear someone quote that, I just cringe, because I know it is only a half truth. To me, the whole truth is, "The only progress we make is by the people we meet, the books we read, the experimenting we do, and what God, Himself, downloads of His truths into our minds, spirits, and hearts."

I would like to give you a small example of what I mean by this, by using my art training and experience in sketching portraits. As I began my third year of college with a major in art at the University of Washington in Seattle, a live model was placed before us thirty students. Our instructor said, "Draw without using lines." Then he left the class, went downstairs to the coffee shop, and had coffee with his friends. In my eighth year of college with a major in art at Peabody College in Nashville, Tennessee, a live model was placed before us thirty students. Our instructor said, "Just draw what you see."

Now compare this art teaching in these two colleges with what was being taught in the best art college in the nation of Art Center College of Design in Los Angeles. One of my beginning classes there was called, "Analysis of Form," and was taught by the world famous instructor, Lorser Feidelson. The class met one day a week for six hours for thirteen weeks. On a Wednesday morning, he gave a three-hour lecture and demonstration on how to draw the eyes. Then on Wednesday afternoon, we drew different people's eyes for three hours. The following Wednesday morning, he gave a three-hour lecture and demonstration on how to draw the nose. That was followed by us thirty students drawing noses for three hours on Wednesday afternoon. In the following Wednesdays for thirteen weeks, we learned to draw the mouth, the ears, the face, and other parts of the body with six hours of lectures, demonstrations, and practices on each part.

In the universities, we learned by our own practice, and from observing the other student's projects.

In books, we learned construction of the eyes and expressions of the eyes. In Mr. Feidelson's class we learned construction, expression, sexual traits, family traits, nationalities, age, size, position in the face, and other things about drawing the eyes and other parts of the head and bodies. We also learned by our own practice, and by the practice of seeing other students' drawings. After taking his class, we should be able to draw one eye, and a trained person should be able to see, "That's the right eye of an eight year old Japanese girl, who is a bit sleepy, who favors her maternal grandmother."

Here is an example of how we learn by experimenting: One year at the Tennessee State Fair, a high school student artist and I were in an art booth for the Tennessee Art League. We were taking turns sketching portraits for free. I saw that every portrait she sketched, she did well on their eyes and mouth, but she put her OWN nose on EVERY portrait she drew. The following year, this same high school student and I were in the same booth, taking turns sketching free portraits for the public. I noticed a fantastic improvement in her sketches from the year before! She was putting the right noses on the right people! I asked her, "You are so much better than last year! What happened to you?!" She said, "I sketched ten to twelve portraits each day all summer in front of the Ryman Auditorium." It was PRACTICE ALONE that improved her sketching skills tremendously!

The fourth way is by God helping us. In my sketching children's portraits, Jesus said to me, **"Just put down the eyes and hairstyles, and I will do the rest."** God's Holy Spirit within me teaches me things like, **"Set your models in the shade, and their eyes won't squint into the sun."** Also things like, **"Draw their right eye first, so you can compare your drawing to draw their left eye."** For a squirming two-year-old, **"Stare at their right eye, memorize it, and draw it from memory."** I'm now writing a book titled, *Art Lessons Beyond The Classes*, of forty things God has taught me after my eight years of college with an art major.

Blessings! Velma

Yes, Our God's beloved Christian children of Our God's beloved Christian pastors and ALL of Our God's beloved Holy Bible teachers, YOUR heavenly Father God does love you, does GUIDE you, and does HELP you to be successful in your walk with, your talk with, and your preaching and teaching about Our God's Holy Triune God, the love of God for ALL of mankind, the power of God to provide for and to protect ALL of Our God's mankind on Our God's planet Earth.

Yes, YOUR God IS all-powerful!

Yes, nothing good and nothing seemingly bad can happen at any time, day or night, on Our God's planet Earth without Our God's knowledge and wisdom permitting it to happen.

Yes, YOUR Holy Triune God is always in full control of everything and every event that happens on Our God's planet Earth at all times.

Yes, Our God spoke the words and Our God's planet Earth was created out of nothing, and Our God hung Our God's planet Earth on nothing, and a God Who can do that can surely do whatever Our God chooses to do.

Yes, Jesus Christ IS the spoken Word of His heavenly Father God. (John 1:1-3)

Yes, Jesus Christ has all power in heaven and earth given to Him after His resurrection from the dead after He had been crucified on Calvary's cruel cross, dying for the sins of mankind. (Matthew 28:18)

Yes, the supreme divine love of Jesus Christ for ALL of Our God's mankind on earth caused Jesus to shed His holy blood and die on Calvary's cross so that each person now alive on Our God's planet Earth could COME to Jesus, could ASK Jesus to forgive ALL their sins and wrongdoings, could make Jesus the Lord, Master, and Savior of their life, could come out of a sinful lifestyle and live for God while alive on earth, and could enter heaven forever AFTER their one life on earth is over.

Yes, do tell people that time on earth is running out!

Soon earth time WILL change to Our God's millennial time, when one day is as a thousand years. (2 Peter 3:8)

Yes, SOON Our God's Jesus Christ will be told by His Father God to, "Go! Go back toward earth for Our God's great catching away to heaven ALL of Our God's saved and sanctified beloved Christians of God; catch them away to the heavenlies in a split second and bring them BACK to their heavenly home for Our God's great wedding supper of The Lamb of God!"

Yes, get ready to go!

Stay ready to go!

Keep your garments spotless from sin!

Come out of a sinful lifestyle and live for God while alive on earth.

Yes, sin will NEVER enter heaven.

Only people who have their sins forgiven and washed away in the holy shed blood of Jesus and who are rebuking sin in their lifestyle, who are living righteously for God, WILL enter heaven with Jesus at Our God's great rapture of Our God's obedient souls on earth.

Yes, God demands holiness in each of mankind's thoughts, words, and deeds.

Yes, do live a holy life on earth to God, with Jesus Christ as your example and Our God's Holy Spirit within you as your Guide.

Yes, Jesus Christ is coming back to Our God's planet Earth SOON, so do get ready, stay ready, and warn others to get ready and to stay ready for the SOON return of Jesus for Our God's great rapture of obedient souls on earth.

Yes, time is SHORT and is growing shorter day by day until

Jesus returns toward earth coming in clouds of great glory with ALL of His holy angels with Him, and EVERY EYE will see Him.

Yes, soon every knee will bow and all will proclaim that Jesus Christ is King of all kings and Lord of all lords to the glory of God the Father in heaven.

Yes, do worship and do praise YOUR Holy Triune God many, many times daily and nightly, as this is WHEN YOUR heavenly Father God does fill you with love, with power, with knowledge and wisdom, with discernment, to make the right choices in your life that you must make daily and nightly.

Yes, before you do make ANY important decision in your life concerning yourself and concerning others, do PRAY about it, pray in Jesus' holy name, do ASK your God for knowledge and wisdom concerning all matters, and YOUR Father God WILL HEAR YOU and WILL GIVE YOU the knowledge and wisdom to make right decisions that will benefit you, benefit others, and will glorify God on earth.

Yes, you cannot out-give God.

When you give to promote Our God's gospel worldwide and give to help the helpless with love to Our God's glory on earth, Our heavenly Father God WILL GIVE TO YOU double and even more than double.

Yes, it is possible for individuals and even for churches to tithe their way out of debt.

Yes, YOUR heavenly Father God is ALWAYS your Provider of ALL good things, and Our God does give to you the power to get wealth, that you will be helped, that others will be helped, that your church will be helped, in order that you and others may be able to help the helpless with love to Our God's glory on earth.

Yes, when you do see another person, another family, and another church or body of believers in need, and you ARE ABLE to help them, do help them in the way that they need it the most, and in return for your good deeds to help them, your loving God WILL HELP YOU in the way that you need it the most.

255

Yes, your God is WELL ABLE to help you, your loved ones, and your church, WHEN you do ASK for Our God's help, when you ask it in Jesus' holy name, when your church congregation ask it in one accord, that you will be helped, that others will be helped, and that Our God will be glorified in your lives and in your church congregation's lives.

Yes, Our God's Holy Spirit is your Helper, sent by YOUR heavenly Father God to ALWAYS help you and help your congregations, when you and they ARE READY to RECEIVE Our God's divine help in any situation, in EVERY situation.

Yes, Jesus Christ is still your physical Healer, so do pray believing prayers for healing for your sick and afflicted members of your family, your other loved ones, for members of your congregations, even for strangers in public places, pray BELIEVING prayers in Jesus' holy name, then WATCH Our God work according to your faith in Jesus Christ as your divine Healer.

Yes, Jesus Christ healed EVERY PERSON who came to Him and who asked Him for healing, when Jesus walked this earth nearly two thousand years ago, and Jesus Christ is now alive in heaven, and Jesus Christ STILL has His same power to heal anyone today who has ENOUGH FAITH in Jesus for their healing today.

Yes, do build up your faith in Jesus for your physical healing by reading, studying, and believing EVERY PART of Our God's Holy Bible, by claiming ALL the promises of God, by obeying the CONDITIONS of all the promises of God, and then WATCH Our God do HIS work in answer to your believing prayer prayed in Our God Jesus' holy name.

Yes, Our heavenly Father God does LONG to show Himself, Myself, strong in people's lives, who love God with their total being, who honor God, who obey God, who are willing to serve and help others with love, that people can know God, can love God, can be benefited by God, can be saved by the shed blood of Jesus to cleanse them of all sin and unrighteousness, that they can come out of ALL unrighteous lifestyle, can live for God, and can be greatly benefited by God.

Yes, it IS Our God's holy will that ALL of mankind prosper and be in good health at all times. (3 John 1:2)

Yes, your prosperity comes from God. (Deuteronomy 8:18)

Your good health also comes from God.

Yes, when you know God, live for God, obey God, and your soul grows more in God, your prosperity, your good health, your good relationships with others, will all prosper as all of this is Our God's rewards to you as your soul grows in God.

Yes, do TRY to grow to be more like Jesus Christ, Who did set the example for you of how to LOVE people, how to HELP people, how to SERVE people, how to OBEY God, how to honor God, how to teach others about the love, power, justice, and forgiveness of THEIR holy Creator, THEIR heavenly Father God.

Yes, do study, do memorize, do live by, do teach others, ALL the words Jesus spoke as recorded in Our God's Holy Bible.

Yes, this whole earth may someday pass away, but ALL the words Jesus spoke in love and in truth when Jesus walked this earth nearly two thousand years ago will NEVER pass away, but they WILL be fulfilled in due time.

Yes, Jesus is God. (John 10:30)

Yes, do love, do honor, do praise YOUR Lord and Savior, Jesus Christ, as you do love, honor, and praise YOUR heavenly Father God.

Do KEEP a holy praise to YOUR Holy Triune God centered on your mind and in your heart at ALL times, and you will be KEPT in perfect peace at ALL times. (Isaiah 26:3)

Yes, your joy comes from the Lord, Who made heaven and earth. (Psalm 121:2)

Praise God continually until your joy and your strength come.

Praise God and depression and anxiety and worry will flee from you.

Rejoice in the Lord!

Again I say, rejoice in the Lord, your Provider, your Giver of ALL good benefits in your life now on earth AND in your future life in heaven with YOUR Holy Triune God.

Hallelujah!

Praises to Our Father God for this wonderful prophetic message for ALL church growth.

Hallelujah!

Praises to Our heavenly Father God!

Dear Christian Pastors and All Holy Bible Teachers,

We have been praying for our pastor's physical healing of his foot problem. I am truly amazed and shocked at how many people in our Oasis Church are now having physical problems.

More than a year ago, the pastor had given me his permission to pass out my monthly family newsletter to the leaders at our church, so they could read the prophetic message in every issue. The Lord had already told me to give them to my Sunday School class so I had been handing them out in class.

Since I am selling my house in Brentwood, Tennessee in December and am relocating to Marietta, Georgia in January 2017, Father God wanted me to take a survey of the people in our church who have been receiving the newsletter and ask them if they wanted to keep receiving the newsletter. If they did want to keep receiving it, to give to me their home mailing addresses. This way, they could continue to receive it after I relocate.

After twenty-eight years of our publishing the monthly family newsletter with a prophetic message in every issue for twenty-five years, the circulation now is about 210 copies going to families in twenty-three states. Now the Lord is slowly changing the family newsletter into a Christian magazine, continuing with a prophetic message from either Father God or Lord Jesus in every issue. The Lord has given to me the Scripture verse for the newsletter of Philippians 4:8 as our guide. He wants me to publish whatever things are true, honest, just, pure, lovely, good report, virtue, and praise, and for us to think on these things.

I especially want to receive and report on people helping people with love to God's glory. I also want to hear from widows and widowers the twelve best things of their marriages when their spouses were alive. I want to collect about forty of each of these Christian testimonies, publish a shortened version in the newsletter, and publish a longer version in book form. I now have about half of the needed forty testimonies for each of these two books. Anyone is invited to submit the good things that God is doing in their lives for publication to encourage people. What God will do for one of His children, He will do for any when the right conditions are met. God is good!

When I began phoning people and asking them if they wanted to continue receiving the newsletter, everyone I spoke with wanted to keep receiving the newsletter, except one lady who said she was too busy to read it.

As I spoke with people from our church, I was amazed at what they were telling me! The amazing part was that EVERYONE I spoke with, with the exception of our Sunday School teacher Betsy Flick, had physical problems that they wanted prayer for healing for themselves and for others. Then I got a phone call from our friend Pam Morris who told me that Betsy had fallen at night, broken her foot, called 911, was in the hospital, and may need surgery! I added Betsy's name and our pastor's name to my long list of people for us to pray for healing on Sunday morning after our Bible teaching and sharing class.

Our Oasis Church now has many Life Groups, where people meet at church or in private homes, for studying specific subjects, making friends in small groups, and praying for their needs. So far as I know now of all the more than forty Life Groups, none of them are listed specifically as prayer groups.

Before the merger of The Lord's Chapel with Oasis Church twelve years ago, our Monday evening prayer meetings were well attended by the leaders and members of The Lord's Chapel. We took turns praying for ourselves, our loved ones, our church, our nation, and other prayer needs. At the merger, this Monday evening prayer meeting was cancelled by Oasis Church.

As I missed this weekly prayer meeting so much, I decided

to try to begin the Monday evening prayer meetings again at Oasis Church as a Life Group. When I asked about it, I was told, "You may have a prayer group, but only in your own home, not at Oasis Church." I was greatly disappointed in this, as there were no other prayer meetings at the church. Also, at that time, I had been paying on that church building for about thirty-six years. Also, doesn't the Bible and Jesus teach, "My house shall be a house of prayer?"

I signed up to have a prayer meeting in my own home. Only one lady signed up to come. After coming a few times, she lost her transportation and was unable to come. Later I signed up again to have a prayer meeting in my own home as a Life Group, and NO ONE signed up to come. Since I had three single ladies living with me at the time, I tried to have a prayer meeting with the four of us. Instead of praying for the needs of the people, they would rather sing and dance during our prayer time. After a few weeks of this, the people's needs were not being prayed for, so we discontinued our meetings. Now my housemate Karen and I pray together often. Sherri Cline and I pray on the phone many times. Joy!

It sounds like to me that with all these sick people at Oasis Church, that there needs to be a weekly prayer meeting there. Have it during the evening at a reasonable hour at the church building and actually PRAY for the needs of the people!

Since I wrote the above message a year ago in April 2016, and have now relocated to Georgia, I read on the internet recently that Oasis Church now has a prayer meeting at the church on Wednesday evenings. This is good, I believe, so that more people are able to attend.

At Mt. Bethel United Methodist Church in Marietta, Georgia where I am now a member, we have a church prayer meeting every first Wednesday evening of each month. We have a time of praise reports and have Communion at the meetings. At the recent time of our praise reports, nine people told of their physical healings by God. One of the healings was recently at our previous prayer meeting. Joy! I also gave a praise report that my daughter, Lori, and her family were able to close on the house that they purchased last week. That house had one hundred viewings and had thirty-five offers to purchase, even some offers above the asking price. Lori's family was able to purchase it at their asking price, because they were able to pay cash and close in only ten days! Joy! God is good!

Blessings! Velma

Yes, Our God's beloved Christian children of Our God's beloved Christian pastors and Our God's beloved Holy Bible teachers, YOUR heavenly Father God does love you, does protect you, and does provide for you, and does meet all your needs, and does meet ALL of your holy desires when you do know God, love God, honor God, and abide in God.

Yes, you do stand on the solid Rock of Jesus Christ with Jesus as your Lord, Savior, and God.

Yes, Jesus Christ NOW has ALL power in heaven and in earth, and YOUR God, Jesus Christ, is now willing and able to HELP meet ALL your needs that enables you to spread Our God's message of salvation in Jesus that forgives peoples' sins and wrongdoings, and enables them to come out of ALL known sin in their lives, and live righteously for and unto THEIR God for the rest of their life on Our God's planet Earth, then enter heaven forever after their one lifetime on earth is over.

Yes, Our God IS a just God, Who does reward the righteous-living people, and Who does discipline, punish, the unjust people who refuse to repent, to come OUT OF a sinful lifestyle, who will NOT come to God Jesus for forgiveness, who will not live a righteous lifestyle unto God.

Yes, sin will NEVER enter heaven.

Yes, even Christians living in a deliberate sinful lifestyle will NOT enter heaven unless they REPENT, come OUT OF ALL sinful lifestyle, ask God for forgiveness, then live righteously for God, for them to enter heaven in their life AFTER their one lifetime on earth.

Yes, Our God WILL NOT TOLERATE for long a person's

living in rebellion against God and against Our God's righteous ways for them to live.

Yes, Our heavenly Father God did send Jesus Christ to Our God's planet Earth to TEACH people about THEIR true God, their holy Creator and Sustainer God, to live a holy lifestyle unto HIS heavenly Father God, for ALL people to know God, love God, obey God, live for God, and be rewarded by God for their obedience to THEIR holy God.

Yes, Our God SENT Jesus to Our God's planet Earth to live a holy life unto God, shed His precious holy blood as a ransom to THEIR Creator God for mankind's sins, transgressions, and iniquities, to reunite Our God's mankind with THEIR holy Creators, for them to know God, fellowship with God, be blessed and rewarded by God, to be connected BACK to THEIR God to have life, abundant life on earth, and have everlasting joyful life in heaven with THEIR Holy Triune God.

Yes, do NOT make a mockery of Our God's Jesus' supreme sacrifice for mankind's sins of the holy shed blood of Jesus, His death and resurrection, that freed ALL of mankind from eternal punishment in hell separated from THEIR true God, but do rejoice in the only true way to YOUR heavenly Father God that Jesus has made available to ALL who will accept Jesus as Lord and Savior from their sins, who will then go and sin no more.

Yes, Jesus is the ONLY TRUE Savior with enough power to save each of mankind from their sins, when they do COME to Jesus and ASK Jesus to save them, accept this free salvation from Jesus, then LIVE a RIGHTEOUS LIFESTYLE for God until the end of their days on earth.

Yes, Jesus is YOUR physical Healer. (Isaiah 53:5)

Yes, ASK Jesus for physical healing, then praise Jesus and your heavenly Father God many times daily until the complete healing manifests itself.

Yes, Jesus Christ IS the same yesterday, and today, and forever! (Hebrews 13:8)

Yes, claim all these good promises to you from Jesus as recorded in Our God's Holy Bible, meet the conditions of these promises, and according to your faith in your Lord Jesus Christ, your desires and all holy requests will be granted to you by your Holy Triune God.

Yes, do draw nearer to YOUR God, and YOUR God WILL draw nearer to you. (James 4:8)

Yes, if Our God be for you, who can be against you? (Romans 8:31)

Yes, become "on fire" for your Holy Triune God, as Our God Jesus Christ said that He will spit out the lukewarm Christians. (Revelations 3:16)

How do you become "on fire" for and with YOUR Holy Triune God?

You become "on fire" for and with your God by PRAYER, FASTING, praising God, by reading, studying, and memorizing Our God's Holy Bible, and by knowing God better, by living righteously with and for God, by living Our God's truth, and by TEACHING Our God's truth.

Yes, seek to know YOUR Holy Triune God better.

Seek to honor and obey YOUR Holy Triune God more.

Put away ALL evil habits.

Redeem the time as time now on planet Earth is running out, as you do know time now to be on earth.

Yes, soon time on earth will be counted in Our God's millennial time, when a thousand years is equal to one day. (2 Peter 3:8)

Yes, what you now do with and for your God MUST be done quickly, before time on earth runs out.

Yes, Jesus DOES come quickly.

Yes, the fields are now even more white to harvest. (John 4:35)

Yes, pray for YOUR heavenly Father God to send MORE FAITHFUL workers into Our God's harvest fields to win more souls to YOUR Lord Jesus Christ.

Yes, winning more and more souls to Jesus Christ is what is NOW important in Our God's harvest fields, as time is now shorter than most people do realize until Jesus Christ splits Our God's great Eastern skies coming back towards earth for Our God's great catching away to heaven ALL of the saved-in-Jesus and right-living-unto-God beloved saints, beloved Christians, children of God.

Yes, do stay prayed up and do stay fasted up and do keep ready to go, to be caught up to heaven in ANY split second.

Yes, do warn others to get right with Our God's ONLY beloved Savior, Jesus Christ, STAY right with God, and do KEEP READY to go at ALL times.

Yes, you do NOT know the day nor the hour WHEN YOUR Lord Jesus Christ WILL RETURN for Our God's great catching away. (Matthew 24:36)

Yes, ONLY YOUR heavenly Father God knows the day and the hour when the time is right for Father God to SEND His only begotten Son Jesus Christ back towards earth for Our God's great rapture of ALL of Our God's saved and sanctified Christian souls, and YOUR heavenly Father God does SAY TO YOU, the time is SHORT and is now growing shorter day by day.

Pray in ALL your lost loved ones.

Do warn the unrighteous to get right with Jesus Christ, come out of ALL sinful lifestyle and live for God, if they do want to go to heaven in their afterlife, after their ONE life on earth is over.

Yes, sin will NEVER enter heaven.

Yes, all people are sinners by their own sin and by their sinful nature they inherited from Adam's sin.

People cannot save themselves without Jesus saving them.

No other being, dead or alive, has the power to save anyone from their eternal soul going to hell except Jesus Christ, Who has paid the price with His holy shed blood on Calvary's cross, His death and resurrection, to pay for all of mankind's sins, transgressions, and iniquities, so that whosoever will, may come to Jesus with a repentant heart, ASK Jesus to forgive their sins and save them, accept this free salvation from Jesus, then go and sin no more, but live a righteous life for and unto God for the rest of their life on earth—THEN they WILL BE on their way to heaven to live for eternity.

Yes, eternity is a long, long time.

Yes, if a person refuses Jesus Christ as their Lord and Savior, and if they die in their sins and lift up their eyes in hell, they can and will be trapped in hell for eternity, where the fire is never quenched and the worm never dies. (Mark 9:44-48)

Yes, do warn the unrighteous people about hell.

Yes, pray for the unrighteous people, who are NOW living in a sinful lifestyle that they WILL come to Jesus for salvation, will COME OUT of ALL their sinful lifestyle, live for God, and avoid going to hell and remaining in hell after their one life on earth.

Yes, Father God and Jesus Christ have provided the ONLY WAY for a person to avoid their eternal soul from going to hell after their one life on earth, as Jesus Christ is the ONLY SAVIOR with enough power to save them, and they MUST accept Jesus while they are NOW ALIVE on earth.

Tomorrow may be too late for them to accept Jesus Christ as Savior.

Yes, do explain Our God's truth to all people you have influence over.

Encourage ALL people to read and study Our God's Holy Bible, as every word in Our God's Holy Bible is true. (John 17:17)

Yes, when people know Our God's truth, it will set them free. (John 8:32)

Yes, Jesus Christ is truth. (John 14:6)

Know Jesus Christ and know the truth.

Know Jesus Christ and know the way of salvation.

Yes, know and teach the truth of Jesus Christ.

Live for God, obey God, love God with your total being, be

rewarded by God, then people will believe your true message and WILL come to Jesus for salvation before it is too late.

Hallelujah!

Praises to Our heavenly Father God for this true message for church growth!

Hallelujah!

Praises to Our God!

Dear Christian Pastors and All Holy Bible Teachers,

Recently I went online on my computer for about six hours and read about what several Christian prophets and prophetesses have to say about the times we are now living in before the soon return of Jesus Christ for our God's great rapture of all the saved and obedient Christians. The Bible Code message found in either the Hebrew of the Old Testament or the Greek of the New Testament reads, **"President B. Obama, re-elected U. S. President, 2012, sworn in twice**." This message was found written in code in the Bible six months before the 2012 U. S. Presidential election.

Another message found in the Bible Code is, **"President B. Obama directs the war from the underground bunker."** Since President Obama is no longer in office, this message did not come true.

It did not come true yet about the war on the United States because our God has had mercy on us Americans, and He has given all of the wicked Americans more time to repent of all of our evil ways, turn to God, seek God's forgiveness, be saved in Jesus and live righteously for God, for our God to forgive our sins and heal America and make America great again with our God the Lord and Ruler of America.

After bringing the Israelites out of their bondage in Egypt, when they rebelled against God, God was ready to slay them all except Moses, who had found favor with God. When Moses interceded for the Israelites, God relented and postponed some of their destruction. I believe that God in His mercy, because of the prayers of the righteous-living Christians who have been interceding for America, God has given these wicked Americans TIME to REPENT. Our God IS a merciful God, but our God is a just God, Who will tolerate sin in the people for only so long, until He will act to wipe them off the face of the earth.

Some of the prophecies that I read online about the future of America is that there will be riots in a lot of the major cities with burning fires, flooding, looting, broken glass, and violence. It is prophesized to be caused by the government cutbacks on welfare benefits of food stamps, health care, and other free benefits.

I read online the seventeen countries worldwide that are the most in debt, and which are believed to be headed for bankruptcy. The top of the list is Japan, which is at 243.2% of GDP, with Greece at second place with 173.8% of GDP, and the United States in tenth place at 104.5% of GDP. I heard a business man on the news being interviewed about the economy of Japan. It is in serious trouble financially as a lot of their manufacturing businesses are now pulling out of Japan and are moving to Brazil. They believe that Brazil is a more stable country now than Japan and other countries for their businesses.

The Bible teaches, "It is God Who gives you the power to get wealth." (Deuteronomy 8:18) When you look at the religions of Japan, you see that Christians in Japan are 2.3% of the population. About 50% are Buddhist and most of the rest are Shinto, or of no religion.

When you look at the religions of the United States, you see that now only about 70% claim themselves as Christians, compared to a few years ago when 85% claimed to be Christians. In 2016 in the U.S. about 23% claim themselves to be unaffiliated with religion. As our American people are turning away from honoring God as head of our lives and head of our governments and schools, and even as head of our churches, our God is slowly turning away from us Americans. When people reject God, they become worthless to their Creator and are headed for destruction!

One prophetic message that I read online, stated that as much as 75% of the United States population could be destroyed, including all of the lukewarm Christians, with only 25% of the U. S. people spared from destruction, who are the strong Christians!

I got on my knees and prayed about this and asked Father

God if this prophetic message is still true? Father God replied something like this, **"Yes, it is still true, unless these wicked Americans repent, turn back to God, come out of all sinful lifestyle, and ask God's forgiveness and ask God to heal their land."** He also said something like this, **"The pastors of the churches are lukewarm and the Christians in the churches are lukewarm. There are the sins of abortion, homosexuality, theft, lying, adultery, and other sins in the churches, and the pastors are not preaching against it."**

Then I asked Father God if even the babies and small children in the families of the 75% of the U.S. people would also be destroyed? He answered me by showing to me in the book of Joshua in the Bible, how when the people of Israel destroyed the city of Jericho, how the man Achan kept some of the items from the spoils of Jericho that were dedicated to God as holy. Because he disobeyed God with this theft, not only Achan and his wife and children were stoned and burned, but also all of his animals and other possessions were destroyed. God showed to me that evil seeds of rebellion against God can be planted even in small children, so they can also be destroyed along with their rebellious parents. God is able to protect ALL of His obedient children.

I found a map of the United States that prophetically shows what ten cities Russia plans to bomb, where nine of the cities are our east and west coast port cities. This would cripple the U. S. foreign trade at our harbors so that we cannot import and export oil, food, and other supplies. Long bread lines have been prophesied for America. One preacher advises people of the U. S. to store up six weeks of food and water for our whole families.

Father God showed to me in a dream that no obedient Christian will have to go without food for more than three days, or God will feed them with manna. In the dream manna looked like boiled oatmeal and it tasted sweet, like honey had been added. Praise God for taking care of all the obedient Christians who live for God.

Blessings! Velma

Yes, Our God's beautiful beloved Christian children of Our God's beloved Christian pastors and ALL of Our God's beloved Holy Bible teachers, YOUR heavenly Father God does love you, does provide for you, and does protect you, your congregations, and all of your loved ones.

Yes, your heavenly Father God does hear ALL of your prayers and all of your petitions to God for yourself, for your church congregations, and for all of your other loved ones.

Yes, your God does ANSWER ALL of your prayers prayed with great faith in Jesus, prayed in the holy name of Jesus that will help you, will help others, and that WILL bring glory to your God on earth.

Yes, do pray, pray, pray, for a long time to YOUR God, pray in the holy name of Jesus, pray with great faith in Jesus as your Lord, Savior, Guide, Provider God.

Yes, Jesus Christ NOW has ALL power in heaven and in earth, and your God, Jesus Christ, is WORTHY of ALL of Our God's mankind's praises and adoration, because of ALL that Jesus has done for mankind, what Jesus is doing now for mankind, and what Jesus will do for mankind. (Matthew 28:20)

Yes, Jesus Christ opened the way, the ONLY way, for mankind to be saved from their sins, live for God, be reconciled to THEIR holy Creator God, and enjoy THEIR heavenly home forever.

Yes, Jesus Christ did come to earth to give each of mankind life, abundant life on earth, and eternal life in heaven.

Yes, Jesus Christ is all in all, and was not anything made that was made, that does not have a part of Jesus Christ now in it. (John 1:1-3)

Yes, Jesus Christ IS the only begotten Son of HIS heavenly Father God. (John 3:16)

Yes, Jesus Christ has been raised from the dead, ascended into Our God's great heaven above, and is now at the right hand of HIS heavenly Father God to tell Him to, "Go! Go BACK toward earth and claim and catch away to Our God's great heaven above ALL of Our God's beloved saved and sanctified children of God!"

Yes, Our God's great rapture of souls is SOON!

Yes, get ready to go, stay ready to go, to be caught up to the heavens in a split second for Our God's RAPTURE of ALL the saved-in-Jesus and all the Christian souls who are living for God.

Yes, do pray in ALL your lost loved ones.

Yes, witness to the people you meet about Jesus and about the SOON arrival of Jesus.

Yes, do encourage people to come OUT OF ALL unholy lifestyle, live completely for God, know God, love God, honor God, and then do love and do help others where they do need it the most.

Yes, when you help meet the needs and holy desires of others, your God WILL help to meet your own needs.

Yes, YOUR God does have UNLIMITED power and unlimited resources to shower down onto each of mankind, when their soul has grown enough in God to handle, use wisely, all of these resources to help themselves, help others, and to bring glory to Our God's name on earth.

Yes, Jesus always brought glory to His Father God's name when Jesus walked this earth nearly two thousand years ago.

Yes, Jesus Christ still brings glory to His Father God's name on earth AND in heaven today.

Yes, soon every knee will bow before Jesus, and EVERY tongue will confess that Jesus Christ is Lord of ALL, to the glory of Our Father God on earth.

Yes, do praise your Father God now for this message for church growth.

Yes, do draw near to YOUR God, and your God WILL draw near to you. (James 4:8)

Yes, you do love and live for and do serve a powerful God.

Yes, YOUR Holy Triune God IS ALWAYS ABLE to build up the righteous and to tear down and destroy the wicked among you.

Yes, unless the habitual sinners in these wicked Americas do REPENT and turn back to God and come out of their sinful lifestyle of rejecting God and rejecting living a wholesome lifestyle unto God, they shall ALL likewise perish, as Our God WILL ALLOW THEIR ENEMIES to come in and crush them.

Yes, Our God's patience IS WEARING THIN waiting for these wicked Americans to repent, to come out of their sinful lifestyle, to come BACK to THEIR true God, to TURN from their wicked ways, to ASK Our God to forgive their sins, and to heal their lands of these wicked Americas.

Yes, Our God is NOW calling for righteous living of ALL of Our God's children who do call themselves Christians.

Yes, Our God cannot and will not reward Christians who do not live for God on a daily and nightly basis.

Yes, Our God's rewards of good health, good finances, good opportunities for advancement in ALL areas of your life, are for those Christian leaders who do know God, who love God with their total being, who live for God, who love others, and who serve THEIR God by loving and by serving others to Our God's glory on earth.

Yes, when Our God's only begotten Son Jesus Christ walked this earth nearly two thousand years ago, He was the only perfect Human Being Who grew to maturity, and Jesus Christ did set the perfect example for you to follow in prayer, in fasting, in honoring His Father God in heaven, in teaching Our God's truth to the crowds and congregations, by healing the sick and afflicted, by obeying Our God's decrees and obeying the laws of the land, by feeding the hungry, and by helping the helpless with love to Our God's glory.

Yes, do go forward and do the works Jesus did in love honoring His Father God and by loving, teaching, and helping others.

Yes, didn't Jesus say to you in Our God's Holy Bible that He is going to HIS heavenly Father God, and that He will send Our God's Holy Spirit to endue you with power from on high, and that you could do the works that He did, and even greater works than these can you do? (John 14:12)

Yes, seek Jesus.

Seek to be filled with Our God's Holy Spirit with power from on high.

Seek to do the works Jesus did, so that others will be taught Our God's great truths, so that others can come out of bondage, be helped spiritually, physically, mentally, emotionally, financially, and be prosperous in EVERY good way to Our God's glory on earth.

Yes, doesn't Our God's Holy Bible teach you that no good gift will be withheld from those who live righteously? (Psalm 84:11)

Yes, Our God does give ALL GOOD GIFTS to Our God's obedient Christian children, who know God, love God, live for God, honor God, and who do love and do help themselves and their fellow mankind.

Yes, you ARE your brother's keeper.

Yes, HELP your neighbors and other loved ones to know God, to love God, to love and help and serve others to Our God's glory on earth, and THEN they WILL BE REWARDED by THEIR loving heavenly Father God.

Yes, Our God IS a great God of rewards, Who does ENJOY showering down ALL GOOD GIFTS on Our God's loving, obedient, and helpful mankind.

Yes, Our God does tell all people who are now alive on earth, does tell them in Our God's book of Deuteronomy in Our God's Holy Bible, what Our God will do for Our God's people who do know God, love God, and obey God, and Our God does tell the people, all the people, what Our just God will do unto the wicked people who turn away from God, who reject God, and who live in a sinful lifestyle by loving and serving objects and people rather than loving and serving the true God.

Yes, you cannot enter heaven if you are living in a sinful lifestyle when you die your one death on earth, as sin will NEVER enter heaven.

Yes, in order for a person to enter heaven, they MUST have Jesus Christ as their Lord and Savior from ALL their sins, transgressions, and iniquities, and they must REPENT from ALL sinful lifestyle and live a righteous lifestyle unto God for the rest of their life on earth.

Yes, do warn the wicked to come OUT of a sinful lifestyle and live for God on earth, if they do want to enter heaven forever.

Yes, Jesus forgives mankind's sins when they REPENT, come out of ALL sinful lifestyle, ASK Jesus to forgive them, ACCEPT this free gift of salvation from Jesus, then go and SIN NO MORE.

Yes, Jesus does give the gift of Our God's Holy Spirit to live within a person to help them to KNOW right from wrong and HELP them to live a righteous lifestyle for God.

Yes, Jesus promised never to leave you nor forsake you, but to always go with you to the end of the world. (Matthew 28:20)

Yes, Jesus loves you.

Yes, Jesus helps you.

Yes, Jesus now intercedes for you with HIS heavenly Father God.

Yes, Jesus comes quickly!

Do WARN people that Jesus does come quickly for Our God's great catching away of ALL of Our God's beloved saved-in-Jesus and obedient Christian children of God!

Hallelujah!

Praises to Our heavenly Father God for this prophetic message for church growth!

Hallelujah!

Praises to Our God!

LETTER NUMBER THIRTY FOUR
FOR CHURCH GROWTH

Dear Christian Pastors and All Holy Bible Teachers,

I have been praying about what to write to you that will encourage you. I know that our pastor is out now with a foot problem and our Sunday School teacher is out now with a foot problem. Usually, when a person is out with health problems, they can take a break from their regular work, rest up, and have time to grow closer to God.

I remember reading once in "Money" magazine that people earn more money when the stock market is going down than they do when the stock market is going up. I wondered, "How can this be, because I always thought the stock market was always played, 'buy low and sell high'?" When I read the article, I realized that the people were making money by selling high first, then buying it back lower as the market dropped. Then God showed to me that more people come to God in their troubles than they do in their prosperity.

Then the Lord showed to me in the Bible how when the Israelites were in bondage in Egypt, they cried out to God to free them as they knew that THEIR God had the power to free them. Then God did free them with great signs and wonders. You know the story of how after God did free them, they didn't trust THEIR God's power enough to defeat their enemies in the Promised Land, and disobeyed God's instructions to enter and claim the Promised Land.

After that older generation died in the wilderness and the younger generation was about to enter the promised land, God warned the younger generation that after they went into the new land, received all these free benefits from God that they had not earned, that when they became well fed and prosperous, for them to NOT forget God as it is God Who gives them the power to prosper. The younger generation promised to obey God. They obeyed God's instructions so long as their good leaders obeyed God's instructions in leading them. However, when their righteous leaders died off, the people began to drift away from God, enjoying their prosperous lives. They began to feel that they didn't need God's help for their prosperity as they could do it all by themselves.

As they drifted farther and farther away from God, God began to drift farther and farther away from them. Since they felt that they no longer needed God, they became worthless to their holy Creator. Then God had the decision to either let them be destroyed, or to let them be punished enough so that they would feel the need for God's provisions and God's protection once again. God had warned them in the book of Deuteronomy what would happen if and when they turned away from God, that there would be droughts, famines, wars, plagues, destruction, bondage, poverty, and that they would be scattered throughout foreign lands. Their leaders failed to obey God and then the people failed to obey God. They failed to teach the younger generation about the love and power and provisions and protection of God.

Each generation drifted farther and farther from loving, honoring, and serving THEIR God. Then when the Israelites were punished by their enemies, with many killed off, and the others were mistreated in the foreign lands where they were driven, they again returned to THEIR true God, Whom they knew had the power to rescue them from their bondage. God gave to them again their homeland of Israel in 1948, and now many of the Jewish people who have been scattered all over the world are returning to their home in Israel.

I believe that now we can see the same things happening in the United States, with the people slowly turning away from our true God, and our true God slowly turning away from the people. A few years ago in the U.S. 85% of the people claimed to be Christians, and now only about 70% of the U.S. population claim to be Christian. Now I read the statistics that in the U.S., 23% of the people have no religion. Even though people now in the U.S. can have their own copy of the Bible that is printed in their own language, most of the Christians don't even read it on a regular basis. If they did they would know about all the rewards from God and about all the punishments from God. If they knew these truths they could at least TRY to live by them, and they could teach their children and grandchildren these great truths.

I always look in the weekly newspaper to see what America is now reading of the top fifty best-selling books. I find that it is always about 90% fiction, and the other 10% is rarely good-character building material. Many of the movies are so filled with violence that they are hard to watch. People seek to be entertained rather than seek for spiritual growth in God. So many people when they do go to the church services seek to be entertained rather than seek to have their souls grow in God. Then the pastors and other leaders tend to give them what they want rather than feeding them the truths of the Bible that God rewards the righteous and punishes the unrighteous. When people are being punished they seek the true God more as they know that only God has the power to help them. People's souls have to be strong in God to survive if evil times overtake America.

Blessings! Velma

Yes, Our God's beautiful beloved children of Our God's beloved Christian pastors and ALL of Our God's beloved Holy Bible teachers, YOUR heavenly Father God does love you, does take care of you, and does take care of your congregations and ALL of your loved ones on Our God's planet Earth.

Yes, YOUR Holy Triune God is NOW calling ALL Christian pastors and ALL Holy Bible teachers to be true to your calling, to preach and teach your messages from Our God's Holy Bible.

Yes, do tell your congregations of Our God's rewards and blessings for their salvation in Jesus, for their answered prayers prayed in great faith, prayed in the holy name of Jesus, for their living righteously for God, and for their helping and comforting the needy among them.

Yes, do warn the wicked-living people among you of their consequences of their destruction by their enemies, unless they REPENT, come out of ALL sinful lifestyle, ask Jesus Christ for forgiveness of their sins, then go and sin no more.

Yes, Our God NEVER sends ANY of mankind to hell, but ANY of mankind can and does send themselves to hell by refusing to COME to the ONLY TRUE SAVIOR of mankind of Jesus Christ and ASKING Jesus to save them from their sins and wrongdoing, then by them refusing to live righteously for God while they are alive on earth.

Yes, the wages of sin is death. (Romans 6:23)

Yes, each person alive now on earth is given a free choice to either accept Jesus or reject Jesus, to rebuke sin from their lifestyle or continue living in a sinful lifestyle.

Yes, Our God does reward all people who choose Jesus and does reward people who live righteously for God.

Yes, people who reject Jesus and who continue living in sin do bring about their OWN PUNISHMENT, punishment in this their one life now on earth and their punishment in hell forever, where there is no hope of ever escaping.

Yes, hell is hot and it is long, and you do NOT want to go there where the worm, the soul, never dies. (Mark 9:48)

Yes, Jesus Christ has NOW prepared beautiful homes in heaven for all who choose Jesus as their Lord and Savior and all who come out of a sinful lifestyle and live for God while they are alive on earth.

Yes, Jesus does return toward earth SOON to claim and to catch away to Our God's great heaven above, for Our God's great rapture of souls that are saved-in-Jesus and are living-righteously-for-God, to abide eternally in heaven with THEIR Holy Triune God.

Yes, get ready to go!

Stay ready to go!

Time on earth is now running out, as you now know time to be on earth.

Yes, soon time on earth WILL convert to Our God's millennial time when one day will become as a thousand years. (2 Peter 3:8)

Yes, TEACH that time on earth is SHORT and is now growing SHORTER until Jesus returns toward Our God's earth for Our God's great rapture of souls of all the saved-in-Jesus and all the righteous-living-for-God obedient Christian saints to take them back to THEIR home in heaven to live eternally with THEIR Holy Triune God.

Yes, do TEACH people to get their minds off of accumulating more earthly possessions and off of entertainment and get their minds focused on spiritual growth in God.

Yes, teach them to store their treasures in heaven by their helping the helpless and needy on earth, and by their helping to promote the good news of Jesus Christ on earth.

Yes, teach people the TRUTH of Our God's Holy Bible, the

TRUTH of Jesus is their only Savior and Healer, the truth of heaven and hell, the truth of their afterlife after their one life on earth is over.

Yes, teach people about eternity where they came from their holy Creators God and where they are going.

Yes, reveal Our God's Holy Trinity to them and teach them that they can have a personal relationship with each One of Us.

Yes, teach them of Our God's promises to them and Our God's rewards to them for their obedience to God.

Teach them of Our God's love for them, of Jesus' sacrifice for their eternal salvation, and Our God's good plans for them both on earth and in their afterlife.

Yes, do teach them of the love, the goodness, and the power of THEIR holy Creators God.

Yes, Our God will NEVER leave you nor forsake you, but Our God Jesus and Our God's Holy Spirit of God WILL GO WITH YOU to the end of the world. (Matthew 28:20)

Yes, Jesus is Our God's holy God, the Ruler and Sustainer of Our God's whole universe.

Yes, nothing good and nothing bad does happen in Our God's whole universe unless Our God causes it to happen and/or Our God allows it to happen.

Yes, when good things and good events happen to a child of God, Our God does give them ALL good things to encourage them and to reward them for their good thoughts, words, and deeds.

Yes, when seemingly bad things happen to an obedient child of God, Our God does allow it to happen to draw the person closer to THEIR God for relief of the bad situation.

Yes, everything good and everything seemingly bad that EVER happens to a child of God IS ALLOWED by God for their soul's growth in God.

Yes, EVERYTHING that a person goes through in their one life on earth IS ALLOWED by God and IS USED by God for their soul's growth in God, as nothing, no experience on earth, is wasted.

Yes, the ONLY thing that you do take to heaven with you after your one life on earth is your soul's growth in God.

Yes, your soul does grow in its relationship to YOUR God, when you do SEEK to know your God better through prayer, praise, fasting, reading and studying and memorizing and applying to your life, Our God's Holy Bible teachings.

Yes, every word of Our God's Holy Bible is absolutely true. (Proverbs 30:5)

Yes, know Our God's teachings to you in Our God's Holy Bible, apply them to your own life, and then do teach them to others, and do encourage others to live by these holy teachings, and they WILL BE REWARDED for holy-living-unto-God by THEIR Holy Triune God.

Yes, Our God does reward Our God's obedient Christian children who know Jesus Christ as their Lord and Savior and who live a righteous lifestyle unto THEIR God.

Yes, won't others be drawn to YOUR God, unless they see your good works and righteous living, and your good rewards to you from your God?

Yes, what Our God does for one of Our God's Christian children, Our God will do for anyone when the right conditions are met as Our God is no partial God. (Acts 10:34)

Yes, Our God does love and does provide for all of Our God's righteous-living children of God, but Our God does give special rewards to Our God's children who have earned them by helping themselves and by helping the needy with love to Our God's glory on earth.

Yes, Our God does watch the motives and actions of EVERY person on earth at ALL times to reward those whose thoughts, words, and actions are pure, lovely, kind, and generous toward all others so that Our very generous God can, is able to, reward these virtuous acts with the good rewards the person needs the most.

Yes, as you do help to meet the needs of others, Our God will then meet your needs in the way that you need it the most.

Yes, you can NEVER out-give YOUR God as whatever love, kindness, and good gifts you do give to others will be returned to you by YOUR God double, and returned to you even MORE than double.

Yes, it IS possible for a person, and possible even for a church congregation, to tithe their way out of debt.

Yes, trust God and try your God with this tithing of ten percent of ALL of your income, with ALL of your increase, give to promote the gospel of Jesus Christ worldwide and give to help the helpless, give with love to Our God's glory on earth, then do WATCH and do SEE ALL of Our God's good benefits on you, on your loved ones, and on your church congregations.

Yes, Our God knows your heart's desires and knows your fondest wishes, and YOUR GOD IS ABLE to fulfill ALL your righteous desires when you know God, love God, obey God, live for God, when you ask Father God in Jesus' holy name, and when you do claim these good gifts and do EXPECT TO RECEIVE these good gifts that will HELP you, will HELP others, and will glorify God on Earth.

Yes, you are your brother's keeper.

Yes, share your love and your possessions with the widows, the orphans, the strangers, the homeless, the addicts, the poor, the hungry, the sick, the neglected, the ones who need your help, and YOUR heavenly Father WILL SEE your good works done with love and will ALWAYS reward you.

Yes, you can NEVER OUT-GIVE your God, as YOUR God will ALWAYS reward you double what you give and will even reward you MORE than double your giving.

Yes, YOUR Holy Triune God ALWAYS has MORE than abundant supplies to shower down on Our God's obedient children.

Yes, YOUR Father God is now, and always will be, more wealthy in ALL good supplies, more than you can even think or even imagine, and YOUR heavenly Father God does love you, does provide ALL GOOD things and all good events for you, and has now made you to be joint heirs with Our God's only begotten Son Jesus. (Romans 8:17)

Yes, worship your Lord Jesus as you do worship YOUR heavenly Father God.

Yes, do draw near to YOUR God, and your God WILL draw near to you and will provide for your every need and your every holy desire. (James 4:8)

Yes, love your God with your total being, and love and serve others to your God's glory.

Yes, let Our God's will be done on earth as it is done in heaven. (Matthew 6:10)

Hallelujah!

Praises to Our Father God for this prophetic message for church growth!

Hallelujah!

Praises to Our Father God!

Dear Christian Pastors and All Holy Bible Teachers,

I have been praying about what to write to you pastors and Bible teachers that will encourage you.

After I finished a March issue of the Garner News, I mailed it out to 228 families in twenty-three states. It always has a prophetic message in it either from Father God or from Lord Jesus that I pray will help people and encourage people in the Lord. I have been passing out copies of them to all of the leaders at Oasis Church where I currently am a member. Now the Lord wants me to mail to each of them a copy of this newsletter so that each leader can read it or not as they choose. Today I mailed to them each a copy.

It is an eight-page newsletter that I have been publishing almost monthly for nearly twenty-nine years. Each month I begin work on it with first printing a prophetic message either from Father God or from Lord Jesus, which fills up the two middle pages. Then I print about 230 copies of that. Then I try to work on the front cover with colored photos and work on the back cover with letters from relatives, or with an interesting article that is Christian related. For the front cover photos, I use the photos that I take with my camera at our yearly Garner Family Reunions in Rawls Springs, Mississippi. I know the names of my cousins who attend and know some of the names of their families. When I don't know the names of the younger generations or the names of visitors, I mail photos to my relatives and ask them questions. They email replies to me. When I make mistakes in the names, or in the correct spelling of their names, I always try to correct the mistakes in the next issue. It would be easier if they lived next door.

Nearly all of my relatives live out of the state of Tennessee. My older sister, Carolyn Hill, and her family live in central California. My younger sister, Pauline McCulloch, and her family live in southern Oregon. My younger brother, Cliff Garner, and his family live in central Florida. My daughter, Lori Davies LaVoy, and her family live in Marietta, GA. My son, Alan Davies, and his family live in northern Virginia. My husband's sister, Marcia Davies, now lives in Maryland. The first ten years of my life, I lived in southern Mississippi, where most of Mom's and Dad's relatives still live although some still live in northern Georgia, Alabama, Louisiana, Texas, and a few in Tennessee. When we have our yearly Garner Family Reunions in Mississippi, we have relatives and friends come from many states.

When we began the newsletter it was just to amuse my dad. After Mom passed away at age fifty-seven from an aneurysm, Dad sold their trailer home in Mississippi and moved to California to be near Carolyn and her family. Since he missed all of his relatives in Mississippi and Georgia and the rest of his children in different states, I asked my relatives to write to me their news. I would then add my news, compile it into a newsletter and mail out twelve copies of it with two letters to each of the six main Garner Families. We continued to do this for several years while the circulation number grew.

After my dad, Grover Garner, passed away at age sixty-four from a stroke, I thought that we would discontinue the newsletter. However my Garner family wanted us to continue it so we did. When we finally got many families using email, I got a great deal more written letters and photos to go into it. Then we decided to publish it on a monthly basis.

I began putting a prophetic message in every monthly issue about twenty five years ago. I alternated them of one from Jesus and one from Father God. I did not know how this would be received by most of my relatives because most of them are Southern Baptist, who are not familiar with current prophetic messages. However, some of our Garner relatives in northern Georgia are members of the Church of God, and they are the ones who encouraged me to receive the baptism of the Holy Spirit with the gift of prophecy. They encouraged me to begin putting the prophetic messages into the monthly newsletter. I now have more than 940 prophetic messages written out and typed up.

For this March newsletter, I needed some articles to fill up the last two of the eight pages. As I was looking through my many photos, I saw one I had taken of the many photos of Habitat Houses on the walls at John LaVoy's Mt. Bethel United Methodist Church in Georgia. I asked him to write an article for us about them, which he did. John has volunteered his work on Habitat Houses for more than twelve years. Their large church usually builds two or more a year.

Then I saw a photo of my cousin's grandchild, Leah Michelle, with an article her Grandmother Fay had written on Facebook, so I used it for one page. Leah has an incurable bone disease with metal rods in her neck, so she can hold her head up. Father God told me that He wants to heal her to show mankind that only God can heal a person that doctors, medicine, and surgery cannot heal! Praise God!

Blessings! Velma

Yes, Our God's beautiful beloved Christian pastors and ALL of Our God's beautiful beloved Holy Bible teachers, YOUR heavenly Father God AND YOUR Holy Triune God do love you and We do, YOUR God does, lead you and feed you daily with ALL GOOD things and with ALL GOOD events in your life, when you do love God, obey God, live for God, and when you do SERVE your God by your loving and serving others to YOUR God's glory on earth.

Yes, your God is a GOOD God.

Yes, taste and SEE that your God IS a good God Who does benefit thousands of generations of those who know God and who honor and obey Our God. (Deuteronomy 7:9)

Yes, Our God NOW has MANY MORE good rewards laid up to give to Our God's mankind when each of Our God's mankind is able to receive all these good gifts from THEIR God without their becoming corrupt when they do receive these good gifts from God.

Yes, Satan in heaven became corrupt when Our God gave to him riches, fame, prestige, and responsibilities that he was unable to handle, unable to use wisely, and he became corrupt and rebelled against Our God.

Yes, Satan is still rebelling against Our God, by coming against Our God's children to steal, kill, and destroy. (John 10:10)

Yes, Satan is a liar and is the father of all lies and is deceitfully wicked. (John 8:44)

Yes, you Christian leaders do not fight against flesh and blood, but you do fight against spiritual wickedness in high places, but all of Satan's followers can be overcome by the shed blood of Jesus and by the power of Our God's words—Our God's Holy Bible—the teachings of God as given in Our God's Holy Bible. (Ephesians 6:12)

Yes, if you WILL spend time daily reading, studying, memorizing, and meditating on Our God's Holy Bible, you will be able to quote the exact Scripture to Satan and his followers when they do TRY to come against you to discourage you, to defeat you, to drag you down.

Yes, the power of YOUR Holy Triune God IS far ABOVE ALL the power of ALL evil forces.

Yes, prayer, believing prayers prayed in the holy name of Jesus is now and always will be the strongest force on earth today.

Yes, Satan only has the power that Our God allows Satan to have on earth.

Yes, the power of evil forces on earth is ALWAYS limited by Our God.

Yes, when people on earth turn away from Our true God and rebel against Our God, the way Our God disciplines these rebellious people is to withdraw Our God's protection of the people, and this does allow Satan and his evil forces to harm people.

Yes, Our God does ALWAYS limit the damage that evil forces can do to harm people.

Doesn't Our God's Holy Bible teach that you will not be tempted above what you are able to withstand, but that Our God will make a way for you to escape, so that you will be able to withstand it, to overcome it, to Our God's glory? (1 Corinthians 10:13)

Yes, ALWAYS remain faithful to your God THROUGH all your trials and troubles, and Our God will bring you THROUGH them safely, and will ALWAYS reward you for your faithfulness to God.

Yes, doesn't Our God's Holy Bible teach you that ALL things

work together for good to those who love God and who are called according to Our God's purpose? (Romans 8:28)

Yes, Our God ALLOWS Satan to test Our God's beloved children to prove the love of Our children for God.

Yes, if Our God's children come faithfully through ALL the testing, this shows Our God the strength of a person's character, how much their soul has grown in God, and shows God to what level a person can be promoted with funds, fame, possessions, and responsibilities that they can and will use wisely to help themselves, help others, and glorify God on earth.

Yes, Our God promotes servants, not dictators.

Yes, Our God sees the hearts, thoughts, words, and deeds of each person, to see if their character as a servant, servant of God and servant of the people, to see if they are READY for Our God's promotion of all good things and all good events on earth.

Yes, Our God does require truths in Our God's Bible teachers as Our God does require that they do LIVE the truth and that they do TEACH the truth to others.

Yes, Jesus Christ is truth. (John 14:6)

Know Jesus Christ and know the truth.

Yes, know the truth of Jesus Christ, and this truth will set you free. (John 8:32)

Yes, preach about the life of Jesus Christ when He walked this earth nearly two thousand years ago, when He LIVED the truth and TAUGHT the truth.

Yes, heaven and earth may pass away, but the words spoken by Jesus Christ when He walked this earth nearly two thousand years ago as recorded in Our God's Holy Bible, will NEVER pass away. (Matthew 24:35)

Yes, do KNOW these teachings of Jesus, do LIVE by these teachings of Jesus, and do TEACH others what Jesus taught for other people to KNOW them and to LIVE by them.

Yes, let your beliefs, your teachings, and your living

standards all be pure, and be in agreement with the teachings, the beliefs, and the righteous living of Jesus.

Yes, Jesus Christ came to earth to teach mankind how to know, love, worship, and live for THEIR holy Creators, to shed His holy blood and give His life on Calvary's cruel cross so that people could be saved from their sins by Jesus, could live a holy life on earth to God, and could spend eternity in heaven with THEIR Holy Triune God.

Yes, Our God did give to ALL of mankind on Our God's earth Our God's Holy Bible to teach them about God and about Our God's ways of how Our God wants Our God's mankind to live their daily and nightly lives, to love and honor THEIR holy Creator God above all else, and to love, help, and serve others to Our God's glory on earth, even as they do love, help, and serve themselves.

Yes, Jesus Christ is the greatest Son of God and Son of Man Who ever lived to a mature life on earth, and He came not to be served, but to serve. (Matthew 20:28)

Yes, Jesus ALWAYS served each of mankind that He did help, He served them with great LOVE.

Yes, this is how people will know if you are a true Christian within your heart is if you serve others with great love, with the love that Jesus shows to you and through you to them.

Yes, do give your love and your service to the needy people around you, expecting NOTHING from them in return for your love and your service, and your heavenly Father God Who sees ALL of your good works unto others WILL REWARD YOU.

Yes, people will know you are a Christian, when they see Our God's love working through you to help the helpless.

Yes, Our God created you, sustains you at all times, loves you, forgives you of sins when you repent of your sins, when you ASK God to forgive you of ALL your sins, and when you come out of ALL sinful lifestyle and live for God.

Yes, you cannot live in a sinful lifestyle and still preach

the Word of God because if you do NOT repent of your sinful lifestyle you can no longer teach the Word of God.

Salt water and fresh water cannot come out of the same fountain at the same time.

Yes, you must COMPLETELY live for God if you are now teaching the Word of God as Jesus said that He will spit out the lukewarm Christians. (Revelation 3:16)

Yes, if you do want to be used by God more in your Christian ministry you must become HOT for God through your more prayer, more fasting, more reading and studying Our God's Holy Bible, by praising Our God more, by honoring Our God more, by loving Our God more.

Yes, do draw near to Our God and Our God WILL draw near to you and as your soul does grow more in God as you obey Our God more, Our God can and will use you in a greater way to serve God and to help others to live a successful life in God.

Yes, your promotion comes from YOUR God.

Yes, your God has the power to promote you for your obedience to God, and your God has the power to demote you for your disobedience to God.

Yes, your Holy Triune God IS a great God, a very generous God, Who shows Himself strong to ALL of God's obedient children.

Yes, your Holy Triune God is also a very just God, Who will NOT ALLOW Our God's Christian children to live in habitual sin without Our God correcting them.

Yes, live for God and be rewarded with ALL good things and all good events.

Yes, do not live for God and be punished and corrected by God.

Yes, doesn't Our God's Holy Bible teach that Our God corrects those He loves? (Hebrews 12:6)

Yes, when Our God does correct your wrong motives and wrong actions and you are punished by God for your sins, when you do repent of your sins, turn BACK to YOUR God for forgiveness of your sins, your God can and will forgive you of your sins and heal you.

Yes, when King David sinned, God took the newborn child from him, then God raised him back up and gave David the son of Solomon to lead the people after David did repent of his sins and confessed his sins to God.

Yes, Our God does forgive people of their many sins when they do REPENT, CONFESS, BELIEVE, then go and sin no more.

Yes, Our God is a good God Who does LOVE ALL of mankind, and Father God and Jesus Christ have made a way for all people alive on earth today to know Jesus as Lord and Savior, live for God, and spend eternity in heaven with THEIR Holy Triune God.

Hallelujah!

Praises to Our God!

LETTER NUMBER THIRTY SIX
FOR CHURCH GROWTH

Dear Christian Pastors and All Holy Bible Teachers,

I have prayed and asked Father God in the name of Jesus to help me to write an encouraging letter to you pastors and Bible teachers. I know for certain that God wants all of you to be completely sold out for God, to be HOT for Jesus Christ, to lead a holy life unto God and encourage others to do the same. Your Christian teaching must reflect your Christian living or it's not successful.

I have been in church services all of my life. I have observed the different sermon topics and ways of preaching by different pastors. Pastor Billy Roy Moore started The Lord's Chapel as a Bible study in a private home until it outgrew three homes then began meeting in a church building. His method of preaching was to teach a chapter of the Bible each Sunday morning until he completed one whole book within the Bible.

Many other pastors will teach on a specific subject and will find some Bible verses throughout the Bible to relate to the subject. Growing up in a Southern Baptist church, I heard many sermons on, "Bring ye ALL the GROSS tithes into the storehouse." When I began reading through the Bible for myself, I was greatly surprised that every third chapter was not on, "Bring ye all the gross tithes into the storehouse," as about every third sermon seemed to be!

My favorite Bible teacher is Pastor Ernest Angley who quotes more Scriptures per sermon than anyone else I have ever heard. In all of his writings, he always has one or two Scripture verses in each paragraph. I think he must have the whole Bible memorized in order for him to do that!

Another favorite Bible teacher of mine is Pastor Perry Stone who has spent more than 23,000 hours studying and researching the Bible. He also studies history a lot, especially history of Israel and the United States. He is able to teach the Bible truths and relate these teachings to the present time in which we are living. He takes a group of people to Israel every year and has teachings about Israel and the Bible while there. It would be great fun to take one of these trips with his group!

Derek Prince, who is now deceased, is one of my Bible teachers that I greatly respect for his testimony, his brilliant mind, his excellent education in England, and his Bible teaching. He has written more than fifty books about the Bible teachings on many subjects. I still listen to his verbal teachings on CDs every week. His many books are now being translated into many foreign languages and are used in Christian colleges and churches worldwide. His teachings are also still on radio.

Other wonderful Christian teaching books that have been written, published, and marketed by Christ For The Nations and by Kenneth Hagin, are some that I enjoy reading. I now help support the ministries of Ernest Angley, Derek Prince, Christ for The Nations, and Kenneth Hagin, along with many other great ministries that promote the Gospel worldwide of Bibles for The World, Bible League, and American Bible Society. I try to read two Christian books a month along with reading through the Bible each year.

The Christian charity that I give the most funds to every month is K. P. Yohannan's Gospel for Asia that especially helps spread Christianity throughout India. I help support four full-time missionaries with them for only $30.00 each, for $120.00 a month. I also co-sponsor a child with them with my sister Carolyn Hill in California, which together we pay $35.00 a month. Carolyn and I also each support children with World Vision for $35.00 a month plus other gifts to them.

I read K. P. Yohannan's book, *Revolution In World Missions*. It is a powerful book on how to spread the Gospel of Jesus worldwide to help people. Recently I finished another book by him titled, *No*

Longer A Slumdog, about the poor people of India. It tells how the millions of children are abused in India with awful child labor, sex trafficking, little food, impure water, illiteracy, inadequate clothes, shoes, housing, sanitation, health care, dental care, as well as extreme spiritual poverty. He tells how Gospel for Asia goes into a poverty-stricken area and begins a Bridge of Hope school for the young children. They find a sponsor for each child for $35.00 a month, with all of these funds going for school uniforms, school supplies and instructions, one meal a day, and Christian instruction. As these children become Christians and are transformed, they take their knowledge, skills, and Christian influence home to their families. This improves their whole families which improves their whole communities.

This book about the Slumdogs of children in India being transformed, written by K. P. Yohannon, told of one man and his wife who sponsored a child in this Bridge of Hope. This man went on a business trip to India and got to meet and visit the child he was sponsoring. Seeing all the needy children in the streets compared to the happy, clean, educated, and fed children in the Bridge of Hope classrooms, impacted his life so much that he went home and told his wife about it. As a result, they decided to sponsor twelve children a month in the program for $10,000.00 a year!

I thought, "How wonderful for them to do that! I would certainly like to do that!" Then the Lord gave me a dream that showed me holding a large oil painting of mine with a black canvas. A voice in the dream told me that a single large oil painting of mine will sell for $10,000.00 and for even more than $10,000.00. Only God can create a miracle like that! God told me that Velma must paint and give God something to work with in order for God to send buyers for my paintings. Praise God!

Blessings! Velma

Yes, Our God's beloved Christian children of Our God's beloved Christian pastors and ALL of Our God's beloved Holy Bible teachers, YOUR heavenly Father God does love you, and your God has called you and chosen you to preach and teach these true messages of love, of salvation-in-Jesus, of right-living-unto-God to all your congregations, families, friends, and even to the strangers you meet along your way.

Yes, everyone alive on planet Earth today does need to hear and see the message of Our God's love for them, Our God's provisions for them, Our God's protection of them, Our God's salvation for them in their knowing Jesus Christ as their Savior, their Healer, their soon-coming holy Bridegroom, their everlasting Lord of ALL lords and King of ALL kings, the holy One of God.

Yes, Jesus is all in all. (Colossians 3:11)

Yes, everything that Our God created does have a part of Jesus Christ in it.

Yes, Jesus Christ IS the spoken Word of HIS heavenly Father God. (John 1:1-3)

Yes, Jesus Christ is God.

Jesus Christ IS Our God's only begotten Son. (John 3:16)

Jesus Christ is the ONLY TRUE SAVIOR of ALL of mankind as Jesus Christ came to earth as Son of Man and Son of God, was conceived by Our God's Holy Spirit, was born of the virgin girl Mary, grew into manhood without any sin, without ANY spot or blemish, but lived a holy life unto God, shed His holy blood and gave His righteous life on Calvary's cruel cross to pay for all of mankind's sins and unrighteousness so that WHOSOEVER WILL MAY come to Jesus with a repentant heart, ASK Jesus to forgive their sins, MAKE Jesus the Lord and Master of their life, RECEIVE this FREE salvation from Jesus, then go and live a righteous lifestyle unto God for the rest of their life on Our God's planet Earth.

Yes, Jesus Christ IS coming back toward Our God's planet Earth SOON to claim and to catch away in the air in a split second to take them BACK to THEIR home in heaven to live eternally with THEIR Holy Triune God.

Yes, the time is now short and is growing shorter until Jesus Christ splits the Eastern skies for Our God's great rapture of ALL of the obedient Christian souls on earth for Our God's great rapture on earth.

Yes, do GET READY TO GO in ANY split second to meet YOUR Lord Jesus Christ in the air.

Yes, yes, yes, SOON, SOON, SOON!

Jesus returns SOON!

Get ready to welcome Him!

Get ready to meet Him!

Get ready to RETURN to heaven with Him!

Yes, yes, yes, do warn the people you teach!

Do warn the people you meet, friends and strangers alike.

Yes, yes, yes, ALL people NOW alive on earth NEED to be WARNED that the time is SHORT until Jesus returns towards earth for Our God's great rapture of Our God's obedient Christian souls.

Yes, when Jesus does come for Our God's great rapture of souls on earth, those living in habitual sin on earth will be LEFT BEHIND!

Yes, sin will NEVER enter heaven.

Yes, in order to go up in Our God's rapture of souls to heaven, a person MUST be saved in Jesus and they MUST be living in a righteous lifestyle unto God.

Yes, Our God will NOT tolerate a Christian or anyone else living in a habitual evil lifestyle for long until Our God will bring judgment and punishment on them.

Yes, in Noah's day, people turned away from their true God and made their possessions and their activities their gods until the rains came, the floods rose, and destroyed all of them, except Noah and his family escaped and were preserved in the ark that Our God helped Noah to build.

Yes, now for all the people alive on earth to escape Our God's punishment, all of mankind must forsake their own evil ways, turn BACK to their first love of God, ask forgiveness of their sins and their rejection of God, accept Our God's forgiveness, come out of ALL sinful lifestyle, live a righteous lifestyle in obedience to God, and ALLOW Our God to heal these lands of these Americas.

Yes, YOUR heavenly God has spoken to ALL the leaders and ALL the people now alive on Our God's planet Earth.

Yes, do go into ALL the world and teach the true gospel of Jesus Christ to everyone, and lo, Jesus is with you now and will always be with you to the end of the world. (Matthew 28:20)

Yes, Jesus will never leave you nor forsake you. (Hebrews 13:5)

Yes, where two or three are gathered together in Jesus' name, Jesus is there with them, hearing them, comforting them, teaching them, and using them to teach others. (Matthew 18:20)

Yes, do ALWAYS preach and teach the many truths given in Our God's Holy Bible.

Know ALL the promises of God to you and to ALL your loved ones, all of Our God's promises to you as given to ALL of Our God's mankind on earth, given in Our God's Holy Bible.

Yes, when there are conditions given for these benefits to be received from YOUR God, do MEET these conditions, then do claim these good benefits from God to you of Our God's good promises to you, to all your loved ones, and to ALL of Our God's mankind now alive on Our God's beautiful earth.

Yes, Our Holy Triune God created all that you see, and Our God saw that Our God's creation was good. (Genesis 1:31)

Yes, Our God created all your known and unknown universe, the whole earth and all on it and all in it.

Yes, Our Holy Triune God did create and still does create each of mankind in Our God's image with body, soul, and spirit.

Yes, at the moment of your human conception, you were given an everlasting soul by YOUR heavenly Father God.

Yes, your eternal soul will live forever in heaven with YOUR Holy Triune God Creators, or it will live in hell forever with Satan as there are NO OTHER PLACES for your eternal soul to live after your one life and one death is over on earth.

Yes, those people alive today who repent of their sins, come to Jesus with a repentant heart, ASK Jesus to forgive their sins and save them, then receive this free gift of salvation from Jesus, then come out of ALL sinful lifestyle and live for God, will go to heaven for eternity to live forever rejoicing with THEIR Holy Triune God.

Those who reject choosing Jesus as their Lord and Savior and those who reject living a righteous lifestyle for God will never enter heaven, but will enter hell and will live forever in hell with Satan, your tormentor.

Yes, you must make your choice of accepting Jesus or rejecting Jesus while you are now alive on earth.

Tomorrow may be too late for you to accept Jesus as your Lord and Savior.

Yes, your allotted time on earth is running out.

Life on earth is uncertain and death on earth is certain.

Doesn't Our God's Holy Bible teach that it is appointed unto each person to die once, and after that is Our God's white throne judgment? (Hebrews 9:27)

Yes, reincarnation, as you do know reincarnation to be, is a complete lie from Satan who is the father of all lies. (John 8:44)

Satan wants you to believe you can WORK your way into heaven, but it is IMPOSSIBLE for ANY human being to work their way into heaven by obeying rules, or by loving others, or by living righteously and/or doing works, either good works or bad works.

The ONLY way for ANY person now alive on earth to ever enter heaven is by the only true Savior Jesus Christ Who has the power to cleanse them of their sins, cleanse them of ALL unrighteousness in Jesus' shed blood on Calvary's cross to pay the penalty for their sins, to give them true freedom from all bondage, to give them a new life to live righteously for God, and to enter heaven forever.

Yes, Jesus Christ is YOUR ONLY Door to heaven in your afterlife after your one life on earth, and you MUST choose Jesus while you are now alive on earth, and you must come out of ALL sinful lifestyle, then go and sin no more in order to enter heaven in your life after your one life on earth. (John 10:9)

Yes, sin will NEVER enter heaven.

Yes, only sinners who have REPENTED of their sins, ASKED Jesus for forgiveness, who then rebuke all sin in their life, and who then live a righteous lifestyle for God, will be the ONLY sinners-who-have-REPENTED will enter heaven for eternity.

Yes, you can no longer straddle the fence and be a lukewarm Christian, but you must choose Jesus over all other temptations, live completely for God, and be HOT for Jesus, if you want to lead others to Jesus and be used by YOUR Holy Triune God in the ministry of God in a bigger and more influential way to help others.

Yes, your promotion in your Christian ministry can ONLY come from YOUR God WHEN you are READY to receive the promotion from God without it corrupting you.

Yes, as your soul grows in God you WILL BECOME more of a servant of the people and become less of a dictator of the people.

Yes, as your love for your God grows your love for people will grow and you will become more like Jesus, when Jesus walked this earth nearly two thousand years ago, when Jesus went about loving people, teaching people, healing people, helping people, and being the true God of the people.

Yes, Jesus was completely faithful to the people and was completely obedient to HIS Father God to the end with His death, burial, and resurrection, now seated at the right hand of HIS Father God in heaven with His eternal reward from HIS heavenly Father God.

Yes, YOUR heavenly Father God will always reward you for your faithfulness and your obedience to God, reward you both on earth and reward you in heaven in your afterlife.

Praise God for this prophetic message for church growth!

Hallelujah!

Praises to Our God!

LETTER NUMBER THIRTY SEVEN
FOR CHURCH GROWTH

Dear Christian Pastors and All Holy Bible Teachers,

I have been praying about what to write to all of you pastors and Bible teachers to encourage you in your work. I want to encourage you to study and memorize all the teachings of Jesus when He walked this earth as given in Our God's Holy Bible. I also want to encourage you to recognize the voice of Father God, Jesus Christ, and our God's Holy Spirit, when each of Them do speak to you, and when they do speak to others. If our Bibles are ever taken away from us, if we do these two things, we will always stay strong in God and will be able to survive no matter what happens.

I went through a period of time in my own life when I was learning to hear from God and learning to obey the voices that I was hearing. I kept hearing three distinct male voices, who were telling me what to do. They were calling themselves "the father," "the son," and "the spirit" and they were pretending to be good spirits, telling me to do seemingly good things, and quoting certain Scriptures to me. I thought that these voices were the Father, the Son, and the Holy Spirit, until God showed to me twelve guidelines to go by in hearing the three voices of the true God of, **MY heavenly Father God, MY Savior Jesus Christ, and our God's Holy Spirit.**

Some of the main guidelines are:

Father God, Jesus Christ, and God's Holy Spirit, will call you by your own name.

Father God, Jesus Christ, and God's Holy Spirit, will tell you that they love you, usually before They tell you anything else.

The name of "Jesus" is protected, and evil spirits cannot use the HOLY name of JESUS.

Father God, Jesus Christ, and God's Holy Spirit, will not contradict the whole Holy Bible teachings but will always agree with true Scripture teachings.

Father God, Jesus Christ, and God's Holy Spirit, will always speak the truth in love.

Father God, Jesus Christ, and God's Holy Spirit, will not tell you to harm yourself or harm others.

Father God, Jesus Christ, and God's Holy Spirit, will not tell you the secrets of others that They know.

Father God, Jesus Christ, and God's Holy Spirit will help you to obey the laws of the land and obey the leaders when they obey God.

When Father God, Jesus Christ, and God's Holy Spirit, tell you of the future, if it comes true in DUE TIME, it is from God. Sometimes God will tell a person a future happening, but with no due date. We must wait until God's timing and not our timing for a future event to happen.

Father God, Jesus Christ, and God's Holy Spirit, always keep their promises to mankind as given in our God's Holy Bible, when the right conditions are met, as God loves all people the same.

God's Holy Spirit will bring certain Scriptures to your mind to correct your walk with God, when you start to stray from God, or when you don't "rightly divide" the word of God.

Satan can quote Scriptures to you, give you dreams, can give you fears and frustrations, but when you seek God in a matter or in a decision, God will give you peace, love, and true guidance.

God gives peace, love, comfort, hope, truth, joy, righteousness, knowledge, wisdom, and all good things and good events that will help us, help others, and will bring glory to God.

God will speak to us when we get on our knees in private, praise God, ask God to speak to us, and wait on our knees until a thought crosses our minds. We must speak out, or write out, that first thought, or the second thought won't come. We continue to speak out or write out the rest of the thoughts that come into our mind. Then we praise God for speaking to us.

Father God once told me, "**In these last days, Christians can be led astray, but if they truly do seek God and keep on seeking God, that they will not be led astray FOR LIONG, as God will reveal our God's truth to them.**" Praise God for His faithfulness to us all who are truly seeking God and seeking to live for God on a daily and nightly basis.

Some people have not heard the true voice of God enough in their lifetime to recognize the true voice of God when they do hear it. I mailed some prophetic messages from Jesus Christ and from Father God to some newspapers. One lady online wrote, "Jesus would never talk like that." One man cracked jokes about my calling them, "Hot Off The Throne," and said that it referred to the toilet. This shows me that they have no respect for God and cannot recognize the true voice of God when they hear it.

One pastor that I know of was being very cruel to a ninety-year-old-sick widow who had helped this pastor a lot in the past. My friend and I wrote to the pastor and requested that he be kind to her. The letter must have made him angry as he immediately became even more cruel to the widow and to her family. The Bible says that we "will know them by their fruits." I am praying for this pastor to become more like Jesus and to love and help others as he loves and helps himself, especially the widows and orphans.

Blessings! Velma

Yes, Our God's beloved Christian children of Our God's beloved Christian pastors and Our God's beloved Holy Bible teachers, YOUR heavenly Father God does love you, does take care of you, and does TEACH you Our God's truths as found in Our God's Holy Bible, and does enable you to live for God and to teach others Our God's truths.

Yes, your God IS a holy God.

Yes, Our God does DEMAND ALL of Our God's Christian pastors and ALL of Our God's Holy Bible teachers to live a righteous lifestyle unto God.

Yes, do love YOUR God above ALL else.

Yes, do enjoy spending time with YOUR God so that you can reveal YOUR God to others.

Yes, doesn't Our God's Holy Bible teach you to draw near to God, and Our God WILL draw near to you? (James 4:8)

Doesn't Our God's Holy Bible teach you to call unto your God, and your God will answer you and show you great and mighty things which you know not? (Jeremiah 33:3)

Yes, do read, study, and meditate on parts of Our God's Holy Bible daily so you will know your God better, know of the love, power, kindness, goodness, and majesty of YOUR God.

Know the justice and fairness of God in handling, rewarding, Our God's obedient people and the disobedient people.

Know how and why mankind was created by THEIR Holy Triune God.

Know the fate of all mankind now living on Our God's planet Earth, how after their one lifetime on earth they will spend eternity in heaven with THEIR Holy Triune God; or if they reject salvation in Jesus and continue living in a sinful lifestyle they will spend eternity in hell with Satan as there are NO other places for their eternal soul to live after their one life and one death on earth is over.

Yes, know Jesus as your Lord and Savior and live in a righteous lifestyle unto YOUR God.

Yes, teach others how to know Jesus Christ as their Lord and Savior, then how to REPENT, come out of ALL sinful lifestyle, then live for God while they are alive on Our God's planet Earth, then be welcomed into heaven FOREVER to rule and to reign with THEIR Holy Triune God.

Yes, teach people that there are winners and there are losers in the heavenly realm just above Our God's planet Earth.

Yes, Our God's good angels, the righteous-unto-God group of good angels, are sent to earth by THEIR heavenly Father God to help answer the righteous prayers of mankind and to HELP mankind live righteously for God. (Hebrews 1:14)

Yes, the losing group of the unrighteous angels, evil demons, and Satan's followers know their time on Our God's planet Earth is now short, and they are now prowling the earth searching for whom they may harm, kill, and destroy.

Yes, Our God's power is higher and stronger than ALL the evil powers of Satan's losing group of his followers.

Yes, prayer in the holy name of Jesus is NOW the strongest force on earth today, so do use it often and do use it in your great faith in Jesus when you do pray to YOUR heavenly Father God, when you do pray for gifts from your God that will benefit you, help others, and glorify your God on earth.

Yes, trust God!

Try God!

Rely on God for all of your provisions of your needs and all of your holy desires for yourself and for ALL of your loved ones, and then WATCH your God come through for you for this with flying colors!

Yes, you ARE with an army of God that has NEVER lost a battle!

Yes, live for God.

Yes, witness for Jesus, the love of Jesus for all of mankind, the saving power of Jesus, the healing power of Jesus, the soon-arrival of Jesus coming from Our God's third heaven back toward earth for Our God's SOON rapture of ALL the Christian obedient souls to take them BACK to Our God's great heaven above to rule and reign with THEIR Holy Triune God forever.

Yes, teach everyone that ONLY Jesus Christ is the true Savior with enough power to save anyone who ASKS Him for salvation, who repents of ALL sinful lifestyle, who then goes and sins no more while they are alive on Our God's planet Earth.

Yes, sin will NEVER enter heaven.

Yes, Jesus Christ is the ONLY Door for any of mankind to enter heaven.

Yes, it is impossible for ANY of mankind to work their way into heaven by good works and by their loving other people.

Yes, ONLY Jesus saves.

Buddha cannot save a person.

Allah cannot save a person.

Mohammad cannot save a person.

Apart from Jesus, no person can save themselves or save anyone else.

Yes, Jesus freely saves ALL who do come to Jesus and who do ASK Jesus to save them, who make Jesus their Lord and Master, who receive this free salvation from Jesus, who REPENT of ALL sinful lifestyle and live a righteous lifestyle unto God, will receive salvation, abundant life on earth, and eternal life in heaven.

Yes, if a person receives Jesus now on earth they will NEVER regret it, not in this their lifetime on earth nor in their life in heaven for eternity.

If a person now rejects Jesus Christ as their Lord and Savior and if they do refuse to come OUT of their sinful lifestyle and refuse to live righteously for God, they can and WILL REGRET IT forever in hell.

Yes, Our God has now created each person now alive on Our God's planet Earth with a free will, and each person now is able to choose Jesus, live for God, and enjoy Our God's beautiful heaven in their afterlife, or they are free to reject Jesus Christ and the salvation He offers, continue to live in a sinful lifestyle, and suffer greatly in hell forever.

Yes, the choice belongs to each person now alive on earth.

Yes, you cannot ride the fence of indecision.

You must choose Jesus and live in a completely righteous lifestyle for God, or you must reject Jesus and not accept Jesus' free offer of salvation from all sins, spend eternity in hell without the true God, in hell where there is no escaping for eternity.

Yes, all Christian pastors and ALL Holy Bible teachers must make it absolutely clear to all they teach that they must make their choice for or against Jesus soon as time on earth is now running out.

Tomorrow may be too late to choose Jesus and live for God.

Yes, YOUR heavenly Father God has NOW spoken to you, Our God's beloved Christian leaders.

Yes, you do serve a great big God, an all-powerful God, an all-loving God, and a very generous God.

Yes, YOUR heavenly Father God is ABLE to meet ALL your needs, ALL your holy desires, ALL the needs of ALL of your loved ones, and meet ALL the needs of ALL of your congregations with ONLY Our God's spoken Words.

Yes, Jesus Christ IS the spoken Word of HIS heavenly Father God. (John 1:1-3)

Yes, Our God's Holy Triune God did make all of mankind in Our God's image with body, soul, and spirit.

Yes, and Our God STILL DOES make each of mankind now in Our God's image.

Yes, at each person's moment of conception in their mother's womb, Our God not only gives them their eternal soul, but also endues them with many gifts to help them be creative in life, to help them be successful in life, to give them enjoyment in life, to help themselves, to help others, and to glorify God on earth with their special talents and gifts given to them by THEIR Holy Triune God.

Yes, when abortions of unborn babies take place, it does grieve THEIR Holy Triune God Who has created them so beautifully and so talented in Our God's image.

Yes, each and every human being born on earth does come to earth for a certain reason, and that reason is for their eternal soul to grow up MORE in God.

Yes, the only thing that a person takes with them after their one life and one death on earth is their soul's growth in God.

Yes, your soul does grow daily as you do seek to know God better, love and honor God more, praise God more, obey God more, witness for Jesus more, live for God daily and nightly in a righteous lifestyle, help the helpless more with love and kindness.

Yes, as you do live a righteous lifestyle unto God and as you do seek to know God better and praise your God more, you will be rewarded by YOUR God more with ALL GOOD benefits for you and your loved ones to enjoy and to share with others.

Yes, look around you with your eyes and hearts filled with Our God's Christian love, and Our God WILL show you WHERE you can be of service and help to others with your prayers, your comforting and uplifting words of encouragement, your money gifts, and your other gifts.

Yes, even as Peter said, "Such as I have I give to you, rise and walk." (Acts 3:6)

Yes, let Our God's Holy Spirit flow through you to do signs, wonders, and miracles for others as you do pronounce their physical healings in the name of Jesus, and you can and WILL see the power of God work MIRACLES to help others to Our God's glory on earth.

Yes, these ARE the last of the last days on earth before Jesus Christ returns toward earth for Our God's great catching away to Our God's great heaven above, ALL of Our God's saved-in-Jesus and right-living-unto-God beloved Christian children of God.

Yes, more and more of Our God's mighty miracles WILL begin to manifest on earth as Our God's righteous-in-Jesus children of God proclaim physical healings in Jesus' holy name to Our God's glory on earth.

Yes, Our God can do all things possible, whereas men, medicine, surgeries, and physical treatments can do little to help people. (Mark 10:27)

Yes, when Jesus Christ walked this earth nearly two thousand years ago, He healed EVERY person who came to Him and did ASK Jesus for their healing, then Jesus told them, "Your faith has made you whole."

Yes, Jesus still heals today ALL the ones who do COME to Jesus, who do ASK Jesus to heal them, who do have ENOUGH FAITH in Jesus to be healed.

Yes, Jesus Christ IS the same yesterday, today, and forever. (Hebrews 13:8)

Yes, preach and teach Jesus Christ.

Yes, do study ALL of the teachings of Jesus Christ given to you and given to all mankind on Our God's earth, given in Our God's Holy Bible.

Yes, know these teachings of Jesus, apply these teachings of Jesus to your own life, and then do WATCH and do see HOW MUCH Our God does reward you, your loved ones, and even your congregations because of your knowledge of and obedience to YOUR Holy Triune God.

Yes, Our God's people do perish from a lack of knowledge of Our God's words to them and Our God's promises of rewards to them. (Hosea 4:6)

Yes, if ONLY Our God's Christian children knew that Our God's tithe from them is holy, and if they only knew that Our God will return to them double and more than double what they give to help spread Our God's gospel worldwide and to

312

help the helpless, they could reap enormous benefits on their work jobs, in their peace of mind, in better relationships, in knowledge, wisdom, creativity, and opportunities to be more successful in life.

Yes, if only people knew of the benefits to be gained by tithing, and if they loved and trusted God enough to tithe with love on a regular basis, in only one year's time of their being faithful to God in this tithing with love to Our God's glory, they could reap enormous benefits as Our God WILL BE FAITHFUL to reward them accordingly.

Praises to Our heavenly Father God for this wonderful, powerful message for church growth given to ALL of Our God's beloved children of God on planet Earth.

Hallelujah!

Praises to Our God!

Hallelujah!

LETTER NUMBER THIRTY EIGHT
FOR CHURCH GROWTH

Dear Christian Pastors and All Holy Bible Teachers,

I want to encourage you to never be weary in well doing as soon you will reap a great harvest if you keep working for God and witnessing for Jesus.

These fifty prophetic messages from our Father God for church growth along with the fifty cover letters will hopefully be finished soon if I continue receiving two a week. They are due to be put into a self-published book by Westbow Press titled, *Church Growth Our Father God's Way.* The cost is $5,075.00 which has already been paid. There will be an additional charge for each book printed. Westbow Press will not only publish the book but will help me to market it to the public in bookstores and online with computers. All of the eighteen pastors and Bible teachers that I am sending these messages to now will receive a free copy of the book.

Father God told me that this book on church growth will be very successful, will go worldwide, and will help many churches to grow in attendance and grow in financial income as the pastors and leaders of the churches grow in God. As their souls grow in God, God will promote them to minister to larger groups of people with greater church incomes.

After this book is complete with the fifty letters and fifty prophetic messages for church growth, Father God told me that He will then give to me fifty prophetic messages about tithing and giving and about God's rewards to people who obey God. I have now received the first five prophetic messages for this new series. This first book on church growth will help the leaders of the churches to grow in God and will help the church congregations grow and church finances grow. The next book on tithing and giving will not only help individuals and families to grow in trusting God and grow in financial rewards, but will help the churches to grow as people give more of their income to helping the churches and helping the needy. The name of this next book on tithing and giving will be titled, *Tithe Your Way Out of Debt.*

The Southern Baptist Churches are all very dear to my heart as I was led to become a Christian, was baptized, was educated, and worked for The Southern Baptists. Once I said something about The Southern Baptist churches don't believe in being Spirit filled with "tongues and prophecies." Father God spoke to me then and said something like this, **"Don't ever criticize any of My Southern Baptist pastors because that is all that the Holy Spirit has to work with."** I know they are doing an excellent job of winning souls to Jesus and I thank them for that. At one time they were the largest denomination of churches in the United States. I read a statistic once that gave the report that the average Southern Baptist church has eighty-five members with only twelve percent tithers. With all those sermons on tithing, I was surprised that there were such few tithers—as I thought, "That's probably only the pastor's family and the choir director's family who are tithers, and the other members just give a few dollars here and there."

I read another report that told what percent of Christians in the United States are tithers, and it was even a lower percent than the Southern Baptist members. Then the report gave a survey on the lifestyle of the tithers, that reported they have longer and healthier lives with less health care expenses, more own their own homes than rent, with their homes paid for, less general debt, are happier and their families are happier, have fewer auto accidents and other harmful accidents, have more friends, more and better vacations that are paid for, are more successful in their careers, have fewer alcoholics and less substance abuse, less lawsuits and prison time, less divorce cases, are respected leaders in their communities, and all live much more successful lives than the general public. More of the general public should know about this report! Maybe more would want to try tithing and see what our God will do for them.

I believe that this book, *Tithe Your Way Out of Debt,* is greatly needed today to help people get out of debt and stay out of debt. God teaches in the Bible, "My people perish from lack of knowledge." (Hosea 4:6) I think this is especially true about tithing. Father God showed to me that the Scripture verse that states, "Give and it will be given back to you, good measure, pressed down, shaken together, running over, will be given back to you," means that you will receive back double and more than double what you give. (Luke 6:38) A person cannot out-give God as God watches peoples' lives who give with love to help others and give to promote the gospel worldwide, and they are ALWAYS rewarded for this by God.

Father God also showed to me that the **tithes are holy.** God showed to me that the holy things are guarded by our **HOLY God.** Jesus' name is **holy.** Marriages are **holy.** Our bodies **are the temple of the Holy Spirit.** God gives to everyone some gifts and inside each of those gifts is a ten percent **holy tithe.** God watches to see what each person does with their **holy tithe,** to see if they CONSUME it, or if they INVEST it in helping others and promoting the gospel. If they consume it, their income growth is little. If they invest it, their income growth is much, because God can trust them with bigger incomes.

There is a story in the Bible in Matthew 5:14-30 that I could not understand the true meaning of until God revealed it to me. It is the story about the three servants who each received some income from their master to invest while the master went on a trip, with one servant receiving five units to invest, another servant receiving two units to invest, and the third servant receiving one unit to invest. You know the story. When the master returned, he found that two of the servants had doubled their amount, but the servant with one unit buried his unit and did not invest it. Then the master took the one unit returned to him, and gave it to the servant who had ten units. I didn't understand why the

316

master didn't give it to the one who had four units, because he had doubled his two units, he deserved as much credit as the one who also doubled his five units. I felt that the master should have given the one extra unit to the person who had fewer units.

Then God showed to me in verse 14 how the original units were given out in the first place, each to the servants according to their abilities. The amounts given to each of the three servants reflected their soul's growth, their character, of each. The servant that was given the original five units could be trusted by the master more than the other two servants because he had already proven himself more than the other two servants to be a good manager, a good worker, a good business person. This illustrates the Scripture verse of Matthew 25:29 that states, "For whoever has will be given more, and they will have an abundance. Whoever does not have, even what they have will be taken from them."

It's amazing to me what our God has done in the life of Dave Ramsey, how he was a multi-millionaire at age twenty-eight, lost it all over a period of three years, then turned to God for wisdom in handling family finances. What God has taught him over the last few years and what he has been able to teach others, has helped many people to get out of debt, stay out of debt, and lead more successful lives. It's amazing to me that God led Dave from the beginning of writing, self-publishing, and marketing his first book, to owning a large building in Franklin, Tennessee. The miracle of this is that God is doing it through Dave using "financially broke" people! Dave gives God ALL the glory for his success. Dave is now helping the church members with their family finances. God is good!

Blessings! Velma

Yes, Our God's beloved Christian children of Our God's beloved Christian pastors and beloved Holy Bible teachers, YOUR heavenly Father God does love you, does take care of you and does meet ALL of your needs and ALL of your holy desires.

Yes, when you do help meet the needs of others, YOUR heavenly Father God does help meet YOUR needs.

Yes, you ARE your brother's keeper.

Yes, do teach people to come to THEIR heavenly Father God, pray to THEIR Father God, pray with great faith in Jesus, always pray in the holy name of Jesus, and let your requests be made known to YOUR God, and you shall have ALL the good and righteous things and events that you ask for that will help you, will help others, and will glorify God on earth.

Yes, your God IS a GOOD God Who does enjoy giving ALL good gifts to ALL of Our God's obedient children when they know God, love God, obey God, and live for God, who does have enough knowledge and wisdom to use all these good benefits from God to enrich their own lives and help enrich the lives of others to Our God's glory.

Yes, you do glorify God on earth when you do help others with love, help the ones who do need your help of the aged, the infirm, the young, the strangers, the prisoners, the lonely, the poor—poor in material things and poor spiritually—yes, help them know the love and power Our God has for them to be strong and healthy in body, soul, mind, emotions, and strength.

Yes, Our God IS ABLE to give each and ALL of Our God's mankind on earth ALL of Our God's good gifts WHEN they are READY to receive all of these good gifts that will enrich their lives, will help them to grow up in God, will help the needy, and will bring glory to Our God.

Yes, Our God does reward servants, those who serve themselves and who serve others with love.

Yes, Jesus Christ, the greatest Servant of all, was the greatest among you as Jesus Christ is God, is Lord of all, and King of all kings.

Yes, worship Jesus Christ, the only begotten Son of the living true God, for a long time and do see how Our God does fill you with more love, joy, creativity, and power in ALL of your many endeavors on earth.

Yes, your joy and your strength do come from YOUR God, Who made heaven and earth. (Psalm 121:2)

Yes, Our God opens His hand and all are fed. (Psalm 145:16)

Yes, Our God is the God of knowledge, of wisdom, of love, of power, of blessing, Who abundantly bestows all good things on all who know God, who seek God, who love God, who worship and praise God, who adore God, who live for God, who instruct others to know God and have a right relationship with God, who set an example for others on how to know God, worship God, and live for God.

Yes, teach others to come out of ALL sinful relationships and LIVE for God, be saved in Jesus, and lay claim to ALL GOOD benefits in your life and in the lives of all of your loved ones.

Yes, Jesus, Father God, and Our God's Holy Spirit of God are three separate Beings, but We are, your God is, always in one accord, yes, the Holy Three in One.

Yes, worship Jesus as you do worship YOUR heavenly Father God.

Yes, worship your heavenly Father God as you do worship your Lord Jesus.

Yes, worship Our God's Holy Spirit, a third part of Our God's Holy Triune God.

Yes, when you do get to heaven, you WILL SEE Jesus Christ

at Our Father God's right hand, just as Our God's Holy Bible explains in several places.

Yes, before Stephen was stoned to death, didn't he see Jesus standing at the right hand of HIS Father God? (Acts 7:55)

Yes, yes, yes, Jesus Christ, Father God, and Our God's Holy Spirit are ALWAYS in one accord, are always in agreement.

Yes, strive to be in agreement with your fellow mankind by forgiving offences that come your way—be slow to offend and be quick to forgive, as all humans have frailties, and ALL humans need forgiveness of their faults, their weaknesses, their sins against others, and their sins against God.

Yes, doesn't Jesus tell you in Our God's Holy Bible to forgive people seventy times seven when they ask for your forgiveness? (Matthew 18:22)

Yes, Jesus forgives those who do COME to Jesus, who ASK Jesus for forgiveness, who ASK Jesus to be their Lord, Savior, and Master, who ACCEPT the free gift of salvation from Jesus, who then go and sin no more.

Yes, Jesus does not clean up a person who does continue to live in a habitual sinful lifestyle, as a person must REPENT, come out of a habitual lifestyle of sin, to be washed clean of all sin in the shed blood of Jesus, then go and sin no more.

Yes, people living in a sinful lifestyle CANNOT enter heaven, unless they REPENT of their sins, accept Jesus as their Lord and Savior, then go and sin no more, in order to enter heaven for eternity.

Yes, sin will NEVER enter heaven.

Yes, your God is holy.

Yes, be ye holy as your God is holy. (Leviticus 19:2)

Live a HOLY lifestyle unto your God after your salvation from sins and cleansing in Jesus' holy shed blood, then be helped and be rewarded by your Holy Triune God to live a righteous lifestyle unto God for the rest of your life on earth.

Yes, ALWAYS do use Our God's Holy Bible as your supreme

divine guide when preaching to others and when teaching others as every word in Our God's Holy Bible is absolutely true.

Yes, despise not small beginnings as ALL GOOD small beginnings do have growth potential. (Zechariah 4:10)

Yes, your church congregations and your church financial income will continue to grow in proportion to your leaders' souls' growth in God.

Yes, as the leaders' souls grow more in God, they do become more trustworthy and more capable of teaching, leading, encouraging, and serving a larger group than the year before.

Yes, it is ALWAYS YOUR heavenly Father God Who promotes you to more influence, more prestige, more financial income, and more possessions, and more fame.

Yes, some people cannot handle any advancement in these ways, or they will become corrupt.

Yes, EVERY individual person does have a level of corruption above them, that they are NOT allowed by God to reach, until their soul growth in God is strong enough for them to cope with, to manage, without them becoming corrupt.

Yes, YOUR heavenly Father God does know your strengths, your weaknesses, your pleasures, your hopes, your dreams, your love for God, your love and your service for your fellow mankind, your desires to win souls for the kingdom of God, your prayers, your reading and study of Our God's Holy Bible, and how you give your tithes and offerings to help spread the gospel of God worldwide, and how you help the helpless with love to Our God's glory.

Yes, Our God sees your heart and sees all the motives for your actions to see if your actions are done with love to help yourself, to help others to Our God's glory, or if they are done for your own glory.

Yes, the scribes and Pharisees said long prayers in public places to be noticed, and wanted choice spots at head tables at banquets, and wanted to be noticed for their fasting.

Yes, didn't Jesus teach you to NOT be like these corrupt

leaders who want to be noticed and praised by the people in public places, but to pray in your prayer closet, give alms and do good deeds and fast in secret, and YOUR heavenly Father God WILL REWARD YOU for these good deeds openly? (Matthew 6:4)

Yes, instead of holding grudges for the wrongs that have been committed against you and against others, do pray for others to know God, grow strong in God, and be used by God to help others—then Our God WILL hear and will HONOR your prayers, will reward you for praying for them, and WILL work with the others to CHANGE them into better, righteous-living people.

Yes, you are your brother's keeper.

Yes, if you do need a physical healing, do pray for others with the same affliction as you have to be healed, and Our God will work for you both to be healed.

Yes, pray to be healed of physical afflictions, and then praise God and thank God daily until your physical affliction is totally healed to the glory of God on earth.

Yes, Jesus Christ is STILL your physical Healer today as Jesus Christ is STILL the same yesterday, today, and forever. (Hebrews 13:8)

Yes, do ALWAYS pray in the name of Jesus, not only for physical healings, but for ALL of Our God's good gifts to you and to others of mental, emotional, spiritual, and financial healings.

Yes, if you are broke financially, in debt and jobless, try tithing for one full year and watch Our God's improvements in your life in only one year.

Yes, Our God can give you better things than what you now have of a job, a better job with better pay with more enjoyment of your work, more opportunities for advancements, better food, better clothes, better transportation, better friends, better sleep at night, better living standard than what you now have.

Yes, your heavenly Father God is ABLE to reward you, your family, and your church family, as you do grow closer to your God, your God WILL draw closer to you, and Our God WILL REWARD YOU with ALL GOOD THINGS and ALL GOOD EVENTS.

Yes, love YOUR Holy Triune God above ALL else, and honor YOUR Holy Triune God above all else, and love and help the helpless as you love and help yourself, then WATCH as YOUR Holy Triune God does pour out so many good benefits on you, on you family, and on your church family, that there will not be room enough to receive it all.

Yes, when you preach to and teach your church congregations, preach the truths that Jesus taught, encourage the righteous to know God, live for God, and be led and fed by Our God's Holy Spirit in their daily and nightly lives; but also do warn the wicked to come out of living a sinful lifestyle and live a righteous lifestyle for God, if they do want to go to heaven in their life after their one life on earth.

Yes, do warn them that sin will NEVER enter heaven.

Warn them that by their living in a sinful lifestyle WILL keep them OUT of heaven, if they do die in their sins.

Yes, they MUST REPENT of ALL sinful lifestyle, live for God with Jesus as their Lord and Savior to enter heaven.

Yes, ALWAYS speak and write the truth in love with the lifestyle of Jesus as your divine Guide.

Yes, ask YOUR Father God, ask it in Jesus' holy name, to meet ALL your needs, meet ALL your holy desires, give you knowledge, wisdom, strength, and guidance in ALL your decision making daily and nightly, and do watch for and do receive ALL of Our God's good benefits showered down on you and on ALL of your loved ones for your daily obedience to YOUR Holy Triune God.

Hallelujah!

Praises to Our Father God for this wonderful prophetic message for encouragement for church growth to Our God's glory!

Hallelujah!

Praises to Our heavenly Father God!

Hallelujah!

Praise God!

Dear Christian Pastors and All Holy Bible Teachers,

I have been praying about what to write to encourage you to "fight the good fight" to keep living for God, keep on witnessing for Jesus, and keep on speaking and writing the truth in love. I know that our God's Holy Spirit helps us with whatever we do that will glorify God, help ourselves, and help others.

I read a report that stated that more than half of the people who work full-time jobs do not enjoy their jobs. They spend such a great part of their lives working on their jobs just to earn a living, that, to me, this is not only very sad, it is very unnecessary to be bored or unhappy on a job. All we Christians have our God's Holy Spirit living within us to HELP us. If only people would just COME to the Holy Spirit and ASK the Holy Spirit to HELP them, our God's Holy Spirit could make their jobs so much easier and so much more enjoyable than how they are working now. Absolutely no job is a drudgery job if it is done with love to help others, help ourselves, and glorify God on earth.

In April of 1965, I moved to Nashville, Tennessee from Washington state to work as an artist at the Baptist Sunday School Board. I was a Graphic Designer creating Sunday School literature to help win the world to Jesus Christ worldwide. I began my job designing the covers of Sunday School quarterlies with a combination of photos, art work, and type. After I had designed a few covers and they were sent off to be printed, hundreds of thousands of printed copies were returned to the Shipping Department to be purchased and shipped all over the world.

I was single at the time and shared an apartment with Emma Jane Vidrine, who was also an artist at the Baptist Sunday School

Board. She had worked there as an artist many years before I came. She showed me around the nearby Baptist Book Store, now named Lifeway, and then showed me around the attached Shipping Warehouse. As we entered the shipping department, my mouth flew open and I loudly said, "WOW!" I was truly amazed at what I saw! There before us were stacked on wooden pallets, several hundred thousand magazines, showing one of the covers that I had designed! I said to her, "WOW! I designed one little cover and look what happened! I'm truly amazed!" She laughed and said to me, "Yeah! Just wait until you see your mistakes in print!" And sure enough, it wasn't long until Velma made one little mistake, and it was multiplied many thousands of times. When this happened, I always praised God that it wasn't a serious mistake. I always tried to be more careful in the future.

I want to tell about an interesting event that happened in that shipping department a few years before I began working there. At the time, the Baptist Sunday School Board owned seven of the largest buildings in downtown Nashville. When I first came, the art department was located on the tenth floor of the eleven-story tower building. Later, the art department was moved across 10th Avenue and located on the second floor above the Shipping Department. It is one large building connected to the public bookstore, across from the Nashville Train Station. Next door to the train station was the main post office. The Baptists had hired three large trucks and nine drivers to load up the printed literature packages to be shipped out, drive a half block away to the post office, and unload the packages. Then drive the half block back to the Shipping Department and reload for their next trip.

One of the workers in the Shipping Department got the idea to build an underground tunnel from the Shipping Department to the Post Office. It had an overhead linked track with mail bags hanging from the track about every ten feet that could be loaded with packages and carried underground under the buildings, under the bookstore, under the five-lane Broadway street, and directly to the post office. It worked very efficiently, but put the trucks and the drivers out of business.

This system worked wonderfully well, until the city moved that main post office from downtown Nashville to out by the Nashville Airport. Then the men and trucks were hired again for shipping the literature. The old post office has been turned into a lovely art museum.

A few years ago, I read in the newspapers that The Southern Baptists sold their buildings and relocated to a new smaller building in a different part of Nashville, as they needed to downsize. That same year, the Methodists also sold their main building. The Methodists had their own printing presses in their building, whereas, the Baptist hired their literature printed with several local printers in the Nashville area.

It's interesting to me that hundreds of people worked in that Shipping Department for the Baptists, but it took just one man's good idea from the Lord to improve that Shipping Department with that under-ground tunnel. When people have jobs that are boring to them, they could pray to Father God in faith in the holy name of Jesus, and ASK Father God how they can IMPROVE their job for service to others and to help themselves, to God's glory. Then be amazed at what our God's Holy Spirit leads them to do! God is good!

As we work on our jobs with joy to the Lord's glory, we are shown how to work faster and better with more fun, like moving with a musical rhythm! We can easily accomplish better quality work in lesser time. I can see the improvements in my artwork in the last few weeks and months as I have been working for a few minutes daily on the acrylic paintings of butterflies. Father God told me, **"Every painting you finish will be better than the last one."** Praise God for the help of our God's Holy Spirit doing the work through us.

Blessings! Velma

Yes, Our God's beloved Christian children of Our God's beloved Christian pastors and ALL of Our God's beloved Holy Bible teachers, YOUR heavenly Father God does love you, does take care of you by providing for you, protecting you, guiding you, and using you to help others to Our God's glory on Our God's planet Earth.

Yes, Our God has NOW created beautiful homes for you in heaven and has provided beautiful homes in heaven for ALL of Our God's faithful, dedicated-to-God Christian children of God.

Yes, do be faithful to YOUR Holy Triune God on earth to the end of the age, and you WILL reap GREAT rewards in heaven after your one lifetime on earth is over.

Yes, the God that you do know, do love, and do serve is a VERY powerful God, a very loving God, a just God, an everlasting God, a very generous God, and a God Who rewards the righteous-living Christian people, and Who does allow evil people time to REPENT of their evil before bringing punishment on them.

Yes, your God is HOLY!

Yes, do live a HOLY lifestyle unto your God.

Yes, preach and teach holy living unto God.

Yes, salvation in Jesus Christ and holy living do bring MANY good rewards to you and to others who know God, love God, and who live in a righteous lifestyle unto THEIR God.

Yes, when others see your holy lifestyle lived unto the glory of God, and when they do see ALL of Our God's rewards to you for your obedience to God, they WILL be drawn to YOUR God for their desire for their prosperous living.

Yes, Our God does give prosperous living to all of His righteous-living Christian people.

Yes, doesn't Our God's Holy Bible teach you that it is God Who gives you the power to get wealth? (Deuteronomy 8:18)

Yes, at the moment of conception of each person now alive on earth, Our Father God gave each one an eternal soul that will live forever, and Our God also gave each person special gifts at their conception that will help them to lead successful and prosperous lives on earth, if they will develop these gifts in their life and use the gifts to help themselves, help others, and glorify Our God on earth.

Yes, EVERY person has at least ONE gift from God and others have many gifts from God given to them at the moment of conception in their mother's womb that if pursued and developed WILL bring success in their life on earth.

Yes, doesn't Our God's Holy Bible teach for each person to bring a gift to God? (Deuteronomy 16:16-17)

Yes, EVERYONE does have a gift that they can give BACK to their God, by developing their gift or gifts from God and then use these good gifts to help themselves and help others to Our God's glory on earth.

Yes, your talents and abilities will grow as you use and develop them.

Yes, Our God does help you to be a success in your life.

Doesn't Our God's Holy Bible teach you that you can do ALL things through Christ which strengthens you? (Philippians 4:13)

Doesn't Jesus Christ teach that apart from Jesus you can do nothing? (John 15:5)

Yes, Our God does give you knowledge, wisdom, skills, opportunities for advancements, and open doors for spiritual, mental, emotional, physical, and financial growth in your life.

Yes, when you do draw near to your God and your God does draw near to you, your advancement and successes in life begin and then continue to grow as you are led and fed by your God daily and nightly.

Yes, do be more sensitive to Our God's Holy Spirit's leading in your life, and as you learn to quickly obey Our God's leadership in your daily and nightly life, the sooner your advancement will come from YOUR Holy Triune God.

Yes, YOUR heavenly Father God has given to each of you a holy calling to preach and teach others from Our God's Holy Bible ALL the great truths written therein.

Yes, every word of Our God's Holy Bible is absolutely true, as it has been proofed seven times. (Psalm 12:6)

Yes, every promise given to mankind in Our God's Holy Bible is absolutely true, and the promises of God will work for any of mankind who will meet the conditions of the promises as you do know and do serve a great God Who does not show partiality to Our God's children as Our Holy Triune God does love all of Our God's children of mankind the same.

Yes, Our Holy Triune God did create and still does create each of Our God's mankind in Our God's image with body, soul, and spirit.

Yes, Our God created and still does create today Our God's mankind of male and female on earth to reproduce of their own kind.

Yes, when any of mankind perverts sexual relations outside of marriage of a man and his wife this does displease God, and it does cause Our God to withhold Our God's many benefits from mankind.

Yes, Our God does send Our God's rain on the just and on the unjust because without Our God's rain on the earth, none of mankind could survive for long. (Matthew 5:45)

Yes, do read of the history of nations in the Bible of how people sinned against God, and how Our God punished and corrected them by withholding the rain, and their food supply became scarce.

Yes, Our God does control the rain supply, and Our God does control all of the weather patterns on Our God's earth.

Yes, Our God controls the sun, moon, and stars and uses them to control all the elements on earth.

Yes, mankind did NOT evolve from monkeys, apes, or other creatures large or small, as Our God did create man in Our God's image, to know God, to fellowship/commune with God, to love and obey God, to be rewarded by God.

Yes, when Eve and Adam deliberately disobeyed God and ate the forbidden fruit in the Garden of Eden, they had been told by God that they would surely die. (Genesis 2:17)

When they disobeyed God, their actions brought sin into the world, so their children and all the following generations were born with a sin nature which would eventually cause the physical death of the person.

Yes, it is appointed unto man to die once, and after that is Our God's judgment. (Hebrews 9:27)

Yes, mankind's fellowship daily with THEIR holy Creator God was broken, but Father God sent His only begotten Son Jesus Christ to restore mankind's relationship with THEIR heavenly Father God by paying for mankind's own sins and paying for Adam's original sin, paying the penalty for their sins with His holy shed blood and death on Calvary's cruel cross.

Yes, Father God raised Jesus Christ from death and the grave in three days, and now Jesus Christ IS seated at His Father God's right hand now in Our God's third heaven where Jesus is now interceding with HIS Father God for each person who is NOW alive on earth, that they will COME to Jesus, ASK Jesus to save them from their sins, ACCEPT this free gift of salvation of their soul from Jesus, then go and sin no more, but live a righteous lifestyle unto God, and then spend eternity in heaven with THEIR Holy Triune God after their one lifetime on earth is over.

Yes, Jesus Christ is your ONLY Door to heaven, and you must accept Jesus as your Lord and Savior and come OUT of

ALL sinful lifestyle and live for God while you are now alive on earth in order to enter heaven in your afterlife after your one life on earth.

Yes, no one else, either dead or alive, has enough power to save a person, keep their eternal soul out of hell, and give a person FREE access to heaven except Jesus Christ of Nazareth.

Yes, Jesus is mankind's ONLY Savior, and Jesus Christ is your ONLY access to heaven in your afterlife.

You cannot WORK your way into heaven by loving and helping others.

You cannot PURCHASE your way into heaven.

You must come in at the ONLY Door to heaven, by coming to Jesus Christ, ASKING Jesus to save you from your sins, ASKING Jesus to be your Lord and Savior, then by going and sinning no more.

Yes, Jesus Christ is your ONLY access to the one true God, YOUR heavenly Father God, Who created you in Our God's image. (1 Timothy 2:5)

Yes, you cannot come into the holy presence of YOUR heavenly Father God except you be first cleansed of ALL unholy filth in the shed blood of Jesus that makes you free from sin, whole, and complete, to enter YOUR heavenly Father God's presence.

Yes, YOUR heavenly Father God is holy and pure and cannot look on sin. (Habakkuk 1:13)

Yes, after you are born-again and saved in the shed blood of Jesus on Calvary's cross, you may enter your heavenly Father God's very presence and ask what you wish for ALL your needs and ALL your holy desires to be met, praying your prayers in the holy name of Jesus, and your prayer requests will be answered according to your faith in Jesus.

Yes, your heavenly Father God spoke this entire universe into existence.

When prayers are prayed to YOUR heavenly Father God, when they are prayed believing in Jesus' holy name, your heavenly Father God does speak the words, "Be it done unto you according to your faith in Jesus Christ," then Father God looks to see which of the prayers are answered.

Yes, do have great faith in Our God's Son Jesus Christ, YOUR divine Savior, YOUR divine Healer, YOUR divine Giver of ALL good gifts along with YOUR heavenly Father God.

Yes, all good gifts that you now have in your life are good gifts from YOUR heavenly Father God and these good gifts are given to you THROUGH Jesus Christ. (Philippians 4:19)

Hallelujah!

Praises to our wonderful heavenly Father God for this prophetic message for church growth!

Hallelujah!

Praises to Our God!

Dear Christian Pastors and All Holy Bible Teachers,

I have prayed for you that Our God's Holy Spirit will help me to write encouraging words to you to help you to grow in the Lord, to be more successful in your daily and nightly walk with the Lord.

I have been in church services all of my life and have always loved our church services and our Sunday School classes. The first ten years of my life, my mother and my four siblings and I attended a small Southern Baptist Church in rural southern Mississippi. Our church then had about seventy to eighty in attendance for our Sunday morning worship service and had about half that many for our Sunday evening worship service. We sang church hymns from our Baptist Hymnal with our volunteer song leader and volunteer pianist. I remember us singing the words to "Amazing Grace" of, "When we've been there ten thousand years, bright shining as the sun, we've no less days to sing God's praise than when we first begun." I was about eight years old when the truth of this song was revealed to me. I thought, "I want to go to heaven and sing praises to God for ten thousand years!"

Shortly after that, a visiting evangelist came and spoke at our church ending his sermon with the plan of salvation, saying, "If you want to be saved by Jesus and go to heaven, just lift up your hand to Jesus." I did accept Jesus then and was the only one at the time who came forward to be welcomed as a new Christian. A few weeks later, I was water-immersed baptized in a nearby river with several other newly converted Christians from our Baptist church.

Since then, now that I am seventy-nine years old and have continued to attend church services all of my life, our God's Holy Spirit has given me another meaning of those words, "We've no less days to sing God's praise than when we first begun." This new meaning is not about the ones in heaven, but the ones in hell. Father God told me that the souls trapped in hell now will be there for eternity. He revealed to me that our human minds are too small to understand how long eternity is. He told me, "**If each leaf in the state of Tennessee equals a thousand years, when that amount of time is up, it begins all over again unending.**" Tennessee is over four hundred miles east to west, and over a hundred miles north to south. It is covered with rolling hills that are covered with trees and bushes that are covered with leaves!

As I was driving the 2½ hours from Nashville to Chattanooga through the lower mountains, I kept looking at all the hills that were covered with trees that were covered with leaves. For all that time, I kept thinking about what our Father God had told me about the people being trapped in a tormenting hell for eternity with NO HOPE of ever escaping. My mind was just boggled at thinking of each of these leaves equaling a thousand years, and when that amount of time is over, it begins over again! Our minds are just too small to imagine just how long of a time that equals! God impressed upon me the seriousness of winning souls to Jesus Christ, for them to come out of all sin, live for God, and enter heaven forever.

I knew that I wanted to devote the rest of my life on earth to winning souls to Jesus Christ! I want to make it the highest priority in my life!

Father God has impressed upon me that if people reject salvation in Jesus from their sins, and if they refuse to repent and come out of a sinful lifestyle, and if they die in their sins, they will end up in hell for eternity, where there is NO ESCAPE from hell. Some people are now deceived into thinking that there is no hell. Father God once told me that, "**Some of the people now in hell did not believe there is a hell when they were alive on earth.**" Now it is too late for them as they are trapped in hell forever!

Father God tells us all about heaven and all about hell in His Holy Bible, and He should know the truth about heaven and about hell as He created them both. He created hell for Satan and all his followers. God does NOT send people to hell. God sent Jesus to save people who would receive salvation in Jesus, and live a righteous lifestyle unto God. People send themselves to hell by rejecting salvation in Jesus and by refusing to come out of all sinful lifestyle and live righteously in obedience to God.

Many preachers today want only to preach their sermons to encourage the righteous, and not preach sermons to warn the wicked. However, the Bible does warn the wicked what will happen to them in their afterlife, after their one life on earth is over, if they do not repent of their sins, come to Jesus for salvation, and live for God while alive on earth.

I believe that God wants all preachers and all Bible teachers to preach and teach the truth, the WHOLE TRUTH, and nothing but the truth. I believe that if preachers and Bible teachers do not teach the whole truth of the Bible, that our God will hold them responsible for not WARNING the unrighteous. When Jesus walked this earth, he told the woman caught in adultery to, "go and sin no more." Yes, God does want ALL the Christians to live righteously, to rebuke ALL sin in their lives, to live for and with God, if they do want to go to heaven for eternity.

Some people believe that "once saved, always saved," but living in a sinful lifestyle after a person is a saved Christian WILL KEEP THEM OUT of heaven if they do die in their sins, because Father God says, **"Sin will never enter heaven."** The Bible states, "The wages of sin is death." It also states that life in hell is known as the second death. It is the job of the Christian pastors and all Bible teachers to warn people of hell, and encourage all people to pray in their lost loved ones, and get ready for our God's great rapture of all the saved and righteous-living souls on earth that will take place soon! Be encouraged!

Blessings! Velma

Yes, Our God's beloved Christian children of Our God's Christian pastors and ALL of Our God's beloved Holy Bible teachers, YOUR heavenly Father God does love you, does provide for you, does protect you and all of your loved ones, and does give to you ALL good things and all good events for you to enjoy on Our God's planet Earth.

Yes, ALL GOOD gifts and all good events that you now have in your life have been given to you by YOUR heavenly Father of lights, and they do come to you through YOUR Lord and Savior, Jesus Christ. (Philippians 4:19)

Yes, Jesus Christ came to Our God's planet Earth and opened up the way for each of mankind to commune with their Holy Triune God one on one, without going through a priest, high priest, or other person to get to YOUR holy God.

Yes, there is one true God and one mediator between men and God, the Person of Jesus Christ. (1 Timothy 2:5)

Yes, when you pray, always pray ALL of your prayers in the holy name of Jesus and pray with great faith in Jesus.

Yes, Our God does answer righteous prayers from righteous people prayed with great faith and prayed in the holy name of Jesus that will help people and will glorify Our God on earth.

Yes, your Father God is righteous.

Your Lord Jesus Christ is righteous.

Yes, Our God DEMANDS righteous living at ALL times for ALL of Our God's obedient Christian children.

Yes, you cannot ride the fence of indecision, but must be HOT or COLD for Father God, Jesus Christ, and Our God's Holy Spirit.

Yes, the people who are led by the Holy Spirit of God are the obedient Christian children of God. (Romans 8:14)

Yes, yes, yes, do LIVE righteously for YOUR God.

Yes, do teach others to come OUT of ALL sinful lifestyle and live for God if they do want to go to heaven in their life after their one life on Our God's planet Earth.

Yes, it is appointed unto each of mankind to die once on earth and after that is Our God's judgment. (Hebrews 9:27)

Yes, the prayers of a righteous person availeth much. (James 8:16)

Yes, live righteously and pray, pray, pray, often and pray long.

Yes, thank Our God's Holy Triune God for ALL of Our God's good benefits to you.

Yes, enter into Our God's courts with praise, be thankful unto God, and bless Our God's holy name. (Psalm 100:4)

Yes, do keep a continual praise to Our God's Holy Triune God on your mind and with your voice, and you will have continual love, peace, and good will in your heart and mind at all times.

Yes, depression, anxiety, fear, worry, and evil thoughts that do try to attack your mind and your emotions will have to flee from you when you center your mind and your thoughts on God continually.

Yes, doesn't Our God's Holy Bible teach you that you will have perfect peace when you center your mind, KEEP your mind centered, on God? (Isaiah 26:30)

Yes, Jesus Christ is Lord and Ruler of all.

Yes, COME to Jesus, ask your Lord and Master for all of your needed help, your comfort, your salvation and redemption, your true knowledge and wisdom in your decision making, and YOUR Lord and Savior will NEVER fail you, but will ALWAYS give to you your needed help always on time.

Trust your God Jesus to help you.

Trust your God Jesus Who loves you, Who has prepared

a way to heaven and to everlasting, joyous life in heaven for eternity to ALL who will receive it from Jesus, who will then go and live an obedient life unto God for the rest of their life on Our God's planet Earth.

Yes, do tell everyone you meet about the free gift of abundant life on earth and free everlasting, joyous life in heaven that is FREE for them in Jesus, when they do come to Jesus with a repentant heart, accept this free gift of salvation from THEIR King Jesus, who will then live a righteous lifestyle to God while they are alive on earth.

Yes, Jesus Christ is the only Being, dead or alive, with enough power to save a person's eternal soul, keep them out of hell, and give them eternal life in Our God's beautiful heaven.

Where is Our God's beautiful heaven located?

Our God's third heaven where Father God and Jesus Christ live is far ABOVE ALL of your known universe.

Yes, Jesus came down to earth from heaven, led a perfect life on Our God's planet Earth, become the ONLY true Savior of ALL of Our God's mankind Who returned to heaven and is now seated at the right hand of HIS heavenly Father God.

Yes, SOON Jesus Christ will return to the heavenlies just above Our God's planet Earth to claim and to catch away ALL of Our God's obedient Christian children to take them BACK to THEIR heavenly home to live with, to enjoy with for eternity, THEIR Holy Triune God!

Yes, when you do know God, love God, serve God, and do love and help your fellow mankind as you love and help yourself, YOUR heavenly Father God does reward you.

Yes, as your soul grows more in God, you will be promoted more by YOUR heavenly Father God with more benefits and more responsibilities to help more people to YOUR God's glory on earth.

Yes, you do now have Our God's Holy Spirit living within you to guide you into all truth, all truthful living and all truthful teaching of others.

Yes, as your soul grows more in God daily, you WILL become a more powerful Bible teacher of the truths contained in Our God's Holy Bible given to ALL of Our God's mankind on earth, for them to KNOW intimately THEIR holy Creator God, to LOVE THEIR Holy Triune God, to fellowship with their TRUE God, to honor and obey THEIR God, to live righteously with THEIR God daily and nightly, and be greatly rewarded by THEIR Holy Triune God in ALL good things and in ALL good events.

Yes, YOUR Holy Triune God now has many excellent benefits created by God and laid up since the beginning of time on earth to give to each and to all of mankind on earth WHEN mankind has advanced enough in God to be able to receive these good gifts from God without their becoming corrupt with these good gifts and good benefits.

Yes, every good gift that any of mankind now enjoys on earth has been given to them FROM their heavenly Father God and has been given to them THROUGH Jesus Christ. (Philippians 4:19)

Yes, your life, your health, your opportunities for achievements, your daily progress, your growth, all that you own or ever hope to own, are ALL good gifts to you from YOUR holy Creator God.

Yes, Our God did create each of mankind in Our God's image with body, soul, and spirit, and placed mankind on earth to live only once, and then Our God's judgment. (Hebrews 9:27)

Yes, after Our God created Adam and Eve and placed them in the Garden of Eden, they fellowshipped daily with God until they disobeyed God by eating the forbidden fruit, and had to be released from the beautiful Garden of Eden, and their daily fellowship with their holy Creator God was broken.

Yes, Our God's only begotten Son Jesus Christ came to earth to restore mankind's broken relationship with THEIR holy Creator God.

Yes, Jesus Christ, the only begotten Son of God, came to

earth as a baby born of the virgin Mary, led a sinless life as He grew in favor with God and man, and shed His sinless, pure blood and gave His life on Calvary's cruel cross, so that mankind's sins could be forgiven, and each of mankind could ask Jesus for forgiveness of ALL their sins, could make Jesus their Lord and Savior, could then live a righteous lifestyle on earth, and their communion and daily fellowship with God could resume.

Yes, when Jesus Christ died on Calvary's cross, when Jesus said, "It is finished," the temple curtain was rent in two, signifying that each of mankind now had power through salvation in Jesus to enter the Holy of Holies in the temple and commune with THEIR holy Creator God.

Yes, after Jesus' death on Calvary's cruel cross, He was in the sealed tomb for three days before HIS heavenly Father God raised Jesus from the dead.

Yes, Jesus' resurrected body ascended from earth into the third heaven where His heavenly Father God now resides, where Jesus is now seated at the right hand of HIS heavenly Father God, now interceding for all of mankind on earth to know Jesus as Savior from their sins, live for God on earth, and enter heaven for eternity after their one life and one death on earth.

Yes, SOON Jesus Christ WILL split the Eastern skies coming back towards earth for Our God's great catching away in a split second ALL the saved-in-Jesus and right-living-unto-God obedient Christians to take them BACK to THEIR home in heaven.

Yes, when Jesus Christ walked this earth nearly two thousand years ago, didn't Jesus say to His followers, "If I go away, I will prepare a place for you, and I will come again, and receive you unto myself; that where I am, there you may be also."? (John 14:3)

Yes, Jesus ALWAYS keeps His promises to mankind.

Yes, Jesus is now listening for the words of His Father God's command to, "Go! Go back towards earth and claim your holy Bride-to-be!"

Yes, the wedding banquet in heaven is NOW ready for the Bridegroom to GO and claim HIS holy Bride, the Bride without spot or wrinkle, the Bride cleansed of ALL sin and wrongdoing, the Bride of Christ awaiting the last trumpet sound for Our God's great rapture of all the saved and obedient Christian children of God.

Yes, soon time on earth is running out as you do know time now on earth to be.

Yes, soon time on earth WILL change to Our God's millennial time, when a thousand years will be as one day. (2 Peter 3:8)

Yes, do GET READY to meet Jesus Christ in the air in ANY split second.

Yes, time on earth is running out.

Stay prayed up.

Stay fasted up.

Stay ready to go.

Pray in ALL your lost loved ones.

Witness for Jesus.

Tell others that Jesus loves them.

Tell others Jesus is the only Being, dead or alive, Who has the power to save them from their sins and give them an eternal home in heaven with Jesus and THEIR Father God and Our God's Holy Spirit.

Yes, your eternal soul will live forever either in heaven with your true God, or it will live in hell with Satan, man's tormentor, as there are NO OTHER PLACES for your eternal soul to live after your one life and one death on earth.

Yes, choose Jesus now and you will NEVER regret choosing Jesus.

Come out of ALL sinful lifestyle and live for God, and you will NEVER regret it.

If you reject Jesus, and if you live a sinful lifestyle, and if you die in your sins, you can and will regret it in hell forever.

Warn the wicked what awaits them if they refuse Jesus and refuse to live for God.

Yes, God does not send people to hell as God has made a way through His only Son Jesus for them to enter heaven.

Choose Jesus now, live for God, and enjoy heaven forever.

Praises to Our heavenly Father God for this prophetic message for church growth!

Hallelujah!

Praises to Our God!

Dear Christian Pastors and All Holy Bible Teachers,

Again, I have been praying that God's Holy Spirit will help me to write an encouraging letter to you not only for your spiritual growth in God, but also for you to preach and teach sermons that are full of the "meat" of the Word of God and not just crumbs.

Once upon a time, in the church where I had been a member for thirty-nine years, the lead pastor had been watching a lot of movies, and he decided it would be fun to have a series of sermons about the movies, complete with costumed actors and actresses on stage in the pulpit. Since he goes on Facebook a lot, he decided to take a survey to find out what movies people had been watching, and requested that the church members tell him their favorite movies, that could be acted out on stage on Sunday mornings, instead of having his regular sermons.

One teenage boy answered him online and said something like this: "Preachers used to preach from the Bible." This made the preacher very angry and he scolded the boy, telling him something like this: "Who are you, a young inexperienced child, to tell an experienced preacher of many years, what I should do!" Then the preacher spread the word about this boy, that the boy made a comment like that because he was having problems at home, and that he should have never said such an insulting thing to this pastor, with his many years of being a pastor of a large church.

One of the costumed stage plays that was presented, the whole message was, "Love those who love you." It had nothing about the Bible and nothing about Jesus. It was entertaining and fun to watch, but nothing about spiritual growth in God. Then the exact same performance was held a couple of weeks later, complete with costumed actresses, with the same message, just entertainment. Some of the older members did NOT like it!

After I had watched that second entertaining performance of the same movie, Father God gave to me a message to give to this pastor, which I wrote out and handed to him after the service. The message read:

Father God says, "When you feed people Jesus and the Bible, you are feeding them steaks.

When you feed them movies, you are feeding them, but you are feeding them crumbs."

Then later Father God said for me to tell him something else, which I wrote out and gave to him:

"People will go where they are being fed. If you feed them Jesus and the Bible, they will return."

Later, Father God said to me, **"He will not listen to a word you say, but he will listen to God."**

Later, Father God said to me, **"You have done your part. God will continue to work with him."**

Then God's Holy Spirit said to me, **"See where he is in one year and see where you are in one year."**

A year after I gave that first written message to this pastor, he again presented five more movies as substitutes for his five sermons, which were NOT about Jesus and the Bible. This pastor is a great friend of Joel Osteen. He preached five sermons from one of Joel's books. The messages were good in that they encouraged the righteous to keep living righteously and be blessed by God. The sermons said nothing about warning the wicked to come out of their sins and live for God. They also said nothing about getting ready and staying ready for the SOON return of Jesus for our God's great rapture, the great catching away to heaven of all the saved-in-Jesus and all the right-living-for-God obedient Christians. Always stay ready to go in any split second to meet Jesus in the air.

For all preachers and all Bible teachers to be on SAFE ground in all your sermons, live like Jesus lived, and preach and teach what Jesus taught. Then the hungry souls in the congregation will be fed their steaks, and will return for more good food, and will bring their friends. Praise God!

When this pastor did preach his lukewarm sermons about Jesus and the Bible, at the end of his sermons, he would ask, "Did you get anything out of this?" And my answer to him in my mind was usually, "No. I could have gotten more out of reading a good Christian teaching book at home."

But, since I had always been attending that church for thirty-nine years, I continued to attend. However, God's Holy Spirit led me to pray this prayer before I attended each church service:

"Father God, please show me what you want me to learn from this sermon." Then an amazing thing happened to me! It became like this pastor's sermon became the first half of the message, and God downloaded to me the second and better half of that same message! I began learning a great deal during and after each of these sermons! Since I have been reading the Bible nearly daily for more than 45 years, God's Holy Spirit began to bring to my memory more Scripture verses that applied to the lukewarm sermons that made the sermons RICH in POWER! I began thanking and praising God for these sermons and thanking God for His teaching me MORE than the sermons, and God teaching me how I can apply these great Bible truths to my own life to enrich my life. In my life now, before I hear any speaker teach or hear any preacher preach, I pray that God will teach me what He wants me to learn from their message, and teach me how I can apply it to my own life, to make my life better. It truly amazes me how my God always answers my prayers for this.

Since I have moved to Marietta, Georgia, have now joined the large Mt. Bethel United Methodist Church, I am thrilled that our main pastor, Dr. Jody Ray, ALWAYS teaches his whole sermons about Jesus and the Bible. He is very consistent in this with every sermon! Maybe this is why this church has over nine thousand members with great outreaches to reach people for Jesus in this area. When he said in one of his sermons, "I would do anything except sinning to win people to Jesus Christ," I knew that I had joined the right church! Praise God!

After I heard Pastor Jody say that in one of his sermons, I wrote him a note that asked: "As pastor of this church, would you be willing to let five thousand families camp out on the church grounds for three days and three nights while Jesus saves the people and heals the maimed?"

There is a young blind man in the choir at Mt. Bethel church, who has been blind since he had brain surgery for cancer at age 13. Since Jesus is our divine Healer, I asked Jesus if he wanted to heal Will Graham of his blindness? Jesus answered me, **"Yes, yes, yes, a thousand times yes, the sooner the better!"** Then I asked Jesus if He would give to me a prophetic message each month to give to Will to increase his faith in Jesus for his healing? Jesus said that He would do so. I have now asked Jesus for and have received three messages from Jesus to Will, instructing Will how to have faith for his physical healing and how to claim and receive his eyesight healed to 20/20 vision. He is to pray to Father God in Jesus' name with great faith asking God for his healing. Then he is to praise God continually daily and nightly and thank God that he is healed, until the healing manifests in the physical. Jesus said that He will raise up Will as a voice testifying that Jesus is alive and well and is still the divine Healer today that He was when He walked this earth two thousand years ago—that Jesus can heal people that mankind cannot heal! I'm praying for this daily, claiming this miracle for Will Graham for God's glory on earth.

I have been giving copies to our Pastor Jody of these messages from Jesus to Will. My latest note to Pastor Jody said, "I see a cloud the size of a man's hand!" (If you don't know what that means, look it up in the Bible. It's an interesting teaching about faith in God.)

Blessings! Velma

Yes, Our God's beloved Christian children of Our God's beloved pastors and ALL of Our God's beloved Holy Bible teachers, YOUR heavenly Father God does love you, does take care of you, does provide for you, does protect you, and does HELP you in ALL of your good works to serve Our God's mankind and to serve Our God on earth.

Yes, your God IS an ALL-POWERFUL God Who is ABLE to HELP ALL of Our God's mankind when they do REACH OUT to their Holy Triune God, THEIR holy Creator God, for help.

Yes, Our God is ready to give ALL needed help to ALL of Our God's mankind on earth when they do COME to Our God, repent of ALL sinful lifestyle, ASK Jesus Christ to forgive their sins and wrongdoing, ASK for Our God's help, ASK for free salvation from Jesus, come out of ALL sinful lifestyle and live righteously for God, THEN Our God WILL help them spiritually, mentally, emotionally, physically, and financially.

Yes, Our Holy Triune God is the total and complete answer to ALL of Our God's mankind's troubles and dilemmas, WHEN mankind does get right with God and does ALLOW Our God to help them.

Yes, symbolically, when a person is slowly sinking in quicksand, if they will reach out their hand to Jesus, He will pull them out without judging how they got there.

Yes, Jesus is a God of love.

Jesus is a God of power.

Jesus is the God with ALL the right answers to peoples' lives on earth.

Yes, Jesus says that apart from Jesus, you can do nothing. (John 15:5)

The Holy Bible teaches that you can do all things through Christ which strengthens you. (Philippians 4:13)

Yes, yes, yes, know Jesus, love Jesus, trust Jesus, pray to Jesus, pray to YOUR heavenly Father God in the holy name of Jesus.

Pray, pray, pray, to your God with great faith in the holy name of Jesus, live for God, and receive, receive, receive, ALL good things and all good events from YOUR heavenly Father God THROUGH YOUR Lord and Savior, Jesus Christ, that will help you, will help others, and will glorify God on earth.

Yes, when you know God, receive God's rewards by living a righteous lifestyle unto God, others WILL SEE your prosperous lifestyle, and will want to know, worship, praise, and live for YOUR God and receive these same blessing from THEIR God.

Yes, ALL who do COME to Jesus Christ with a repentant heart, who ASK Jesus for forgiveness of sins, will be received by Jesus, will be forgiven by Jesus, will be given a portion of Our God's Holy Spirit to live within them that will help them to live for God, and they will be enabled to live for God, and honor God by living in a righteous lifestyle for God.

Yes, Our God does reward Our God's mankind who knows Our God, loves Our God, honors Our God, does live for Our God, and who does help their fellow mankind with love to Our God's glory on earth.

Yes, know God.

Love and honor God.

Live for God.

Teach others of the love, mercy, goodness, justice, and power of God, power to help them when they can't help themselves and when no one else can help them.

Yes, teach them that Jesus is ALWAYS the BEST answer for anything that troubles them.

Yes, Jesus is ALWAYS ready to help them when they do COME to Jesus and ASK Jesus for His help.

Yes, Jesus is ALL-POWERFUL in heaven and in and on Our God's planet Earth. (Matthew 28:18)

Yes, call on Jesus!

Trust Jesus to help you!

Yes, Jesus loves you!

Yes, Jesus paid the price of His shed blood and holy life on Calvary's cross for your cleansing of ALL SIN and ALL wrongdoing that does open the door to heaven for you in your life after your one life on earth ends.

Yes, Jesus Christ is the ONLY Door to heaven, and you must ASK Jesus for it while you are NOW alive on earth.

Tomorrow may be too late to choose Jesus, repent of your sinful lifestyle, live for God, and enter heaven.

Yes, choose Jesus now, choose to live for God now, and NEVER regret your choices, never regret it in your one lifetime on earth, nor regret it in heaven after your one lifetime on earth ends.

Yes, NOW is the right time to get right with your ONLY Lord and Savior, Jesus Christ, and live for God.

Yes, if you reject Jesus and the FREE salvation Jesus offers and if you refuse to come out of ALL sinful lifestyle and live for God, you WILL regret it in hell for eternity where there is no hope of escaping.

Yes, choose Jesus now.

Repent of sins and live for God now and be rewarded by God now.

Enter heaven forever!

Yes, YOUR Holy Triune God IS all-powerful, all-loving, is very generous, and does have all things and all people WELL in Our God's control at ALL times, both in the heavens AND on and in Our God's planet Earth.

Yes, do come to YOUR heavenly Father God daily, even hourly, and ask YOUR heavenly Father God to meet ALL your many needs and ALL your holy desires, always praying in the holy name of Jesus, praying with your GREAT FAITH in Jesus;

then praise your God often until your answers to your prayers are manifested in the physical.

Yes, YOUR heavenly Father God does DELIGHT to answer ALL your believing prayers prayed in Jesus' holy name that will benefit you, will benefit others, and WILL bring glory to YOUR God on earth.

Yes, is any prayer request too difficult for the power of God to perform?

No, Our God's power is unlimited and is able to do what is impossible for mankind to do, is very easy for Our God to do.

Yes, no prayer request is too difficult for Our God to accomplish, and no prayer request is too small for Our God's love to accomplish, when prayed in faith in the name of Jesus.

Yes, the holy name of Jesus is above every name, and at the name of Jesus every knee will bow and every tongue will confess that Jesus Christ is Lord of all. (Philippians 2:10-11)

Yes, Father God raised the body of Jesus Christ from the dead and gave all power in heaven and in earth into the capable hands of Jesus. (Matthew 28:18)

Yes, Jesus has commissioned all people, whosoever will, to go into all the world and spread the gospel of Jesus Christ, that whosoever will MAY come to Jesus with a repentant heart, ASK Jesus to save them from ALL their sins and wrongdoing, accept this free gift of salvation in Jesus, then go and live a holy life unto God.

Yes, tell everyone you meet about the love of Jesus and the saving grace of Jesus.

Yes, Jesus is the ONLY Being now, dead or alive, with enough power to save their soul, forgive their sins, and give them FREE entrance into heaven in their life after their one life on earth.

Yes, when Jesus Christ ascended into heaven after His resurrection from the dead, He sent Our God's Holy Spirit to earth to woo people to Jesus Christ for salvation, and for living a righteous lifestyle unto God by living within the Christians, and for entering heaven forever after their one lifetime on earth.

Yes, as each person does give their life to Jesus Christ to be cleansed of their sins in Jesus' holy shed blood, Our God does give each new Christian a part of Our God's Holy Spirit to live within them to guide them into ALL holy living for God, to comfort them, to pray with and for them, to give them Our God's knowledge, wisdom, and strength to lead successful lives on earth and to prosper in ALL their good endeavors to help themselves, to help others, and to glorify THEIR God on earth.

Yes, you are NOT ALONE if you have given your heart and life to Jesus Christ as your personal Lord and Savior as you have Our God's Holy Spirit living within you as your divine Guide and divine God, directing your thoughts, your steps, and your deeds.

Also, you do have the promise of Jesus given to you that when you spread the gospel worldwide that Jesus does go with you even to the end of the world. (Matthew 28:20)

Yes, you also have the wonderful promise of Jesus that where two or more are gathered in Jesus' name that He, Jesus, is there with you. (Matthew 18:20)

Yes, Jesus gave to you His wonderful promise that He will never leave you and that He will never fail you. (Hebrews 13:5)

Yes, Jesus Christ is ALWAYS faithful to ALWAYS keep ALL His many promises to ALL of mankind, when mankind is faithful to meet the conditions of the promises of Jesus.

Yes, Jesus NEVER fails.

Yes, Jesus LOVES you and always wants your happiness, your joy, your success in ALL your good endeavors to help yourself, help others, and to glorify God on earth.

Yes, TRUST Jesus.

ASK Jesus to speak to you, praise Jesus, and wait on your knees patiently until JESUS speaks to you, then PRAISE Jesus for speaking to you.

Yes, evil forces are ABLE to speak to you pretending to be good forces, but evil forces are NOT ALLOWED to use the holy name of Jesus when they speak to you.

Yes, evil forces do have the power to speak to you, so do learn to "try" the spirit voices you do hear, to compare what they tell you to see if it agrees with what Our God's Holy Bible teaches you. (1 John 4:1-3)

Yes, do read, do study, do memorize parts of your Holy Bible daily, and make ALL the teachings of Our God's Holy Bible so much a part of your life so that when you do hear a voice in your mind speaking to you, you will know immediately if it agrees with the WHOLE teachings of the Bible.

Yes, Satan quoted the Scripture of the 91st Psalm to Jesus, but Jesus answered Satan with a Scripture that showed to Satan that he was NOT using rightly the Scripture.

Yes, do know how to "rightly divide" the word of God.

Yes, Our God's Holy Spirit working within you will bring more Scriptures to your mind to help you to "rightly divide" the word of God, if people quote Scriptures to you, and if they do give to you the wrong interpretations to specific Scriptures.

Yes, you will know the truth and the whole truth of Scripture, and the truth will set you free. (John 8:32)

Jesus Christ is the way, the truth, and the life. (John 14:6)

Praises to Our holy God Jesus!

Praises to Our heavenly Father God for this prophetic message for church growth!

Hallelujah!

Praises to Our Holy Triune God!

Hallelujah!

Dear Christian Pastors and All Holy Bible Teachers,

Again, I have been praying and asking our God's Holy Spirit to give to me some encouraging words to all of you to keep on fighting the good fight of faith, to keep on encouraging your people to know our God better, love our God more, honor our God more, and witness for our Lord Jesus more. We know that time is short until Jesus returns towards earth to claim all the saved and obedient Christians to take us home to heaven for the grand and glorious wedding supper of the Lamb. Since Father God has already told us that the wedding supper is now already prepared in heaven, we know that it won't be long! Since only Father God knows the day and the hour, we should ALL pay attention to what He tells us!

Some people believe that Jesus, Father God, and the Holy Spirit are the same person, and that when we all get to heaven, we will see Jesus only. I believe that what they believe and teach is not true. For this very reason alone, They are three separate Beings: Jesus does not know the day of the return of Jesus for the rapture, and ONLY Father God knows the day and the hour when Jesus returns toward earth for the rapture. (Mark 13:32) I believe the Bible that teaches, "Jesus is at the right hand of Father God in heaven." We will know for sure when we get to heaven and actually SEE Jesus at the right hand of our Father God, exactly as the Bible teaches us now to believe.

Father God, Jesus Christ, and God's Holy Spirit are three separate Beings Who are always in one accord. Jesus is now at HIS Father God's right hand, now waiting for His Father God to tell Him, "GO!" Jesus wants us all to get ready to go and to stay ready to go, to meet Jesus in the air in a split second! Some preachers that I know never even mention this from their pulpits, while other preachers tell of it in nearly every sermon.

I have now asked for, received, written out, and typed up more than 940 prophetic messages from our Lord Jesus Christ and from Father God with the help of God's Holy Spirit in the past thirty years. Nearly every one of them give the plan of salvation of Jesus forgiving people of their sins, helping them to come out of a sinful lifestyle and live for God, and go to heaven for eternity. I believe that now is the time for us to all emphasize soul winning in Jesus, living righteously for God, and praying in all of our lost loved ones.

I also believe that now is the time for us to work, give, pray, and teach that these wicked nations of the Americas must repent, turn back to God, and let our God heal these nations. I greatly admire what Franklin Graham is now doing, visiting each of the fifty state capital buildings and encouraging people to turn back to God and pray for America that God will heal our land. I heard that he had a wonderful turnout in Nashville a few months ago of several thousand people attending. His Samaritan's Purse is one of my favorite charities that I give to monthly. They do a great deal of good in the world by aiding disaster victims after earthquakes, tsunamis, floods, severe drought, mud slides, and other natural disasters. They not only help here in the USA, but fly needed supplies into many foreign countries, wherever the greatest needs are. He also has his Christmas shoe box ministry to millions of children in foreign lands, giving the children delightful Christmas gifts and giving the saving gospel of Jesus Christ.

To me, it is just amazing what our God is able to do through one completely dedicated Christian like that of Franklin Graham. When Franklin was a teenager, he was such a rebel! When his dad, Billy Graham, was traveling as an evangelist and his mom Ruth thought he was upstairs in his bed asleep, he crawled out a window, across the roof, down a tree, and went partying. His life got totally turned around after Billy convinced Franklin to give his life to Jesus. Then Franklin flew on some mission trips delivering needed supplies to disaster areas in foreign countries. Then he became hooked for life, knowing he can help the helpless. I know that all those prayers that Ruth and Billy prayed for Franklin's life are even now still being answered!

Jesus tells us, "If you will lose your life for My sake, you will find it." Let us all honor God by losing our lives in loving, teaching, and serving others, especially the ones who desperately NEED us to love them and to help them. Some of us just need to start small, and when we are faithful to do so, Our God's Holy Spirit will help us improve our services daily with love and joy! The Bible teaches, "Despise not small beginnings." Father God told me recently, **"Small beginnings have growth potential."** A mustard seed is small, but it has great growth potential. Our faith in God can grow. Our hope in God can grow. Our peace and joy in God can grow. Our service to others can grow. Our love for God, for ourselves, and for others can grow. Our success in life can grow. God is always the source of our good growth. He leads us, guides us, gave us Jesus to save us, gave us His Holy Spirit to help us, and God gives us many good opportunities for growth. We just have to step out in faith and RECEIVE all of our God's goodness to us.

A newborn baby is small, but it has wonderful growth potential. A new mother may look at her newborn baby and see only a mouth that needs feeding and a diaper that needs changing. But when our heavenly Father God looks at the newborn baby that He has created, He sees their growth potential, perhaps another Albert Einstein, Bill Gates, Billy Graham, Dave Ramsey, or other successful person! Father God knows not only their growth potential because He gave them ALL special gifts at their moment of conception in their mother's womb that will help them to be successful in their life as they grow and develop these gifts, but our Father God can actually SEE and KNOW their future success before it happens! God creates every baby with love and with all great growth potential, and it grieves our God when ANY abortion takes place! I feel like putting a bumper sticker on my car that reads, "What if your mom had aborted YOU?" Only God creates life, and only God should be allowed to take the life of people on earth! A fetus is a living child created by God in our God's likeness with body, soul, spirit, and great growth potential!

God creates and owns all the children of the world, and we parents, grandparents, and other helpers, are only the caretakers for them. Let's all pray for the success and prosperity of our children, our grandchildren, and for all children that they will love our God above all else, will love and help their fellow mankind as they love and help themselves, will be healthy and prosperous in body, soul, and spirit all of their lives, and will enter heaven with us and with our God forever. Yes! Our God is good!

Blessings! Velma

Yes, Our God's beloved Christian children of Our God's beloved Christian pastors and ALL of Our God's beloved Holy Bible teachers, YOUR heavenly Father God does love you and does love ALL of your loved ones and does take care of you and them at ALL times, all daytimes and all night times.

Yes, your God IS a good God, a merciful God, a God slow to anger, a righteous God, a just God, a God without beginning and without ending, a God Who never slumbers nor sleeps, an all-powerful God, a God Who has ALL knowledge, all wisdom, and all knowledge of mankind's past, present, and future.

Yes, Our God does know the future of Our God's planet Earth, and does know the future of each person now alive on Our God's planet Earth.

Yes, Our God did create and is still creating each of mankind in Our God's image with body, soul, and spirit.

Yes, each person's soul that was given to them from THEIR holy Creator God at the moment of their conception in their mother's womb is an eternal soul that WILL live forever either in heaven with their Holy Triune God, or it will live forever in hell with Satan as there are no other places for their eternal soul to live after their one life on earth is over.

Yes, Our heavenly Father God has made a pathway for every person now alive on earth to enter heaven in their life after their one life on earth is over by Our God sending His only begotten Son Jesus to earth to pay the penalty for mankind's sin so that whosoever will MAY COME to Jesus, ASK Jesus to save them from their sins, make Jesus the Lord and Master of their life, accept this free gift of salvation from Jesus, then repent of ALL sinful lifestyle, live righteously for God while alive on earth, and enter Our God's heaven forever to rule and reign with THEIR Holy Triune God forever.

Yes, Our God did create and still does create Our God's mankind with a free will which allows them to choose Jesus, live for God, and enter Our God's heaven forever, or reject Jesus as Lord and Savior, continue living in sin, and enter hell forever with Satan.

Yes, there are no other choices, and a person cannot ride the fence of indecision for long as they must make their choice to be HOT for Jesus, or cold against Jesus.

Yes, you must make your decision for Jesus and live for God while alive on Our God's planet Earth, because if you reject Jesus and continue living in sin and die in your sins and lift up your eyes in hell, it will be too late to choose Jesus as your Savior and live for God as you will be trapped in tormenting hell forever with no hope of escape.

Yes, Jesus loves you and Jesus wants Our God's best for you, best for you while alive on earth, and best for you in Our God's great heaven above in your afterlife.

Yes, Jesus is the ONLY Door to heaven, and Jesus does offer this free entrance into heaven in any person's afterlife, if only they WILL COME to Jesus NOW while they are still alive on Our God's planet Earth, ASK Jesus to save them from their sins and wrongdoing, then come OUT OF ALL sinful lifestyle, and live righteously for God for the rest of their life on earth, THEN they are able to enter Our God's beautiful, sin-free heaven forever.

Yes, sin will NEVER enter heaven.

Yes, sinners who have rebuked all sin from their lifestyle, who have made Jesus Christ their Savior, their Lord, their King, and their God, who live righteously-for-God on earth will be allowed to enter heaven forever, as ONLY Jesus Christ and HIS holy shed blood, death and resurrection MAKE them worthy to enter heaven forever.

Yes, Jesus shed His holy blood, gave His holy life, to be the holy propitiation, the righteous substitute, for mankind's sins that cleanses a person of sins, transgressions, and iniquities and allows them to enter heaven clean and pure.

Yes, Jesus Christ has restored man's fellowship with God that was broken when Adam sinned in the Garden of Eden, by Jesus paying the awful price of His holy shed blood and death on Calvary's cruel cross, when the curtain in the Holy of Holies was rent in two from top to bottom at the moment of death of Jesus Christ on Calvary's cross that has allowed any of mankind to come into the holy presence of THEIR Creator Father God, to come through the cleansing power of Jesus to THEIR heavenly Father God.

Yes, doesn't Our God's Holy Bible teach you that there is one true God and one mediator between God and men, the Man Jesus Christ? (1Timothy 2:5)

Yes, ONLY Jesus saves.

ONLY Jesus has paid the price for FREE salvation for mankind, to ALL who will choose salvation in Jesus while they are now alive on earth, who will then live a HOLY life unto God for the rest of their life on earth.

Yes, do live for God and do honor YOUR Holy Triune God in all that you are and in all that you think, say, and do, so that YOUR Holy Triune God IS ABLE to reward you for your living righteously and teaching righteously.

Yes, YOUR heavenly Father God IS a great God of rewards.

Yes, as you do all your good deeds to help yourself, help others, and glorify YOUR Holy Triune God on earth, it will not cause YOUR Holy Triune God to LOVE you more, but it WILL cause YOUR Holy Triune God to REWARD you more.

Yes, YOUR heavenly Father God does know you, know ALL about you, does hear and does answer you when you pray for yourself and for others, does accept ALL your praises to YOUR Holy Triune God, and YOUR Holy Triune God does see ALL your good deeds done with love to help yourself, help others, and to glorify God, and YOUR Holy Triune God does ALWAYS REWARD you for ALL of your good works.

Yes, doesn't your God Jesus teach you in Our God's Holy Bible that even a cup of cold water given with love to help a person will be rewarded? (Matthew 10:42)

Yes, do look around you and do see the many needs of others and do reach out to them with your Christian love to help the sick, the tired, the lonely, the grieving, the poor, the hungry, the naked, the fearful, the lost, the strangers, the widows, the orphans, the ones who not only need spiritual guidance, but need emotional encouragement, and do let them know that as YOUR Holy Triune God has met ALL your needs and met ALL your holy desires, that YOUR God is also able to help them in EVERY way that they need help.

Yes, do let all other people know that as YOUR God has met ALL your needs, that YOUR God is also able to meet ALL THEIR needs, when they know God, love God, honor God, live for God, and do obey God.

Yes, do let them know that Jesus Christ is the ONLY true Savior, Who is able to forgive their sins, save their eternal soul, help them to come out of all sinful lifestyle and live a righteous lifestyle unto God, will heal ALL their diseases, will answer ALL their many prayers prayed to THEIR heavenly Father God prayed with faith in Jesus' holy name, will help THEIR heavenly Father God give them a peaceful, happy, prosperous life on earth, and will give them an eternal home in heaven with THEIR Holy Triune God in their afterlife, after their one lifetime on earth.

Yes, YOUR heavenly Father God and YOUR Lord Jesus Christ ARE the complete source of YOUR life on earth, your ABUNDANT life on earth, and your eternal life in heaven.

Do praise your heavenly Father God daily, hourly, even at all times, do keep a praise-to-God and a heart-of-thanksgiving to your God attitude on your mind and in your heart, and YOUR Holy Triune God will not only give you perfect peace, but will "download" into your mind, heart, and spirit Our God's knowledge, wisdom, love, joy, and spiritual enrichment beyond measure, for ALL your needed success in your life.

Yes, as you praise God for Who God is, and as you thank YOUR God for what Our God does, that is the time that Our God uses to enrich spiritually, emotionally, and physically EVERY part of your total being.

Yes, your physical body was designed by God to heal itself of all diseases, when you obey Our God's rules of proper food, proper sleep, proper exercise, keeping free from substance abuse, keeping free from a sinful lifestyle, honoring God by living for God, by loving and helping the helpless, by obeying God by giving your holy tithes and offerings, by loving God above all else, and by worshiping, praising, thanking God; YOUR Holy Triune God WILL GIVE TO YOU ALL of Our God's good benefits to you and to your loved ones.

Yes, YOUR heavenly Father God does DESIRE to GIVE to you and to ALL of your loved ones ALL of Our God's good gifts for you and for them to enjoy when your soul is built up enough in God so that you and they are able to enjoy all these good gifts without becoming corrupt through them, and then turning away from YOUR God because of them.

Yes, your God will NOT give you a good gift that will lead to your corruption, to your rejecting your God because of it.

Didn't Jesus tell you in Bible Scripture that if you love your family more than you love God, that you are not worthy of God? (Matthew 10:37)

Yes, do LEARN to love God MORE than you love anything else, learn to put YOUR God FIRST above ALL else.

Yes, Our God IS ABLE to look on your heart, your emotions, and SEE the love you have for God and the love and service you have for others, and Our God is able to promote you accordingly, with power, with prestige, with service, so long as you are able to withstand the promotion without your becoming corrupt because of it.

Yes, read and study daily Our God's Holy Bible to draw closer to Our God, to know more about God, about Our God's ways, Our God's dealings with Our God's obedient children and Our God's dealings with Our God's disobedient children.

Yes, know Our God better, love Our God more, obey Our God more, seek to be used by Our God more to love, help, teach others better how to grow up more in God, and be rewarded more by God to lead better and more prosperous lives in God.

THEN people WILL be attracted to your successful lifestyle and attracted to YOUR GOD, Who gives you ALL GOOD benefits so richly to enjoy.

Do praise YOUR heavenly Father God now for this prophetic message for church growth.

Hallelujah!

Praises to Our heavenly Father God now for this prophetic message for church growth!

Hallelujah!

Praises to Our heavenly Father God!

Hallelujah!

362

LETTER NUMBER FORTY THREE
FOR CHURCH GROWTH

Dear Christian Pastors and All Holy Bible Teachers,

I have been praying about what to write to you to encourage you in your faith in God and in your work to help build up the Kingdom of God on earth. I will write to you about My family's life and about the sale of my home in Brentwood, Tennessee and the purchase of my home in Marietta, Georgia.

When I moved to Nashville in 1965 to work as a Graphic Designer, I always rented an apartment until I got married. After Hugh Davies and I got married on Thanksgiving weekend in 1970, I moved in with Hugh who was living in a two-bedroom rented duplex at the time. Our daughter, Lori, was born in 1972 when we lived in the duplex. We lived there until just before Christmas in 1974 when we purchased our first house in Franklin, Tennessee and relocated just before our second child, Alan, was born in February 1975. We were able to pay cash for this three-bedroom house with 1/3 acre. We had borrowed $3,000.00 from Hugh's parents in order to pay cash for this $30,000.00 house. One year later, on our fifth wedding anniversary, we had paid back the loan to Hugh's parents, owned our house outright, and had our two healthy, wonderful children. God is good! Hugh and his father converted our two-car garage into three rooms of a play room, an office, and a small laundry room. We lived there until 1983.

With me being a stay-at-home mom with our two children, with only Hugh working at Vanderbilt and with no mortgage on our house, we were able to save some extra funds. We decided to invest these funds into a larger house in Brentwood, Tennessee. We found the perfect house, two-story, four bedrooms, two bathrooms, one acre, on a quiet street, on a hill, that we both

363

liked. Three offers were made on this house at the same time, but we were able to purchase it because we could pay cash for most of it and assume the $18,000.00 mortgage on it until we could sell our Franklin house. We paid off this mortgage about seven months later when our Franklin house sold.

After we had moved our furniture and other items into our Brentwood house, we were planning to paint and fix up our Franklin house to put it onto the market to sell. Hugh's parents were retired and were living in Delmar, New York at the time. They decided to relocate to be near us and our two children, their only grandchildren. After they sold their house in New York, they purchased our Franklin house for cash and moved in during the Fall of 1983. They took the house "as is" without us even painting it. Later, Hugh and the children helped them build a sun deck on the back of the house. Hugh's parents lived in that Franklin house about sixteen years. Hugh's father passed away while they lived there. When Hugh's mother became ill with Alzheimer's, his sister, Marcia, came down from Maryland, cleared out her house and sold it. She moved her mother's things and her mother to Maryland, where she bought another house for her mother. She took care of her until her mother passed away.

Hugh and I had a 600 sq. ft. addition built to the back of our Brentwood house with a computer room, a third bathroom, and a sun room that had an outside entrance with a small porch.

Hugh's mother and Hugh both became ill at the same time. Hugh was diagnosed with Lupus and his mother was diagnosed with Alzheimer's. Five years later, Hugh's sister asked us to have Hugh's health checked again to see the progress of the Lupus. When it was checked, the report came back that he had Alzheimer's as the Lupus had turned into Alzheimer's. Hugh's mother was ill for eight years, and Hugh was ill for eleven years. Hugh became ill at age fifty eight and passed away at age sixty nine in February, 2010. We were married for thirty nine years. He had enjoyed his Vanderbilt job and wanted to continue.

When we moved into our Brentwood house in the summer

364

of 1983, Lori entered the sixth grade and Alan entered the third grade at nearby Lipscomb Elementary School in the Fall. They finished Lipscomb Elementary school, Brentwood Middle School, and Brentwood High School. Lori graduated class of 1990 in the top ten percent of her class, then attended Vanderbilt University for 1½ years. She then transferred to Middle Tennessee State University in Murfreesboro, Tennessee for her last 2½ years. She graduated with a Bachelor's degree in math. She got a job out of state and never came home again.

Alan graduated from Brentwood High School class of 1993. He went to college at Tennessee Technical Institute in Cookeville, Tennessee. He earned a Bachelor's degree in Computer Science. He got a job out of state and never came home again.

Hugh and I lived together in our Brentwood home until I could no longer take care of him, and he needed to go into assisted living. He was in assisted living for 2½ years in Nashville, and for another year in assisted living in Franklin. He was on medication for Alzheimer's. He became very angry at times and would throw things at the other residents. They upped his medication to try to get rid of his angry spells. He was overly medicated which caused him to fall several times. Each time he fell, he was taken by ambulance to the nearby emergency room at the hospital. When they found scars on parts of his body from several falls, they ruled that he must be put into a nursing home, where he would have constant care.

He was in the nursing home in Nashville for one year until he passed away in February, 2010.

With Hugh in assisted living and later in the nursing home for 4½ years, I was living alone in our Brentwood home. During this time, I met four ladies who needed a temporary place to live, so I invited them to live with me. Since the house was paid for, I did not charge the ladies any rent, but we did share expenses of the utilities and taxes. We each had our own bedroom and own food. My friend Karen lived with me the longest and chose to live in the sun room. When we had guests from out of state for

Hugh's funeral, Karen helped gather up all of Hugh's things, and we offered them for people to take with them.

In 2016, six years after Hugh passed away, I decided to sell my large house and relocate to Marietta, Georgia to be near my daughter, Lori LaVoy and her family of husband John and sons, Joshua age thirteen and Jacob age eleven. I also wanted to be near my son Alan and his wife Michelle and their family of five who were also living in Covington, Georgia. They soon moved to northern Virginia.

I prayed about me hiring a realtor to advise me on how to get my house and yard ready to put on the market to sell. Father God told me to hire a realtor, so I hired one that my friend Karen knew. She advised me to do new landscaping, refinish many of the hardwood floors, get new carpet in the dining room, update one bathroom, and replace two doors. I hired all of this done. I also replaced the front shutters, hired the outside trim and porch columns painted, and repaired the roof. I hired some trees removed and some stumps ground. My son-in-law John came up and removed one large pine tree. My son Alan came up and removed two large pine trees. John had updated and installed a new kitchen for me a couple of years before. Karen agreed to paint most of the inside of the house in exchange for a place to live. I painted my bedroom, walk-in closet, hallway, and my bathroom. Before Karen painted the rest of the inside of the house, she packed up everything in the closets, drawers, kitchen, and bathrooms and put the boxes into the two-car garage. She packed up the attic and garage items. Later I rented a U-Haul truck and hired Karen to drive a load of boxes to Marietta, Georgia. I stored them for months in Georgia.

Lori and John came up and hauled another U-Haul truckload to Manchester, Tennessee for storage.

My house finally sold and the closing was set for December 19, 2016. The day before the closing, I hired two men and a U-Haul truck to move the rest of my things and Karen's things to two storage units in Manchester, Tennessee. We closed on December

19, and I drove to Marietta, Georgia. I spent the next three weeks with my daughter, Lori and her family, until I purchased my house on January 6, 2017 in Marietta, Georgia. Later, John and some other hired workers helped me to empty my two storage units in Manchester, Tennessee and my storage unit in Marietta and move the items into my new home. Lori helped me to get settled into my new home. I praise God for helping me to relocate in Georgia, where I am enjoying my family and my new church, Mt. Bethel United Methodist Church. God is so good to me!

Blessings! Velma

Yes, Our God's beloved Christian children of ALL of Our God's Christian pastors and ALL of Our God's beloved Holy Bible teachers, YOUR heavenly Father God does love you, does love ALL of your loved ones, and ALL of your congregations, and YOUR heavenly Father God is and does take care of you and them at ALL times, all daytimes and all night times.

Yes, your God never slumbers nor sleeps, your God does hear ALL of your many prayers at ALL times. (Psalm 121:4)

Do pray long, pray often, pray with your great faith in YOUR all-powerful Lord and Savior, Jesus Christ.

Yes, ALWAYS pray in the holy name of YOUR Lord and Master, Jesus Christ.

Yes, the holy name of Jesus Christ is above ALL names and is NOW totally worthy of ALL of the praises and worship of mankind.

Yes, the JOY of the Lord is your strength. (Nehemiah 8:10)

Yes, the praises of your God Jesus Christ bring to you joy, love, peace, your strength, your well-being, your prosperity, your opportunities for advancements.

Yes, YOUR Lord Jesus is all in all. (Colossians 3:11)

Yes, it is Christ in you, the hope of glory. (Colossians 1:27)

Yes, prayer and fasting unto God does bring your eternal soul closer to God.

Yes, your believing prayers prayed in the holy name of Jesus is NOW the strongest force on earth today.

Yes, your hope, your trust, your faith is in Jesus Christ that delivers to you ALL good things and all good events to you FROM YOUR heavenly Father God. (Philippians 4:19)

Yes, your life, your loved ones, your possessions, your

abilities, your opportunities, all you are and all you have, are all good gifts to you coming down from YOUR heavenly Father of lights, coming to you through YOUR Lord and Savior, Jesus Christ of Nazareth.

Yes, Jesus is now alive and well, and is now seated at HIS heavenly Father's right hand, now awaiting the command of HIS Father God to, "GO! Go back towards earth for Our God's great rapture of ALL living and obedient Christian souls and BRING them BACK to Our God's great heaven above for Our God's great wedding supper of the Lamb of God!"

Yes, Jesus Christ is the Lamb of God.

Yes, Jesus Christ is God.

Yes, Jesus Christ is the holy Bridegroom.

Yes, Jesus comes quickly for ALL His own, ALL His beloved holy Bride-to-be, all the saved-in-Jesus from their sins and are living-righteously-unto-God, who are READY TO GO in Our God's great rapture of souls, to be caught up into the heavenlies in a split second, to join Jesus and all His holy angels in the air, to be taken BACK to THEIR heavenly home, to live with, to rejoice with, THEIR Holy Triune God forever.

Yes, time is short until Jesus returns!

Pray in ALL your lost loved ones!

Preach and teach for ALL people now alive on Our God's planet Earth to get ready and stay ready for the return of Jesus for Our God's great rapture of souls on earth.

Yes, come to Jesus.

Repent of sins and live righteously in obedience to God.

Sin will NEVER enter heaven.

Only sinners saved in Jesus and them living righteously in obedience to God will be able to enter heaven.

Yes, Father God sent Jesus to be born of the virgin Mary, conceived by Our God's Holy Spirit, grow sinless into manhood, shed His holy innocent blood, and give His righteous life on Calvary's cruel cross so that each of mankind who COMES to Jesus, ASKS Jesus for salvation, makes Jesus the Lord and

Master of their life, comes out of ALL sinful lifestyle, lives for God, could join Our God Jesus forever in heaven AFTER their one lifetime on earth is over.

Yes, Jesus Christ, raised from the dead by HIS heavenly Father God, is the ONLY Savior, dead or alive, with enough power to save a person's soul and take them to heaven forever, and keep their eternal soul OUT of hell forever.

Yes, Jesus Christ is the ONLY Door to heaven in any person's afterlife, after their one life on earth is over.

Yes, Jesus does hold the keys to death, hell, and the grave. (Revelation 1:18)

A person cannot save themselves by doing good works as salvation is by faith in Jesus and the grace of God and by living righteously unto God while alive on earth.

Yes, Jesus Christ has ALL power to forgive sins and give eternal salvation to ALL people who COME to Jesus with a repentant heart, ASK Jesus to forgive their sins and save them, who then rebuke ALL sinful lifestyle from their life and live for God while alive on earth will be headed for heaven after their one life on earth is over.

Yes, your life on earth is uncertain and death on earth is certain.

Accept Jesus now as your Lord and Savior before it is too late.

Yes, NOW is the day of salvation.

Yes, Our God's Holy Spirit is NOW wooing people to Jesus Christ for salvation and for righteous living unto God.

Yes, Jesus Christ does hold ALL the good and excellent answers to any and to ALL of Our God's mankind's problems and dilemmas on Our God's earth today.

Yes, try Jesus.

Pray to Jesus.

Ask Jesus to help you and praise Jesus many times daily and nightly until the right answers come and ALL your problems on earth are solved, then praise, thank, and worship Jesus for the mighty help Jesus has given to you in solving ALL of your problems.

Yes, Jesus is God.

Yes, Jesus has ALL power in heaven and earth.

Yes, Jesus is WELL ABLE to heal you physically, mentally, emotionally, spiritually, financially, and give you abundant life on earth AND eternal life in heaven.

Yes, praise Jesus now!

Choose Jesus now!

Yes, YOUR Holy Triune God does have a great work for each of you to do to HELP bring in Our God's last great harvest of souls for salvation from their sins in the saving shed blood of Jesus Christ, and to help people come OUT OF ALL sinful lifestyle and live for God in order for them to go to heaven in their afterlife, after their one life and one death on earth.

Yes, time is now short and is now growing shorter day by day until Jesus Christ returns towards earth for Our God's great catching away of ALL of Our God's saved-in-Jesus and right-living-for-God beloved Christian children of God.

Yes, do WARN ALL people to come OUT of ALL sinful lifestyle, if they do want to enter heaven for eternity after their one life and one death on earth.

Yes, sin will NEVER enter heaven.

Yes, Jesus Christ paid the awful price on Calvary's cruel cross of His holy shed blood and death so that people could REPENT of their sins, ASK Jesus to forgive them of their sins, make Jesus Christ THEIR Lord and Savior, then go and sin no more.

Yes, Jesus Christ has been raised from the dead by HIS heavenly Father God, has been given the keys to death, hell, and the grave, has ascended on high into the third heaven, is now seated at the right hand of HIS heavenly Father God, and is now making intercession to HIS heavenly Father God for ALL the people now alive on earth, that ALL people now alive on earth will COME to Jesus for salvation from their sins, will accept Jesus Christ as their Lord and Savior, will come out of ALL sinful lifestyle, will live for God, and will enter heaven for eternity.

Yes, preach Jesus saves.

Preach that Jesus is the ONLY Being, dead or alive, that can forgive their sins, help them to live righteously for God, and give them a FREE one-way ticket to heaven in their life after their one life on earth.

Yes, after Father God raised Jesus' body from the dead, Jesus was given ALL power in heaven and in earth. (Matthew 28:18)

Yes, Our God Jesus is now calling all who will to go into all the world and preach the good news of Our God's saving grace to all people, bringing them to Jesus for salvation from their sins, helping them to come out of all sinful lifestyle and live a righteous lifestyle unto God, have an abundant life on earth, and enter heaven forever in their afterlife, after their one life on earth.

Yes, when you go into all the earth and preach the good news that Jesus saves and delivers, Our God Jesus does go with you even until the end of the world. (Matthew 28:20)

Yes, when you became a Christian with Jesus Christ as your Lord and Savior, Our heavenly Father God gave a part of Our God's Holy Spirit to live within you as your daily and nightly holy Guide, your Teacher, your Comforter, your holy God to lead you into ALL of Our God's truth, to apply to your own life to set a good example for others, and to teach others of Our God's holy truths as found in Our God's Holy Bible.

Yes, do read and do study Our God's Holy Bible daily, and do make ALL the promises of YOUR God to all of mankind part of you, and do claim these promises of God for your life, for the lives of your loved ones, and for all the people you teach.

Yes, do know the conditions for each promise and do encourage people to KNOW the promises, CLAIM the promises, and MEET THE CONDITIONS of the promises.

Yes, do draw near to God, and Our God WILL draw near to you. (James 4:8)

Yes, Our God is ALWAYS ABLE to meet EVERY need you have and every need your congregation has with only Our God's spoken Word.

Yes, Jesus Christ IS the spoken Word of His heavenly Father God. (John 1:1-3)

Yes, ALWAYS pray ALL of your prayers to YOUR heavenly Father God, pray them ALL in Jesus' holy name with your great faith in Jesus.

Yes, when Jesus walked this earth nearly two thousand years ago, didn't Jesus tell the people who were healed, "Your faith has made you whole"? (Mark 10:42)

Yes, your faith in Jesus Christ is what heals the sick and sets the captives free.

Yes, Jesus Christ IS the same Healer today as He was nearly two thousand years ago, when He walked this earth and healed the lame, sick, and blind, and raised the dead back to life.

Yes, TODAY Jesus is NOW looking for trustworthy Christians to NOW work His miracles through, who will NOW give God ALL the glory for answering their prayers for peoples' salvations, for peoples' healings, for miracles that ONLY Our God can perform, that mankind cannot perform.

Yes, Our God will NOT give Our God's glory to another. (Isaiah 42:8)

Yes, Satan tried to claim some of Our God's glory, became corrupt, and had to be punished.

Yes, do give ALL glory, all honor, all worship, and ALL your praises to YOUR Holy Triune God, Who are the only Ones WORTHY to receive ALL of Our God's mankind's praises.

Yes, God is sovereign above all.

Yes, God has all power, all love, all majesty, and does ALWAYS DESERVE first place in man's body, soul, and spirit, and YOUR Holy Triune God is to be first in YOUR life above all.

Yes, when you are loving, worshiping, praising, adoring,

and thanking YOUR Holy Triune God, that is the time when YOUR Holy Triune God is filling your mind, body, and soul with all good things of knowledge, wisdom, good health, correct guidance, and all good things and events in your life.

Yes, love your God more and be filled more with Our God's love, joy, peace, and comfort.

Yes, do draw near to God and do receive ALL of Our God's good benefits for you and for all your loved ones.

Hallelujah!

Praises to Our heavenly Father God for this message for church growth!

Hallelujah!

Praises to Our God!

Dear Christian Pastors and All Holy Bible Teachers,

I have been praying and asking our God's Holy Spirit to show to me what to write to all of you pastors and Bible teachers to encourage you in the Lord. Whenever I write anything, I am only the TYPIST, and God's Holy Spirit is the WRITER.

As I was growing up, I never read a single book all the way through, that I can remember. As a child, the only two books that I can remember being in our home were the Bible and the Sear's catalogue. In elementary school, I heard some of the children's books that were read to us by our teachers. I don't ever remember visiting a library until I was in high school, which was only for research on specific topics.

Even during my eight years of college, I don't ever remember reading a single college book all the way through. I would attend class and listen to the lectures. For the books that were required reading in my World Literature class, I would read the first and last chapters in each book, then ask some smart student in class about that middle part. That system didn't get me an A for the class, but it got me a lot of B's. My reading for my history classes were ALWAYS very difficult for me, as I was a slow reader, and the vocabulary word meanings were unfamiliar to me as they were not spoken at home by my family or my friends. I must have had a vocabulary of about 200 words at the time I was in high school and in college. Also, I had little time for reading as I always had part-time jobs, was attending church two evenings a week, and dating some evenings. When I did try to read, I was usually too sleepy to concentrate on my required reading assignments. I always got excellent grades in art and math, which always helped to offset the lower grades in the history and literature classes.

Even though I could see the value of printed Christian literature to win the world to Jesus Christ, which was always my heart's desire, I knew that I did not have command of the language enough to become a writer. Therefore, I decided to become an artist, a Graphic Designer, to decorate the Christian literature that other people would write. Christian literature could be mailed worldwide and could be used to win people to Jesus Christ for salvation.

I always wanted to do something to help win people to Jesus Christ. The only other things that I could think of to do was to play the piano for church worship singing, marry a pastor and pray for him, go to the missions field and pass out printed tracts, or become a writer of Christian tracts and other good literature. Since I could not do any of those things and since I enjoyed art work, I doubled up on my art assignments in high school and went on to work my way through college with an art major.

After I had completed two years of Junior College and my Junior year at the University of Washington in Seattle with an art major, I wrote to the Baptist Sunday School Board in Nashville and asked them about the possibility of my working for them when I graduated in one year. Mr. Herman Burns, the Head of the Art Department, wrote back to me, "Do not take your senior year at the University of Washington, but go to The Art Center College of Design in Los Angeles." I knew that Art Center was the best art college in the nation at the time and desired to go there. I had rejected the idea as I knew it was very expensive and that I would have to work my way through. I knew it was located in the big city of Los Angeles, a thousand miles south of my home in Washington state. When I heard from Mr. Burns, I thought that I had heard from God, Himself, so I decided to go there.

I lived with my sister Carolyn and her family in central California for the summer, worked as a waitress, and saved up enough money to enter the college. I submitted a portfolio of samples of my art-work and was accepted as a student. Before I left to take the bus to Los Angeles to enter the college, the Lord spoke to me and said, **"Don't come home until you have to."** Since the first semester was four months long, and I had only enough funds for the first two months, it really was an experiment of my stepping out in faith to trust God to meet all my needs.

I took the bus one way to Los Angeles. Upon arrival, I took a city bus to Art Center. A worker there gave me the location of a home within walking distance of the school where some of the Art Center ladies were living. I found the last vacant room in that house and lived there for the first semester, paying cash for room and board for the first two months.

Classes began, and I did fine for the first two months. The very day that I spend my last dollar, I was drawing in my fashion illustration class when someone came to me and said, "You are wanted in the office." My first thought was, "They know I spent my last dollar today, and they are going to kick me out!" Then I thought, "They CAN'T kick me out! I've already paid my tuition for this whole semester!"

When I got to the office, I was told, "We see on your application that you do typing. May we hire you to do some typing for us?" I gladly accepted and earned enough funds for another month of expenses. Then some other lady art students and I worked at the local post office sorting mail during the Christmas rush which enabled me to finish my first four months at Art Center! Joy!

For the next three semesters, I attended Art Center with a Government loan for tuition, with my brother Cliff loaning me funds for art supplies, and with my sister Carolyn making all my free clothes. I lived with a family and helped take care of their three children for room and board. This family lived within easy walking distance to the college building. Since Art Center classes go year round, with three semesters a year, I was able to attend for four semesters straight.

When I applied for tuition funds for a government loan for my fifth semester, only part of the loan amount needed was granted. I knew that I would have to drop out of college and earn some more tuition funds before I could continue. I was contemplating, "If I go home and work, I can save more money. If I stay in Los Angeles and work, I will be able to save less money, but I will be able to attend night school at Art Center." I was contemplating what to do, when a very wonderful opportunity came my way, straight from my heavenly Father God!

My best girlfriend and fellow art student, Helen Twentyman, told me that she had been offered a Graphic Design position at Gospel Light Publications in Glendale, but was unable to take it. Her parents from Peru were arriving, and they were all planning a month's boat trip to New Zealand to visit with her maternal grandparents. She asked me if I would like to take the job, have the use of her car for transportation, and live in her apartment in Hollywood with her two roommates, until she came home. Yes, indeed! I showed my art portfolio samples at Gospel Light Publications and was hired with my very first job as a full-time Graphic Designer, where I worked on Vacation Bible School literature. I drove Helen's car round trip from Hollywood to Glendale daily and lived with Helen's two housemates, Frances and Audry. We lived in a rented upstairs apartment in a large house across the street from the very large Hollywood Presbyterian Church where we attended. We were located only two blocks from the famous "Hollywood and Vine" streets. I was able to take a printmaking class at Art Center during the evening.

On Helen's boat trip to New Zealand, just after they headed south after stopping in Hawaii, they got a cable that her grandmother had passed away! So Helen and her parents stayed an extra month to help settle her grandmother's estate. I was able to live in Helen's rented room and drive her car to work until she returned. Then the ladies let me live in their living room for a few more months. I continued working at Gospel Light for a total of one year and four months, taking the city bus for transportation, until I could save enough money to enter Art Center full time. I was able to save half of my earnings.

When I was able to enter Art Center again full-time, I was able to live with a very wonderful Jewish family, work for room and board, and walk only three blocks to school. They had only one little girl living at home, Vicki, who was in sixth grade at the time. I was able to stay with her when her parents went out socially in the evenings. Their older son, Jack, was away at college. I lived with them for my last four semesters at Art Center, receiving some funds from government loans for tuition, and using my savings for art supplies. Carolyn still made all my clothes for me, which I greatly appreciated!

After I graduated from Art Center, as I took the bus a thousand miles north to home in Washington State, Father God spoke to me, **"Did you lack anything?"** When I thought back on my 4½ years in Los Angeles, I realized that I did not lack anything! I lived in the best houses that I ever lived in my whole life, usually with a private room with a private bathroom. I ate the best food I had ever eaten in my life.

I attended the best art college in the nation at the time. I wore all new clothes tailored to fit me free from my professional seamstress sister, Carolyn. I attended the largest and best church I had ever attended.

I had the most girlfriends that I had ever had. I had dates with young Christian men from the college and from the church. I had access to the largest library in Los Angeles and the best art galleries and museums in the city. I rode in the best cars and city buses I had ever been in. I had the best art supplies and camera use I had ever had in my life. I attended the best church camp, Forest Home, I had ever been to. I attended socials monthly with the large College Department at the church and took a boat trip to Catalina Island for one day with them. I never missed a single meal in 4 ½ years, except for one day that I chose to fast at church camp. I was able to get some good Graphic Design work experience at Gospel Light, which helped me to know which classes at Art Center would help me most in my future career of magazine publishing, when I returned for my last four semesters at Art Center.

All of my needs and good desires were more than abundantly met by my heavenly Father God in the time I was in Los Angeles. When I returned, I had only about $4,000.00 in government college debt, which I was allowed ten years to pay off. I learned to trust God during that time, and my God NEVER once failed me in all that time!

When I got off the bus in Longview, Washington my dad met me at the bus station to give me a ride home. He and Mom had never visited me all the time that I was in Los Angeles. He asked, "What have you got in the fishing tackle box?" I replied, "That's my art supplies." He asked, "Have you been taking art?" I laughed and said, "Dad, I just graduated from the best art college in the nation, and you didn't know I was taking art? What did you think I was taking?" He replied, "I thought you were going to be a teacher or a nurse." I said, "No, Dad. I'm an artist."

I stayed at home for six months while waiting for a Graphic Design position to open at The Baptist Sunday School Board in Nashville, Tennessee. I taught an evening art class in the same Junior College from which my brother Cliff and I had graduated. I was hired as a Graphic Designer at the Baptist Sunday School Board in Nashville and began work on April 1, 1965. I had the pleasure of working on Christian literature to help win the world to Jesus Christ. Joy!

Blessings! Velma

Yes, Our God's beloved Christian children, ALL of Our God's beloved Christian pastors and ALL of Our God's beloved Holy Bible teachers, YOUR heavenly Father God does love you, does take care of you, and does guide you into all good living for your God and in all good teaching to others about Our God and Our God's way on earth.

Yes, you must LIVE for God at all times, and you must teach Our God's truth in love as you do teach others, to be successful in your life on earth.

Yes, always use Our God's Holy Bible as your Guide when you teach others.

Yes, know Jesus, walk with and talk with Jesus daily, do preach and teach what Jesus taught to others as recorded in Our God's Holy Bible when Jesus walked this earth nearly two thousand years ago.

Yes, these great truths that Jesus taught then are still true today for they have always been true throughout time and will always be true throughout time in the future.

Yes, heaven and earth may pass away, but Our God's words of Jesus, Our God's truth of the words of Jesus, will NEVER pass away. (Luke 21:33)

Yes, people need to know these treat truths that Jesus spoke as recorded in Our God's Holy Bible, and these truths will set them free. (John 8:32)

Yes, doesn't the psalmist say, "Thy word have I hid in my heart that I might not sin against Thee"? (Psalm 119:11)

Yes, do hide Our God's word in your heart, do memorize parts of Our God's Scriptures, live a holy life unto Our God, and all will go well with you.

Yes, Our God does watch over ALL of Our God's own to provide for them, and to protect them, and protect ALL that belongs to them.

Yes, doesn't Our God teach you in Psalm ninety-one that Our God sends Our God's angels to protect you? (Psalm 91:11)

Yes, if ONLY you could see Our God's angels protecting you, you would trust your God more for your safety daily and nightly.

Yes, Our God does control ALL that happens to you and to all of your loved ones at all times.

Yes, Our God showers benefits on you and your loved ones when you are obedient to God.

When you or your loved ones are disobedient to God, Our God does correct you and may punish you for you to have a learning experience with God, to draw you into a closer relationship with YOUR God.

Yes, doesn't Our God's Holy Bible teach that Our God corrects those He loves? (Proverbs 3:12)

Yes, the more you love God, the more you worship and obey God, the more you do love and do help the helpless, the more your soul WILL GROW in God, the more Our God WILL reward you with ALL GOOD things and all good events that WILL enrich your life, will help others, and will glorify Our God on earth.

Yes, your good deeds of helping the helpless will not cause Our God to love you more as Our God does love you for who you are—Our God's child made in Our God's image—but your good deeds for others WILL cause Our God to reward you more.

Yes, Our Holy Triune God STILL has many good gifts stored up to give to all of mankind when their strength of character, their soul, has grown up enough in God to use wisely these good gifts from God, gifts for mankind that Our God created for them before your God created Our God's planet Earth.

Yes, Our God Jesus Christ was able to heal the sick, blind, maimed, and crippled, and even raised the dead when He walked this earth nearly two thousand years ago, and Jesus Christ is now alive and is still the same God yesterday, today, and forever. (Hebrews 13:8)

Yes, it is Christ in you, the hope of glory. (Colossians 1:27)

Yes, didn't Jesus promise His followers that even greater works than He did, you will do when you know Jesus, live for God, and ALLOW Our God's Holy Spirit to work through you to help others, to bring others closer to Our God for healing and miracles for Our God's glory on earth? (John 14:12)

Hallelujah!

Yes, know Jesus, live for Jesus, preach Jesus saves, Jesus heals, Jesus does miracles, signs, and wonders, Jesus is God, Jesus is Father God's ONLY begotten Son, Jesus has ALL power in heaven and in earth, Jesus rules and reigns supreme, Jesus returns soon for Our God's rapture of ALL saved and right-living-unto-God Christian saints, to take them BACK to Our God's great heaven above, to rule and reign with Our God Jesus forever.

Yes, you are joint heirs with Jesus so do claim ALL good things and ALL good events from YOUR God that will enrich your own life, will enrich the lives of others, and will bring glory to Our God on earth.

Yes, your God IS a GOOD God Who does ENJOY giving ALL good gifts to ALL of Our God's precious obedient children of God who do love God and who do love and do help the helpless on earth.

Yes, you are your brother's keeper on earth.

Yes, what you give to help the helpless, your love, your time, your expertise, your skills, your supplies, your funds, ALL you give, whatever you give, will be returned to you doubled and more than doubled, given BACK to you from YOUR God to HELP YOU in the ways you need it the most. (Luke 6:38)

Yes, all your possessions and all your opportunities do come from YOUR heavenly Father God, and they do come to you through YOUR Lord Jesus Christ so do keep a heart and a mind focused on the goodness of Our God to you and to your loved ones at all times—then do SEE WHAT Our God will do for you and through you for your obedience to God in this.

Yes, do MAKE it your daily habit in all you think, say, and do to be thankful to YOUR Holy Triune God for ALL of your successes in life.

Yes, doesn't Jesus Christ tell you in Our God's Holy Bible that apart from Jesus, you can do nothing? (John 15:5)

Yes, when you do continually ABIDE in YOUR Holy Triune God through praise, worship, honor, and thankfulness, you can do all things through Christ which strengthens you. (Philippians 4:13)

Yes, YOUR heavenly Father God is the divine Being Who gives to you knowledge, wisdom, strength, courage, new creative ideas, and does send to you ALL your needed HELP to be successful in life so when you are given a measure of success in your life, do give to YOUR Holy Triune God the glory and honor for your success.

Yes, many people begin projects in a small way, and they do seek God and do seek Our God's help in the start-up phase, and Our God does answer their many prayers and does give to them their needed help.

However, as the person becomes more and more successful in their life, in their business, and in their ministry, they get busy with their own efforts, and drift away from their relationship with God, and drift away from seeking Our God's help in seeking their endeavors to prosper.

Yes, you shut out your relationship with God when you seek to be successful without Our God's help, you begin to become corrupt, and unless you repent, you are headed for a downfall, you become worthless to YOUR holy Creator God and need to be destroyed.

Yes, when you ABIDE in Jesus, you do bring forth much fruit that does PLEASE YOUR heavenly Father God. (John 15:8)

Yes, when you do NOT abide in Jesus through worship,

praise, and thanksgiving, you have cut off ALL your substance to a prosperous life, you are then unable to bring forth good fruit that glorifies YOUR Holy Triune God, decay sets in, and you become WORTHLESS in YOUR holy Creator's sight, and end up being destroyed.

Yes, do consider what happened with the people at the Tower of Babel in the Bible when the people became self-righteous and tried to ascend into heaven on their own without God, when Our God had to intervene in their plans by confusing their language in order to preserve mankind then. (Genesis 11:1-9)

If the people of Babylon had continued with their plans without God in building the Tower of Babel, they would have encountered total swift destruction.

Yes, whenever Our God does see a child of God or see a nation on earth beginning to drift away from God, Our God does send warning signs to them for them to REPENT and turn BACK to their true God as they are headed for total destruction drifting away from their true God.

Yes, when Our Holy Triune God does look down on these wicked Americas and Our God does see the government leaders, church leaders, business leaders no longer honoring God, no longer living for God, no longer teaching the whole truths of God, Our God does send righteous leaders, Bible teachers, preachers, and prophets to warn people of ALL their corrupt ways—then Our God does give these unrighteous leaders time to repent, time to come back to their true God, live for God, and teach ALL the truths of God to mankind as given in Our God's Holy Bible.

Yes, Our God is NOW holding our preachers, prophets, and Bible teachers accountable to teach ALL the truths of Our God's Holy Bible, and not only to teach ALL of them, but to live by them with Our God's Holy Spirit as their divine Guide.

Yes, there is a heaven and there is a hell.

Yes, encourage the righteous-in-God to keep living for God and also warn the wicked to repent, turn to God, to Jesus for salvation from their sins, come out of ALL sinful lifestyle and live for God, if they do want to enter heaven in their life after their one life on earth.

Yes, doesn't Our God's Holy Bible teach that it is appointed unto man to die once, and after that is Our God's judgment? (Hebrews 9:27)

Yes, life on earth is uncertain, and YOUR death on earth is certain.

Yes, you MUST accept Jesus now while you are now alive on earth as your Lord and Savior, ASK Jesus to save you from your own sins and save you from the corrupt sin of Adam that you were born into, accept this FREE salvation from the ONLY true Savior of Jesus Christ, come out of ALL sinful lifestyle, and live righteously for God for the rest of your life on earth, if you want to enter heaven for eternity after your one death on earth.

Yes, sin will NEVER enter heaven.

Yes, Jesus Christ IS the ONLY Being, dead or alive, Who now has paid the awful price of His holy shed blood and death on Calvary's cruel cross, to pay the penalty for YOUR sins, to give you freedom to live for God, and to enter heaven for eternity.

Yes, Father God did raise Jesus Christ from the dead, and ALL power in heaven and in earth has been given to Jesus. (Matthew 28:18)

Yes, Jesus is now alive in the third heaven, seated at His Father God's right hand, now making intercession with HIS Father God that people on earth will repent of sins, come to Jesus for salvation, live for God, and enter heaven forever.

Hallelujah!

Praises to Our wonderful heavenly Father God for this prophetic message for all church growth!

Hallelujah!

Praises to Our Father God!

LETTER NUMBER FORTY FIVE
FOR CHURCH GROWTH

Dear Christian Pastors and All Holy Bible Teachers,

I have been praying about what to write to you to encourage you in the Lord. I know of many pastors, especially young pastors, who begin with small churches, who struggle financially. I also know of many pastors who began with small congregations, and when they remained faithful, their congregations grew yearly, until they reached large sizes, with large congregations with large incomes.

The Bible states, "Despise not small beginnings." (Zechariah 4:10) A mustard seed is small, but locked inside it is great growth potential planted there by God. Father God told me recently, **"Small beginnings have growth potential!"** With the help of God, this is true with any person, any project, and any church. Habitat for Humanity has as its theme, "Commit to the Lord whatever you do, and your plans will succeed." (Proverbs 16:3)

I have often wondered why some churches grow and why others do not seem to grow, since they all worship the same Holy Triune God. This prophetic message number forty five answers this question. It is God Who promotes people. God puts each person through seven trials designed for each trial to bring the person closer to God. If the person endures faithfully through the length of the trial, and the trial brings them closer to God, then God is able to promote the person without the person becoming a corrupt dictator.

In the past, I have noticed some of the ways some pastors have tried to increase their church services' attendance. One pastor put all the visitors on the mailing list for the church newsletter. The circulation of the newsletter increased, but the church congregation did not grow. I know of another pastor who offered free Starbucks coffee coupons to visitors, but the congregation did not grow. Another pastor offered free money to the children if they would bring their friends. Another pastor had the congregation shout, "I'm a bringer!" at the end of every service. Another pastor preached from Joel Osteen's book and gave Joel's free books to all the visitors to try to build up the congregation. I'm not sure that any of these methods worked for church growth.

I believe that people attend the church services where they are getting fed "steaks" (the Bible and Jesus Christ), so that their souls can grow in God. If people attend church services where they are being fed "crumbs" (other things instead of the Bible and Jesus), their souls are not able to grow in God, and they will not return and will not bring their friends.

My heavenly Father God has taught me through these prophetic messages for church growth, the church's attendance grows and the church's financial income grows in direct proportion to the leaders' souls' growth in God. If the church leaders do NOT live for God, and do not love God with their total being, and do not love and SERVE themselves and others, and do not spend daily time studying the Bible and worshiping, praising, and thanking God, their soul is not growing in God. Their sermons are weak and the people are not being fed enough spiritual food for their souls to grow in God. Their church congregations and church finances are not growing. When the church leaders' souls grow in God, THEN God is able to promote them and their ministry, without these leaders becoming corrupt.

Dr. Henrietta Mears told her pastors-in-training to always spend four hours a day in prayer and Bible study. Dr. Bill Bright with Campus Crusade for Christ was one of the successful Bible students she mentored.

Recently online on the computer I saw a list of the top fifty world ministers with the greatest financial net worth. Since I know that their great net worth comes from God, I knew that their souls had grown in God enough that God could trust them with great wealth, without their becoming corrupt because of it.

Here are the top fifteen in net worth in millions:

#15 **Rick Warren** ($25) in USA
#14 **Billy Graham** ($25) in North Carolina
#13 **Kenneth Copeland** ($26.5) in Ft. Worth
#12 **Creflo Dollar** ($27) in Atlanta and New York
#11 **John Danforth** ($30) in St Louis
#10 **Joel Osteen** ($40) in Houston
9 **Benny Hinn** ($42) in Texas
8 **Robert Tilton** ($50) in Texas
7 **Jan Crouch** ($50) in Florida (passed away)
6 **Chris Oyakhilome** ($50) in Nigeria
5 **Enoch Adebye** ($55) in Nigeria
4 **David Oyedepo** ($150) in Nigeria
3 **George Foreman** ($250) in Houston
2 **Pat Robertson** ($500) in Virginia
1 **Edir Macedo** ($1.1 billion) in Brazil

Since I give to 118 charities and since seven of my charities that I give to have these leaders with big financial net worths in the top fifty, I wondered if I should stop giving to these seven ministries? I prayed and asked Father God about if I should stop giving funds to Reinhard Bonnke ($4), Ernest Angley ($15), Benny Hinn, Samaritan's Purse, TBN, Kenneth Copeland, and The 700 Club? Father God answered me something like this: **"What you are giving is going to their MINISTRY, not to them. Your gifts ARE being used to build up the Kingdom of God on earth, which is your heart's desire, so do keep giving to these ministries that you are now giving to."** Praise God!

I realize that most of these pastors with large amounts of financial net worth have received them from the books, CDs, DVDs, and music they have produced and sold worldwide. Father God also once told me, **"Your greatest income will be from the sale of your books."** This is my third book to self-publish, and I have four more planned. Joy!

Blessings! Velma

PROPHETIC MESSAGE FORTY FIVE FROM
FATHER GOD FOR CHURCH GROWTH

Yes, Our God's beloved Christian children of Almighty God, Our beloved Christian pastors and ALL of Our God's beloved Holy Bible teachers, YOUR heavenly Father God does love you, does love ALL of your many loved ones, and does love ALL of your congregations that you minister to, and YOUR God does take care of you and them at ALL times.

Yes, YOUR Holy Triune God is a good God, a loving God, a majestic God, an all-powerful God, a God Who does meet all the needs of Our God's created mankind on Our God's planet Earth.

Yes, doesn't Our God's Holy Bible teach you that when Our God opens His hand, all the needs are met of all living things? (Psalm 145:16)

Yes, YOUR heavenly Father God can ALWAYS do exceedingly abundantly above all that Our God's mankind on earth can ask God for or can even imagine! (Ephesians 3:20)

Yes, do COME to YOUR heavenly Father God in prayer and do pray GREAT and MIGHTY prayers to YOUR heavenly Father God, pray with great faith in YOUR Lord and Savior, Jesus Christ, always praying in the holy name of Jesus, ASK WHAT YOU WILL that you will be helped, others will be helped, and YOUR Holy Triune God will be glorified on earth.

Yes, YOUR God can do the possible that it is impossible for man to do, impossible even for all mankind working together to do.

Yes, YOUR God is an all-powerful God.

Yes, YOUR heavenly Father God spoke the words, and Our God's planet Earth was created out of nothing, then God hung planet Earth in space on nothing, and a God Who can do that is

390

an all-powerful God, Who greatly deserves all the love, worship, praise, and honor from ALL of mankind that Our God has created with Our God's spoken words and has placed on Our God's created earth.

Yes, Our God has created and still does create mankind in Our God's image with body, soul, and spirit to inhabit Our God's planet Earth.

Yes, Our God created ALL of mankind on earth to know Our God, fellowship with Our God, honor Our God, love Our God, be taken care of by Our God, and enjoy Our God in Our God's heaven above forever.

Yes, when mankind deliberately refuses to know God, love God, fellowship with God, and obey Our God—when mankind drifts away from God and puts other things and other events in first place in their hearts and minds and lives, decay sets into their lives, they become worthless to Our God and are headed for destruction, unless they do REPENT and come BACK to their first love and give Our God FIRST PLACE in their hearts, minds, and daily life.

Yes, mankind was created and is still being created on Our God's planet Earth to know Our God and to enjoy Our God forever.

Yes, Our God's Holy Bible was written for Our God's mankind to teach mankind about Our God, about heaven and hell, and how to know salvation-from-sins in the holy name of Our God's only begotten Son, Jesus Christ, how to come out of ALL sinful lifestyle, live for God, and enter heaven forever.

Yes, Jesus Christ, Our God's only begotten Son, has been raised from the dead by HIS heavenly Father God, is now in heaven seated at HIS Father God's right hand, now making intercession with HIS heavenly Father God for ALL people now alive on earth, that they will know Jesus Christ as their Lord and Savior from their sins, will REPENT of all sinful lifestyle in their life, come out of ALL sin and live in a righteous lifestyle in obedience to God, and enter Our God's heaven forever after their one life on Our God's planet Earth is over.

Yes, it is appointed unto each of mankind now alive on earth to die only once, and after that IS Our God's judgment. (Hebrews 9:27)

Yes, come to Jesus and ASK Jesus to save you.

Yes, now is the time to come.

Tomorrow may be too late to come.

Yes, life on earth is uncertain, and death on earth is certain.

Yes, come one and come ALL to Jesus Christ for forgiveness of sins, repent of a sinful lifestyle, come OUT of ALL sin in your life, live for God while alive on earth, and enter heaven forever.

Yes, Jesus refuses no one, Jesus accepts EVERYONE who does come to Jesus with a repentant heart, and who asks Jesus for salvation from their sins, who makes Jesus the Lord and Master of their life, who comes OUT of ALL sinful lifestyle and lives for God, who then goes and sins no more, WILL join THEIR Lord and Savior Messiah Jesus in heaven forever.

Yes, Jesus Christ is the ONLY Savior, dead or alive, Who has enough power in His supreme sacrifice of His shed blood, death, and resurrection to forgive a person's sinful lifestyle, cleanse them of ALL unholy filth, help them come out of sin, live righteously for God, and enter heaven forever.

Yes, ONLY Jesus saves!

Yes, Jesus saves ONLY the repentant sinner who ASKS Jesus for salvation, who does RECEIVE this free salvation from Jesus, who then goes and sins no more.

Yes, a person cannot work their way into heaven as salvation is by Jesus Christ, the saving grace of Jesus Christ by their faith in Jesus Christ, by their rebuking their sinful lifestyle and living for God while they are alive on earth.

Yes, after salvation in Jesus by faith through grace for forgiveness of all sins, Our God does call each person to rebuke sin from their life and live a righteous lifestyle in obedience to God.

Yes, Jesus does hold the keys to death, hell, and the grave. (Revelation 1:18)

Yes, ONLY Jesus holds your one-way ticket to heaven away from hell for eternity, and it is FREE for the asking as ONLY Jesus' holy shed blood and righteous life, death, and resurrection have already paid the required price for each person now alive on earth to have life, abundant life on earth, and eternal life in heaven. (John 10:10)

Claim it now!

Live it now!

Yes, YOUR heavenly Father God does have a great work for you to do on earth to teach people about God and about Our God's way for them to live to love God, love themselves, and love and help others.

Yes, as YOUR Holy Triune God does lead you and does feed you daily, you are to HELP lead and feed others daily so that people will know THEIR Holy Triune God, will love God with their total being, will honor God, will praise God, and will live for Our God so that Our God IS ABLE TO pour out ALL of Our God's good benefits on all of mankind.

Yes, when each of mankind does know God, does love God, does honor, and does obey Our God, Our God is able to shower down ALL of Our God's good benefits on mankind without them becoming corrupt and drifting away from their true God.

Yes, Jesus Christ, your heavenly Father God, and Our God's Holy Spirit are the true and only God, three separate Beings, but are ALWAYS in one accord.

Yes, Allah is not the true God.

Mohammad is not God.

Buddha is not God.

Allah cannot save you and take you to heaven.

Mohammad cannot save anyone.

Buddha cannot save anyone.

Allah is a liar and is the father of all lies. (John 8:44)

Jesus Christ is the way, the truth, and the life. (John 14:6)

Know Jesus Christ and know the truth.

Yes, ONLY Jesus Christ, the only begotten Son of the true heavenly Father God, is the ONLY Savior of mankind with enough power to save a person's eternal soul, help them to live a righteous lifestyle unto God, and take them to heaven for eternity. (Acts 4:12)

Yes, Jesus Christ is the only Being, dead or alive, Who has paid the price of HIS holy shed blood and death on Calvary's cruel cross to pay for each of mankind's sins and unrighteousness, Who forgives a person's sins when they DO COME to Jesus, ASKS Jesus to forgive their sins, accepts this free salvation from Jesus with a repentant heart, then does go and sin no more.

Yes, ONLY Jesus Christ has enough power to save a person, help them to live for God, and take them to heaven for eternity to live with THEIR Holy Triune God forever.

Yes, when a person does accept Jesus Christ as their Lord and Savior, a measure of Our God's Holy Spirit is given to them to live within them, to comfort them, to guide them in righteous living for God, to teach them Our God's truth, and to help them to live successful and prosperous lives to Our God's glory on earth.

Yes, Our Holy Triune God is a righteous God, and Our God does expect Our God's pastors and Bible teachers to live a righteous lifestyle unto Our God.

Yes, Jesus Christ, when He walked this earth nearly two thousand years ago, did set the perfect example of how Our God wants you to live in loving others, teaching others, helping others, and in revealing your/His heavenly Father God to others.

Yes, do go about loving others, teaching others Our God's holy truths from Our God's Holy Bible, praying for others, and do HELP others where they do need YOUR help the most, and YOUR heavenly Father God will see your love for them, and the help you do give to them, and WILL REWARD YOU accordingly.

Yes, you cannot out-give YOUR Holy Triune God as it is ALWAYS Our God's rule to ALWAYS return to you double and even MORE than double, what you do give to others with love to Our God's glory on earth. (Luke 6:38)

Yes, do LEARN to be very generous givers, and YOUR Holy Triune God WILL BE very generous Givers back to you.

Yes, YOUR heavenly Father God does have unlimited supplies of ALL good gifts and all good events to shower down on each of mankind WHEN they are ready to receive all these good gifts from God without these good gifts leading to their corruption.

Yes, all promotions in your businesses and in your careers do come from God.

Yes, Our God does put each of Our God's mankind through seven tests, with each test designed to draw a person's soul closer to God.

If each person does pass each test with the desired result bringing them closer to God, they are ready for promotion in wealth, prestige, and power, without their becoming corrupt.

Yes, doesn't Our God's Holy Bible teach that mankind falls seven times, but he gets up? (Proverbs 24:16)

Yes, doesn't Our God's Holy Bible teach that it is God Who does give you the power to get wealth? (Deuteronomy 8:18)

Yes, doesn't Our God's Holy Bible teach you to read your Bible daily, live for God, keep away from evil influences, and whatever you do will prosper? (Psalm 1:1-3)

Yes, ALL your prosperity does come to you as your reward from God for your soul's growth in God.

Yes, with Our God's holy love for each of mankind, Our God does work with each person to help form them into the likeness of their holy Savior, Jesus Christ.

Yes, as your eternal soul grows in the likeness of your holy Savior, Jesus Christ, so will your success and prosperity grow, and as you do become more trustworthy, Our God is able to

trust you with more success without your becoming corrupt
and turning away from YOUR true God.

Hallelujah!

Praises to Our heavenly Father God for this teaching
prophecy!

Hallelujah!

Praises to Our God!

Dear Christian Pastors and All Holy Bible Teachers,

Greetings in the holy name of **Jesus** that is above every name. Soon every knee will bow and every tongue will confess that **Jesus Christ** is Lord of lords and King of all kings to the glory of God on earth!

I have finished reading another one of Merlin Carothers' books about praise titled, *Bringing Heaven into Hell.* This is my fourth book by him that I have read. The other three books are, *Prison to Praise, Power in Praise,* and *Let Me Entertain You.* He has many other books on praising God that he has written with over eighteen million in print in 53 languages. He passed away a few years ago. Some of his family members are now running his organization. This is one of my favorite charities that I give to monthly, **Foundation of Praise** in Escondido, California, because they send free Christian books into many of the prisons in several states in the U. S. A. I wrote to them once and asked them why they didn't send any books into the prisons in Tennessee, my home state at the time. Their reply was, "We send them only to the prisons where the Prison Chaplains request the free books." If they would only give these free books on praising God to the Tennessee prisoners, they probably would have fewer repeat offenders in the Tennessee prisons!

I have been a member of the same church for 39 years now, with Pastor Billy Roy Moore for the first 13 years, other pastors for 14 years, and Pastor Danny Chambers for the last 12 years. When Pastor Billy Roy taught us about praise where the Bible teaches us to "praise God in all things," he taught us that when we are going through any kind of trial for us to praise God for **Who God is,** NOT to praise God for the trial we are going through.

However, Merlin teaches people to praise God FOR the trial that they are going through because our God Who loves us has brought us to the specific trial for our own good, for us to learn something from the trial. He quotes the Scripture, "All things work together for the good, for those who love God."

Merlin quotes many examples in several of his books about certain people being in pain trials, financial trials, relationship trials, in prison, and in other bad circumstances, who, after reading one of Merlin's books on their praising God FOR their trials, have immediately come out of the trials victorious!

He explains in his books that complaining about a bad situation is a SIN against God as God is the One in His divine wisdom Who has placed us in the exact places for our souls to grow in God. As "iron sharpens iron" some difficult people who rub us the wrong way and cause disharmony in families and in work places, can actually HELP us to get rid of the flaws in our own character and make us better people and help us to grow closer to God. When the Israelites in the desert complained about having to eat only manna, God became angry about their complaints! When he sent birds to them, many of them died because of their complaining. Paul said, "Whatever state I am in, I have LEARNED to be content." I believe that this state of being has to be LEARNED. It is learned as our soul grows up in God when we can truthfully say, "The Lord is my Shepherd, He provides all that I need."

Father God has told me several times in other prophetic messages that God uses all the GOOD things and all the seemingly BAD things that a person goes through on earth to build a person's character. Father God said that nothing that you go through on earth is ever wasted as God uses it to build your character for your soul to grow in God. He said that the only thing that you take to heaven with you after your one life and one death on earth is your soul's growth in God. He said that our character continues to grow in heaven throughout eternity.

Merlin has some chapters in his book about submission to

authority. He tells about him being in the military service for twenty years. The first five years, he hated submitting to their authority as he didn't want them telling him when to get up, what to wear, what military drills to do, what to eat. Later, Merlin learned that some of the greatest benefits from God come from submitting to God's will, God's instructions for us. He learned great JOY in submitting to God's authority over him. That's when he learned to praise God FOR the military authority over him, and then he began to have great JOY in submitting to the military's authority. His life became transformed because he learned to praise God FOR the circumstances that annoyed him.

Merlin goes on to teach how wives are taught in the Bible to submit to their husband's authority. But husbands must submit to God's authority in order to have the knowledge, wisdom, and kindness to relate to their submissive wives. He also teaches that children are to submit to the authority of their parents as their parents submit to the authority of God in their own lives. He gives many proven examples of how praising God improves people's lives and how submitting to God's authority improves people's lives. He teaches for us to submit to government's and to the IRS's authorities as they are there for our benefits.

About twelve years ago when the merger of The Lord's Chapel and Oasis Church took place, The Lord's Chapel had very strong weekly prayer meetings, but had only about forty active church members. Oasis Church had practically NO prayer meetings with over a thousand church members. For me, the regular Monday evening prayer meetings were where I was getting my main Christian growth. I could not see what made the difference in the attendance in the two different churches. Then God showed to me that the PRAISE SINGING in Oasis Church was what made the difference. God showed to me that when a person is praising God is when God is filling them with love, faith, power, knowledge, wisdom, guidance, and all good things. When we praise God FOR our trials is when God begins to erase the trials we are in. Praise God!

Something else that could possibly be happening, which I suspect is happening, is that if a trial is being caused by an evil spirit, like depression can be caused by an evil spirit, praising God FOR the trial will make the evil spirit flee from you, because the evil spirit does not want to be the cause of your offering MORE praise to Jesus Christ and the true heavenly Father God! When I was suffering severely from depression, God gave me a dream to show me how I could get rid of it by the words to the song, *"This is my story, this is my song, praising my Savior all the day long."* Continually praising God can get rid of evil spirits that cause depression! In the Bible, when King Saul was tormented by an evil spirit, he called for David to play harp music for the king's relief. David was probably playing some of his praise music on his harp. The Bible teaches that God has given us the garment of praise for the spirit of heaviness. (Isaiah 61:3) In many of the books about people visiting heaven, they have reported on the continual praise music in heaven as there is continual praise music to God in heaven. Joy!

Blessings! Velma

Yes, Our God's beloved Christian children of Our God's beloved Christian pastors and ALL of Our God's beloved Holy Bible teachers, YOUR heavenly Father God does love you and does love ALL of your congregations, and YOUR heavenly Father God does take care of you and them at ALL times.

Yes, you do serve a great God, a mighty God, an all-powerful God, a merciful God, a God with no beginning and no ending, an enduring God, a God Who has GREAT LOVE for ALL of Our God's mankind on Our God's planet Earth that Our God has created and still does create in Our God's image with body, soul, and spirit.

Yes, your holy high God has created each of mankind on Our God's earth who is alive now, created each with a free will to choose Jesus or reject Jesus, choose to live for God or not to live for God on earth.

Yes, the ones who do choose Jesus Christ as their Lord and Savior, who ASK Jesus to forgive their sins, who then do come out of ALL sinful lifestyle and live for God, will be REWARDED by Our God as they will have abundant life on earth and will have eternal life in heaven rejoicing forevermore.

Yes, heaven is joyful!

Yes, heaven is beautiful!

Yes, the continual praises of Our God's Holy Triune God do ring throughout heaven continually which brings more love, hope, peace, and joy to the people now in heaven.

Yes, doesn't Our God's Holy Bible teach you to keep your mind centered, focused, on Jesus Christ, and you will have perfect peace at all times? (Isaiah 26:30)

Yes, doesn't Our God's Holy Bible teach you that the JOY of the Lord is your strength? (Nehemiah 8:10)

Yes, doesn't Our God's Holy Bible teach you that you can do all things through Jesus Christ which strengthens you? (Philippians 4:13)

Yes, DO ALLOW Our God to strengthen you and fill you with love, joy, peace, comfort, knowledge, wisdom, good health, and ALL GOOD benefits THROUGH your praises to YOUR Holy Triune God!

Yes, your God strengthens you and does give to you ALL good benefits through your praise and worship to YOUR Holy Triune God.

Yes, do praise YOUR God until the power comes, until your good health comes, until the answers to your righteous prayers come, until your joyful breakthrough comes, until your problems are solved.

Yes, Jesus is the ANSWER so do ASK Jesus then praise Jesus until ALL the RIGHT answers come that will benefit you, will help others, and will glorify Our God on earth.

Yes, nothing is too difficult for your God working through you and through your believing prayers, prayed in the holy name of Jesus, to accomplish on Our God's planet Earth.

Yes, Jesus Christ has been given ALL POWER in heaven and in earth so do go forth and win this whole world to a saving grace in Jesus.

Yes, Jesus Christ and Our heavenly Father God do desire that ALL mankind now alive on Our God's planet Earth know Jesus Christ as THEIR Lord and Savior, that they come out of ALL sinful lifestyle and live a righteous lifestyle in obedience to God, and enter heaven forever after their one lifetime on earth is over.

Yes, yes, yes, do tell EVERYONE to get ready to go and to STAY READY TO GO in Our God's great rapture of souls on earth that WILL take place soon!

Yes, Our heavenly Father God has spoken that the rapture

on earth is imminent, is SOON, and Our heavenly Father God does know the exact day and hour that Our God's great rapture of ALL of the obedient Christian souls WILL be caught UP to Jesus in the air to go BACK to THEIR glorious home in heaven, to live with, to rule and reign with, to enjoy being with forever, THEIR Lord Jesus Christ.

Yes, do choose Jesus now.

Do live for God now and NEVER regret it.

Yes, Jesus is God.

Jesus is all in all. (Colossians 3:11)

Jesus is the word of God. (John 1:1-3)

Yes, Jesus will judge the quick and the dead at Our God's white throne judgment.

Yes, Jesus comes soon!

Yes, whatever you do go through in your life on earth, all the good times and ALL the seemingly bad times, YOUR heavenly Father God does use it ALL for your soul's growth in God.

Yes, do NOT be discouraged by bad circumstances in your life, but do rejoice in Our God's bringing you THROUGH these bad situations, and Our God giving to you MORE of your soul's growth in God so that Our God is able to reward you with greater benefits in your life for your faithfulness to Our God THROUGH these trials.

Yes, Our God's obedient children have NEVER lost a battle.

Yes, Our God's obedient children are ALWAYS victorious in the end.

Yes, YOUR Holy Triune God has ALL power over ALL your enemies, and YOUR Holy Triune God will NOT ALLOW harm to come to you, EXCEPT what you need to experience for your soul's growth in God.

Yes, when a child of God IS in ANY kind of trial, ALL trials ARE ALLOWED by God to bring the person closer to THEIR Holy Triune God for love and for solutions.

Yes, each person's time on earth is allotted for their soul's growth in God.

Yes, Our Father God does know the extent of each person's allotted time on earth.

Yes, Our heavenly Father God is the great I AM, Who does know the beginning to the ending of all things.

Yes, all good things and all good circumstances and good events in your life now ARE from YOUR heavenly Father God, and they do come through your Lord Jesus Christ to you. (Philippians 4:19)

Yes, YOUR heavenly Father God does know what good benefits to give to each person now alive on earth to help bring each person into a closer relationship with their Holy Triune God, for their soul to grow in God.

Yes, YOUR Holy Triune God has all knowledge on ALL subjects and does have all divine wisdom, and Our God does give to mankind knowledge and wisdom when they do ASK for it and will use it to help themselves, help others, and glorify God on earth.

Yes, doesn't Our God's Holy Bible tell you that if anyone lacks wisdom to come to God, ASK God for it, and they will be given wisdom from Our God? (James 1:5)

Yes, Our God is a GOOD God Who does LOVE to shower down ALL of Our God's good benefits to mankind when they are able to receive all these good benefits without these good benefits bringing them to corruption and bringing them away from God.

Yes, do learn to TRUST YOUR Holy Triune God to bring about your specific set of circumstances for YOUR soul to grow in God.

Yes, do you have physical health problems? If so, bring them to Jesus, your Healer.

If you have shortages of supplies, finances, and need help in any situation, do ASK for your Father God's HELP in sending to you ALL your needed items on time, when you know God, honor God, love God, and obey God.

Yes, YOUR heavenly Father God does have unlimited

supplies and unlimited resources that are available with only Our God's spoken Word.

Yes, Jesus Christ IS the spoken Word of His heavenly Father God. (John 1:1-3)

Yes, Jesus Christ has been raised from the dead by HIS heavenly Father God, has been given the keys to hell and the grave, and has been given ALL power in heaven and in earth. (Matthew 28:18)

Yes, when you pray your prayers to YOUR heavenly Father God, do pray ALL your prayers in Jesus' holy name.

Yes, in answer to your believing prayers prayed in Jesus' holy name, Our heavenly Father God does speak the words, "Be it done unto you according to your faith in Our God's Son, Jesus Christ," and then Our God watches to see which prayers are answered.

Yes, your faith in Jesus Christ does heal the sick, and your faith in Jesus Christ does get your prayers to YOUR heavenly Father God answered.

Yes, Jesus Christ is God.

Yes, love, honor, and praise Jesus Christ as you do love, honor, and praise YOUR heavenly Father God.

Yes, Father God, Jesus Christ, and God's Holy Spirit are three separate Beings, but are always in one accord.

Yes, love Our God's Holy Triune God with your total being and do LEARN to keep a praise to your God on your heart and mind at ALL times, and Our God will infill you with love, joy, peace, and happiness at ALL times, regardless of your good or bad situations at ALL times.

Yes, do REJOICE in God at ALL times, knowing God does give you victory in and THROUGH every good and every seemingly bad situation in your life.

Yes, everything good and every good situation outcome are possible when you do submit to your God's divine authority in your life.

Yes, commit your life and commit everything and every

situation in your life to God, keep trusting God, and do watch your life emerge through trials victoriously with YOUR GOD'S guidance in your life.

Yes, your God is perfect, and your God has a perfect will for your life, for your soul's growth in God.

Yes, as your soul does grow in God year by year, you will prosper, and your ministry will prosper, and whatever you do will prosper.

Praises to Our God for this prophetic message for church growth!

Hallelujah!

Praises to Our God!

Joy!

Dear Christian Pastors and All Holy Bible Teachers,

Many people all over the world now are suffering persecutions for their belief in and worship of Jesus Christ and our heavenly Father God. Many of them are having their blood shed and even killed because of their faith in and worship of Jesus and Father God. Many people in the United States now are being criticized and punished for passing out Christian literature, for witnessing for Jesus, and for praying in Jesus' name. One of the strongest Christians that I know, my cousin Inez Ingram who recently passed away, told me, "We Christians in America have not yet shed any blood because of our Christianity." With my giving to seven military organizations to help the wounded, I receive many letters in response to my giving that tell how the military chaplains are not allowed to pray in Jesus' name and are not allowed to pass out Bibles in the military hospitals. With our new President Donald Trump, many new organizations have come into being to fight against this and restore to our people the freedom of religion that we in America are guaranteed in our U. S. Constitution.

There may come a time in our lives when we must stand up against the evil in people that come against our faith in Jesus in us. I believe that we as Christians must know Jesus personally and know what the Bible teaches in order to be strong to withstand the evil that comes against us and comes against our faith in Jesus and the true God. My God has had me in training for this all my life, I believe.

I married a non-Christian and listened to his scoffing against my Christian beliefs for over 33 years until he finally became a Christian. I prayed for Hugh Davies to become a Christian for five years before we were married and for most of the 39 years of our married life. He finally became a Christian just before he went into assisted living with Alzheimer's. In the nursing home where he passed away, I was told that he had died with a smile on his face! I know that God answered my prayers for him and that I will see him again in heaven. After living with a habitual scoffer of my Christianity for all those years, there is nothing now that a non-Christian can say to me about my Christianity that will upset me. I will just give them a soft answer and tell them, "You need prayers. I will pray for you."

It is one thing to have a non-Christian scoff at you for your Christian beliefs, but it is something else to have a Christian Pastor scoff at your Christian beliefs, believe lies that were told about you, tell you to leave the church, tell you not to join their church, and tell you to not even visit their church. Four times in my life, Christian Pastors have come against me for my service conduct and for my Christian beliefs. The first time this happened, I was shaken to the core. The last three times that this happened to me, they happened at the time when I was Holy Spirit filled and could ask God to speak to me about the situations. God did speak to me and told me what is going on in those particular situations. It greatly comforted my heart to hear the true voice, the true wisdom, knowledge, love, patience, and power of God that is at work in the different situations. What grieved my heart so much is that I know that I was innocent in these four situations when these pastors came against me. Going through these four trials with these four Christian Pastors coming against me when I was innocent in the situation, has taught me to identify more with Jesus Christ and the trials He went through with the leading priests of the synagogues coming against Him when he walked this earth, when Jesus was the only perfect person who ever lived on earth, totally innocent! It also helped me to relate more to Joseph in the Bible when he went through the twelve-year trial of being sold into Egypt as a slave and being put into prison, when he was totally innocent! Both of them remained faithful to God and both were rewarded by our heavenly Father God as Jesus was given all power in heaven and in earth, and Joseph became second in command in all of Egypt.

Father God once told me, **"Listen not to man, because man can lead you wrong. Trust God to work out all details for this project, and God will lead you and guide you."** After my going through these trials with these four Christian pastors coming against me, it has brought me closer to God and has made me more determined to hear from MY God in every seemingly bad situation, especially with non-Christians and with Christian leaders coming against what MY God is leading me to do in my Christian service to my fellow mankind and to my God on earth. God tells us in the Bible to pray for those who come against us, so I am praying for those pastors, that our God will reveal our God's truth to them and the truth will set them free.

I believe that when a Christian worker can get to the place in their life where they are willing to take abuse from non-Christians and from Christian leaders when they are totally innocent in a situation and still remain faithful to God and pray for the people who wrongfully abuse them is when our God can use the person in a great way in service to God and to all mankind on earth.

I wish that EVERY Christian could get to the place in their life when they can get on their knees in their prayer closet, praise God, ask God to speak to them, wait on their knees until God answers them, praise God for speaking to them, then act on the excellent advice that our God gives to them. Father God said, **"If people would pray about the decisions they are to make, they could save themselves a lot of heartache."** After my making many wrong decisions in my life, I am finally learning to do that! I praise God for speaking to me whenever I ask Him to. Joy!

Blessings! Velma

Yes, Our God's beloved Christian children of ALL of Our God's Christian pastors and ALL of Our God's beloved Holy Bible teachers, YOUR heavenly Father God does love you, does love ALL of the congregations you do preach to and teach to, and YOUR heavenly Father God does take care of you and them at ALL times.

Yes, YOUR Holy Triune God is a good God, a righteous God, a never-ending and never-beginning God, a God with all power, a God with all love, a God Who does rule with love, power, justice, and mercy.

Yes, YOUR heavenly Father God does desire greatly to give to each of you Christian-workers-for-God all of the good gifts and ALL of the good events that you WILL use wisely to help yourself, to help others, that will glorify Our God on earth that will NOT fill you with pride, conceit, selfishness, and evil.

Yes, each person of mankind now alive on earth does have a threshold above them, that if they are raised up too quickly and too high with money, fame, possessions, and prestige, they will begin to become corrupt and will be headed for their destruction, UNLESS THEY DO REPENT and come back to their first love of THEIR Holy Triune God.

Yes, do read about the king in Our God's Holy Bible who became so prideful that Our God reduced him to living like an animal eating grass for seven years until he gained the wisdom that Our God rules and reigns on earth, exalting the faithful-in-God and bringing down the prideful, self-centered, evil people who turn away from God. (Daniel 4:30-37)

Yes, Satan had wealth, prestige, honor, and beauty when he was first created by God in heaven, but when Satan became selfish and corrupt and was leading others to become corrupt, Our God had to punish him for his corruption because he would not REPENT of his corruption and turn back to honoring his very Creator God.

Yes, when mankind puts other things and other events in first place in their hearts and minds and turns away from giving Our God first place, they begin to drift away from God, with these other things and other events becoming their gods.

Yes, in the days of Noah while Noah was building the ark for 120 years, God was giving all the people TIME to REPENT, time to turn back to their first love of knowing God, loving God, honoring God, and living for God, but none turned back to God, back to knowing God, loving God, and living for God—when they became so selfish and so prideful, they became worthless to Our God and did DESERVE Our God's wiping all of them off the face of the earth with the great flood, sparing only Noah and his family who loved Our God, honored and obeyed Our God.

Yes, Our God does examine the thoughts, words, and deeds of each person now alive on earth, to reward the righteous-in-Jesus and to give the unrighteous TIME to repent, TIME to turn to God, ask God's forgiveness for their sins, come back to honoring and loving and obeying God, before Our God has to bring their enemies to destroy them from off the face of the earth.

Yes, Our God is a merciful God, Who does give each of mankind TIME to repent of their sins, TIME to turn to Jesus and ASK Jesus to save them from their sins and wrongdoing, TIME to come out of a sinful lifestyle and live righteously for God so that they DO become valuable to Our God, and their total destruction can be avoided.

Yes, Our Holy Triune God did create and still does create ALL of Our God's mankind in Our God's image on earth with body, soul, and spirit, created them to know Our God, fellowship with Our God, enjoy the goodness of Our God, be provided for by Our God, and to enjoy Our God forever in heaven.

Yes, whenever mankind turns away from the goodness of God, turns away from knowing God, loving God, fellowshipping with God, and honoring God, he neglects God, becomes prideful, self-centered, unloving, unhelpful to others, and evil, and no longer deserves to live on Our God's planet Earth, and Our God does allow their destruction.

Yes, Our God does send warnings to evil mankind who are now living in a sinful lifestyle on earth and does give evil people TIME to REPENT of their evil lifestyle, TIME to turn back to the true God, TIME to seek forgiveness from God, time to turn BACK to their true God, come out of sin, live for God, give God first place in their hearts, minds, and lives, and avoid their total destruction on Our God's planet Earth.

Yes, life on earth is uncertain and death on earth is certain.

Yes, each person now alive on Our God's planet Earth will face Our God's white throne judgment and WILL give an account of their one life they lived on earth, the decisions they made and the works they did while they were alive on earth.

They will be judged for the decisions they made and the works they did while alive on Our God's planet Earth, and will then be given access to heaven or will be turned into hell for eternity.

Yes, choose Jesus as your Lord and Savior, repent of all sin and all unrighteous lifestyle, live for God, help your helpless mankind, enter heaven forever, and enjoy Our Holy Triune God forever!

Yes, YOUR heavenly Father God has called each of you out to do a very great work for and WITH YOUR Holy Triune God to win the lost to Our God's only begotten Son of Jesus Christ for salvation from ALL their sins, and to teach people HOW to come out of ALL sinful lifestyle and live for God, in order for them to enter heaven in their life after their one lifetime on earth.

Yes, Our God's only begotten Son, Jesus Christ, is the only Being alive Who has enough power to forgive a person's sins and cleanse them of ALL unholy filth that does enable a person to enter heaven for eternity.

Yes, ONLY Jesus Christ has paid the penalty for ALL of Our God's mankind's sins with Jesus' holy shed blood and cruel death on Calvary's cross, that does enable whosoever will to come to Jesus with a repentant heart and ASK Jesus to forgive their sins, transgressions, and iniquities, and ASK Jesus to be their Lord and Savior of their soul, to cleanse them, to help them come out of all sinful lifestyle, to live for God for the rest of their life on earth, and give them everlasting life in heaven with THEIR Holy Triune God.

Yes, only Jesus Christ does have enough power to forgive a person's sins, cleanse them of ALL unrighteousness, and take them to heaven in their afterlife, after their ONE life on earth.

Yes, Jesus Christ is your ONLY true access to YOUR heavenly Father God, the only true God, Creator of heaven and earth, all in heaven and all in earth. (1Timothy 2:5)

Yes, Jesus Christ has been raised from the dead by HIS heavenly Father God, has been given the keys to hell and the grave, has been given all power in heaven and in earth, has ascended into the third heaven, and is seated at the right hand of HIS heavenly Father God, and is now making intercession with HIS heavenly Father God for all people now alive on earth to know Jesus as their personal Savior and Lord, will live for God on earth, and will enter heaven forever after their one life on earth.

Yes, Jesus Christ IS coming back towards earth soon to claim and to catch away to Our God's great heaven above, all the saved-in-Jesus and right-living-unto-God beloved children of God.

Yes, sin will NEVER enter heaven.

Yes, in order to enter heaven in a person's afterlife, they

413

MUST accept Jesus Christ as their Lord and Savior, and they must live a righteous lifestyle unto God.

Yes, Jesus Christ saves.

Yes, Jesus Christ saves completely when people REPENT, come to Jesus and do ASK Jesus to save them from their sins, and do ASK Jesus to help them to live for God.

Yes, Jesus is all powerful.

Yes, Jesus has the power to heal your body and save your soul.

Yes, Jesus Christ is the same yesterday, today, and forever. (Hebrews 13:8)

Yes, when your faith and trust in Jesus is strong enough for you to be healed in Jesus, and you do ASK your Lord Jesus for healing, you will be totally physically healed by Jesus, because didn't Jesus say to the ones in the Bible that Jesus healed, "Your faith has made you whole"? (Luke 17:19)

Yes, when you do pray TO your heavenly Father God, ALWAYS pray in the name of Jesus, and always do pray with great faith in the healing power of your God Jesus.

Yes, Father God, Lord Jesus, and Our God's Holy Spirit do hear you when you pray with faith in Jesus Christ.

Yes, Our heavenly Father God does desire to ANSWER ALL your holy prayers prayed with faith in Jesus Christ.

Yes, Our heavenly Father God does desire to give ALL of Our God's obedient-to-God mankind on earth ALL of Our God's great gifts that Our God created for all of mankind even before Our God created planet Earth, and Our God WILL give them to all of Our God's mankind when mankind is ready to receive them.

Yes, Our loving holy high God will NOT give to any of mankind a gift that will harm them or will lead them away from God.

Yes, do read and do study Our God's Holy Bible that does teach ALL of Our God's mankind about God, about how to know God, how to honor and love God above all else, and how

414

to live for God, and how to love and help yourself and others to Our God's glory.

Yes, Our God's ways ARE higher than man's ways. (Isaiah 55:8-9)

Yes, learn from OUR Holy Triune God the more perfect way, the more righteous way, the way that does please your God the most, and then YOUR heavenly Father God WILL REWARD YOU with the most excellent of gifts and benefits for you to enjoy, to share with others, and to glorify Our God with.

Yes, it does please Our God when you seek to know God better, live for God better, and do help the people who need your help.

Yes, ALWAYS keep a cheerful attitude as you go about your daily work and needed chores, knowing that ALL things do work together for good for all the ones who know God and are called for the purpose of God. (Romans 8:28)

Yes, know YOUR heavenly Father God does have ALL power in YOUR universe, including Our God's earth, and NOTHING can harm a child of God EXCEPT what Our God does allow for the person's soul growth in God.

Yes, do keep your mind centered on Jesus Christ, and you will have perfect peace of mind at all times. (Isaiah 26:3)

Yes, praise God without ceasing for a long time and do see HOW YOUR heavenly Father God does reward you for this with more love, knowledge, wisdom, kindness, better physical health, more opportunities for advancement on your jobs and in your careers, and more success in ALL areas of your life and in your loved ones' lives.

Yes, your God is a good God Who enjoys rewarding Our God's obedient children.

Hallelujah!

Praises to Our heavenly Father God for this prophetic message for church growth!

Hallelujah!

Praises to Our God!

Dear Christian Pastors and All Holy Bible Teachers,

I always pray about what to write to you Christian pastors and teachers that will encourage you in your work for the Lord.

I want to share with you some of the good things that our God is now doing in my life. All good gifts do come to us from our heavenly Father God and they do come to us through our Lord Jesus Christ. Jesus explained it to me like this: Father God gives to you a package, Jesus Christ is the mailman that delivers the package to you, and your praise to God is what pays the postage for the delivery. He said that the more we praise God, the sooner the package is delivered to us!

Jesus gave us this explanation about a blind young man in our Mt. Bethel United Methodist Church. He has been blind since age thirteen when he had surgery for a brain tumor. He has been blind for 21 years. I first met this young man at the Mt. Bethel UMC's annual arts and crafts fair where we had each rented booths to sell our art work on the first Saturday of November, 2016.

Since I know that Jesus is our divine Healer, that He heals blind eyes, that Jesus is now alive in heaven at the right hand of HIS heavenly Father God, and that Jesus always speaks to me when I asked Him to, I asked Jesus if He wanted to heal Will Graham's blind eyes? Jesus answered me, **"Yes, yes, yes, a thousand times, yes! The sooner the better!"** Praises to our God Jesus!

Then I asked Jesus if He would give to me a prophetic message each month from Jesus to Will to increase Will's faith in Jesus for the physical healing of his eyesight? Jesus replied to me that He will when I ask Jesus for the messages. I asked Jesus for the first one, which He gave to me, which I wrote out and read to Will over the phone. Will was happy to receive the message and happy to know that Jesus wants to heal his eyesight. Later, after one of our church services, I gave to Will the printed copy of the prophetic message from Jesus and invited Will to come to our first Wednesday of the month evening church prayer meeting where he could be anointed with oil and prayed for his physical healing. Will replied that he is able to come to the 6:00 p.m. prayer meeting and then go to his 7:00 p.m. choir practice on Wednesday evenings. He has not yet been able to attend one of our monthly prayer meetings.

A month later, I asked Jesus for the second prophetic message from Jesus for Will to encourage him to have faith in Jesus for his complete healing of his eyesight. Jesus gave to me a long prophetic message for Will that I wrote out and typed up and finally was able to deliver to Will at church. It was three typewritten pages long and was very encouraging. Jesus told Will to praise Jesus and Father God many times daily, and that the more he praised God, the sooner his eyesight will be restored to 20/20 vision!

Jesus told Will that after Jesus heals Will's eyesight that He will raise up Will as a powerful testimony of what God can do for mankind that mankind cannot do. Copies of the two prophetic messages from Jesus to Will about the healing of Will's eyesight have been given to Pastor Jody Ray and his father, Pastor Glenn Ray, at Mt. Bethel UMC. I told Pastor Jody, "I see a cloud the size of a man's hand!"

I have been praising God daily for several weeks for the healing of Will's eyesight to the glory of God on earth. I plan to keep asking Jesus for a prophetic message each month to give to Will, written out and typed up, so that Will can have it read to him daily, to be encouraged for what our God will do for him, to build up Will's faith in Jesus for Will's complete physical healing. Jesus said, "Your faith has made you whole," when He healed people on earth as He walked this earth nearly two thousand years ago.

I have put out my Garner family newsletter for more than 28 years with a prophetic message in every monthly issue for the past 25 years. Now that our older parents' generation has passed away, and more than half of our cousins' generation has passed away, and the younger generation has turned to Facebook for their news and information, I believe that the printed family newsletter is no longer needed. Now I have decided to begin a monthly Christian magazine named, "Evidence," which will give evidence that Jesus Christ is alive and well with a prophetic message from Jesus in every issue. I have also asked Father God to give to me at least three personal testimonies of physical healings by Jesus to be included in each issue. At our last monthly prayer meeting at Mt. Bethel UMC, nine people gave verbal testimonies of how God had physically healed them when mankind was unable to heal them! I would like to publish some of these wonderful testimonies of what our God Jesus is now doing for His precious needy people! Praise God for healing these people and for them giving their testimonies of the goodness and greatness of our God!

I claim this Scripture for this new Christian magazine, "I shall not die, but live, and declare the works of the Lord." (Psalm 118:17)

Blessings! Velma

Yes, Our God's beloved Christian children of Our God's beloved Christian pastors and ALL of Our God's beloved Holy Bible teachers, YOUR heavenly Father God does love you, does help you to be successful in life, and does take care of you and ALL of your loved ones at ALL times.

Yes, do PRAISE YOUR Holy Triune God for a long time daily, and Our Father God WILL USE this time to strengthen you, teach you knowledge and wisdom, will fill you with more love, joy, kindness, meekness, and ALL good things to make you MORE successful in your daily and nightly life on earth.

Yes, as your soul does grow more in your God, you can be trusted more by your God, and this enables Our God to open more doors for your promotion and advancement.

Yes, Our God can open doors that no man can open, and Our God can close doors that no man can close. (Revelation 3:7)

Yes, ALL promotions do come from YOUR heavenly Father God.

Yes, Our God does test the heart of each person seven times to prove the love that each person has for Our Holy Triune God. (Proverbs 24:16)

Yes, Our God does NOT make each test too difficult for the person, but will ALWAYS make a way of escape for the person so that if they make the right choices, they WILL be ABLE to come THROUGH each test with flying colors! (1 Corinthians 10:13)

Yes, when a person goes through a time of testing, it usually is not a pleasant experience, but if the person endures through the test and emerges victorious with their strong faith in THEIR

Holy Triune God, they will be promoted to the level that their faith has grown in God.

Yes, Joseph was sold as a slave and was carried off to Egypt where he endured trials for twelve long and difficult years, but his faith in HIS God never wavered when Our God was with him and HELPED him endure all of the trials, when he was innocent of wrongdoing to cause the trials.

Yes, during the twelve years of Joseph's trials as a slave and then in prison, Our God was building the character of Joseph, having his faith in God to grow, having his soul to grow up in God, preparing Joseph for the great task ahead of him to be second in command next to Pharaoh in Egypt to store up food in the coming seven years of plenty followed by seven years of drought on the land.

Yes, Our God's divine plan for Joseph's whole life was worked out daily by God as God used the works of Joseph to help bring Jacob and all of his family to Egypt.

Yes, Our God's plans and activities are ALWAYS perfect, and Our God's actions in any of mankind's life will ALWAYS work out for good for all the people who are called according to Our God's purpose. (Romans 8:28)

Yes, now mankind sees through a glass darkly and sees only part of the whole plan and purpose Our God has for each life, but soon they will be able to see the entire history and purpose of their life on Our God's planet Earth, and they WILL REJOICE IN GOD knowing and understanding Our God's plan, purpose, and execution of their time on earth. (1 Corinthians 13:12)

Yes, in all your ways do acknowledge Our God, and Our God will ALWAYS direct your path. (Proverbs 3:5-6)

Yes, a man plans his way, but Our God directs his steps. (Proverbs 16:9)

Yes, ASK for Our God's directions in your life, the path you are to take, the decisions you are to make, the rules you are to follow that will help you, will help others, and will glorify YOUR God on earth.

Yes, the two hardest trials that humans on earth seem to go through are financial shortages and poor health.

Yes, THEIR God is their divine answer to these two problems, as well as, ALL of their problems on earth.

Yes, Jesus Christ IS your physical Healer so do claim your physical healing in Jesus name, then praise your God Jesus until your healing is manifested in your body, then praise your Lord Jesus for your physical healing.

For finances, ask God to help you to tithe your way out of debt.

Yes, tithes are holy unto God, and each person is given a gift from God that does contain a holy tithe built into it, and Our God does watch each person's life to see what they do with THEIR holy tithe from God that has been LOANED to them by God.

Yes, if a person RETURNS their holy tithe and offerings BACK to Our God in helping the poor and helpless, and if they give to promote Our God's gospel to mankind, Our God sees their good work and WILL REWARD them double and more than double what they give. (Luke 6:38)

Yes, doesn't Our God teach you in Our God's Holy Bible that it is God Who gives you the power to get wealth? (Deuteronomy 8:18)

Yes, Our God will help you overcome all hardships from lack of finances and lack of supplies as YOUR heavenly Father God is ALWAYS your divine Provider!

Yes, YOUR Father God is in heaven, and you shall never lack any good thing when you know God, love God, obey God, and live righteously. (Psalm 84:11)

Yes, do know Jesus as your Lord and Savior, live a holy life unto God, help and serve your fellow mankind, ask YOUR heavenly Father God to meet ALL your needs and meet ALL your holy desires, always praying in the holy name of Jesus with great faith in Jesus, then praise your God many times daily until the answers to your prayers are manifested in the physical, and you SHALL HAVE the answers to your righteous prayers that will help you, help others, and will glorify Our God on earth.

Yes, time on earth is soon running out as you do now know time to be on earth, and soon time on earth will be marked as Our God's millennial time where one day is as a thousand years, and a thousand years is as one day. (2 Peter 3:8)

Yes, Jesus Christ is NOW READY to split the great Eastern skies above earth coming back to claim and to catch away ALL of Our God's saved-in-Jesus and right-living-unto-God beloved Christian children of God to claim them and to take them BACK to THEIR eternal home in Our God's third heaven above to enjoy, to rule, and to reign with THEIR Holy Triune God forever.

Yes, time on earth is now short, and what you do with and for YOUR Holy Triune God MUST be done QUICKLY!

Yes, it is time to work and witness for and with YOUR Holy Triune God to HELP BRING IN ALL lost souls on Our God's planet Earth to know Jesus Christ as THEIR Lord and Savior, to come out of ALL sinful lifestyle and live for and with THEIR true God, and get ready to GO to heaven and SPEND eternity in heaven with THEIR Holy Triune God.

Yes, witness, witness, witness for Jesus to everyone you meet.

Tell ALL the physically sick people that Jesus is THEIR divine Healer, that Jesus had 39 stripes on His back to pay for the physical healing of all 39 kinds of diseases and afflictions.

Just COME to Jesus, PRAY to Jesus with your repentant heart, ASK Jesus to save you from ALL your sins, ACCEPT this forgiveness from Jesus, ASK Jesus to help you to LIVE for God, ASK Jesus to CLEANSE YOU of ALL unholy filth, and ASK YOUR LORD Jesus to completely heal your entire body of ALL diseases, all afflictions, all pain, and ALL deformities.

Do ASK Jesus and then do praise Jesus many times daily and nightly until your complete healing is manifested in your body, then do THANK YOUR Lord Jesus Christ daily that He has completely healed you.

Yes, if anyone has EVER offended you in ANY WAY, do FORGIVE them of ALL offenses towards you, and if YOU have ever offended anyone in ANY way, either intentionally or unintentionally, go to them, ask their forgiveness, and make your relationship right with them as much as it is possible with yourself.

Yes, make ALL your relationships right with others so long as you are able to do so.

As you forgive others who have sinned against you, THEN YOUR heavenly Father God WILL forgive YOU of ALL YOUR sins. (Matthew 6:12)

Yes, sin will NEVER enter heaven.

Yes, ALL people in heaven now do have a right relationship with THEIR Holy Triune God and do have a right relationship with others there in heaven.

Yes, do let Our Father God's will be done on earth as it is in heaven. (Matthew 6:10)

Yes, there are no maimed, crippled, blind, sick, unhealthy people in heaven.

All people now in Our God's third heaven with THEIR Holy Triune God are happy, whole, restored to perfect health, and are now living righteously with unto THEIR Holy Triune God.

Yes, now in hell are people who rejected being saved in Jesus and rejected living for God while they were alive on earth who have carried their illnesses, their deformities, and their maimed bodies with them to be tortured in hell forever.

Yes, if only people knew the whole and complete truth of who will go to hell forever and who will go to heaven forever, surely THEY WOULD MAKE the right decision to accept the ONLY TRUE Savior of all of mankind, would come OUT of ALL sinful lifestyle and live for God while they are alive on earth, and spend eternity in heaven forever with eternal bliss, with THEIR Holy Triune God, and with their saved-in-Jesus family and friends.

Yes, do warn others about their spending eternity in hell by their rejecting Jesus Christ as their Lord and Savior, and by their refusing to come OUT of living in a sinful lifestyle.

Yes, God is holy.

Yes, marriages of one man and one woman are holy.

Yes, praising God, loving God, obeying God, living for and with YOUR Holy Triune God does glorify YOUR God.

Yes, ALL GOOD THINGS and ALL GOOD EVENTS in your life now are FROM YOUR heavenly Father God and are now given to you THROUGH YOUR Lord Jesus Christ. (Philippians 4:19)

Yes, do praise and do thank your holy high God daily, many times daily, for Our God's good gifts to you, to your family, and to ALL your loved ones.

Yes, as you do praise and thank your God for ALL your good gifts, Our God does use this time to fill you with Our God's love, kindness, joy, peace, knowledge, wisdom, and ALL good things to enrich your life on earth, to make you successful in all your good deeds and kind benefits you do and give to others with love to YOUR God's glory on earth.

Yes, do ALWAYS encourage others to ALWAYS grow closer to God, and Our God will ALWAYS grow closer to them, and will ALWAYS give to them ALL the good benefits in their life for them to use to improve their own life and to improve the lives of others.

Yes, ALWAYS have a helpful and joyful and truthful relationship with ALL others, especially to all the ones who NEED your help, the lonely, the discouraged, the tired, the fearful, the sick and hurting, the hungry, the naked, the ones in prison, the ones who NEED your encouragement, and who NEED your prayers, and who NEED your help.

Yes, Our heavenly Father God sees your heart (emotions), your thoughts, your encouraging words, and ALL your good deeds to love and help others, and Our God WILL REWARD YOU in the ways that you need it the most as Our God is always a GOOD God Who ALWAYS has unlimited resources to shower down on you and on ALL your loved ones.

Hallelujah!

Praises to Our heavenly Father God for this prophetic message for all church growth!

Hallelujah!

Praises to Our God!

Dear Christian Pastors and All Holy Bible Teachers,

I always pray about what our God would have me to write to you in these letters for church growth.

I have never thought of myself as a professional writer, but have just always thought of myself as a typist. However, Father God told me recently that He is going to train me to be a writer as He is going to give to me writing skills, as wells as, my graphic design skills. Father God told me, **"Always speak and write the truth in love."** I responded to God by saying to Him, "All right, God, with your help, I will always try to do that." I usually don't even read fiction books, but always try to read good Bible teaching books.

I especially like to read biographies and autobiographies. When I read true stories about the lives of people who have lived on earth, I like to see what kind of environment they were born into, the abilities and skills they were born with, how they developed their talents, and how they used their special talents to help themselves, help others, how they lived for God, loved God, obeyed God, loved others, helped others, and became successful in life. I especially enjoy reading how God helped them to overcome the difficulties in their lives, how God helped them overcome their mistakes and solve their problems, how God brought them through their difficult trials in life victoriously. Even the books that I read about the lives of non-Christians, I can see how God worked in their lives, how our God rewarded them for their good works, and how God allowed them to be punished for their evil works. It shows to me that God is in control of their ENTIRE life, whether or not they believe in Him!

More than a year ago, Father God told me that I was going to be one of the winners in the Guidepost's annual writing contest, where the twelve winners receive a week's paid vacation trip to Rye, New York, where they are trained by professional writing teachers to be writers of Christian literature. Since I was not chosen for this honor this year, I thought that maybe I had not heard Father God right, when He had spoken to me about it. Then God showed to me that when God promised Abraham that God would give him a son that God did not tell him that he would have to wait twenty years for it to happen! When God revealed this to me about Abraham and his waiting period for God's promise to be fulfilled, I realized that I did hear God correctly in this, that I am a future winner, but the time is not yet right for the trip for me.

In May of 2016 when I was very busy getting my house ready to put on the market to sell, I felt a strong urge from God's Holy Spirit to enter the contest again, before their deadline of June 10 for entries. God's Holy Spirit helped me to write a true story about my artist friend, Carolyn Andrews, that I worked with at Gospel Light Publications for a year between my fourth and fifth semesters at Art Center College of Design in Los Angeles.

The story that I wrote about my friend Carolyn Andrews began by showing how jealous I was of her exceptional skills and abilities she was gifted with. Although we were both hired as Graphic Designers at Gospel Light Publications, Carolyn also had the wonderful abilities of writing, singing, piano playing, sewing, and working with children. When I saw the quality of her art work, I realized that she was also a MUCH BETTER ARTIST than I was when I compared my five years of college with an art major compared to her four years of college with an elementary school teacher major. She volunteered as a Children's Choir Director at the church she attended. She was always cheerful and had a happy smile for everyone. She often brought snacks to share with our group of five of us artists who worked together in two rooms. Her kindness, gentleness, and patience were not usually returned by me, UNTIL …!! One day Carolyn came up to me and another of our workers named Gloria and said, "I want to treat both of you to lunch today." We agreed to go so at noon we three walked to a nearby restaurant, where we ate our good food, became better acquainted, and had a good time.

On our way back to the office, we stopped by the apartment where Carolyn lived. She showed to us some of the fun projects she was working on. For her Children's Choir at church, she had designed and was making 25 little choir robes. The design was very cleaver—made of a top square of green satin fabric with a bottom square of gold satin fabric, with a hole in the center with a collar, with a small opening with a hook and eye for closing. They were reversible and so very pretty! She also showed to us two little dresses full of pretty ruffles with pretty "girl colors" she had just finished for her two little nieces. She had also designed the dresses and made them in two sizes, matching, for the two little sisters. Her cleverness just amazed me! All of a sudden, I became very PROUD of her, her kindness in helping others, and her ability to share.

After we three walked back to the office, I asked Carolyn, "Why did you treat Gloria and me to lunch today?" She replied, "Because today is my birthday!" I was amazed and said, "We should have been treating you!!" She just smiled her usual sweet smile when we told her, "Happy Birthday!"

Later as I was talking with our Art Director, Joyce Thimsen also an artist, about how creative and how talented Carolyn is, Joyce told me things about Carolyn that I did not know. She said that everything that Carolyn does, she does with a severe headache! Since she is pre-diabetic, her doctor has her eat extra sweets every day to combat the extra insulin her body produces, which gives her bad headaches and causes her weight gain. She has written, illustrated, and produced some Christian children's books. The greatest desire of her heart is to go to the mission field, create more children's Bible teaching books, and work with the children's choir in a church there. She has applied to several foreign mission's groups, but none will take her because of her poor health. Her poor health requires her to be near medical facilities, and most of the mission fields in foreign countries are in remote places. I felt bad for her that she could not have her heart's desire to serve children and serve the Lord on the mission's field.

After a year and four months working with Carolyn at Gospel Light Publications, I left and returned to Art Center to finish my last four semesters and graduate. Before I graduated, I heard the latest information about my friend Carolyn. She had been accepted by a foreign mission board that had sent her to the capital of Brazil, locating her near a hospital in case she needed medical care. She was very happy there writing and illustrating children's Bible story books written in Spanish. God had finally given her heart's desire to her! I also heard that her health had improved when she was taken off ALL sweets and was treated for pre-diabetes with medicine. Her headaches were gone, and she got back to her normal weight! God is good!

That is the personal story that I had submitted to Guideposts Magazine for their yearly writer's contest.

After myself receiving and reading Guidepost's magazine over the years, I have noticed their writing style. They like to show the negative part of a situation, contrast it with the turnaround of the good situation, all with a happy outcome in the end. This approach is like the lights in a painting contrasted with the darks in a painting. To control the focal point, make the lightest light next to the darkest dark.

When I receive the monthly Guidepost's in the mail, I usually read the first half the first day then read the rest in the next few days. Some of the endings of the articles did not give enough glory to God for solving the problems, I believed. But God warned me before I ever take their writing course, **"Do not criticize what they are teaching you as God's Holy Spirit has been working with them over the years to develop their successful style of writing."**

This is similar to what God told me once when I had criticized the Southern Baptist preachers that they didn't believe in prophecies and praying in tongues. God said to me, **"Don't ever**

criticize Our God's Southern Baptist preachers because that's all Our God's Holy Spirit has to work with." I praise God for our Southern Baptist preachers because they won me to salvation in Jesus. Praise God!

Blessings! Velma

Yes, Our God's beloved Christians of Our God's beloved Christian pastors and ALL beloved Holy Bible teachers, YOUR heavenly Father God does love you, does train you, does teach you to live for God and teach you to help others know Our God's great truths that are given to you in Our God's Holy Bible that will benefit you in your own life, will benefit others in their lives, and WILL BRING GLORY TO OUR GOD on Our God's planet Earth.

Yes, time on earth as you do now know time on earth to be is quickly drawing to a close, when time on Our God's planet Earth will become Our God's millennial time, when one day is as a thousand years. (2 Peter 3:8)

Yes, SOON Jesus Christ WILL split the great Eastern skies coming back just above earth to claim and to catch away ALL of Our God's saved-in-Jesus and sanctified, right-living-unto-God, beloved Christian children of God to take them BACK to THEIR glorious home in Our God's great heaven above.

Yes, no sickness, no sorrow, no hunger or thirst, no pain, no unhappiness do await them in THEIR heavenly home where Our God's Holy Triune God does rule and does reign for eternity.

Yes, preach Jesus saves!

Preach Jesus heals!

Preach Jesus is coming soon!

Preach get ready and stay ready to go!

Preach time is running out!

Preach the rapture awaits the just!

Preach living a righteous lifestyle is God's will for ALL people's lives!

Preach sin will NEVER enter heaven!

Preach God is good!

Preach heaven and hell are real!

Preach who will go to heaven!

Preach who will go to hell!

Preach on the beauties of heaven!

Preach on the horrors of hell!

Preach life on earth is uncertain and death on earth is certain!

Preach that in hell there is never any escape from the torments of hell!

Preach if they reject choosing Jesus and continue living in their sinful lifestyle, and if they do die in their sins, and lift up their eyes in hell, they will be trapped in hell for eternity with no hope of ever escaping where they will REGRET their choice forever!

Yes, preach God is a loving, all-powerful, just, and merciful God, Who gives people enough time to REPENT of their sins, turn to Jesus Christ and be saved, then live in a righteous lifestyle unto God.

If people do REFUSE Jesus and do refuse to come OUT of sin and live for God in a given amount of time for their repentance, Our God has no choice but to allow their destruction from off the face of the earth.

Yes, America and the Americans have been slowly turning away from their true God and have replaced their true God with their businesses, their entertainments, their daily activities that ignore Our God exists, Our God created each of them in Our God's image, Our God controls Our God's planet Earth, all on it and all in it.

Yes, Our God created Our God's mankind on earth to know Our God, to love Our God above ALL else, to fellowship with Our God, to love and help their fellow mankind, to be provided for and to be protected by Our God, for them to know Jesus Christ as their Lord and Savior, live righteously for God, and to enjoy Our God's Holy Triune God in heaven forever.

Yes, when mankind drifts away from God and tries to be independent from God, Our God does try to woo them BACK to God, to their first love of God, but when they fail to repent and turn BACK to God, they become USELESS to God and do not DESERVE to live on Our God's beautiful planet Earth.

Yes, people bring about their OWN destruction when they do turn away from Our God and give things and events FIRST PLACE in their hearts and lives.

Yes, America and these wicked Americans who have turned away from their true God are NOW on the verge of destruction, UNLESS they repent of all of their evil ways, turn back to THEIR true God, ASK Our God's forgiveness of ALL of their sins and wrongdoing, come out of ALL sinful lifestyle and live righteously for God, and ALLOW Our God to heal these lands of these Americas. (2 Chronicles 7:14)

Yes, Christians are becoming lukewarm in their relationship to God, in their Bible study, in their church attendance, in living for God, in loving and helping the needy among them, in witnessing for Jesus, in seeking a deeper relationship with God, in not honoring marriages as holy, in not honoring tithes and offerings as holy, in not obeying authority and not obeying the laws of the land, in pursuing possessions and pleasures, and not giving Our God the praise, worship, honor, and glory to Our God that Our God deserves.

Yes, Our God does deserve honor, glory, praise, and worship from ALL of Our God's created mankind on earth as all they are, all they have, and all they will ever be and will ever have, their life and all the good things and all the good events in their lives now, are ALL good gifts to them FROM THEIR heavenly Father God given to them through Jesus Christ.

Yes, TEACH people to be thankful to God for ALL of Our God's good gifts to them that they now enjoy in their lives.

Yes, TEACH people to come out of ALL sinful lifestyle, live for God, and enjoy MORE GOOD benefits from THEIR heavenly Father God.

Teach people to put Our God's Holy Triune God in FIRST place in their hearts, minds, bodies, and souls, and to praise and worship and thank Our God MANY times daily, and then do see MORE of Our God's goodnesses in their lives AND in the lives of their loved ones!

Yes, DO KEEP your faith in YOUR Holy Triune God strong, DO PRAY many, many prayers to YOUR heavenly Father God, pray ALL your many prayers in Jesus' holy name, believing that what you do ask for, that you will receive all good gifts to enrich and to prosper your own life, the lives of others, and that YOUR Holy Triune God will be glorified on earth, and you SHALL HAVE ALL good things and all good events that you do ask for, receive them FROM YOUR heavenly Father God and receive them THROUGH YOUR Lord and Savior, Jesus Christ of Nazareth.

Yes, you in your human frailty and limited knowledge and limited wisdom do not yet realize ALL the good things and good events that you should pray for and ASK YOUR God for so do pray TO Our God's Holy Spirit and ASK Our God's Holy Spirit to pray FOR you and THROUGH you to YOUR heavenly Father God.

Yes, Our God's Holy Spirit does know your needs and ALL the needs of your loved ones and does know ALL the righteous desires of your heart, and Our God's Holy Spirit WILL pray for these needs and these holy desires to be met on time by YOUR heavenly Father God and by YOUR Lord and Savior, Jesus Christ.

Yes, Jesus Christ IS ALL powerful! (Matthew 28:18)

Do praise Jesus Christ as you do praise YOUR heavenly Father God.

Yes, do know, do realize, that YOUR Holy Triune God does desire for you and ALL your loved ones to prosper and always be in good health as your soul and as their souls prosper in God. (3 John 1:2)

Yes, do draw near to YOUR Holy Triune God with prayers,

fastings, praises, worship, and thankfulness to Our God, and THEN YOUR God WILL draw near to you and to ALL your loved ones, and THEN YOUR God will shower down on you and on ALL of them Our God's good benefits to help you and help them to lead successful and prosperous lifestyles on earth to Our God's glory on earth. (James 4:8)

Yes, do let YOUR Father God's will be done on earth as Our Father God's will IS done in heaven where all the people now living in heaven are happy, completely healthy, contented, joyful, and do lead a prosperous lifestyle, where ALL their needs and ALL their holy desires are being met at ALL times.

Yes, people now located in hell, the people who have refused Jesus Christ as their Lord and Savior from their sins, and the people who refused to come out of a sinful lifestyle on earth and live a righteous lifestyle unto God are now tormented in hell, and they WILL REMAIN in hell forever as there is now NO hope of them EVER escaping from hell and escaping from the torments of hell.

Yes, do read and do study what Our God's Holy Bible teaches you about heaven and about hell, and do preach and do teach ALL your congregations and Bible students about heaven and about hell.

Yes, heaven is real and hell is real, and each person now alive on earth WILL LIVE ETERNALLY either in heaven or in hell as there are no other places for each person's eternal soul to live after their one life and one death on earth.

Yes, each person now alive on earth does have an eternal soul that WILL live forever given to them at their moment of conception in their mother's womb.

Yes, each person now alive on earth was once alive in heaven, and each person did desire to come to earth to learn from their experiences on earth how they can go through trials, learn to TRUST THEIR God more so that their souls can grow more in God, and they can be promoted to a higher level of service to THEIR Holy Triune God now in heaven.

Yes, your eternal soul WILL continue to grow in heaven as you do learn better how to obey God, love God more, and love and help others.

Yes, there are many ways that your soul can grow up more in God as you experience your one life and one death on earth.

Yes, read about and study the life of Jesus Christ in Our God's Holy Bible of Our God's New Testament, and do STRIVE to live a holy life unto YOUR heavenly Father God as Jesus lived His one life on earth: Love God, teach others the holy truth of YOUR holy God, heal the sick, the blind, and the crippled, comfort the lonely, the painful, the downtrodden, the poor, the hungry, the strangers, the orphans and widows, and do be a servant to everyone, even as YOUR Lord and Master, Jesus Christ, served everyone who asked Jesus for help.

Yes, do be generous with everyone and do let Our God's love, truth, and obedience-to-God flow THROUGH you to love and help and instruct others.

Yes, the greatest among you IS the greatest SERVANT among you. (Matthew 23:11)

Yes, Jesus came to save and to serve all of mankind, to give them life, abundant life on earth, and give EVERYONE an eternal life in heaven to ALL who do choose Jesus as their Lord and Savior from their sins and who choose to live a righteous lifestyle unto God while they are alive on earth.

Yes, there is only ONE way to YOUR heavenly Father God, YOUR holy Creator God, and that is through the shed blood of Jesus Christ for cleansing of ALL unholy filth. (1 Timothy 2:5-6)

Yes, Father God cannot look on sin so you must come spotlessly clean through Jesus to enter heaven and to come into YOUR heavenly Father God's presence. (Habakkuk 1:13)

Yes, Jesus Christ is the ONLY true Savior of the world Who is able to forgive each person's sins and save them when they do come to Jesus Christ with a repentant heart and do ASK Jesus to forgive them of their sins and wrongdoing, help them to come

436

out of ALL sinful lifestyle, live for God while alive on earth, and go to heaven for eternity.

Yes, do preach the truths of Jesus Christ and of Our God's Holy Bible, and you will NOT lead people astray.

Yes, do LIVE a holy life unto YOUR God and do be rewarded for this by YOUR God.

Hallelujah!

Praises to Our heavenly Father God for this good message for church growth!

Hallelujah!

Praises to Our God!

Dear Christian Pastors and All Holy Bible Teachers,

I always pray about what to write to you in these fifty letters for church growth that will encourage you in your work for our Lord and in your service to others. I never know what to write about until I begin typing and God's Holy Spirit helps me. Now that this book project for church growth is nearly finished to help the churches' attendance to grow and churches' finances to grow, Father God has given to me another book project to work on.

The next book project that Father God will help me to work on will be fifty prophetic messages for the book titled, *Tithe Your Way Out of Debt.* He has already given to me the first five prophetic messages for the book. I would like to do an experiment with fifty families over the next year. I would like to find fifty Christian families who are now in debt who are not tithing. I would like for them to meet weekly for a discussion about tithing and giving based on one of these prophetic messages from God each week. I would like for these families to begin tithing and see what our God will do for them in one year concerning bringing them out of debt. I would then like to put these findings in the book with a one-page report from each of the fifty families between each of the fifty prophetic messages. I believe that the book will be a powerful witness to the faithfulness of God. People can argue religion "until the cows come home," but it's hard to argue with a person's personal experience of our God's faithfulness to them and their family.

The results of this year-long experiment with fifty families could be very powerful. Tithing and giving in the Holy Bible is the only place where our God says to test God in this and see if God will not pour out such benefits on you that you will not be able to receive them all. (Malachi 3:10) Father God told me that the Scripture that states, "Give and it will be given back to you, good measure, pressed down, shaken together, and running over will be given back to you, means that it will be given back to you double and more than double what you give." (Luke 6:38) God has also told me that the tithes are holy, and that God gives something to every person that does have a holy tithe built into it. Then God watches what each person does with this holy tithe that God has LOANED to the person. If the person consumes the tithe selfishly, his gifts from God do not increase much. If the person gives BACK to God the HOLY TITHE that God has loaned to him, gives it to help the helpless, or gives it to promote Christianity, God then increases God's gifts to the person, by giving to the faithful person more funds with a bigger HOLY TITHE included. God says, "If a person is faithful with little, he will be faithful with much." (Luke 16:10) The Bible teaches, "Despise not small beginnings." (Zechariah 4:10) Father God said, **"Small beginnings have growth potential!"** With tithing, a person could begin small, then grow into tithing the whole amount. People need to learn to give it FIRST, right off the top when they receive their income. This book on tithing and giving will not only help families financially, but will also help the churches financially as more people learn to give and as people learn to give more.

When my Financial Planner at my Fifth Third bank and I were discussing my investments, I asked him, "Do you know of any financial investments that pay a one hundred percent return that is guaranteed?" He replied, "No. There are none." I told him, "I know of only one and it's called tithing. God says in the Bible to give and it will be given back to you double, and God cannot lie, so it is guaranteed!"

Father God has been teaching me a great deal about what He wants to do for the Christian families who do pay their holy tithes and give their offerings to promote the gospel worldwide and to help the helpless. God will change their hearts from being more self-centered to being more others-centered and more

God-centered, then when they see the helpless, they will WANT to help the helpless with love, when they are able to help them. God will see their good works and will reward them in the way that they need it the most. As their character grows more in God, God is able to trust them with more income and more benefits.

Here are some of the benefits that our God gives to Christian people who are faithful tithers over the years, when they know God and live for God. God plugs up the leaks in their wallets and purses, and they do not have expensive accidents and other-than-normal living expenses. He shows them where to find reduced prices, when they need to purchase items. He gives them knowledge and wisdom in living their lifestyle with less impulse purchases that are not needed. He shows them where the greatest needs are to help the helpless with love to God's glory. When they need help with any project, he sends to them the needed help with DEPENDABLE people, who will treat them fairly. If they have a paying job, He will give them more strength, wisdom, and knowledge to work better, smarter, and happier on their jobs, so that they DESERVE and will receive a raise from their employers. He will improve their health, so that they miss fewer days of work because of illness. He will provide opportunities for their advancements on their jobs. He will give them better ideas on how to serve others on their jobs with love and joyfulness. He will teach them how to be more loving, more giving, and more helpful, and when they learn this, their relationships with others will improve. Their marriage' relationship will improve, their childrens' relationships will improve, their co-workers' relationships will improve, their friends' and extended families' and neighbors' relationships will improve. Their sleep will be sounder, and they will not have anxieties that tend to keep them awake at night. Their lifestyle will improve, and their food, clothing, shelter, transportation, and vacations will improve over time.

Their praise and thankfulness to God will increase as they do see all of our God's rewards to them for their tithing and their giving. When they do grow closer to God, God will grow closer to them, fill them with joyfulness, and cause them to prosper in all good things and in all good ways. God looks on their hearts and does see their fondest desires, and God delights to GIVE to them their fondest desires when they know, love, and obey God, and love and help others.

Marriages are holy unto God, and our God wants them to survive and prosper. But it's like Art Linkletter always said, "Whether you are rich or poor, it's always nice to have a little money." Our God says in Deuteronomy 8:18, "But thou shalt remember the Lord thy God: for it is he that giveth thee power to get wealth." Let's all be faithful to do that with love and faithfulness to our Holy Triune God!

Blessings! Velma

Yes, Our God's beloved Christian children of Our God's beloved Christian pastors and ALL of Our God's beloved Holy Bible teachers, YOUR heavenly Father God does love you, does take care of you and all of your loved ones on Our God's planet Earth, and Our God Jesus Christ WILL go with you even to the end of the age on earth. (Matthew 28:20)

Yes, YOUR heavenly Father God is a God of love, of power, of truth, of righteousness, Who does hold all things, all beings, and all powers that be, WELL in the full control of Our God at ALL times.

Yes, nothing good and nothing seemingly bad is allowed to happen on Our God's planet Earth at any time unless Our God does give Our God's permission for it to happen.

Yes, YOUR heavenly Father God NEVER slumbers nor sleeps. (Psalm 121:4)

Yes, Our God's planet Earth is Our Father God's footstool, and Our God continues to watch every part of it at all times. (Isaiah 66:1)

Yes, daylight and dark are the same to Our God, and Our God is able to see and know ALL happenings in the dark times, as well as, the daylight times. (Psalm 139:12)

Yes, YOUR heavenly Father God does see and does know ALL the things and all the events done in secret, and when Our God sees your good deeds done in secret, Our God WILL reward you openly. (Matthew 6:4)

Yes, some things that have been said in secret WILL BE shouted from the rooftops! (Luke 12:3)

Yes, witness for Jesus.

Tell of the love of Jesus for all of mankind on earth, tell

of the sinless life and virgin birth of Jesus, tell of the supreme sacrifice of Jesus with His shed blood, holy death, resurrection, and ascension into heaven, tell of His power to save ALL sinners who ASK Jesus for salvation from sins, tell how Jesus gives them new life to sin no more, tell them how Jesus will RETURN towards Our God's planet Earth SOON to claim and to catch away to heaven ALL of Our God's obedient Christian saints for THEIR eternal reward in heaven.

Yes, time on earth is now short and is now growing shorter until Our God Jesus returns toward earth for Our God's great rapture.

Yes, do look around you at the many signs of the times that will take place right before Our God Jesus returns for ALL of His own, all the signs of the times listed in Our God's Holy Bible that WILL take place on Our God's planet Earth that signify the time of Jesus' appearing in the heavenlies is near.

Yes, do read and do study and do teach and preach on the signs of the End-times now taking place on Our God's planet Earth, and do realize how SHORT the time is until Jesus returns!

Yes, time IS SHORT and is now growing SHORTER day by day, and what you do for and with your God MUST be done QUICKLY!

Yes, yes, yes, do TELL PEOPLE, tell ALL people, to GET READY, to STAY READY to meet THEIR Lord Jesus Christ in the air in ANY split second to be taken BACK to THEIR heavenly home to live with their holy Creators God throughout eternity in total happiness and bliss!

Yes, make no mistake; every word written in Our God's book of Revelation in Our God's Holy Bible is absolutely true.

Yes, believe and teach others the book of Revelation in Our God's Holy Bible.

Yes, Jesus Christ is truth.

Teach the truth of Jesus Christ, how He lived, what He did, and what He taught.

Yes, Jesus lived the truth, and Jesus taught the truth.

Yes, teach ALL the truths that Jesus taught, leaving NOTHING out that he taught, when He walked this earth nearly two thousand years ago.

Yes, do the works in helping others that Jesus did to help others when Jesus walked this earth as recorded in Our God's Holy Bible.

Yes, Jesus came to give life and to give it more abundantly to ALL of Our God's mankind on earth who will receive Jesus as their Messiah, Savior, God, and King, who will confess their sins and unrighteousness to Jesus, ASK Jesus for forgiveness, receive this free salvation from Jesus, then go and sin no more, but live in a righteous lifestyle in obedience to God.

Yes, you MUST be saved in Jesus and living in a righteous lifestyle in order to receive ALL good gifts from your heavenly Father God and receive them through Jesus Christ.

Yes, Jesus Christ is the way, the truth, and the life, and no man is able to come to THEIR holy Creator, THEIR heavenly Father God, except they first go through the cleansing power of the holy shed blood of Jesus Christ that cleanses them of ALL unholy filth and makes them clean, pure, and whole to enter the presence of THEIR HOLY heavenly Father God for their answered prayers and all good gifts from THEIR heavenly Father God. (1 Timothy 2:5)

Yes, Jesus is righteous, and the shed blood of Jesus makes people righteous who go to Jesus and who ASK Jesus to make them righteous.

Yes, only the righteous-in-Jesus will see THEIR heavenly Father God. (Hebrews 12:14)

Yes, Father God is holy and cannot look on sin of any kind. (Habakkuk 1:13)

Yes, the wages of sin is death. (Romans 6:23)

Yes, God calls for each of mankind to come OUT of ALL sin and live righteously for God.

Yes, sin will NEVER enter heaven.

Yes, only the sinners who have repented of their sins, who

444

choose Jesus as their Lord and Savior from their sins, who then live righteously for God, will be the only sinners--who are ex-sinners--who will be allowed entrance into heaven THROUGH JESUS in their life after their one life on earth ends.

Yes, choose Jesus NOW and never regret it!

Yes, live righteously for God with Jesus as your Savior and God and NEVER regret it!

Yes, Our God did create each of you for a specific reason and that is to know your God, enjoy your God, love, honor, and obey your God, and be rewarded by your God with ALL good benefits for your enjoyment and prosperity in your life.

Yes, your main purpose in your life is to know God and to enjoy your holy Creators God forever.

Yes, at your moment of conception in your mother's womb, YOUR holy Creator God did give you at least 32 gifts to make you very successful in your one life on earth.

Yes, at your moment of conception when Our God gave you the beginning of your earthly body, your heavenly Father did give to you your eternal soul, and your eternal soul WILL live forever either in heaven or it will live forever in hell after your one life on planet Earth is over.

If while you are now alive on earth, you choose to COME to Jesus Christ with a repentant heart, ASK Jesus to forgive you of ALL your sins and wrongdoings, ASK Jesus to be Lord and Savior of your life, do ACCEPT this free gift of salvation from Jesus, then go and sin no more, you WILL be on your way to heaven after your one life on earth ends.

However, if you refuse to ask for and accept the cleansing power of Jesus Christ for your sins and for your wrongdoing, and if you do continue to live in unrepentant sin without Jesus Christ as your Lord and Savior, you will be on your way to hell after your one life on earth is over.

Yes, Jesus Christ is NOW the ONLY Being, dead or alive, with enough power to cleanse you of ALL sins and wrongdoing, cleanse you with Jesus' shed blood shed on the cruel cross of

Calvary, cleanse you of all unholy filth, and make you spotlessly pure enough to enter heaven after your one lifetime on earth.

Yes, sin will NEVER enter heaven.

In order for any person now alive on earth to go to heaven in their afterlife, after their one life on earth ends, they must accept this free salvation and free cleansing of all their sins from the ONLY TRUE Savior of the world, Our heavenly Father God's only begotten Son of Jesus Christ, then come out of ALL known sin in their life, and then live a holy life unto God for the rest of their only one life on earth.

Yes, Jesus is holy.

Yes, Jesus does expect ALL Christians to live a holy life unto the only true God, Our God's Holy Triune God.

Yes, Jesus came to earth born of the virgin Mary, conceived by Our God's Holy Spirit, lived a holy life unto God, shed His holy blood on Calvary's cruel cross to pay the ransom for ALL of mankind's sins, so that whosoever will MAY come to Jesus for forgiveness of their sins, then live for God while alive on earth, then enter the bliss of heaven forever.

Yes, Jesus Christ, Who never sinned, paid the awful price for sinners to have life, abundant life on earth, and have eternal life forever in heaven, and have all of this FREE for the asking, IF they will REPENT of their sins, come out of their sinful lifestyle and live for God while they are still alive on earth.

If a person dies in their sins without Jesus as their Lord and Savior, and they lift up their eyes in hell, it can and will be too late for them as their eternal soul can and will be trapped in hell forever.

Yes, those souls trapped in hell now, who did refuse to accept Jesus as Lord and Savior of their sins, and who did NOT live for God while alive on earth, will REGRET their decision in hell forever.

Yes, come to Jesus now, ask Jesus to save you now and be Lord and Master of your life now, come out of ALL sinful lifestyle NOW, and you will NEVER regret it, not in your present lifetime on earth, nor in your eternal life in heaven.

Yes, Buddha cannot save you.

Mohammad cannot save you.

Allah cannot save you.

You cannot save yourself by trying to work your way into heaven by loving people and doing good deeds.

Your ONLY one-way ticket to heaven is through the only true Savior of mankind of Jesus Christ of Nazareth.

There is NO other name given among men whereby you MUST be saved except Jesus Christ of Nazareth. (Acts 4:12)

Yes, come to Jesus Christ now, and you will NEVER regret it.

If you do reject the ONLY TRUE Savior of mankind, Jesus Christ, you could regret it forever in hell.

Yes, Jesus Christ has ALL power now in heaven and on earth. (Matthew 28:18)

Yes, Jesus Christ IS appearing in the heavenlies soon just above earth at the last trumpet sound, coming back towards earth for Our God's great rapture of ALL of Our God's saved-in-Jesus and right-living-unto-God beloved Christian children of God, to catch them up from earth in a split second, to meet Jesus in the air, to be taken BACK to their eternal home in heaven, to live forever with THEIR Holy Triune God.

Yes, time is SHORT and is growing SHORTER until Jesus returns for Our God's great rapture of souls on earth.

Do GET ready to go and do STAY ready to be caught up into the heavenlies to meet YOUR Lord Jesus Christ in ANY split second WHEN the last trumpet sounds.

Pray in ALL your lost loved ones.

Witness for Jesus.

Live for God.

Proclaim the good news daily that Jesus is alive, that Jesus is coming SOON, GET ready to go, STAY ready to go in ANY split second!

Hallelujah!

Praises to Our heavenly Father God for this prophetic message for all church growth!
Hallelujah!
Praises to Our holy God!
Amen.

ABOUT THE AUTHOR

Velma Garner Davies' Mother took her and her four siblings to a little Southern Baptist church in rural southern Mississippi from birth. Velma became a Christian at an early age and was baptized in a river.

At Velma's age ten their family of seven moved from Mississippi to Washington state, where they continued to attend a Southern Baptist church.

Velma completed high school, completed Junior College with an AA degree, completed Art Center College of Design in Los Angeles with a Certificate of Completion, and completed Peabody College in Nashville with a BFA degree. Velma worked her way through college twice, always with a major in art, as she wanted to illustrate Christian literature to win the world to Jesus Christ.

Velma worked one year as a Graphic Designer for Gospel Light Publications in Glendale, California. She worked as a Graphic Designer at the Baptist Sunday School Board in Nashville, Tennessee for four years. She free-lanced Graphic Design work for the Southern Baptists and Methodists for three years.

She taught an adult beginning art class for two years at Watkins Institute in Nashville.

Velma and Hugh Davies were married in 1970. Their daughter was born in 1972 and their son in 1975. Velma and the children began attending The Lord's Chapel in 1977, where both children became Christians and were baptized by Pastor Billy Roy Moore. Velma continued attending this church through the building relocation in 1988 and with the merger with Oasis Church in 2003. Velma continued her active membership in this church for 39 years, leaving in 2016 when she relocated to Marietta, Georgia.

Velma became Holy Spirit filled at The Lord's Chapel, with evidence of her own prayer language and with the gift of prophecy. At The Lord's Chapel she published their newspaper monthly for twelve years. From the articles published in the church newsletter, 44 Christian testimonies were gathered and were published in her first book titled, *Victory in Jesus*.

Velma published her family newsletter monthly for 28 years, with a prophetic message in every issue for 25 years, titled, "The Garner News." She self-published her second book titled, *Christmas in The Bible Belt*, in 2012. *Church Growth Our Father God's Way* is Velma's third book.

Velma has built up her fine-art painting skills in watercolors, oils, and acrylics, and has had several art exhibitions in the Nashville area. Some paintings and some prophetic messages may be seen on Velma's website: www.HotOffTheThrone.com.

Velma now is a member of Mt. Bethel United Methodist Church in Marietta, Georgia. She continues to work on four more books, as well as, continues to paint beautiful art scenes from nature.

Velma's husband passed away in 2010. She now has three grandsons and three step-granddaughters.

Printed in the United States
By Bookmasters